D0989830

The Contemporary American Short-Story Cycle

The Contemporary American Short-Story Cycle

The Ethnic Resonance of Genre

James Nagel

LOUISIANA STATE UNIVERSITY PRESS

Baton Rouge

Copyright © 2001 by Louisiana State University Press
All rights reserved
Manufactured in the United States of America

cloth
10 09 08 07 06 05 04 03 02 01
5 4 3 2 1

paper
13 12 11 10 09 08 07 06 05 04
5 4 3 2 1

Library of Congress Cataloging-in-Publication Data

Nagel, James.
    The contemporary American short-story cycle : the ethnic resonance of genre / James Nagel.
        p. cm
    Includes bibliographical references and index.
    ISBN 0-8071-2660-8 (cloth); ISBN 0-8071-2961-5 (pbk.)
    1. American fiction—20th century—History and criticism. 2. Short stories,
American—History and criticism. 3. American fiction—Minority authors—History and
criticism. 4. Cycles (Literature) 5. Literary form. 6. Ethnicity in literature. 7.
Ethnic groups in literature. I. Title.
    PS374.S5 N34 2001
    813'.0109920693—dc21   00-048654

The paper in this book meets the guidelines for permanence and durability of the Committee on
Production Guidelines for Book Longevity of the Council on Library Resources. ∞

To
Gwen
for all the years

Contents

Acknowledgments

Every work of serious literary criticism is fundamentally collaborative, building on the work of previous scholars while at the same time being enriched by interactions with stimulating students and colleagues. My own work on the short-story cycle, which reaches back many years, was initially stimulated by an attempt to come to terms with some of the great works of American modernism, particularly Sherwood Anderson's *Winesburg, Ohio*, Ernest Hemingway's *In Our Time*, Jean Toomer's *Cane*, and William Faulkner's *Go Down, Moses*. For a time, that attempt led me backward in time to antecedent works of interrelated stories in American literature, to Washington Irving's *The Sketch Book*, Augustus Baldwin Longstreet's *Georgia Scenes*, Louisa May Alcott's *Hospital Sketches*, and many of the great works of American Realism and Naturalism, among them Hamlin Garland's *Main-Travelled Roads*, Kate Chopin's *Bayou Folk*, Sui Sin Far's *Mrs. Spring Fragrance*, and Sarah Orne Jewett's *The Country of the Pointed Firs*. An earlier book on Stephen Crane had involved some thinking about his two collections of stories and sketches about Sullivan County and Whilomville, and the invitation to write the introduction for John Steinbeck's *The Pastures of Heaven* enlivened my interest and caused me to consider again the role of the genre in modern fiction. This book begins with that consideration. This study represents not the final word about the genre, by any means, but rather an attempt to sharpen the definition of the form in terms of the aesthetics of fiction, to suggest something of the importance of the cycle in American literary history, and to begin the exploration of the multi-ethnic utilization of an ancient tradition in contemporary literature. The eight examples of the genre I have chosen to discuss in depth in this book are only a selection of the hundreds of such volumes that have appeared in the last two decades. Indeed, I hope that my

ix

book will stimulate the observation that the short-story cycle is coming to be understood as an unjustly neglected literary form in the literary canon, a genre that has produced some of the most important books in our national literature.

Over the period of my most intense work on the short-story cycle, I have enjoyed the encouragement of a number of university presses and scholarly journals that have published essays of mine related to this book. I was honored when Columbia University Press chose me to write "The American Short-Story Cycle" for *The Columbia Companion to the Twentieth-Century American Short Story*, ed. Blanche Gelfant. Another essay, on F. Scott Fitzgerald's Basil and Josephine stories, appeared in *New Essays on F. Scott Fitzgerald's Neglected Stories*, ed. Jackson R. Bryer, University of Missouri Press. My introduction to John Steinbeck's *Pastures of Heaven*, which conjoins Naturalism and the short-story cycle, is in the edition published by Viking/Penguin. My articles on Hemingway's *In Our Time* have been published in the *Hemingway Review* and in *American Literary Dimensions: Poems and Essays in Honor of Melvin J. Friedman*, ed. Jay L. Halio and Ben Siegel, University of Delaware Press. "The American Short-Story Cycle and Stephen Crane's Tales of Whilomville" came out in *American Literary Realism*, and a previous essay on Jamaica Kincaid's *Annie John* and *Lucy* and the cycle tradition found a home in *Traditions, Voices, and Dreams: The American Novel since the 1960s*, ed. Melvin J. Friedman and Ben Siegel, University of Delaware Press. The death of Mel Friedman, a brilliant scholar, an honorable gentleman, a treasured friend, is a loss I must live with every day.

It is with humble appreciation that I acknowledge a debt to a few of the many scholars who have worked in the same field, beginning with the monumental sweep of knowledge of Fred Lewis Pattee, who read more fiction than anyone else, and whose tradition inspired all of us who studied at Pennsylvania State University, where the profession of American Literature originated. Every serious scholar in the field should know James J. Martine's *Fred Lewis Pattee and American Literature*. In more recent periods, Forrest L. Ingram's *Representative Short Story Cycles of the Twentieth Century* (1971) will forever be regarded as a ground-breaking study, followed by Susan Garland Mann's *The Short Story Cycle* in 1989, *Modern American Short Story Sequences*, edited by J. Gerald Kennedy in 1995, and *The Composite Novel*, by Maggie Dunn and Ann Morris, the same year. Many other scholars, Robert Luscher and Karen Weekes among them, have contributed in important ways to the developing understanding of the genre, and I am indebted to all of them. George Monteiro read the manuscript and offered many valuable suggestions, and I admire his knowledge of fiction and his generous professionalism. I owe my colleagues in the American Literature Association a special note of recognition, especially Alfred Bendixen, Gloria Cronin, Wilfred Samuels, Jacqueline Brogan, Jeanne Reesman, Leo LeMay, and Laura Skandera-Trombly. Together we have worked to preserve the profession as a haven of cordial multi-ethnic collaboration in the study of American culture. My work on the short-story cycle has been enriched over the years by interaction with scores of dedicated graduate students, and their energy and inspiration revitalizes my own endeavors. I wish to express a special note of gratitude to John W. Easterly, Jr., Executive Editor of Louisiana State University Press, for his unflagging support and wise counsel, and other members of the press also contributed to this study, among them Trudie Calvert and Margaret Hart. Whatever success this book enjoys will be due in part to the efforts of all of them. My most enduring gratitude is for the companionship and inspiration of my wife, Gwen, who knows better than anyone else the value of art. In small measure of my abiding indebtedness to her, I express my gratitude in the heartfelt dedication of this book.

James Nagel
Athens, Georgia

The Contemporary American Short-Story Cycle

Introduction

From the beginning of the professional study of American fiction, the role of the short-story cycle has been largely unrecognized in literary scholarship, overlooked and misunderstood despite its essential role in the development of the national literature. Literary historians of the early twentieth century ignored the genre, and even the most sagacious readers of the ensuing decades seemed innocent of the long tradition of celebrated collections of interrelated stories. In reviewing Ernest Hemingway's *in our time* in 1924, for example, Edmund Wilson was inspired to observe that the author had "almost invented a form of his own."[1] Similarly, in 1949 Malcolm Cowley remarked in a review of William Faulkner's *Knight's Gambit* that the book is "something more than a mere collection. It belongs to a genre that Faulkner has made peculiarly his own by the artistic success of such earlier volumes as *The Unvanquished* and *Go Down, Moses*."[2] But what was "peculiar" was not the notion of a volume of stories with unifying characters and themes but the fact that such eminent commentators on the current state of modern letters should have been oblivious to the important role the short-story cycle had recently assumed. Sherwood Anderson's *Winesburg, Ohio* had appeared in 1919, for example, and Jean Toomer's celebrated volume *Cane* was published only a year before *in our time*. In the years between Wilson's review and Cowley's, some of the most remarkable fiction of the era had appeared in this genre, including John Steinbeck's *The Pastures of Heaven* and *Tortilla Flat*, Zora Neale Hurston's *Mules and Men*, Djuna Barnes's *Nightwood*, and Eudora Welty's *The Golden Apples*. Nevertheless, Cowley seemed to regard the form as anomalous, uniquely Faulkner's, an invention of the moment.

But the fact of the matter is that the short-story cycle is a rich genre with origins decidedly antecedent to the novel, with roots in the most ancient of narrative traditions. The historical meaning of "cycle" is a

1

collection of verse or narratives centering around some outstanding event or character. The term seems to have been first applied to a series of poems, written by a group of Greek writers known as the Cyclic Poets, that supplement Homer's account of the Trojan war. In the second century B.C., the Greek writer Aristides wrote a series of tales about his hometown, Miletus, in a collection entitled *Milesiaka*. Many other early classics also used linked tales, Homer's *Odyssey*, Ovid's *Metamorphoses*, the Arabian *A Thousand and One Nights* among them, as Forrest Ingram has pointed out.[3] In medieval literature, the "cycle" concept of works that are independent but enriched by inclusion in a group of related pieces became widespread. Among the foremost was Boccacio's *The Decameron*, published in Italy in the fourteenth century, but there were many similar volumes: Sacchetti's *Trecente Novelle*, Fiorentino's *Il Pecorone*, Masuccio's *Novellino*, and Bandello's *Novelle*. In British literature, such masterpieces as Chaucer's *The Canterbury Tales* and John Gower's *Confessio Amantis* exemplified the concept, Gower employing a personal confession as the framework for the stories, Chaucer a pilgrimage. Throughout these early works two ideas became clear in the concept of a cycle: that each contributing unit of the work be an independent narrative episode, and that there be some principle of unification that gives structure, movement, and thematic development to the whole.

In another genre, the cycle plays of medieval England were done in verse, unified by setting, character, and theme. As Arnold Williams has explained, the underlying philosophy of the era lent a unifying doctrine to these plays: "Medieval man was sure that the cause of evil is original sin. On this he could be quite specific, enumerating the vices to which each condition of man was specially vulnerable, seeing in every region and time applications of the general rule that man is naturally prone to sin. . . . Apparently, too, there was an implicit belief that the higher the man, the worse the sin. . . . What we find in the cycles is a constant calling attention to the vices of the great."[4]

Rosemary Woolf described the unifying elements in even more explicit terms in speaking of the medieval mystery plays:

> The construction of the cycles resembles that of *The Canterbury Tales*: small pieces are so juxtaposed that the whole work has a vitality and significance which abundantly overflow that of the sum of the individual parts. Similarly, varieties of style and metre coexist

equably so that the tone ranges among the lyrical, satiric, homiletic, comic, and narrative or functional, without conveying a disunified effect. The cohesion, which in *The Canterbury Tales* is provided by the framework, in the cycles is supplied by the unity of subject-matter, and in both the material is bound by recurring thematic patterns in situation and character.[5]

These central ideas of the unification of smaller works into linked groupings, into "cycles," became part of the literary tradition in English, manifested in Mallory's epic *Le Morte D'Arthur*, the sonnet sequences of the Renaissance, and the lyric and epic verse cycles of the nineteenth century: Robert Browning's *The Ring and the Book*, Elizabeth Barrett Browning's *Sonnets from the Portuguese*, and George Meredith's *Modern Love* in 1862, a cycle of sixteen-line poems.[6]

Although there are many complexities in tracing a literary history that crosses genre and nationality boundaries, it is perhaps not too much to say that the central idea of the short-story cycle, the linked set of short narratives, with origins in such works as Boccaccio's *The Decameron* and Chaucer's *The Canterbury Tales*, antedates the concept of the formal novel, which developed in the eighteenth century. In another sense, the basic unit of a cycle, the story, is a far more ancient and fundamental narrative unit, more closely linked to the oral tradition than the extended narrative line of the traditional novel. The modern concept of the "short story" did not appear until the nineteenth century, evolving in the early decades as a form distinct from the "tale," a loosely organized account of strange and often mysterious events, and the "sketch," which stressed character description with little development of plot and little sense of narrative closure.[7]

Accordingly, in the United States, the earliest manifestations of linked narratives appeared in the form of related sketches and tales, among the first of which were Washington Irving's *The Sketch Book* (1820), Sarah Josepha Hale's *Sketches of American Character* (1829), Augustus Baldwin Longstreet's *Georgia Scenes* (1835), and Eliza Buckminster Lee's *Sketches of a New England Village, in the Last Century* (1838), all of which were unified by the depiction of localized characters in regionalized settings.[8] Nathaniel Hawthorne lent depth and sophistication to the development of the form in his "Legends of the Province House," a section of *Twice-Told Tales* (1851), as did Herman Melville in *The Piazza Tales* (1856). As the sketch and the tale evolved into the more realistic "story" in the wake of the Civil War, the market for short fiction burgeoned with the emergence of popular magazines and the inception of the newspaper syndicate. As a result, the genre became increasingly popular, finding expression by writers of both genders and a broad spectrum of ethnic groups. Harriet Beecher Stowe dealt with the personalities and dialects of Maine in *Sam Lawson's Oldtown Fireside Stories* (1871), and Frances E. W. Harper depicted African American characters in *Sketches of Southern Life* (1872) as did Charles Chesnutt in *The Conjure Woman* (1899) and Alice Dunbar-Nelson in *The Goodness of St. Rocque and Other Stories* (1899).

Many of the best "local color" writers used linked stories to describe regional customs and characters, as is the case in George Washington Cable's *Old Creole Days* (1879), Constance Fenimore Woolson's *Rodman the Keeper: Southern Sketches* (1880), and Mary Noailles Murfree's *In the Tennessee Mountains* (1884). Grace King structured her *Balcony Stories* (1892) around the device of having them related by women sitting out of an evening telling their tales after the children had been sent to bed. Kate Chopin also wrote about New Orleans and Louisiana, emphasizing courtship, marriage, and ethnic identity in such volumes as *Bayou Folk* (1894). Hamlin Garland, writing under the sway of the early Populist movement, linked his stories in *Main-Travelled Roads* (1891) with themes of economic and social injustice on the middle border and created one of the milestones of literary Naturalism. For her part, Margaret Deland's stories in *Old Chester Tales* (1898) all relate aspects of small town life in Pennsylvania. Sarah Orne Jewett did the same thing for coastal Maine in *The Country of the Pointed Firs* (1896), unifying the episodes with a portrayal of the citizens of Dunnett Landing and the deepening understanding and sympathy of the urbane narrator for them. James William Sullivan focused on an urban setting in *Tenement Tales of New York* (1895). For his part, Stephen Crane used upstate New York in his posthumous *Whilomville Stories*, investing the stories of children with troubling adult themes. "The Monster," which deals with race and ethical conflict in a small town, is one of the most important works in American literature. By the turn of the century, nearly a hundred volumes of story cycles had appeared in the United States, and the genre was yet to enter its most important phase.

The short-story cycle in modern American fiction is patently multicultural, deriving, perhaps, both from ethnic cross-fertilization within the literary community and from a shared legacy reaching back to ancient oral traditions in virtually every society throughout the world, uniting disparate peoples in a heritage of narrative tradition. The evolution of the genre in this rudimentary form would naturally have derived from the desire of speakers to relate their tales in some meaningful way to those told before, a wish that would accommodate repeated characters, settings, and situations as well as the dominant ideas of a community of tellers. The English "novel," as an extended narrative with a primary central character and a main plot that extends from beginning to end, is not as universal a form as a group of short tales linked to each other by consistent elements, whether ongoing characters, places, or situations. As the tradition evolved, often the stories would be told by a spectrum of speakers relating episodes about a group of characters, each narrative having its own resolution and yet building in some way on the others. Scores of narrative cycles appeared in each decade of the new century, some of them containing individual works that are among the best ever published in English, preeminent among them William Faulkner's "The Bear" from the volume *Go Down, Moses.*

In the early years of the century, for example, Susie King Taylor's *Reminiscences of My Life: A Black Woman's Civil War Memories* (1902) presented an African-American perspective on the most cataclysmic event in the history of the new republic. Mary Austin's *The Land of Little Rain* provided a discerning treatment of life in the American West. Zona Gale's *Friendship Village* (1908) perpetuated the emphasis on localized settings in a small town, using her native Wisconsin, while in *O Pioneers!* (1913) Willa Cather depicted the harsh struggle for survival on the Nebraska prairies. Sui Sin Far's *Mrs. Spring Fragrance* (1912), a compilation of stories she had begun writing in the 1890s, was the first significant Asian-American work of fiction. In a series of episodes set in either San Francisco or Seattle and linked by ongoing characters and themes, particularly the struggle of the titular character not only to assimilate but to be a considerable social force, the author was able to explore the issue of cultural dualism and the process of social adaptation for Chinese immigrants. Zitkala-Sa served something of the same function in her *American Indian Stories* (1921), writing out of her own Lakota background, and Jean Toomer's *Cane* (1923) quickly came to be regarded as a classic work of African American literature. This volume, however, might be better regarded as a "composite narrative" in that it contains verse and drama as well as short fiction, all of the works sustaining a continuing portrait of a people in migration from south to north.

In this period, however, it is Sherwood Anderson's *Winesburg, Ohio* (1919) that remains preeminent among the short-story cycles of the period, both for its contributions to literary history and for the attention it has attracted. This volume of twenty-five stories, all set in a mythical midwestern town, further developed the traditional theme of the "village virus," depicting submerged lives, sexual frustration, and thwarted hopes and aspirations. Unified by a consistent narrative voice, by setting, and by coalescent motifs, these stories also feature a primary protagonist, George Willard, whose struggle for self-realization and growth creates a paramount line of development for the volume, a strategy used successfully in such volumes as Ernest Hemingway's *In Our Time* (1925), John Steinbeck's *The Red Pony* (1937), and William Faulkner's *Go Down, Moses* (1942). Hemingway used not only the continuing character of Nick Adams, who progresses from adolescence to adulthood in somewhat less than half of the thirty-two narratives, but also the synthesizing theme of the longing for "peace in our time" in a world of senseless violence, barbarous war, gratuitous cruelty, and ubiquitous disillusionment. In his book, Steinbeck traced the experiences of a young boy, Jody, growing up on a ranch in California and learning about the realities of life and death. Faulkner's volume is unified by setting, theme, and family relationships, the central characters all being descendants of Carothers McCaslin. As the title would indicate, a continuing issue is the fate of African American characters in the wake of the Civil War. In "The Bear," a young white boy, Ike McCaslin, grows to moral maturity under the guidance of an older man of color, and in the end Ike relinquishes an inheritance of wealth acquired on the basis of slavery, severing his ties to a legacy of cruelty and injustice.

In the years between the two wars, the short-story cycle became an even more popular genre among serious writers of fiction. John Dos Passos's *Manhattan Transfer* (1925), Thornton Wilder's *The Bridge of San Luis Rey* (1927), and Djuna Barnes's *Ladies Almanac* (1928) appeared in rapid succession, followed by Michael Gold's *Jews Without Money* (1930). John Steinbeck's *The Pastures of Heaven* (1932) is important both in itself and because it portrayed the plight of the families living in a mythical valley in California while developing the Naturalistic themes that would inform his masterpiece, *The Grapes of Wrath*. Steinbeck used the genre again for his stories about an Italian neighborhood in Monterey in *Tortilla Flat* (1935). This period was filled with important volumes of interrelated stories, among them Mourning Dove's *Coyote Stories* (1933), Caroline Gordon's *Aleck Maury, Sportsman* (1934), Zora Neale Hurston's *Mules and Men* (1935), and Djuna Barnes's *Nightwood* (1936), illustrating the cross-cultural appeal of the genre. Richard Wright's *Uncle Tom's Children* (1938), unified by themes of white oppression of black families, and William Faulkner's *The Unvanquished* (1938), held together by a continuing protagonist, were indicative of the various unifying elements within the genre.

There was great variety in the story cycles that appeared in the 1940s and 1950s. Following Faulkner's approach to the genre, Erskine Caldwell used a continuing narrator, a regional setting, and the unifying nucleus of a southern family and their servants in *Georgia Boy* (1943). Edmund Wilson apparently had learned a great deal about volumes of interrelated stories since his earlier review of *In Our Time* since he produced his own *Memoirs of Hecate County* in 1946. More significant, however, was the appearance of Eudora Welty's *The Golden Apples* (1947), an exceptional group of stories set around Morgana, Mississippi, in the first half of the twentieth century. As the allusion in the title to W. B. Yeats's celebrated poem "The Song of the Wandering Aengus" indicates, all of these stories in some way relate to themes of longing and searching for fulfillment. In a "composite" volume in the tradition of *Cane*, Peter Taylor included a drama along with eight stories, all dealing with family relations in a small southern town, to comprise *The Widows of Thornton* (1954). Paule Marshall's *Brown Girl, Brownstones* (1959) is a highly unified sequence of stories, set in Brooklyn, about an immigrant family from Barbados.

Flannery O'Connor assembled nine southern stories about the violent conflicts between parents and children to form *Everything That Rises Must Converge* (1965). In *Going to Meet the Man*, published the same year, James Baldwin collected eight stories about successively older black men confronting transitional conflicts. Reflecting the enthusiasm of the age, John Barth offered fourteen metafictional stories about the process of composition in *Lost in the Funhouse* (1968). In one of the most important recent Asian American books, Maxine Hong Kingston published *The Woman Warrior* in 1976, a widely celebrated volume of five long narratives based on Chinese mythology. In *Speedboat*, Renata Adler gathered seven stories about a journalist in New York, a book that, rather ironically, won the Ernest Hemingway Award for the best first "novel" of the year. Russell Banks's *Trailerpark* (1981) was tightly unified in that it presented thirteen stories about people living in mobile homes in New Hampshire, characters who interact in the course of the book.

In the last two decades of the twentieth century, it has become increasingly clear that the tradition of the short-story cycle is one of the most important in the history of American fiction and that the obdurate critical innocence of this legacy has brought about misunderstandings, misinterpretations, and a distortion of literary history. That fact has remained true even in the context of award-winning volumes of interrelated stories written from a spectrum of racial and cultural points of view. For example, Gloria Naylor won the American Book Award for *The Women of Brewster Place* (1982), a collection of seven African American stories unified in setting and theme. Another celebrated story cycle is Harriet Doerr's *Stones for Ibarra* (1984), a comic yet tragic series of episodes about life in a Mexican village as related from an Anglo-American perspective. Consistent with the norms of the genre, each of these stories is complete in itself and yet serves as part of a developing narrative that moves, inexorably, toward a riveting and unifying conclusion. Writing out of her Japanese American tradition, Hisaye Yamomoto depicted in *Seventeen Syllables* (1985) the painful yet strangely deepening experience of life in internment camps during World War II. Denice Chavez focused on Chicano experience in *The Last of the Menu Girls* (1986), which presents seven stories set in New Mexico all dealing with the maturation of a unifying central character.

Of particular significance in contemporary American fiction is a series of books that have won significant literary awards and are widely acknowledged as stellar examples of the richness of modern literature, and yet these volumes have been consistently misconstrued as "novels" because of the lack of awareness of the history of the short-story cycle. Written from a variety of ethnic perspectives, by writers from differing sections of the country, about characters from vastly different social and economic backgrounds, these books are nevertheless united by the use of a common literary tradition and by a commitment to the integrity of literary art. These are all volumes that deserve to be read in detail within the context of an understanding of the genre and the role it has played in American literary history. Only from that perspective can these books be fully understood and assessed for their contributions to the growing multiethnic canon of the fiction of the United States.

Louise Erdrich's *Love Medicine*, which portrays the complex struggles of Native American characters living on or near the Turtle Mountain Reservation in North Dakota, was honored with the National Book Award for the Best Work of Fiction in 1984. The *New York Times* called it one of the eleven best books of the year and, within a remarkably short period of time, it was in print in ten languages, and yet it has been consistently read as a "novel" and judged within the normative expectations of that genre. But in fact the volume is a series of fourteen stories, ten of which had been previously published in magazines, and one of which had won the Nelson Algren Award for the best short story of the year. Some of these episodes used different names for the characters in original publication, and many of them contained events and conversations quite different from those in the published volume, and yet scholars have been largely oblivious to the publication history of the book and have persisted in reading it as a single sustained narrative. Sandra Cisneros's *The House on Mango Street*, a rich and subtle depiction of Latino society in Chicago from the perspective of a young girl, was given the Before Columbus American Book Award for 1985. In that it consists of forty-four compressed vignettes, there has been less confusion about the nature of the genre of this volume, although there has been little appreciation of the fact that it appeared as part of a long literary tradition and not as an anomalous production, mirroring the publication of both *Winesburg, Ohio* and *In Our Time*.

All eight of the stories that went into Jamaica Kincaid's *Annie John* (1985) appeared independently in the *New Yorker*, some of them with variant names for the characters and with altered family relationships. When she brought them together as a story cycle, she arranged them chronologically for the first time and coordinated details so that they now constitute a feminine *Bildungsroman* for a young girl growing up in Antigua under her mother's tutelage and moving through rebellion to her initial independence. Susan Minot insisted on having the word "novel" deleted from her contract for *Monkeys* (1986), since it was clearly a volume of stories, but it has nevertheless been widely read in those terms. In fact, it is a brilliant series of nine minimalist stories about salient moments in the lives of the Vincent family, particularly regarding a daughter named "Sophie," who serves as a point of normative sensibility. The conflict in this volume is not that of race but of class: "Mum" grew up in the Irish Catholic section of South Boston, while "Dad" enjoyed life in the tony suburbs in an Episcopal family with long ties to Harvard.

Another cycle often read as a novel is Amy Tan's *The Joy Luck Club* (1989), a tightly organized series of sixteen stories, divided into four groups of four, with one story told about each of four families in each set, and with alternating episodes told by mothers and daughters. At issue throughout are the unifying details of Chinese emigration into the United States and the desire of the older women to preserve the language and heritage of their native land. The daughters, on the other hand, are preoccupied with cultural assimilation and with "modern" life in America. Julia Alvarez developed similar themes for a family from the Dominican Republic in *How the García Girls Lost Their Accents* (1991), which once again focuses on the transition of young daughters to life in the new country. In fifteen stories, arranged in reverse chronological order, she explores not the consequences of the actions of the family but the precipitating motivation that led them to leave their homeland. Tim O'Brien used the methodology of the story cycle for *The Things They Carried* (1990), a searing revelation of the ethical and emotional culpability borne by young American soldiers in the Vietnam War. A fascinating companion volume is *A Good Scent from a Strange Mountain* (1992) by Robert Olen Butler, which contains fifteen stories about Vietnamese immigrants living in Louisiana after the conclusion of the war. These episodes are unified by the shared heritage of the characters, their vivid memories of the conflagration, and the dramatic ways in which memories of the conflict continue to shape their lives.

There are scores of other examples of the genre in modern American literature, but even these few examples demonstrate how important the short-story cycle has become in contemporary fiction. It is a convention that needs to be recognized and understood as not simply ancillary to the more significant "novel" but as integral to literary history, with an ancient origin and a set of narrational and structural principles quite distinct from other fictional modes. That for the last century many of the most important works of this kind were written by authors from differing ethnic backgrounds suggests that despite its ancient history, the story sequence offers not only a rich literary legacy but a vital technique for the exploration and depiction of the complex interactions of gender, ethnicity, and individual identity. It is an important genre, and it deserves to be defined and studied in terms of its vital and continuing contribution to twentieth-century American fiction.

The process of defining a tradition as rich and diverse as that of the short-story cycle in American literature is inherently problematic and ultimately imperfect, but that is not to say that a general description of the form is impossible. Indeed, the previous scholarship on the subject, most richly represented in four important books, offers a substantial base upon which to build an understanding of the contemporary manifestations of the genre. It is astonishing, however, that such an important class of fiction, which has produced an impressive list of volumes in virtually every period of American literary history, should have occasioned so little direct study. Not until 1971 did a book appear on the subject, Forrest Ingram's *Representative Short Story Cycles of the Twentieth Century*, a seminal attempt at a systematic definition of the genre and a discussion of such books as James Joyce's *Dubliners*, Faulkner's *The Unvanquished*, and Anderson's *Winesburg, Ohio*. Ingram's influential discussion differentiated among volumes "composed" from the beginning as a cycle, those "arranged" or "collected" after the fact to form a series, and those "completed" by adding additional stories to existing ones in a pattern that may have "subconsciously" begun.

Although it may often be the case that data about the knowledge and intentions of the author are not available, it would seem that all three of these stratagems would be richly represented in modern literature. With regard to a formal definition, Ingram offers the clear assertion that "a short story cycle [is] a book of short stories so linked to each other by their author that the reader's successive experience on various levels of the pattern of the whole significantly modifies his experience of each of its component parts."[9] The problem with this approach to a definition is that it has its inception in assumptions not about the works themselves but about the consciousness and intentions of the author and in speculations about the responses of prospective readers. It would seem more felicitous to attempt a definition based on the stories and volumes themselves rather than on authors and readers. For all of his insightful observations about the story cycle in modern literature, Ingram's definitions are ultimately unsatisfying and do not provide a viable, practical understanding of the nature of the genre.

Susan Garland Mann's *The Short Story Cycle* in 1989 was also valuable in that she discussed nine important volumes (including Hemingway's *In Our Time*, Eudora Welty's *The Golden Apples*, and O'Connor's *Everything That Rises Must Converge*) and she provided an annotated listing of over a hundred short-story cycles in the twentieth century.[10] She did not broach a comprehensive definition in her study, however, although she did offer some useful descriptions of the common aspects of cycles, including such unifying features as "repeated and developed characters, themes or ideas, imagery, myth, setting, plot or chronological order, and point of view." Differentiating the cycle from a novel, she observed that "as far as character is concerned, there is much less emphasis on a protagonist in the short story cycle than is generally the case in other fiction."[11] Ultimately, she observed that "there is only one essential characteristic of the short story cycle: the stories are both self-sufficient and interrelated."[12] Although these comments are not definitive, they are based on the cycles themselves and address discursive issues, matters that can be debated among scholars without speculation about motives and affective responses.

Two other books emerged in 1995, both important and both problematic in certain respects. *The Composite Novel: The Short Story Cycle in Transition*, by Maggie Dunn and Ann Morris, is a challenging and controversial study that links brief analyses of individual works with an attempt at defining the parameters of a new genre that contains poetry and drama as well as fiction, Jean Toomer's *Cane* being representative of the form. But for works of interrelated stories, the term "composite novel" would not seem to work in either of its terms, "composite" seeming best left to describe extended narratives composed of works from multiple genres and "novel" to indicate a sustained fictional narrative, with a continuing protagonist, supportive motifs and subplots, and a comprehensive thematic structure, a form quite distinct from a story cycle. The other book, *Modern American Short Story Sequences*, edited by J. Gerald Kennedy, is a collection of twelve essays on the subject exploring a century of works from Henry James's *The Finer Grain* to Raymond Carver's *Cathedral*.[13] It is an excellent collection of engaged criticism, but it is possible to question the concept of interrelated short stories constituting a "sequence" rather than a "cycle." Indeed, in most such collections, "sequentiality" is the least important aspect of the groupings of stories within a volume. The relationships among stories in a short-story cycle is far more complex than the simple following of one another in sequence.

But it should be stressed that the term "cycle" also carries misleading suggestions, at least in its workaday sense of "circularity." In literary history, however, that is not the definition that is applied to this term. As Ian Reid has observed, probably the impulse to combine individual tales into larger wholes has its origin in the very nature of imagination itself, a "coadunating" power as Coleridge described it. Certainly many old story-clusters show that the impulse goes far back into oral tradition, while conventions of the written word have introduced also a practical need to mediate between normal short-story size and normal book size. To group separate stories together cohesively, two sorts of constructive method may be used: internal linking and external framing.[14]

Writers in American literature have used both of these modes, Jewett's *The Country of the Pointed Firs* illustrating a volume in which the integral stories are linked by the psychological progression of the central character, and King's *Balcony Stories* representing how the initial external framework can unify constituent tales about an array of characters.

However useful the distinction between these two kinds of cycles might be, the concept of the "short-story cycle" remains to be sufficiently defined in literary scholarship. Any attempt at a systematic definition, however provisional, ultimately encounters not only the concept of "story," differentiating this form of short fiction from other modulations, but of "cycle," distinguishing this model from loose collections of stories on one side and "novels" on the other. Perhaps it is axiomatic in scholarship that the most common terms and concepts are the most difficult to define. Many scholars, Norman Friedman among them, have despaired of the difficulties of giving the short story precise definition: "For my own part, I do not really believe there is any such thing as *the* short story more specific than 'a short fictional narrative in prose.' Within that definition we cannot logically or empirically rule out actions of any kind or size, any techniques, or any end effects."[15] Where definition fails, however, sometimes description serves. Within the concept of "a short fictional narrative in prose," the short story since the early nineteenth century has evolved a number of continuing attributes which, if not universal, are certainly common in the genre. Most short stories involve the presentation of one or more central characters involved in some kind of conflict, whether internal or external, and this conflict undergoes resolution in the conclusion of the story, leading to some kind of overt or implied transformation in the central character. Given the brevity of the story, there are few subplots, rarely any conflict within a subordinate character, and few secondary issues introduced. In this sense, the well-crafted story is a brief fictional narrative, sharply focused on a central character, with a unified plot and a progressive intensity of action.[16]

Although there has been great historical variation in the implementation of the story, with the tales of American Romanticism employing symbolization and personification in ways totally foreign to Modernist tendencies, particularly to minimalist fiction, still the "story" has become an identifiable genre in American literature despite the difficulties of precise definition, and the works of short fiction that have been part of larger cycles have been among the best in the form. Indeed, it would have to be said that some of the most memorable stories in American literature are component parts of larger cycles: Hemingway's "Big Two-Hearted River," Faulkner's "The Bear," Garland's "Under the Lion's Paw," Chopin's "Désirée's Baby," Steinbeck's "The Red Pony," for example. Recent short-story cycles have also contained individual stories that are brilliant achievements: Minot's "Hiding," Harriet Doerr's "The Red Taxi," Jamaica Kincaid's "Columbus in Chains," and Tim O'Brien's "The Things They Carried" among them.

Because the constituent stories of cycles often appear individually in magazines before being anthologized, they pose special interpretive problems for scholars. These narratives are not always the same in the magazines as they are in the collected volumes, suggesting that adjustments had to be made in setting, character names, and chronology to synthesize independent works into a unified whole. The most obvious of these kinds of changes would be the modification of clarifications of family relationships, descriptions of locations and their distances from other places, and explanations of time parameters, matters essential in the appearance of individual stories published in separate places months or years apart from one another but redundant in a collected volume. For this and other reasons, the analysis of publication history is particularly important in the study of the genre.

If the definition of a "story" is difficult, so is that of the "short-story cycle," particularly with regard to distinguishing it from the "novel," a rather different artistic entity. For example, in the novel there is generally a continuous narrative line, often a single narrative stance, and one climactic resolution of plot, although there are many variations. As an extended fictional narrative with a continuing line of action, the novel has clear principles of unity: continuing characters or situations; patterns of images or allusions that resonate as the action develops; subplots that converge on a core set of issues. Unlike the stories in a cycle, the subordinate units of a novel, its episodes or chapters, are incomplete in themselves, dependent for artistic completion on the other units that comprise the whole. When chapters from novels were published in magazines in the nineteenth century, they were inherently incomplete, requiring chapters in subsequent issues of the magazine for the completion of the plot or situation. In contrast, the stories that comprise cycles were nearly always complete aesthetic works by themselves.

Indeed, a central point is that in the short-story cycle each component work must stand alone (with a beginning, middle, and end) yet be enriched in the context of the interrelated stories. In contrast to the linear development of plot in a novel, the cycle lends itself to diegetical discontinuities, to the resolution of a series of conflicts, to the exploration of a variety of characters, to the use of a family or even a community as protagonist, to the exploration of the mores of a region or religion or ethnic group, each story revealing another aspect of the local culture. One of the most fascinating aspects of the contemporary fictional cycle is that writers from a wide variety of ethnic groups have used the form for the depiction of the central conflicts of characters from their own race or nationality. As "American" narratives, these stories often involve the process of immigration, acculturation, language acquisition, assimilation, identity formation, and the complexities of formulating a sense of self that incorporates the old world and the new, the central traditions of the country of origin integrated into, or in conflict with, the values of the country of choice.

The lack of understanding of the story cycle throughout the profession of literary study may result from its subordination into the concept of "novel," the implicit assumption being that the novel is the highest form of expression in fiction, and the attribution of "novel" to a work of fiction is thus perceived as a compliment. It is time that the genre of the cycle be appreciated as a separate form and that clear distinctions between it and the novel be established. Although there have been myriad variations on the concept, the unifying tendency of the genre of the cycle has been the collection of a group of independent stories that contain continuing elements of character, setting, action, imagery, or theme that enrich each other in intertextual context. What Helen Mustard described as the "cyclic principle" of the lyric in German literature holds true for modern fictional cycles, the idea of "establishing 'such relationships among smaller entities as to create a larger whole' without destroying the identity of the smaller entities."[17] The most obvious and common of these linking devices are a continuing protagonist, such as George Willard in *Winesburg, Ohio* or Nick Adams in Hemingway's *In Our Time*; a consistent setting, even when dealing with multiple characters, such as the verdant valley in John Steinbeck's *The Pastures of Heaven*;[18] or the progressive development of a theme, such as the narrator's deepening identification with, and appreciation of, the people of Dunnet's Landing in Sarah Orne Jewett's *The Country of the Pointed Firs*. As Robert Luscher has pointed out, Hamlin Garland's *Main-Travelled Roads* is thematically unified by the motif of the return to the place of origin, the description of an idyllic nature set against the squalor of social poverty, and the consistent motif of the need for socioeconomic reforms.[19] The recurrence of people, places, objects, and situations also helps unify stories, just as continuing ideas provide thematic resonance, whether in reinforcement, juxtaposition, or counterpoint. Ingram calls this device "the dynamic pattern of recurrent development."[20] Many cycles present the stories within "framing" episodes that begin and end the collection, and often the frame takes the form of a prologue and epilogue, as it does in *The Pastures of Heaven*.

The stories in a cycle normally have less chronological coherence than the chapters of a novel; since each episode tends to focus on a specific incident, the relationship of that incident to previous ones can present interpretive complexities. The relationship may simply be discontinuous, with no attempt to supply the missing action between events; time may move backward to depict temporal simultaneity, the events involving these characters taking place at the same time as the action in another story; or the time may constitute a simple sequence, each occurrence following the events of the previous ones, albeit with occasional flashbacks or references to earlier events, as in Susan Minot's *Monkeys*. As a result of these temporal variations, characters do not necessarily exhibit the same kind of continuity of development found in most novels, a point made all the more clear by the fact that many cycles feature a different protagonist in each succeeding story.[21] Once again, as Mann has pointed out, "as far as character is concerned, there is much less emphasis on a protagonist in the short-story cycle than is generally the case in other fiction."[22] Although the cycle format can be used for the *Bildungsroman*, as Jamaica Kincaid does in *Annie John*, just as frequently it lends itself to the exploration of a family or a community, as in *Love Medicine*, rather than the internal life of a single individual.[23]

There is a similar discontinuity possible in the narrative perspectives of the stories in a cycle: although it is possible for all of the stories to be told from the same point of view, as Jewett did in *Pointed Firs*, more frequently there is a narrative modulation of perspective, with the continuing elements of the collection portrayed from a number of angles of vision. As is true in the novel, the historical progression of perspective in the cycle has been away from omniscience to more personalized modes of perceiving and registering the events and feelings of the stories.[24] The result is that there is a good deal of narrative modulation in cycles, presenting a series of first-person narrators or a third-person narrator deriving information and impressions from a changing series of central characters in each episode. The resultant genre is rich in artistic and ideological possibilities, arming a writer with a broad spectrum of devices with which to present the constituent elements of the total volume.

The short-story cycle thus has a long and complex history and a diversity of implementation so broad as to escape limited definition. To some extent its central components are best described through critical triangulation: a cycle is less unified than a novel but has much greater coherence and thematic integrity than a mere collection of unrelated stories. It can focus on the development of a single character, but it is more likely to involve scenes devoted to a series of characters who interact with each other throughout the episodes, so that the major character of one story may function in the background of another. In the history of the genre, the most persistent continuity in the form has been in setting, so that all of the shorter works constituting a cycle occur in the same general location, with prominent landmarks recurring throughout, tying the events to an enduring sense of place, as in Irving's *The Sketch Book*, Grace King's *Balcony Stories*, Crane's Whilomville series, Kate Chopin's *Bayou Folk*, Zona Gale's *Friendship Village*, and Margaret Deland's *Old Chester Tales*. But never has the genre of the short-story cycle been used with greater force or variety than in the American fiction of the 1980s and 1990s, when it became the genre of choice for emerging writers from a variety of ethnic and economic backgrounds. These authors have created works with ideological force and impressive artistic richness, establishing a legacy that needs to be explored not only in general terms but with a detailed examination of some of the exemplary volumes that are representative of the contemporary short-story cycle.

1

The Ethnic
Resonance of Genre

Louise Erdrich's *Love Medicine*

When Louise Erdrich's *Love Medicine* appeared in 1984, it could hardly have had a more exuberant reception, particularly considering that it was her first volume of fiction. It received unrestrained accolades in the most eminent newspapers and magazines and a host of prestigious honors as well. The first story, "The World's Greatest Fisherman," was given the Nelson Algren Award for short fiction before the publication of the book. When the initial hardback edition came out, *Love Medicine* won the National Book Award for the Best Work of Fiction in 1984, the American Academy and Institute for Arts and Letters Sue Kaufman Prize for the Best First Novel, the Virginia McCormick Scully Prize for the Best Book of 1984 dealing with Indians or Chicanos, and the *Los Angeles Times* Book Prize for Fiction in 1985. The *New York Times* named it one of the eleven best books of the year and, within a remarkably short period of time, it was in print in ten languages. It quickly became the subject of sustained scholarly attention in the academy, and it is taught in contemporary American literature courses throughout the world.

Despite the ebullient interest in *Love Medicine*, the book has not been well understood, as is often the case with collections of interrelated short stories. There was widespread confusion among reviewers about the genre of the volume, and none of them made reference to it as a short-story cycle. Most of them judged it according to the normative expectations of a novel, including D. J. R. Bruckner in the *New York Times*, Marco Portales in the *New York Times Book Review*, Linda Taylor in the *London Times Literary Supplement*, and Harriett Gilbert in the *New Statesman*.[1] This confusion about form caused Robert Towers, writing in the *New York Review of Books*, to make a classically faulty judgment about the book. Approaching it as a novel, he was understandably critical of its "structural problems." He explained that "the book achieves its effect through moments of almost searing intensity rather than through the rise, climax, and closing of a sustained action. . . ."[2] He did not realize that the cycle format does not present "sustained action" but a conflict and resolution in each of its constituent stories. Writing in *Newsweek*, Gene Lyons protested that "*Love Medicine* has as many as a half dozen first-person narrators, and several stories are told in the third person. No central action unifies the narrative, and the voices all sound pretty much the same. . . ."[3] In a later critical article, Catherine Rainwater complained that "*Love Medicine* defies the reader's effort to locate a conventional plot—a temporal sequence of characters' actions traceable along a 'constant curve' with a teleological aim (the notion of plot as consisting of beginning, conflict, rising action, resolution, ending). Erdrich's novels conspicuously lack plot in this traditional sense of the term."[4] In a sense she was right: as a short-story cycle, *Love Medicine* lacks the comprehensive plot of a sustained novel, but that does not mean it is without a complex structural pattern. Indeed, it can be demonstrated, the 1984 edition of the book is a highly organized collection of fourteen interrelated stories that coalesce into an artistic pattern of remarkable thematic and aesthetic integrity.

Many of the initial reviewers were more accepting of the book on its own terms. In a particularly insightful review, Andrew O. Wiget observed that "*Love Medicine* is a set of short stories, like Joyce's *The Dubliners* or Faulkner's *As I Lay Dying*, interrelated by their common tone and setting, by their different points of view in narrating the same event, and by evolving relationships between a common set of characters."[5] Joseph Bruchac, apparently unaware of the tradition of the story cycle, confessed that he was not sure that the book was a novel since half of the contents were previously published as short stories. But he went on to say that "the initial uncertainty I felt about the exact genre of *Love Medicine* disappeared completely as I read further. Though the chapters each may work as fine short stories on their own, together they make up a larger story. . . ."[6] He apparently assumed that any collection of fiction with an overarching framework must constitute a novel. Jay Parini hedged his bet in the *Saturday Review* by describing the book as a "novel" but one made up of "fourteen interlocking stories."[7] Thomas L. Kilpatrick suggested, somewhat more perceptively, that "*Love Medicine* might be characterized as a series of short stories rather than a novel, for any one of its 14 chapters can be read on its own merits."[8]

The reviewers of the book might well have been uncertain about the genre of *Love Medicine* not only because of their ubiquitous innocence of the tradition of interlinked narratives but also because the title page of the 1984 edition declared that it was "a novel by Louise Erdrich," an assertion notably absent from the 1993 edition, which added four additional stories. There was also little information available about the composition history of the volume, which helps a good deal in clarifying the nature of the genre. As is often the case in the developmental history of a short-story cycle, when Louise Erdrich published the first story in the book, there was no idea for a volume entitled *Love Medicine*. There were, however, two previous stories already in print, "The Red Convertible" in the *Mississippi Valley Review* and "Scales" in the *North American Review*.[9] In response to a call for short fiction to be considered for the new Nelson Algren Award, Erdrich wrote "The World's Greatest Fisherman" in two weeks and submitted it, eventually winning the $5,000 prize in 1982. It was only at that point that the notion arose of forming a volume of interrelated stories based around the three already published.[10] By the time the book was completed, ten of the fourteen episodes that made up the 1984 edition were previously published as independent short stories, a point that caught the attention of none of the initial reviewers save for Bruchac. These stories were warmly received by the reading public, two of them winning prizes for fiction ("Scales" was reprinted in *The Best American Short Stories of 1983*), and it was clear that they were independent artistic entities in themselves. The inescapable challenge for the author of a story cycle is to bring the individual narratives together in such a manner so as to construct a larger aesthetic work that is greater than the sum of its parts, each story enriched in artistry, theme, and character by the juxtaposition of the surrounding stories. Louise Erdrich did this with remarkable creative sensitivity.

In a series of interviews subsequent to the publication of *Love Medicine*, she commented on the process of assembling fourteen separate stories into a unified whole, a task undertaken with the collaboration of her husband, Michael Dorris, with whom she worked closely on the book. As she recalls, "we read it out loud to each other when it was finished[,] twice, slowly[,] and did some integration between the various stories to tie them together and figure out the chronology and the relationships and all that stuff in a way that would be comprehensible to someone who didn't know these people as well as we did."[11] On another occasion she confessed that the original organizational pattern for the stories was not what was actually published, with an initial story in 1981, then a shift backward to 1934, and a progression forward from that point. The embryonic form was more haphazard because, as she formulates it, "I did not really think of it as a book. I thought I was writing these disjointed little bits. . . ."[12] As is frequently the case in the cycle format, each of the stories in original publication had its own narrative strategy, its own protagonist, its own internal chronology. Although most of the stories required only minimal modification to fit into the volume, the synthesis of these separate works into a unified whole was something that required careful deliberation. Reflecting on the process, Erdrich has commented that the form of *Love Medicine* "reflects a traditional Chippewa motif in storytelling, which is a cycle of stories having to do with a central mythological figure. . . . One tells a story about an incident that leads to another incident that leads to another in the life of this particular figure. Night after night, or day after day, it's a storytelling cycle."[13] Indeed, it is artistically and culturally significant that the interrelated narrative sequence, far from being an artificial aesthetic construct, is the traditional form of extended fiction among Native Americans.

There are other elements of the genre that suggest that the short-story cycle is more congruent with traditional narratives among Native Americans than is the novel. Much of Chippewa storytelling is in the form of communal gossip, with multiple speakers relating portions of the plot, duplicating and contradicting one another, and covering the activities of many members of the tribe. The relating of a story is in many senses a group activity, one that binds a people together in a matrix of repeated communal sagas. Michael Dorris observed that *Love Medicine* "is a story cycle in the traditional sense. One of the interesting reviews of the book was talking about the fact that nobody in the book is right, that . . . the point of view is the community voice and the means of exchanging information is gossip, and so consequently there is no narrator; there is no single protagonist, but rather it is the entire

21

community dealing with the upheavals that emerge from the book. . . ."[14] Although this practice was part of the oral tradition of storytelling, it is also significant that the Chippewa were historically the only Native American people north of Mexico who told their oral stories with the aid of hieroglyphics inscribed on bark, thus preserving, somewhat more permanently, the central structure of the tales and songs to be presented, a fact recorded by Father Frederick Baraga in 1847.[15] He went on to describe the communal nature of storytelling within the tribe: "Their oral tales are very common and numerous. Every Indian who is old may tell those tales; there are no privileged tale-tellers amongst them."[16] The traditional Chippewa method of narration was to have various stories, or alternative parts of a single story, told by different narrators, a stratagem that lends itself perfectly to a series of interlinked stories, told by multiple narrators, with the tribal family as the central figures.[17] It is a methodology that grew out of the ancient conventions of her people that Erdrich refined into some of the most challenging fiction in contemporary American literature.

The narrative method of *Love Medicine* is congruent with this tradition. Although the fiction of Louise Erdrich need not be read as an exemplum of a single ethnic tradition (she is more German than Chippewa), her works are primarily about Native American characters who live on or near the reservation, who think of themselves in the context of tribal history, and who collectively tell their stories as part of a community of speakers. The implications of their doing so are aesthetically and thematically complex, but the general effect is to convey a fragmentation of knowledge with incomplete information distorted from each teller's point of view. This method of multiple narrators, of narrative parallax, in which reality appears to shift depending upon the vantage point from which it is perceived, functions nicely even within individual stories, but it has its most dramatic effect on the volume as a whole. Each individual story, no matter how dramatic the events it portrays, or how self-sufficient its diegetical structure, ultimately contributes only one design to the mosaic of the book. Given the unreliable nature of the narrative voices in these fourteen stories, the information conveyed can be assessed and understood only in the context of the method of their "telling," a matter of considerable complexity.

Love Medicine is a collection of fourteen interrelated stories told by a shifting spectrum of fifteen narrative perspectives, all but one of them unreliable and biased.[18] Five of the stories are told in first person by Albertine, Marie, Nector, Lyman, and Lulu. Eight of them employ a third-person voice with data and interpretation limited to the mind of a single character even though formulated by an external narrational intelligence. Only two stories, "Crown of Thorns" and "A Bridge," have sections related from an omniscient point of view, with access to the minds of multiple characters, with a knowledge of communal history beyond the grasp of any individual, and with an authoritative judgment that seems beyond reproach. To add to the complexity, five of the stories employ multiple narrative strategies, juxtaposing alternative perspectives on the continuing events so that, in "Lulu's Boys," for example, the events are described as Lulu sees them, then as perceived by Beverly, and then as interpreted by the synthesized consciousness of the community.[19] "Crown of Thorns" opens with an omniscient section but then shifts to a limited point of view identified progressively with the minds of Gordie, Eli, and Sister Mary Martin. "A Bridge" also contrasts an omniscient perspective with the imperfect, even naive, views of Albertine and Henry Jr., neither of whom grasps or articulates the significance of what happens to them. The result is a book that presents a communal voice related to the transmission of gossip in that, save for a few omniscient passages, no one speaker knows or can relate the truth of the matter. Reality must be approximated from imperfect and incomplete information, adjusted for bias and self-interest, and assessed in terms of probabilities rather than narrative certainties. As Kathleen Sands has said, "the gossip tradition within Indian communities is . . . elliptical, relying on each member's knowledge of every individual in the group and the doings of each family (there are no strangers). Moreover such anecdotal narration is notoriously biased and fragmented, no individual privy to the whole story. The same incidents are told and retold, accumulating tidbits of information."[20] This is precisely the method of *Love Medicine*, as the stories in the first edition patently demonstrate.

The opening story in the volume, "The World's Greatest Fisherman," was originally published in *Chicago* magazine in October 1982, where it was clearly an independent work and not a chapter in a novel. For one thing, some of the key characters have different names from those in the collected volume: King and King Jr. are known as "Delmar" and "Delmar Jr.," for example. Albertine, who narrates three of the four sections in the book, is known as "Patsy" in the magazine. Several important passages, some extending for several pages, were added to the story after its initial publication, material that helps link the episode to the rest of the volume, including Albertine's reflections beginning the second section that provides the background for the family (pp. 6–11).[21] Albertine was not a nursing student in Fargo in the magazine; she had not learned of June's death in Zelda's letter, and Zelda is referred to as her aunt rather than as her mother; there was little information about Zelda's marriages to Swede Johnson and Bjornson; and there was no background about June's attempt to be a beautician, her disastrous marriage to Gordie, or the desperation that led her to a life of prostitution. These elements are crucial to the assembled collection of stories in that June's death is the central unifying element for the entire book, something that was not true when the story was published independently.

There were many other alterations as well, including important aspects of family history: in the magazine the grandparents received the allotment of 160 acres of land in 1929 and raised six of their own children along with four they adopted. In *Love Medicine*, the land was owned not by "Grandma Vitaline" but by Rushes Bear, the mother of Nector and Eli Kashpaw, and she raised eighteen children (p. 17). In the book there is an important distinction between the twin boys: Nector was sent to the government school and acculturated into white society while Eli remained in the woods, sustaining his Native American traditions. This difference is mentioned only in passing in the magazine, perhaps because, in the absence of the other stories, no dramatic consequences flowed from it. Another important section added to the volume was the opening three pages of section four, in which Albertine attempts to tell Lipsha that his mother was June, not Grandma Kashpaw, a matter with important resonance for the concluding story, "Crossing the Water," in which Lipsha's psychic reconciliation with his parents is the central issue. Since that story had not been written at the time "The World's Greatest Fisherman" was first published, there was no need to establish a context for this conclusion. This story was clearly an independent fictional narrative in *Chicago* magazine; as the opening story of a cycle, however, it provides a motivational network and point of reference for the other thirteen stories in the collection.

In the magazine text, the story is divided into only three sections: the first, about June's death, and two others, narrated by Patsy, about the family reaction to it. In *Love Medicine*, it has a similar structure, but it consists of four numbered sections, the first, in which June Kashpaw dies in a snowstorm, constituting the motivation for the subsequent three, told by Albertine, in which the family gathers at the homestead on the occasion of June's death. The narrative method of the first section is third-person limited, allowing access to the mind of June but maintaining sufficient distance for objective description: "She was a long-legged Chippewa woman, aged hard in every way except how she moved." It is clear that June, in her early forties, has become a prostitute, working the riggers from the oil fields around Williston, North Dakota, with considerable ambivalence and self-loathing, which leads her into an unsatisfying assignation with a man named "Andy." In geographic context, the name is a clear reference to the surname "Anderson" and an ethnic indicator of the multitude of Scandinavians now living in what had originally been Sioux and Chippewa land, a matter that Erdrich gave greater emphasis in the revised text than in the magazine.[22] Later in the story it becomes evident that Zelda's first husband, the father of Albertine, was Swede Johnson (obviously Swedish) and her second a man named Bjornson (Norwegian), suggesting the frequency of marriage across ethnic lines. In the magazine text, Zelda is defensive about her Swedish husband, defending him against Aurelia's taunts, saying "I will thank you not to take His name in vain" (p. 162); in the book, Zelda dislikes anyone who is not a Native American, and she maintains that "never marry a Swedish is my rule" (p. 14). Her relatives rarely adhere to her proclamations, and the characters in *Love Medicine* produce children of complex racial mixtures, reflecting the historic social patterns of the area.

The first section of this story is also the motivational impetus for the rest of the book, for virtually everything that happens is linked to June's death, either part of the motivational history of her suicide or of the consequences that flow from it. In this sense, and in many others, *Love Medicine* parallels the structural and narrational design of William Faulkner's *As I Lay Dying*, in which the death of the central woman in the book provides the stimulus for the ensuing events. Faulkner's volume is also a series of brief episodes, told by different narrators, concerning a family's responses to a transitional event, and both works contain dark humor and grisly events.[23] In neither case is the woman herself a principal narrator (Addie Bundren tells one brief section), and the other family members who speak have only an uncertain understanding of the events, resulting in narrative parallax, with reality changing shape depending on the angle of vision from which it is perceived.

It is also significant that June's death occurs on Easter Sunday just as she was about to go "home" to the reservation. Easter is the one Christian holiday that unites life and death, and in Native American culture the mythology of Christianity came as an overlay on a traditional religion closely associated with the processes of nature, in this case with the advent of spring. The imagery of this first episode is emblematic of the dual religious matrix, with references to Easter melded with June's sense that she is going "underwater," an allusion to the historic Chippewa legend of the water deity who brings death. As June stumbles in the snow, freezing to death in the storm, the suggestion that "the pure and naked part of her went on" and that "the snow fell deeper that Easter than it had in forty years, but June walked over it like water and came home" evokes the ethereal mythology of the Native American return to the homeland, not the Christian ascendancy into the realm of heaven. As Catherine Rainwater has explained, on the reservation, "her spirit, according to Native American beliefs, mingles with the living and carries out unfinished business." Rainwater goes on to comment that "one of the earliest patterns of Christian references concerns Easter and resurrection. This Christian notion, or code, of death and transfiguration is counter-balanced by Native American notions of immortality."[24] This issue is only the beginning of a rich pattern of cultural duality.

The next three sections of the story are narrated in first person by Albertine Johnson, who proves to be a digressive but effective storyteller. In 1981 a nursing student in Fargo, she resumes the story a week after June's death and fills in the family history amid observations on the vagaries of human existence. For example, in observing that her textbook is turned to "patient abuse," she reflects that to a Kashpaw the implication would refer not to medical mistreatment but to their sense of persistent violation in the sense that European immigrants appropriated their land. But the second section is devoted primarily to memories of June: how she had studied to be a beautician; how she was never much of a mother; how she had an unstable marriage with Gordon Kashpaw; and how, by implication, Albertine adored her. The most important revelation of this section, however, is Albertine's rejection of her mother's interpretation of June's death ("probably wandered off too intoxicated to realize about the storm") in favor of her own assumption that it was a suicide: "But June grew up on the plains. Even drunk she'd have known a storm was coming. She'd have known by the heaviness in the air, the smell in the clouds" (p. 9). Albertine's empathy for June reveals sensitivity, compassion, and an awareness of inner turmoil, appropriate qualities for someone embarking on a nursing career.

Another important element of this episode is the description of the situation on the edge of the reservation, where Albertine's mother, Zelda, lives with her second husband. Albertine remembers growing up "on the land my great-grandparents were allotted when the government decided to turn Indians into farmers." She goes on to reflect that "the policy of allotment was a joke. As I was driving toward the land, looking around, I saw as usual how much of the reservation was sold to whites and lost forever," by which she means, of course, lost to Native Americans. The reference here is to a historically significant series of events beginning in the 1850s when the commissioner of Indian affairs, Francis Amasa Walker, reasoned that the federal government should manage the affairs of Native Americans, giving them sufficient support to make the transition to a modern, increasingly industrialized, society. A decade earlier, Father Baraga had remarked, specifically of the Chippewa, that virtually every winter brought starvation to the tribe and yet they made no effort at agriculture, despite the excellent soil in their area.[25] Edmund Jefferson Danziger Jr. has also assessed this Native American group from a European perspective: "Remarkably functional though it was, Chippewa culture at the time of first European contact was static: archaeological records reaching back two millennia suggest that technical knowledge was passed from generation to generation with little change. Anthropologists classify their way of life as early Neolithic, comparable to the technological progress found in the eastern Mediterranean between 4000 and 3000 B.C."[26] It was thinking of this sort, as Ronald Takaki has explained, that led Walker to conclude that Native Americans should be put on reservations and instructed in "self-improvement" until they were capable of assimilation. Walker reasoned that there was no way to sustain a viable Native American culture outside a protected area, and this assumption led to the establishment of a reservation system that lasted until 1887.[27]

In that year, Senator Henry Dawes introduced the Indian Emancipation Act aimed at getting Native Americans off the reservation as quickly as possible and making them citizens of the country. Known as the Dawes Act, the provision allotted 160 acres to every Indian family, the same size plot of land as made available to European settlers by the Homestead Act, and the assumption was that they too would become prosperous as farmers. To protect Native Americans from unscrupulous land traders, there was a provision in the law that prohibited sale of the property for twenty-five years, a crucial specification rescinded in the Burke Act of 1906. Since Native Americans had no tradition of farming, and the men saw labor of that kind as ignominious compared to the romance of hunting, the Allotment Act was a failure, its central effect being to reduce the area originally established in the reservation system, and gradually much Indian land was purchased by eager European settlers.

These policies persisted until the crucial year of 1934, when John Collier, then the commissioner of Indian affairs, established the Indian Reorganization Act eliminating the allotment provisions and effectively abandoning the efforts at assimilation, attempting instead to acquire more land for the reservations where local tribal governments could be established. None of these strategies proved to be effective in improving the lives of the Chippewa. It is not by accident, in other words, that the second story in *Love Medicine* goes back to begin the action in 1934, a key year in the modification of the Allotment Act that had so diminished the territory under the control of Native Americans. That would be the logic behind Erdrich's assertion that "contemporary Native American writers have therefore a task quite different from that of other writers. . . . In the light of enormous loss, they must tell the stories of contemporary survivors while protecting and celebrating the cores of cultures left in the wake of the catastrophe."[28]

The third section of the story elaborates on the theme of fading Indian lore, on Eli being the "last man on the reservation that could snare himself a deer" (p. 27). That Eli here refers to himself as Cree (elsewhere in the volume he is clearly Chippewa) recalls the historical situation that the Turtle Mountain Reservation in North Dakota brought together Chippewa and Cree tribes along with many French-speaking people of mixed race who came from Canada (p. 30). It is also important, within the ethos of the volume, that of the two Kashpaw brothers, it is Eli, the one who retained a close association with traditional ways, who remains strong into old age; Nector, who was educated in the white schools and lived in "civilization," grows feeble (p. 17). Albertine reflects that "perhaps his loss of memory was a protection from the past, absolving him of whatever had happened" (p. 18).

Many of the memories of June have to do with encounters with death, such as the childhood "hanging" game in which she was saved from strangulation by Zelda's frantic appearance at the last moment. Even the new car that King drives is associated with death, since it was purchased with the money from June's life insurance (p. 21). June's son King, his white wife (Lynette), and their son King Jr., who arrive in the new car, are a particularly complex group. Zelda exhibits her own brand of racism, disliking Lynette for being white. King is obviously violent and destructive, beating his wife even before their arrival at the Kashpaw home (her face is stained and swollen [p. 15]); later in the story he vandalizes his own car, presumably projecting his grief for the death of his mother (p. 32); then he tries to drown his wife in the sink (p. 38). His violence seems less an attempt to express his will than to externalize overwhelming emotions. His love with Lynette is passionate, demanding, sustained, and at the end of the story they are making love in the car (p. 39). The final image, however, is one of irredeemable loss, as Albertine attempts to put together the pies King has destroyed. Her comment that "once they smash there is no way to put them right" seems as appropriate for the lives of her family as for the pies themselves (p. 39). "The World's Greatest Fisherman" is ultimately a story of death and loss, of the disordering of an extended family, of tragedy at a time of renewal. The next nine stories move backward in time to establish the thematic context for these events.

It is significant that "Saint Marie" (pp. 40–56), which won an O. Henry Award, was originally published in the *Atlantic Monthly* in March of 1984 with the designation "A Short Story" and with no indication that it would be part of *Love Medicine*, which was mentioned in a blurb as a forthcoming "novel."[29] The original version carried no indication that the action takes place in 1934, as does the revised text, but beyond that, and some minor stylistic modifications ("Old she-devil bitch!" was changed to "Bitch of Jesus Christ!"), the story was placed unchanged into the volume. As isolated fiction in a magazine, however, there was no access to certain crucial lines of information contained in Erdrich's other work, the most important of which is that Sister Leopolda, who so cruelly receives Marie at the convent, is in fact her mother. Published independently, the story presents simply the relationship between Marie Lazarre and Sister Leopolda; as part of a short-story cycle, however, it initiates a causal history, a psychic context, that is part of the etiology of June's death. This is one of the most obvious ways in which narratives are enriched by the intertextual resonance from the others in a story sequence.

Unlike the desultory structure and chaotic focus of "The World's Greatest Fisherman," this story is a more traditional narrative: it is told in first person by the central character, Marie;[30] it has a linear plot based on a pivotal conflict; and there is a resolution to the primary line of action. As a first-person, retrospective narrative, it has a dual time scheme: the time of the action, specified as 1934; and the time of the telling, an indeterminate moment many years later in that Marie, in relating her initial walk up the hill to the convent, says "that was a long-ago day" (p. 41). Some of the events she reveals have a biographical origin in Erdrich's own family, such as the reference to "those bush Indians who stole the holy black hat of a Jesuit and swallowed little scraps of it to cure their fevers. But the hat itself carried smallpox and was killing them with belief" (p. 42). Erdrich descends from the Pillagers, who got their name by ransacking the supplies of a white trader, goods that later were discovered to have carried the smallpox that infected nearly the entire tribe.

The heart of the story concerns the inner life of Marie and her complex relationship with Sister Leopolda, whose name commemorates the fact that Christianity was brought to the Chippewas by the Leopoldine Society of Austria in 1829. A severe nun who exudes extremes of love and hatred swirled together in images of Satan and brimstone and the bliss of paradise, her feelings are echoed by Marie: "But I wanted Sister Leopolda's heart. And here was the thing: sometimes I wanted her heart in love and admiration. Sometimes. And sometimes I wanted her heart to roast on a black stick" (p. 45). Her ambivalence is all the more telling in that these are the attitudes she has toward her own mother, a fact Marie does not realize but that is embedded in the irony of the text, such as when Marie tells Sister Leopolda, "I'll inherit your keys from you" (p. 46) and when Leopolda declares, "She is mine. . . . A very good girl" (p. 51). Their conflict becomes gruesome as Leopolda steps on Marie's neck, holding her to the floor, or when she scalds her with boiling water, ostensibly to purge her of evil.

Opposed to this dour Christianity, Marie has her own magical vision out of Chippewa mythology, an image of herself with the capacity to walk through windows and with naked breasts tipped with diamonds. Inherent in the situation is the cultural duality of conflicting mythological paradigms, an inevitable ideological dissonance created by the imposition of European values on an existing way of life. Equally gruesome is Marie's attempt to kill Sister Leopolda by kicking her into a flaming

30

stove, an act that results in Marie's being stabbed in the hand by a cooking fork. There is dark humor in the ironic misinterpretation of the
wound by the sisters of the convent, inspired by Leopolda's report that
a stigmata appeared spontaneously. Thus, through a lie, Marie becomes
revered, but she feels no satisfaction, thinking "there was no heart in
it" (p. 56). As an individual story, that sentiment ends the narrative;
within the context of the volume, however, these events are only the
beginning of a line of action that begins in 1934 and leads to June's
death in 1981.

"Wild Geese" (pp. 57–62) continues the action of "Saint Marie" in
1934, picking it up just before Marie leaves the convent to walk down
the hill. When this story was published in *Mother Jones* in 1984, the
magazine gave no indication that it was linked in a crucial way to another story, that, indeed, the motivation for Marie's determined walk
down the hill, and the explanation for the bandage around her hand,
were in another story.[31] This is one of the ways in which a short-story
cycle contains incremental resonance from the ensemble of narratives.
Another way is in narrative dissonance. In the magazine, the story is
told by Nector Kashpaw, and the events are related from his point of
view. In the book, however, although this entire story is narrated by
Nector, his judgment is revealed to be flawed, and the encounter with
Marie is disclosed to be a persistent misinterpretation on his part.

There are essentially two important elements in this brief story.
The first is the beginning of a distinction between Nector Kashpaw and
his older brother, Eli. Eli is the embodiment of the old ways, of a close
identification with nature, and he lives in the woods and eschews the
modern, industrial world. Nector, on the other hand, was sent into the
government school system, and he is much more a product of the white
world, although he still hunts with Eli. His narration, some of it in present tense even though it is retrospective, is subjective and self-revealing.
It is in this story that he acknowledges his sexual obsession with Lulu
Nanapush, and he formulates his lust in the imagery of nature: "She is
a tart berry full of juice, and I know she is mine. I cannot wait for the
night to start. She will be waiting in the bush" (p. 58). Although this
imagery might seem appropriate if it derived from Eli, he of the ancient
ways, Nector uses such tropes even to describe Marie Lazarre, who is
mostly white, thinking of her as having eyes like a mink's, of looking
like a birch, of speaking like a crow (pp. 59–61). Despite his education,

the imagery would suggest, Nector thinks of women and sexuality as being part of the "natural" world.

Of course Nector has no way of knowing about Marie's encounter with Sister Leopolda in the convent. When he starts up the hill, seeking to sell two geese, he encounters the teenage Marie with a pillowcase bandage on her hand where the nun had stabbed her, the wound that gave Marie a temporary "saintly" status. Nector's erroneous assumption is that she has stolen valuables from the convent and is running away with them, a conjecture animated by his conviction that she comes from "a family of horse-thieving drunks" (p. 58). He never understands what has really happened, creating a narrative irony in the book that is absent in the magazine version of the story. As he wrestles her to the ground, she begins responding to the fleshly side of her nature, the spiritual dimension having so recently been celebrated, and they engage in sexual intercourse on the hillside in front of the convent. When they recover, she reveals her cut and swollen hand to him, and he is filled with compassion, holding her hand tenderly. Ambivalent, he protests "I don't want her, but I want her, and I cannot let go" (p. 62). This is the beginning of a relationship that becomes a long marriage producing many children, some of whom play crucial roles in *Love Medicine*. The second and third stories are thus linked to the first not only by providing the prehistory of June's death but because Nector and Marie eventually adopt June and raise her as a daughter. The dominant narrator of the first story, Albertine, is their granddaughter. In family and causal history, as well as in theme, the first three stories are closely linked.

"The Beads" (pp. 63–73) is a crucial story for defining June's character and for explaining how Marie came to adopt her. It was originally published in the *North Dakota Quarterly* in 1984 in a version with only minor differences from the book.[32] As an isolated narrative in a magazine, there was no indication that Marie and Nector were united because of a chance encounter when he came to deliver geese to the convent, that the point of the story is to establish a background and personality for June that will help explain her death, or that June would eventually kill herself in 1981. These elements, the crucial contribution of the story to the assembled volume, are nowhere to be found in the periodical text. It is a good illustration of the intertextual resonance of the cycle format and why the genre, in a sense, often has a dual existence: the magazine stories in isolation; the collected ones enriched by the presence of the surrounding tales.

32

Set in 1948, the action is told by Marie in retrospect at an indeterminate moment but apparently a long time after the events take place. (Throughout her fiction, Erdrich rarely does much with the temporal duality of action and telling.) By the time the story begins, Marie has married Nector Kashpaw, and in the intervening fourteen years since she left the convent, they have had seven children, two of whom died. Marie here reveals herself to be a warmly maternal figure who seeks to explain how she adopted her deceased sister's daughter, June, and how she lost the child when the girl chose to live with Eli in the woods. The narrational motivation would seem to be a coming to terms, Marie's clarification of how she felt about June, the issue that unites all of the stories in the volume. Although Marie begins by indicating that she did not want June at first, she took her in to rescue her from the drunken Lazarres, who brought the nine-year-old girl to the Kashpaws. The key fact about June, and one that relates to her death in "The World's Greatest Fisherman," is that she, like Eli, is an embodiment of Native American traditions, particularly with regard to her relationship with nature. There is even a mystery about her birth and early childhood, for her mother, Lucille, died in the woods, and the child purportedly survived by eating pine sap and gathering food in the wild. Marie thinks it possible that June is a child of the "Manitous, invisible ones who live in the woods," and there are indications that there is a inherent sacredness about her (p. 65).

When she arrives at Marie's home, June is wearing beads, "black beads on a silver chain" (p. 64). Marie, who reasons from a Roman Catholic perspective even after she has relinquished her faith, assumes they are rosary beads, which prompts the Lazarres to laughter. The beads were given to June by the Crees who found her in the woods, and hence the beads are emblems of the irretrievable past, of the fading religion and traditional life of a people who had lived in the region for thousands of years.[33] Since the Crees were an Algonquin clan who lived on the prairies of Canada, the suggestion is that June was found in southern Canada or in northern North Dakota, near the Turtle Mountain Indian Reservation, where they had blended with the Chippewa. June's natural affinity is not for Nector but for Eli, who lives in a shack in the woods and shares with her a knowledge of the ways of the forest. Nector has intelligence and a knowledge of how to survive in the white world, but he has lost touch with the old ways; Eli has retained his heritage: "Eli would sing his songs. Wild unholy songs. Cree songs that made you lonely. Hunting songs used to attract deer or women" (p. 69). It is no surprise that June ultimately goes to live with him.

The story also reveals, with significant foreshadowing, June's affinity for death. The scene in which Marie discovers Gordie and Aurelia about to hang June from a tree has extraordinary psychological dimensions, for it is evident that June cares more for the integrity of the game the children were playing than for her own life. Since it is she who has insisted on the hanging, she reveals a penchant for suicide, and her criticism of Marie for rescuing her, and her persistent defiance even during severe punishment, suggest a determination that will not bend (p. 69). June is implicated in another incident, when Marie has clearly grown to love Eli, and they seem ready to embrace, Eli leaves and Marie holds June in her arms, the girl of nature serving as a surrogate for the man of the woods (p. 71). Marie loves them both, as is suggested in the final passage, which depicts her as caressing the beads that June has left behind. It is a poignant episode darkly foreboding of events to come.

"Lulu's Boys" (pp. 74–88) advances the temporal setting to 1957, with some internal flashbacks reaching back to 1950, when Henry Lamartine committed suicide on the Northern Pacific railroad track. Originally published in the *Kenyon Review* in 1984, where it had more emphasis on the seven-year lapse between Henry's death and his brother Beverly's appearance at Lulu's house in 1957, the story is most dramatic in its revelation of the sexual avariciousness and fecundity of Lulu Lamartine, the feminine embodiment of the reproductive urge of nature.[34] She has had eight children, none of them fathered by her husband, which explains why there are so many hair colors among her children and which might explain why her husband killed himself. "Lulu's Boys" is the first story in *Love Medicine* narrated in third person, in this case with a shifting identification with the minds of Lulu, Beverly, and the collective consciousness of the community. There is also the clear implication that the time of the telling is many years after the events, an odd narrative stance for third person (p. 85). The narrative assumptions are blatantly unreliable, as in the explanation of Henry's "car wreck," when he collided with a train: "Drunk, he had started driving the old Northern Pacific tracks and either fallen asleep or passed out, his car straddling the rails." But the dramatized evidence is that his death was not an accident: he had stated directly in a bar that when "she comes barreling through, you'll never see me again" (p. 75).

The emphasis, however, is not on death but on the origins of life and the irresistible lure of human sexuality, ubiquitous themes whenever Lulu is present in Erdrich's fiction. The closest thing to a death scene is Lulu's melodramatic fainting into her husband's open grave in 1950, almost immediately after which she made love to his younger brother in the shed. Death is linked to the origin of life. Ironically, the product of this untimely coupling was named "Henry Jr.," and it is he Beverly has come to retrieve, to bring him home to live in the Twin Cities (Minneapolis and St. Paul) of Minnesota, a haven for Native Americans who have learned to thrive in a modern economy. The flashback to the past seven years in the cities reveals much about Beverly's life there, how he makes a living selling educational materials, how he has created a fantasy life for his son, and, especially, how his white wife denies his ethnicity, passing him off to her family in St. Cloud as having a perfect tan. The couple is childless, but Beverly dreams of bringing his son home from the reservation, a son he has never seen. That is the motivation that brings him under the sway of Lulu (he is unable to resist her sexual allure), and the conclusion features him sliding into bed with her.

"Lulu's Boys" not only moves the action to 1957, the time of three of the stories, it also shifts the tone to black comedy and the central motif to the linkage between sexuality and death, the thematic issue of the opening episode. Although this story is perfectly suitable for separate publication and, more clearly than the previous ones, contains a central conflict and resolution, there is also a great deal of intertextual resonance from the previous four. Sex and death are linked in "The World's Greatest Fisherman," which also stresses the issue of suicide, as does "The Beads." "Saint Marie" and "Wild Geese" are heavy with religious themes, but both emphasize sexuality in Sister Leopolda's hidden child and Marie's impromptu tryst on the side of a hill outside the convent. In "Lulu's Boys," however, sexuality has become overt, both the enactment of it and its harvest. As an almost vaudevillian naughty lady, Lulu is the subject for much humor in the volume, but she is also an important agent of life, a countervalence to the forces of destruction and self-immolation that pervade the reservation, that tend toward depression and alcoholism and death. That, perhaps, is the significance of her sexual dalliance with Beverly on the day of her husband's burial, for Henry terminated his own existence, surrendered to his worst impulses, whereas Lulu's lust for Beverly is life-affirming, a commitment to the future, the personification of which is the children playing outside the house.

"The Plunge of the Brave" (pp. 89–110) is connected to the stories on either side of it in crucial ways, and yet it was also a self-contained work of fiction when it appeared in the *New England Review* in 1984.[35] The second story in *Love Medicine* narrated by Nector Kashpaw, it is one of the most complex in the volume, especially temporally. The time of narration and present action is identified as 1957, and yet many of the crucial scenes take place in 1940 and 1952, and one of the "past" episodes is told in present tense, as is one of the "present" scenes, with the rest in past tense. On one level, this methodology violates narrative logic, skewing the relationship between the telling and the tale; in the context of traditional Chippewa stories, however, it is an expression of the nonlinear conception of time that guided their lives.[36] For a people to whom time was cyclical and accretive, it would seem natural that in telling a story, as Catherine Rainwater has explained, "linearity is often disrupted by many flashbacks, lateral narrational pursuits, flights of free association, and other indications of the failure of chronology to contain the story."[37] Although there is a clear line of plot involving Nector's marriage to Marie and his lust for Lulu, the memories he relates drift forward and back in time: as he explains it, "events loop around and tangle again" (p. 95). Thematically, however, it concentrates on a nucleus of issues: the personality of Nector; his abiding lust for Lulu; his enduring marriage to Marie.

The title "The Plunge of the Brave" is rich in ambiguity and timbre, referring at once to the painting for which Nector posed as a young man, and which hangs in the North Dakota state capitol in Bismark, and to Nector's decline, driven by his lust for Lulu. The titular reference to "the brave" is also ambiguous, suggesting, somewhat anachronistically, Nector's role as a Native American warrior while also referring to his fortitude as a man in the modern world. In the manner of Nick Carraway's self-revelatory narration in *The Great Gatsby*, Nector begins with a definition of himself: "I never wanted much, and I needed even less, but what happened was that I got everything handed to me on a plate" (p. 89). He is proud of his stature as one of the last hereditary Chippewa leaders (he becomes tribal chairman).[38] He reveals that he was educated at the Flandreau Indian School in South Dakota, where he became intrigued with *Moby-Dick*, an allusion that suggests another meaning for "plunge," as not simply descent but sudden immersion in water, the traditional place of death for the Chippewa. He is pleased with his physical appearance, and his handsome physique leads to his brief career as a model and motion picture actor. But the central focus is on his romantic entanglements, especially with regard to Lulu. What Nector relates about Marie has to do with domestic obligations: he briefly recounts the events of "Wild Geese" and then goes on to describe the next seventeen years of their marriage. He emphasizes that they have a house full of children, some natural, some adopted, and he supports them by working as a farmhand (p. 93). His account of Lulu, on the other hand, has to do with romantic longing and erotic fulfillment, beginning when they were children in boarding school. There is also a philosophic element to his fascination for her: as he contemplates the transience of life, it occurs to him that his love for Lulu has been sustained and that to reclaim their relationship of two decades ago he would have to "swim against the movement of time" (p. 94). That is the thought that is transforming in Nector's life, and his account of his effort to revitalize his romance with her is central to his reflections.

Perhaps Nector, in 1957, narrates the events of 1952 in the present tense because they are so immediate to him; in any event, this retrospective episode is related as though happening in the moment. As he recounts the day he enlisted Lulu into helping him distribute surplus butter to the community, his emphasis is on her sensuality, on his "ache" for her. Her husband, Henry, committed suicide in 1950; she made love with her brother-in-law, Beverly, on the day of the funeral; she gave birth to their child, Henry Jr., nine months later, in 1951; now, in 1952, she makes love with Nector in a Nash Ambassador Custom. When he returns home to Marie, his narration shifts to past tense: the suggestion is that he does not recall these events with the same immediacy as he does the lovemaking with Lulu. He continues his surreptitious affair with Lulu for five years, 1952–57, during which time she has a child. Nector is afraid to ask if it is his, knowing that he may not be able to live with the answer (p. 101). All of this connects to the events in "Lulu's Boys" when Nector sees Beverly Lamartine's car parked outside Lulu's house. Part of the resonance of *Love Medicine* comes from this technique of duplicative time, of circling back to recount an experience from alternate points of view. In the magazine version of the story, of course, there was no way to know that Lulu was inside the house making love to Beverly, that Henry Jr. was his child, and that they would, on this day, begin living together. In the context of the volume, however, this parallactic view of the situation creates a dramatic irony totally missing from the magazine account.

For one thing, in the book it is clear that Nector's actions from this point on, with regard to keeping Lulu, are moot. There is thus a deep irony in his leaving a note for Marie informing her that he is leaving her for Lulu and another note to Lulu proposing marriage. There was no referential base for this irony in the magazine account. When he goes to Lulu's house to propose to her, there is no one at home and, pondering his situation, Nector realizes that he is preoccupied with her, likening his fixation on her to Ahab's obsession with Moby Dick (p. 108). There is a further irony in that he throws down his note to her and then accidentally sets it on fire with a cigarette, eventually burning down Lulu's house. It is at this moment that Nector looks into the bush and thinks he sees Marie standing there, not the Marie he has just left but the Marie of "Wild Geese," fourteen years old, thin, and innocent. The girl he sees, it becomes evident in "Flesh and Blood," is his daughter Zelda, the eventual mother of Albertine Johnson.

The next story is a temporal overlay of "The Plunge of the Brave," relating the same time period from Marie's point of view. She narrates these events on the same day they happen, on August 7, 1957, giving this story a synchronicity of telling and action unlike any of the previous narratives.[39] When "Flesh and Blood" was originally published in *Ms.* in 1984, it carried the title "Love Medicine," which is not what the story is about.[40] The plot actually concerns two separate subjects: Marie takes Zelda to the convent to see Sister Leopolda, who is dying; when they return home, Zelda reads the note Nector left on the table for Marie in "The Plunge of the Brave," and she leaves to bring him home. That is why she is standing in the bushes waiting for Nector at the end of that story. There are thus layers of intertextual allusions to Marie's fight with Leopolda in "Saint Marie," to the combative seduction of Nector by Marie when she leaves the convent in "Wild Geese," and, most overtly, to Nector's decision to leave his family for Lulu in "The Plunge of the Brave."

Marie's decision to return to the convent to see Sister Leopolda is emotionally complex, particularly in the context of the information, not mentioned in this text, that the two are mother and daughter. Marie still carries the scars of her encounter with the nun in 1934; the physical wound to her palm is now healed, but the religious hurt lingers on, causing Marie to perceive the world in terms of hatred and damnation. Leopolda's condescending reception of her daughter is without warmth or sensitivity, although her eyes do linger on Zelda, her granddaughter (a relationship never acknowledged), and only the nun knows the truth (p. 118). The conflicts of more than two decades ago flare again, and Marie and Sister Leopolda fight as they had before, with hatred on both sides. And so they part, in bitterness and condemnation and denial, emotions not lost on the young Zelda.

It is Zelda who first finds Nector's note, and the clear implication is that her reading of it inspires her to rush to Lulu's house to retrieve her father. Marie reads it as well, and her reflections on his infidelity have meaning for the entire volume. For one thing, she thinks of Lulu's indiscretions that compelled Henry to drive onto the railroad tracks and commit suicide. She says, with determination, "I wouldn't park myself on the tracks for Nector" (p. 125). The story opened with Marie canning apples, with domestic preserving, as it were; another form of family preservation now comes into play, as Marie decides not to acknowledge Nector's note, allowing him to return home with no consequences for his impropriety. She also insists on scrubbing the floor in her best dress, cleansing hygienically what she cannot expunge emotionally: "Love had turned my head away from what was going on between my husband and Lamartine. There was something still left that Nector could hurt me with, and now I hurt for love . . ." (p. 128). Nevertheless, when he returns, her comments are only about her work on the floor, and thus she makes a gesture of reconciliation, allowing him to return without humiliation: "I put my hand through what scared him. I held it out there for him. And when he took it with all the strength of his arms, I pulled him in" (p. 129). Marie has preserved what matters to her most. Her means of doing so, however, is not through the magic of "love medicine" but by an understanding of the contradictions and vagaries of "flesh and blood," a much better title for the story than the original.

The eighth story in *Love Medicine*, "A Bridge" (pp. 130–42), is the first in the volume not previously published, the first set in 1973, the first to take place in a city, and the first narrated from an omniscient perspective. The narrative voice is anomalous among the stories, giving a prehistory of the present action, drifting in and out of characters' minds, offering unmediated thought in italics at the closest levels of narrational identification. The action is simple: Albertine Johnson, fifteen in 1973, has run away from the reservation to make her life in Fargo, the largest city in North Dakota and the place where, in "The World's Greatest Fisherman," she is a nursing student in 1981. She knows no one, and she is drawn to Henry Lamartine Jr. by his familiar Chippewa features. Henry Jr. is just back from the war in Vietnam, where he has been a prisoner of war, and he is emotionally unstable. They make love in a cheap hotel before he turns violent, unable to separate present reality from the mental anguish he endured in the war. It becomes clear in this scene that what is important about the story is not the plot but the psychological implications of the characters' responses to their circumstances.

Albertine's trip "down" to Fargo clarifies that the reservation is in the northern part of the state, most certainly the Turtle Mountain Reservation of Erdrich's own family. In geographic reality, from there the closest city is Grand Forks, with Fargo well to the south. Albertine could be from the Devil's Lake Indian Reservation, but that is Sioux and she is clearly Chippewa. Most likely, Erdrich eliminated Grand Forks and the Devil's Lake Reservation from her fictional map. In her description of Fargo, Erdrich is good with local details, the seedy streets along Northern Pacific Avenue, the Herbst department store. She is also good in portraying the vulnerability of the young Albertine, away from home for the first time, comforted by the discovery of another Chippewa who knows her family.

In intertextual context, of course, it is not surprising that Henry Jr. is a randy sort. He is the child born of the tryst in the shed between Lulu and Beverly the day of her husband's funeral. His turmoil derives not so much from American ethnic history as from his recent experiences in Southeast Asia: "He had been a soldier, was now a veteran, had seen nine months of combat in the Annamese Cordillera before the NVA captured him somewhere near Pleiku. They kept him half a year" (p. 134). As is true of the protagonists of Ernest Hemingway, Henry Jr. has his psychological and physical wounds, and that is the most important fact about him. During their night together in the hotel, Albertine realizes that he is emotionally unstable, as his unjustified violence the next day indicates. When he makes love to the young girl, in his mind he sees a woman in Vietnam. His weeping at the end of the story is another indication of the psychic anguish that torments him. In a sense "A Bridge" moves the volume forward to 1973 and into the modern world in which the central issues are not so much the allotment and the historical treatment of Native Americans as the international political configuration, matters far removed from the interactions of the Kashpaws and Lamartines on the Turtle Mountain Reservation.

"The Red Convertible" (pp. 143–54) relates directly to the previous story both temporally and thematically in that it follows the activities of "The Bridge" and continues the presentation of the psychological effect of the Vietnam War on Henry Jr. The second of the *Love Medicine* stories to appear in print (it was published in the *Mississippi Valley Review* in 1982), it is also an indicator of the complex composition history and publication record of a short-story cycle. In the collected volume, the story is narrated by Lyman Lamartine, younger brother of Henry Jr., and it concerns Henry's return home from the Vietnam War. The magazine account, however, is narrated by a character named "Marty" and concerns an older brother named "Stephen."[41] It is very clear that at the moment of its initial publication, this was an independent story and not part of a larger unit. As a consequence, many details (including the names of the characters and the dates) had to be revised when it was merged into place among the other stories, and some important information, including the observation that the two boys have the same mother (the promiscuous Lulu) but look quite different from each other, was added to the text.

This is the first of Erdrich's stories narrated by Lyman, and his ironic tone and sly observations are unique among her narrators, who often sound indistinct from one another. The opening paragraph reveals his acerbic indirection: "I owned that car along with my brother Henry Junior. We owned it together until his boots filled with water on a windy night and he bought out my share. Now Henry owns the whole car, and his younger brother Lyman (that's myself), Lyman walks everywhere he goes" (p. 143). What the ensuing action reveals is that Henry's boots filled with water when he committed suicide by jumping into the Red River of the North during flood stage; he purchased Lyman's share of the car with his life in the sense that Lyman pushed the car into the river when he realized his brother was dead. Henry thus owned the whole car by being in the water with it. Lyman, who is lucky with money and succeeds in one job after another, walks not out of poverty but of despondency, not yet, at the time of the telling, having recovered from his brother's death.

This story, particularly in its original publication, also clearly locates the "reservation" at issue as the Turtle Mountain Indian Reservation in northern North Dakota, not far from the Canadian border. In the magazine text, the younger brother shines shoes at the legion hall in Rolla, a small town on the eastern edge of the reservation. Erdrich removed this specific designation in the book, referring instead to simply the American Legion Hall, leaving it uncertain as to the community in which it is located (p. 143). When the boys take their trip to Alaska, they return home from the West through Bottineau County, which locates precisely the Turtle Mountain Reservation.[42]

The heart of the story concerns the implications of "the red convertible" and Henry's suicide. The car is very clearly an artifact of the industrial world, not at all traditional in the Native American world, and it signifies that the children of Lulu are moving rapidly into the international world, traveling to foreign countries. As Erdrich has commented, "when Henry gets in the red convertible, the red convertible can stand for something like assimilation; it's a very loaded symbol."[43] Although not a formal "symbol," the car is an expression of modernity in the "white" world and an emblem of pride for the boys. Lyman uses that fact when Henry returns home after three years in Vietnam, some of it as a prisoner of war, and Lyman can see the psychic damage that has been done to him: "When he came home, though, Henry was very different, and I'll say this: the change was no good" (p. 147). Lyman damages the car to give Henry some purpose to his life, knowing that he will repair it. When he first arrives home, he is without direction: "Henry was jumpy and mean" (p. 148). His pathology is evident as he bites through his own lip, but Lyman and Lulu (unnamed in the story but obviously Lulu) know that there are no psychiatrists on the reservation, and he receives no help for what is probably post-traumatic stress syndrome. When his repair of the car is finished, he gives it immediately to Lyman, who refuses it, leading to a fight between the two brothers. Henry jumps into the Red River, swollen in springtime from the annual melting of snow and also by the fact that the river flows north into waters that are still frozen, causing a backflood along its entire length. Henry's only comment is "my boots are filling," and then he goes under. Lyman's sacrificing the car in the river that has taken his brother is a gripping conclusion, one somewhat different in the magazine text, which ends not with the "running and running" of the water but with the younger brother saying "Marty you must walk home. They are waiting."

In the integrated volume, "The Red Convertible" has layers of implications missing from the magazine text. There was no indication in the *Mississippi Valley Review* that Henry was the product of a tryst between his uncle and his mother on the day of his father's funeral. There was no implication that the father's suicide foreshadows the son's. There was no suggestion that between his release from the Marine Corps and his return home he had made love to the young Albertine in Fargo or that his pathology had emerged in his relationship with her. Only in the published volume does it become evident that the energy of "love" that produced life in the first half of the book has been transmogrified into a sexual force that brings death in the second half. Lyman survives the story, of course, but his retrospective rehearsal of these events suggests a painful attempt to integrate the death of his brother into his experience, to accept what has happened, and that is presented as being deeply problematic.

The first published story of the *Love Medicine* group was "Scales," which appeared in the *North American Review* in March of 1982 before its inclusion in *The Best American Short Stories of 1983*.[44] In each instance it was clearly presented as a short story, not as a chapter in a novel, and many of the details were changed between magazine and book publication, including the gender of the child born to Dot Adare.[45] But the central plot of the story is essentially the same in each case, as is the narrative stance, a first-person retrospective by Albertine Johnson. Although she has interaction with both Dot Adare and Gerry Nanapush, they, not Albertine, are the focus of the events. As Erdrich has indicated in an interview, she chose the name "Nanapush" as an allusion to "Nanabozho," the legendary Chippewa trickster who had formidable cravings for food and erotic gratification.[46] That he has no regard for the law or any other superimposed social order is another traditional aspect of this allusion, as is the capture and escape cycle that dominates his life.[47] Dot, on the other hand, is portrayed from Albertine's perspective as bovine and docile, with breasts so large she sometimes carries them with her forearms.

As the title "Scales" suggests, the themes of the story relate to the weighing of things: the literal weighing of gravel trucks, the attempt to weigh the baby Shawn, and the figurative weighing of justice and law. At thirty-five, Gerry has been in prison, off and on, for half of his life, beginning with a conviction for a barroom fight with a cowboy over "whether a Chippewa was also a nigger" (p. 161). Albertine exhibits a comic flair in describing the fight, which begins with Gerry's kicking the other man in the scrotum: "Gerry also said he had nightmares sometimes that the cowboy did manage to have little cowboys, all born with full sets of grinning teeth, Stetson hats, and little balls hard as plum pits" (p. 163). But as the events progress to the trial, rather more serious issues begin to emerge: "Gerry's friends, you see, had no confidence in the United States judicial system" (p. 162). The Chippewa perspective, of course, would be that European law had been imposed upon their people, a legal construct that was formulated against their interests and that resulted not in fair dealings but in yet another bureaucracy with which they had to contend. All of this becomes grim as Gerry kills a state trooper while trying to avoid arrest to join Dot and their daughter. Albertine's considered judgment is that Gerry believed in justice but not in American law (p. 161). From this perspective the story is not about a renegade Native American who violates and eludes the law but about the persecution of a Chippewa on his own territory by an invading European population with no sense of proportional justice. The scales are tipped from the beginning against Gerry Nanapush.

But the narrative also concerns the origin of life, with conception occurring in the visiting area of a prison and birth in Saint Adalbert's Hospital near the reservation. It is interesting that in the magazine version the child was born in the "Saint Francis Hospital," an actual facility in Breckenridge, Minnesota, the sister town to Wahpeton, North Dakota, where Erdrich spent her childhood. The two towns are separated only by the Red River of the North, the river in which Henry Jr. drowns himself in "The Red Convertible." In the magazine, Dot gives birth to a boy she names Jason, the name resonant of the Greek leader of the Argonauts who captures the golden fleece. In *Love Medicine*, the child is a daughter and is named Shawn, a masculine name suggestive of the Shawnee people. The action ends with her being weighed on the truck scales and failing to register any substance at all, a wonderfully metaphoric expression of the value of a people who do not count in the scheme of things.

"Crown of Thorns" (pp. 172–88) is the last of the stories in *Love Medicine* to have been published previously, appearing in essentially the same form in *Chicago* in 1984.[48] In a sense its importance is temporal, for it is the first story since "The World's Greatest Fisherman" to post-date the death of June, the unifying event in the book, and its central theme is the emotional devastation her death brought to Gordon Kashpaw, her estranged husband. The action takes place in the spring of

1981, one month after June died on Easter Sunday. If the emotions of the story are complex, the events are simple: Gordie has become an alcoholic, refusing Eli's offer of food, hallucinating that he sees June's face everywhere. When he hits a deer on the way to town, he puts the animal in the back seat; it regains consciousness and Gordie sees it in the rearview mirror and assumes that it is June. Late at night, he stumbles toward the Sacred Heart Convent, the same institution where Marie first confronted Sister Leopolda in "Saint Marie," and he frightens Sister Mary Martin, who eventually calls the police. When they arrive, Gordie is weeping uncontrollably in the open fields.

What makes all of this interesting is not just the depth of emotion that Gordon expresses but the narrative perspectives from which the events are related. Basically, the point of view is shifting and unreliable, varying from omniscient formulations to third-person identifications with the minds of Gordie, Eli, and Sister Mary Martin. An omniscient narrator sketches in the background: that Gordie had married his cousin June, with whom he had been raised. After the wedding, they had a passionate and violent relationship that produced King. The situation and cast of characters are thus resonant of the opening story, in which King and his wife come to the reservation after June's death. The shift to Eli's more limited perspective allows the revelation of his memories of June when she left the home of Nector and Marie and came to live with him, sleeping on a cot next to the stove, learning some of the Native American lore he had to teach her.

The subsequent shift to a perspective allied with Gordie's mind also allows for retrospection, for his assessment of their troubled marriage, for "he both missed June and was relieved to be without her" (p. 176). He remembers how they ran off to South Dakota to get married, choosing a state with no waiting period, but their impulsive romance proved to be emotionally troubled. Despite his bitterness, his obsession with her memory and his hallucinations of her face reveal that she has meant everything to him, so much that he cannot face life without her. The incident with the deer manifests his Chippewa heritage as a hunter, a tradition defiled in the modern world with mechanized methods of killing. In his derangement he believes that when he kills the animal he has actually killed June, and he assumes the guilt for her lonely death in a spring storm.

The concluding narrative modulation showing the perspective of Sister Mary Martin allows for someone outside these events to witness the effect of them, someone who is herself lonely and troubled, unable to sleep at night. She moves from fear to concern to compassion, thinking at first that Gordie has actually killed his wife and has her body in the back seat of his car. When the nun discovers that it is really a deer, her tension breaks, and she weeps: "It came out of her with hard violence, loud in her ears, a wild burst of sounds that emptied her" (p. 187). Her lament would seem to be part relief and part compassion for Gordie and June, with a good deal of the release of her own inner turmoil as well. It is she who witnesses and describes Gordie's final breakdown in the fields near the convent, when the tribal police carry him away, deepening the emotional response he displayed in the opening story to June's death.

The final three stories in the volume were not previously published, presumably having been written for inclusion in the book rather than for magazines. They all take place after June's death in 1981, expanding on the consequences of the tragedy and the psychological responses to it. The first of these is "Love Medicine." Of course Erdrich had already published a story by that title in *Ms.* magazine, but in the compilation of her stories into a volume, she changed that title to "Flesh and Blood" and wrote a new titular story, one that deals with the Chippewa tradition for concocting magic potions thought to evoke romantic longing. That sentimental idea is made into black comedy by having Lipsha Morrissey narrate the events. His digressive intelligence (a throwback to the regional humor technique of the late nineteenth century), his grim humor, and his obtuse attempt to improve the lives of the central characters give this story an absurd tone not present elsewhere in *Love Medicine.*

The events of the story are simple if grotesque. By 1982 Marie and Nector and Lulu are all living in public housing for senior citizens, Nector having declined to the point of near-imbecility. His libido has remained youthful, however, and Lipsha comes upon him making love to Lulu in the laundry room. Realizing that Marie still loves him desperately, he improvises a love potion of turkey hearts that Marie feeds to him, only to have him choke and die attempting to eat them. But "Love Medicine" (pp. 189–215) is more a story of perspective than action, and Lipsha's musings on his life play a unifying role for the entire volume at the same time the events conclude the romance between Nector and Marie that began in "Saint Marie." Lipsha is the son of June Morrissey, whose death drives all of the stories to some degree, but he seems not to know the truth, for he refers to her as "Aunt June." Since her concept of motherhood was somewhat "irregular" (she wanted to drown her son), he was raised by his aunt and uncle, Marie and Nector Kashpaw, to whom he feels intense devotion. He especially admires Nector, who has assumed the status of archetypal Indian, with his image on the tourist guides to North Dakota (p. 191).

In this story, as throughout the volume, love and death are inter-twined, unifying the fourteen stories into one thematic construct. As Erdrich has indicated, "this 'love medicine' is all through the book, but it backfires on the boy who tries it out because he's kind of inept. It's funny what happens until it becomes tragic."[49] Indeed, there are at least three dimensions to "love" in this story: Lipsha's devoted service to his adoptive parents; Marie's sustaining emotional commitment to her hus-band, despite a lifetime of his indiscretions; and Nector's perpetual lust for Lulu. His randy impulses get the better of him in the laundry room scene, and Lipsha is sensitive to how much it hurts Marie: "And that's when I saw how much grief and love she felt for him. And it gave me a real shock to the system" (p. 192). Lipsha is aware of Nector's motiva-tion, however, for, as he describes it, the "Lamartine was jacked up, lat-ticed, shuttered, and vinyl sided, while Grandma sagged and bulged on her slipped foundations and let her hair go the silver gray of rain-dried lumber" (p. 196). The comic formulation of this insight is rendered amusingly grotesque when, during the tryst, Lulu's wig slides off, re-vealing her bald head (p. 197).

Lipsha's desire to direct Nector's craving back to his wife initiates his attempt to devise a love medicine, a plan that goes wrong in every respect: rather than using goose hearts (he misses his shots at the geese), he selects frozen turkey hearts at a local supermarket; when they cannot be blessed by the church, he dips his hand in holy water and blesses the hearts himself; and Marie, seeking to maximize the effectiveness of the medicine, serves them to Nector raw. In a sense, Nector dies *of* love and *for* love, the victim of his charisma, and death is the product of his erotic desire. On the other hand, Marie's selfless love for him is so deep that she fantasizes his presence after his death, as does Lipsha himself (p. 213).

There are important thematic elements that are only tangentially related to the central plot, however. Lipsha's earlier attempts to make his love medicine sacred reveals his cultural duality in that he attempts to receive Roman Catholic sanction for a Chippewa potion, uniting his two religious traditions. It may be simply an attempt to hedge his bets, for his musings on religion reveal his notion that "God's been going deaf. Since the Old Testament, God's been deafening up on us" (p. 194). In his reflections contrasting Christianity with Chippewa mythology, particularly with regard to the trickster Nanabozho and the water deity Missepeshu, Lipsha is led to prefer Native religion: "Our Gods aren't perfect, is what I'm saying, but at least they come around" (p. 195). He ponders the divine injustice of what has happened to his family, including his mother, whom he thinks of as Aunt June, misinterpreting that she was "left by a white man to wander off in the snow" (p. 195). In "The World's Greatest Fisherman," of course, it is she who does the leaving. Lipsha is also off on Henry Jr.'s death in "The Red Convertible," for he reports that "Lyman and Henry went out of control in their car, ending up in the river. Lyman swam to the top, but Henry never made it," which may be the account Lyman gave to the family after the incident (p. 198). Lipsha is the quintessential unreliable narrator, misconstruing much of what happens around him, but he does not deceive himself. Erdrich's handling of point of view here reveals the inherent tendency for narrative parallax in the short-story cycle, reality being described differently from a spectrum of narrators, none of whom have witnessed or understand the entire chain of events.

That method is at the very center of "The Good Tears" (pp. 216–36), in which parallactic narration (allowing Lulu Lamartine to give her version of events) and duplicative time (reaching backward to cover previous scenes once again) constitute nearly the entire story. The only "new" action of substance is the reconciliation of Marie and Lulu after Nector's death, Marie caring for the nearly blind Lulu in the senior citizen apartments. But the heart of the narrative is retrospective and self-revelatory, Lulu illuminating much about herself in the process of explaining her life from her point of view, including her three marriages. What she says is that she always loved Nector from the time they were in school together, but when he began his relationship with the young Marie (in "Saint Marie"), Lulu "married a riffraff Morrissey for hurt and spite" (p. 217). Then she married Henry Lamartine for "fondness" and had eight sons, none of them by Henry. She seems oblivious to the idea that he might have found that humiliating, and she interprets his death not as suicide but as an accident: "He stalled in the middle of a soybean field, or maybe the train did not blow its warning whistle" (p. 218). She seems unaware of what is revealed in "Lulu's Boys," that

Henry announced his intention to commit suicide to his friends in a bar (p. 75), and she is clearly unreliable on this point and many others. Then she indicates that she married Henry's brother Beverly, with whom she had begun an affair on the day of her husband's funeral, out of friendship rather than passion: "I had a fond spot in my heart for Beverly. He was a smooth, mild man, and I thought he wouldn't give me any trouble once I had him" (p. 222). What she leaves unspoken is that her romantic longings over the years were always for Nector.

Almost all of her explanations offer more information and another perspective on events covered in the earlier stories. Her baldness, reported but unexplained in "Love Medicine," turns out to have been the result of Nector's burning her house in "The Plunge of the Brave," a point unknown to him when he told that story. Nor did he know that Lyman, Nector's own son, was in the burning house at the time and that Lulu lost her hair when she crawled through the flames to rescue him. She also clarifies her bitterness, blaming the man she loved for the loss of her house, in that the tribal government ruled that a factory was going to be built on that property and she would have to vacate. That leads to a marvelously humorous scene when Lulu appears before the local government and threatens to reveal the fathers of her children, at which point the tribal leaders immediately shout out "restitution for Lamartine," attempting to purchase her silence (p. 224); she is eventually given a new property. She never understands that it was Nector who started the fire that destroyed her house, but she offers endlessly fascinating perspectives on the crucial events in the previous stories. This kind of incremental enrichment is characteristic of the story cycle, and it functions best when the stories are assembled, not when they appear separately in magazines.

The second half of the story is less retrospective, although she goes back to explain the tryst in the laundry room in "Love Medicine" as "dreamstuff," done for historical reasons, not for immediate fervor: "What I felt for Nector was just elusive dreams but no less powerful for being false" (p. 232). She also reveals her pain at the death of Henry Jr., especially since he died in the river, Chippewa legend holding that those who die in the water are denied heaven and "forced to wander forever, broken shoed, cold, sore, and ragged" (p. 234). But it is the present action that dominates this section, particularly the mutual mourning of Marie and Lulu for Nector, an emotion that unites previous rivals for his amorous affection. It is here that the title develops its final meaning. Initially its significance is in negation, that Lulu did not weep throughout the tragedies of her life (p. 217). When she did weep it was for someone she never knew, the dead man she found in the woods near her childhood home (p. 220). Now, in her dotage, she has lost the physical capacity of tears, probably as a result of the fire, and Marie must put drops in her eyes, caring for her tenderly, as a mother for a child (p. 236). The emotional significance of this situation is fully apparent only in the context of the other stories, through intertextual referentiality, which might explain why the story was never published separately.

The concluding story in the 1984 edition of *Love Medicine* is "Crossing the Water" (pp. 237–72), which is, in effect, Lipsha's quest for identity in the context of the revelations of the thirteen previous stories. It is an episodic narrative, told from two contrasting perspectives: a third-person section in which the narrational intelligence is identified with the mind of Howard Kashpaw (young King Jr.) and three first-person sections told in retrospect by Lipsha. Previously unpublished, this story would have made little sense outside the volume in that the referential base for interpreting even factual matters would have been lost without the antecedent episodes. After describing Howard's impressions within the bathroom, the narration records that "his father" kicks a table, without clarifying that Howard's father is King Kashpaw. Similarly, the reference to "his mother" clearly means Lynette, the white woman who is part of the violent marriage to King documented in "The World's Greatest Fisherman." When he says that "he's busted out again," there is no compensating information to indicate that it is Gerry Nanapush who is at issue, the Gerry whose escapes are celebrated in "Scales." In this section, what is significant is that King Jr. is also seeking an identity for himself, a matter introduced with his taking the name "Howard" at school and in his isolation in the bathroom during a quarrel between his parents. Howard seeks a more tranquil world in which the police are not pursuing his relatives and his parents are not battering each other.

Their tumultuous relationship is much in evidence in the three sections narrated by Lipsha, who, it is revealed in a flashback, has stolen his grandmother's savings to run off to the Twin Cities of Minneapolis and St. Paul (p. 245). There, in his secret search for the truth about who he is, he visits his half-brother King, who knows, but does not acknowledge, that they are both the sons of June. The nexus with the other stories is thus a tangled web of themes and family lineage reaching back to June's death in the opening scene of the volume. Lipsha lived not knowing who his parents were until Lulu, no paragon of judicious restraint, informed him of the truth, which inspired him to enlist in the army (p. 240). Since Lulu's son Gerry is Lipsha's father, Lulu is his grandmother. It is interesting that as Lipsha contemplates all of this, his narrative stance becomes remote, describing himself from the outside: "Lipsha Morrissey . . . was now on the verge of knowing who he was" (p. 244).

The mythic dimension to all of this is Gerry's role as Nanabozho, the trickster, a "famous politicking hero, dangerous armed criminal, judo expert, escape artist, charismatic member of the American Indian Movement, and smoker of many pipes of Kinnikinnick in the most radical groups" (p. 248). Lipsha is forced to a new realization: "Dad." Consistent with Chippewa tradition, Lipsha has a connection to supernatural powers that invest him with a "vision," a sense that his father has broken out of prison yet again. That feeling proves to be both powerful and correct, as a television announcement indicates, and Gerry is soon climbing in the window of King's apartment. When Gerry asks Lipsha his name, he can only laugh at the reply, realizing that here is the son he has never known. As they play cards with King for the "Firebird" (an appropriately Native American referent) purchased with June's life insurance, it is Lipsha who wins, who ends up spiriting his father away in the trunk of the car purchased with his mother's money. Lipsha takes Gerry to the Canadian border, where he plans to cross to see his wife and daughter in Manitoba, fulfilling a parental obligation he had neglected with Lipsha; the son is thus obliged to act as protector for the father. In this inverted relationship they find solidarity: "We held each other's arms, tight and manly, when we got to the border" (p. 271). Lipsha contemplates the Red River, the one in which Henry Jr. drowned himself, and reflects on the legend that it "was the last of an ancient ocean, miles deep, that once had covered the Dakotas and solved all our problems" (p. 272).

Lipsha's garbled allusion is to prehistoric Lake Aggasiz, which was never "miles deep" but which covered the vast Red River Valley of Minnesota and North Dakota and extended north past Winnipeg. This was ancient Chippewa territory, and it has mythic resonance for Lipsha. He is going home to the reservation, but his final comment is enigmatic: "So there was nothing to do but cross the water, and bring her home." The "her" could refer to the car, to Grandma Kashpaw (whose handkerchief is in his pocket), or, most richly, to his mother, June, whose desire to return home animates the opening episode of *Love Medicine*. The conclusion suggests that Lipsha finds some measure of health and peace in his reconciliation with his father and in his fulfillment of his mother's wish to be brought home, at least emotionally: "Lipsha will not be consumed by depression, by loss, by drowning and destruction. Instead, he returns to the reservation to face his life with a sane and philosophical outlook."[50] Significantly, it is the abandoned Lipsha, who never knew who he was, who forges an integrated personality at peace with his family and the world around him and whose final comments conclude the story with optimism: "The morning was clear. A good road led on" (p. 272). He has completed his quest in a definition of self and a psychic reconciliation with his parents, and most importantly, with a bonding to his father, love proving to be the strongest medicine of all.

It is a strong conclusion to a series of fourteen stories that individually are complete within themselves but relate in important ways to the surrounding narratives, which often contain lines of motivation or resolution not in a single story. As an assembled short-story cycle, however, there are issues of structural organization that transcend simple linkages between individual stories, giving shape and coherence to the entire volume, an important element of the aesthetics of the genre. In the case of *Love Medicine*, the fourteen stories are assembled in the mirror image of each other, the first and last dealing with similar issues, as do the second and thirteenth, the third and twelfth, and so on to the pivotal seventh and eighth stories, which swing the structure around.[51] It is a subtle and complex pattern that seems to have developed only in the late stages of Erdrich's organization of the volume, for she has said that when she first set the stories in order, "I had no real theory behind the form. I started it way in the past with 'St. Marie,' then went to the present, and then back and forth without any real structure, just a kind of personal liking."[52] What eventually evolved is a highly organized pattern of stories that gives structure and design to seemingly disparate stories, all of which relate in some way to the death of June, the signal event that begins the volume.[53]

The first and last stories in the collection deal, at least in part, with June's dying wish to return home and with her son Lipsha's ultimate fulfillment of that desire as, having reconciled with his wayward father, he turns his car homeward, the death in the first story having been transmuted into an affirmation of life in the final one. Stories two and thirteen, moving inward from the perimeter, deal with Marie, with her aborted entry into the convent, her pseudo-saintliness, and her genuinely humane virtue as she cares for the elderly Lulu after the death of Nector, a particularly meaningful thematic reflection. Related to these issues are stories three and twelve, focusing on the romance of Nector and Marie, from their impromptu tryst on the hill in front of the convent to Lipsha's attempt to concoct a love medicine to redirect Nector's amorous designs back to Marie from the erotically avaricious Lulu. The next set of matching stories, four and eleven, both deal with June, with her childhood, when Marie adopts her only to have her elect to live with Eli, and with Gordie's inebriated reaction to the news of June's death. Stories five and ten deal with the power of sexual desire and the related issue of fathers wishing to be united with their children. Beverly comes to claim his son, Henry Jr., in "Lulu's Boys" and Gerry Nanapush escapes from prison to be with Dot when their child is born in "Scales." The next set of stories, six and nine, balance on the issues of self-destruction, as Nector decides to leave Marie for Lulu and ends up burning down Lulu's house in "The Plunge of the Brave" and Henry Jr. commits suicide in the river in "The Red Convertible." The two pivotal stories, seven and eight, both deal with pathological love, with Marie's effort to reconcile with the insane Sister Leopolda in "Flesh and Blood" and with Albertine's romantic interlude with Henry Jr. in Fargo, a scene that reveals the depth of his traumatic emotional damage from the Vietnam War. In a book about "love medicine" in its various forms, it is appropriate that the heart of the action turns on love, on destructively familial, intensely erotic, but deeply important affection. The structural pattern of *Love Medicine* thus reveals a volume with a good deal of aesthetic integrity that gives shape to the assemblage of fourteen independent stories.

If this symmetrical structure is subtle and unobtrusive, there are other elements that reveal a more readily discernible coherence to the stories, the most obvious of which is that the major characters are all associated with three Chippewa families: the Kashpaws, the Lamartine-Nanapush family, and the Morrisseys. In depicting the dramatic turbulence of their lives, the temporal arrangement also follows a distinct pattern: The first story, "The World's Greatest Fisherman," takes place in 1981; the second, "Saint Marie," regresses to 1934, and the next eight stories move the action progressively forward through "Scales," which takes place the year before June's death in 1981. "Crown of Thorns" is clearly subsequent to that event since it deals with Gordie's reaction to it, and the last three stories move from 1982 to 1984. Within that time scheme, the same narrative voices recur, linking stories in perspective. Marie tells three stories, for example; Lulu tells one but has another related in third person from her point of view; Albertine Johnson is the narrator of at least part of three stories, and Lipsha is a narrator twice, as is Nector. Even when the point of view is omniscient, it is often identified with the communal values of this society, speaking in its tones and lexicon, focusing on the collective concerns that unify all the stories, which might explain why there are five stories with multiple narrators. Thus, despite the temporal discontinuity within stories, and the lack of transitional bridges between them, there is a comprehensive pattern to the volume and strong threads of unification, a special issue for the structure of short-story cycles.

The most enriching unification comes through thematic linkages, of course, the most ubiquitous of which is the multifaceted concept of "love" ranging from Eros to agape, love profane, familial, spiritual, and brotherly.[54] Lulu is certainly the embodiment of erotic desirability, and three of the stories cast her as seductress, most importantly "Lulu's Boys." Three stories focus on Nector's driving desire for her, and several others allude to his handsome physique and irresistible masculinity. Other stories also involve erotic love, from Marie's impromptu tryst with Nector in "Wild Geese" to Beverly's succumbing to feminine allure in "Lulu's Boys." Albertine has a disturbing night in a hotel with Henry Jr. in "A Bridge," Gerry Nanapush makes love to Dot in a prison visiting room in "Scales," and Nector and Lulu enjoy geriatric fulfillment in "Love Medicine." Marie is perhaps the strongest representative of familial love, with all her biological and adoptive children, her abiding devotion to Nector and tolerance of his philandering, and her concluding gesture of caring for her rival Lulu in the nursing home, a supreme expression of selfless love. Henry Jr. cares enough for his brother Lyman to repair their red convertible before he commits suicide. Gerry's abiding affection for June is manifest in his hallucinatory perception that the deer he hit with his car was June reincarnate. Lipsha's reconciliation with his father, Gerry Nanapush, in "Crossing the Water," is an affirmative conclusion to a series of stories of death, disarray, and self-destruction. Throughout *Love Medicine*, these tendencies seem always to have had their inception in the fact that Native Americans were stripped of their land and their cultural heritage, cut off from their traditional tribal legends and religious ceremonies, and severed from their sacred relationship with nature. At the same time, they have had only marginal success in assimilating into a transplanted European society.[55]

This motif is implicit throughout the stories, always present as a residual motivating force, but it is not such a dominant theme so as to become propagandistic, in accord with Erdrich's attitude toward polemicism: she has said directly that "everyone should be politically and socially committed in personal life, but not in art. Political art is polemic and boring."[56] She has also maintained throughout her career that Native American literature should not be regarded as a tradition separate from the flow of American literary history: "Setting it apart and saying that people with special interest might read this literature sets Indians apart too."[57] She has been consistently emphatic on this point: "I don't think it's right to put everything off in a separate category. All of the ethnic writing done in the United States is American writing, and should be called American writing."[58]

One implication for *Love Medicine* in this line of thinking is that it represents not simply an expression of Native American literature but a manifestation of the extended tradition of the short-story cycle in American fiction. That this genre is consistent with the communal mode of narrative traditional among Chippewa peoples, with multiple speakers, myriad central characters, and an overlapping of narrative time covered from contrasting perspectives, simply lends ethnic congruence to Erdrich's choice of form. *Love Medicine* is a contemporary expression of an ancient literary mode of linked narratives, as she has reflected: "I suppose it goes back to before the Bible; that storytelling cycle is in [the] oral traditions of all cultures."[59] It is only in this broad historical context, and with an understanding of the normative tendencies of the tradition of the short-story cycle, that the rich contribution of Erdrich's remarkable book can be fully appreciated.

2

Jamaica Kincaid's
Annie John

Genre and Cultural Duality

J amaica Kincaid's *Annie John* is a quintessential example of the contemporary short-story cycle.
The volume consists entirely of eight previously
published stories arranged not in order of publication but in terms of
the developmental stages of the central character, who serves as the narrator for all of the stories. The collection is thus unified by narrative
perspective, characterization, temporal progression, and the theme of
the embryonic independence of the protagonist. On another level,
however, the text exists in two independent states: as individual stories
in *The New Yorker*, separated by months and even years from each other;
and as a collected volume, a story cycle often misinterpreted as a novel.
As might be expected, there are sometimes significant differences between the original magazine text and that printed in the collected volume, a matter that has gone almost entirely unnoticed. Despite the fact
that Kincaid's work has attracted scores of reviews and critical essays, as
well as two books, the scholars addressing her subtle and complex fiction have paid no attention whatever to the differences between the two
versions of the stories, notwithstanding the implications of these dis-
crepancies for critical interpretation. Nor have they been insightful
about the genre they were reading, for the temporal leaps, thematic discontinuities, and structural shifts of *Annie John*, often criticized as infe-
licities in a novel, are normative in the traditional story cycle and not

an artistic weakness at all. Kincaid's fiction has become an important part of the scholarly discourse of American literature, and her first book deserves to be read on its own terms and judged in accord with the normative aesthetic of the appropriate genre. The component stories need to be regarded both as independent entities and as part of a complex interrelated volume.

The stories that now constitute *Annie John* all appeared in *The New Yorker* between May 9, 1983, when "Figures in the Distance" was first published, and November 5, 1984, when "A Walk to the Jetty" was printed.[1] Between those two dates the other six stories did not come out in the order in which they are now assembled. A faithful admirer of Kincaid's magazine fiction would have observed Annie moving quickly from her childish fascination with death in the opening story directly to her rebellions at age twelve against the restrictions of her mother in "The Red Girl" and her even more dramatic realization of her cultural duality and gesture of protest in "Columbus in Chains." Then the action moved backward in the next two stories in *The New Yorker* to earlier episodes about Annie's struggle against the confining love of her mother in "The Circling Hand" and "Gwen." From that point onward, the stories resumed the childhood history of Annie and portrayed her as growing progressively older to her final departure from Antigua in "A Walk to the Jetty." One implication of this publication sequence is that, as separate artistic constructs, each of the eight stories presents a conflict, a resolution, and a sense of closure. Another is that, unlike the collective volume, the stories appearing in the magazine did not constitute a progressive feminine *Bildungsroman* depicting the development of a young girl toward her final assertion of independence when she leaves her native island. An informed reading of *Annie John* needs to take into account the dualistic state of this complex literary text.[2]

From another perspective, as a series of interrelated short stories that appeared in *The New Yorker*, the volume has a somewhat different structure from that of the more common novel. Beyond sequentiality, its sections develop thematic depth through intertextual resonance, as each story deepens the layers of Annie's conflicts, adding dimensions to the formation of her personality and cultural identity. Of equal moment, however, is the rendition of the stories from a first-person retrospective stance, for how and where and why the stories are told necessarily conditions not only the events that are related but their ultimate significance. Retrospective narration inevitably employs temporal duality: the time of the action rendered from the time of the telling, and a given event can have very different emotional and thematic values in each perspective. In other words, it is a mature Annie, who has gone to London to become a nurse, who tells the stories about her painful but exciting development from age ten to seventeen, when she left home forever. This is also an important insight that was not apparent in the magazine texts, published out of order, but central to the assembled volume, which more dramatically demonstrates Annie's incremental development.

The action progresses through seven years of Annie's young life, through her dependent childhood to a fierce declaration of sovereignty when she leaves home. The time of the telling seems constant, at an indeterminate point anterior to her departure from home, from a wiser and less strident perspective that allows her to reveal her life in its full complexity. Although her story constitutes a traditional *apologia pro vita sua*, it is less a polemical treatise than a confessional, for much of what Annie reveals about herself and her family does not, ultimately, redound to her credit.

There are two other implications to this narrative strategy: the first is that although there is only one voice that speaks in these stories, that of the "narrator" Annie, she nevertheless artfully renders the childhood scenes in progressively more sophisticated language, so that the eight sections of the book mature linguistically at the same rate as the young Annie's development.[3] The second is that there is a continual narrative irony, as the older teller depicts reality from the perspective of the child, as when she relates the view that dead people would occasionally "show up standing under a tree just as you were passing by" (p. 4). The underlying assumption of this technique, however, is that what is told, the principle of selection of scenes from a multitude of possibilities, would be determined not by the child but by the adult narrator, who seems motivated by a desire to depict the most salient crises of her voyage toward self-realization. In the process, she comes to focus on two central issues: her relationship with her mother, and her sense of cultural duality, a matter somewhat more subtle but thematically as important as the first. Both of these matters are given psychological expansion in each successive story.

The first story in *Annie John*, "Figures in the Distance," was also the first to appear in *The New Yorker*.[4] In both cases it deals with the childhood preoccupations of Annie at age ten, and there are only minor differences between the two texts. In the magazine version, however, Annie suggests that the problem with Mr. Oatie was that he "was such a leech he made you pay for everything," which would seem to reflect negatively on her family as feeling entitled to things without paying for them. Kincaid changed the passage in the volume to "Mr. Oatie was such a leech he tried to suck you dry by making you pay for everything twice," which shifts the negative values to Mr. Oatie.[5] Oatie is Mr. John's business partner in *The New Yorker* but not in the collected volume, where his more negative character would call into question the father's own values.[6]

The story begins by establishing the facts of Annie's childhood circumstances, her home, the people in her neighborhood, the world of her daily interactions. The emphasis is on her fascination with death, a subject with somber values set off against the sunny and carefree world of her everyday life. Throughout a progression of expirations, her interests are in the world of the supernatural, in the imponderable causal forces that live in shadow and sign, that wrest a comforting meaning from random events. Her preoccupation with death is a normative fixation, an attempt to understand the most profound developments around her. As Ike Onward has formulated it, "her naive but none-the-less wise judgments concerning the nature of the universal and permanent amid transience are artfully expressed in the idiom of childhood. But the ambivalence of her love for her mother, her realization of the inevitability of suffering and death, are trials which she must successfully overcome."[7] Beyond the charm of innocent grotesquerie is the revelation of Annie's character, of a lively and creative mind, a love for storytelling, an unsentimental confrontation with the most unpleasant realities, a child's faulty logic that accepts folklore as transcendent reality.

On one level, Annie must reach outward for conflict because the world she lives in is prelapsarian, an antediluvian feast of family love and lore. Her mother is not so much long-suffering as long-rejoicing, so in love with her daughter and with life as to celebrate even its most minute details, from routine household tasks to the bark she uses to scent Annie's bathwater. Indeed, although some scholars, Moira Ferguson among them, have seen Annie's father and mother as projections of a dominating colonial power, the artifacts of the young girl's existence speak of adoration.[8] Her father built the house she lives in with his own hands: he lovingly crafted the furniture in her room, the spoon she eats with, the entire household. It is a brilliant context in which to begin the story, for this caring home is the world that Annie will come to resent and rebel against in her final departure. It is a still point against which to measure the progress of the narrative. Beneath the surface, however, Annie's fascination for death suggests a need for escape, a need for separation and an independent identity that will intensify as she grows older.[9]

Although as narrator she stresses these details, at the time of the action Annie seems oblivious to them, obsessed instead with her immediate concern for a series of deaths, from Nalda to Sonia's mother to Miss Charlotte and the humpback girl, whose passing inspires not compassion but Annie's desire to rap on the hump to see if it is hollow (p. 10). Even these episodes bring her back under the sway of her mother, however, for it is she who tells the stories of death in the family, and it is she who is holding Nalda in her arms at the moment of expiration, a tragedy given cruel interpretation by Annie: "I then began to look at my mother's hands differently. They had stroked the dead girl's forehead; they had bathed and dressed her and laid her in the coffin my father had made. . . . For a while, though not for very long, I could not bear to have my mother caress me or touch my food or help me with my bath. I especially couldn't bear the sight of her hands lying still in her lap" (p. 6). It is the first negative transformation in Annie's attitude toward her mother, one highly ironic from the time of the telling when Annie has left for England to become a nurse, caring for the sick and dying. At the time of the action, Annie begins to visit funeral parlors, an obsession that brings her home late one evening without the fish she was supposed to deliver. Although she lied about the incident, her mother was characteristically lenient: "That night, as a punishment, I ate my supper outside, alone, under the breadfruit tree, and my mother said that she would not be kissing me good night later, but when I climbed into bed she came and kissed me anyway" (p. 12). It is a warm and forgiving world Annie lives in, but it is a childhood paradise, one she will have to leave to become an adult.[10]

The second story in the volume, but the fourth in appearance in *The New Yorker*, is "The Circling Hand" (pp. 13–33), which takes place two years later in Annie's life at a moment of psychic transition.[11] In the first of four stories about Annie at age twelve, the issues that dominate her early adolescence are introduced as she enters the first stages of the love-hate relationship with her mother that informs the central plot of the narrative.[12] Ironically, it is not the terrors of death that lead to the schism but the act that brought her life, for she discovers her parents making love and is revolted. To provide a context for this event, the narrator sketches a background of familial closeness, how mother and daughter would bathe together in water scented with flowers and oils. Annie tells of her mother's departure from Dominica with the trunk and of the many times she later removed Annie's things from it, caressing each item as an emblem of her daughter's precious growth: "As she held each thing in her hand she would tell me a story about myself" (p. 21).

The father's background is rich in affection of a more perverse and complex variety, for he has loved and abandoned a series of women, leaving several with children he does not now acknowledge, a fact that hangs over their lives, seeking expiation. Abandoned as a small child, he grew up with his grandmother, sleeping with her until he was eighteen, when she died. The father weeps when he relates this story, and Annie experiences a sudden growth of sensibility in her compassion for him (p. 24). But Annie's father is thirty-five years older than her mother, of another generation, casting both Annie and her mother into the role of children relative to him, a fact that further binds the two of them together.[13] This temporal distance parallels the psychic space between the practical carpenter father and the sensitive and imaginative daughter who, in many respects, lives in her mother's world, a matriarchal construct of deep emotional bonds. It is significant that throughout her later adolescent rebellion, Annie struggles against the controls of her mother, rather than her father, who lives on the periphery of the family unit.[14]

If the central issue from start to finish is Annie's relationship with her mother, the central image is that of a trunk, one that contained the artifacts of life in Dominica when the mother ran away from home at sixteen, which then comes to hold the treasured reminiscences of every stage of Annie's childhood, and a similar one that Annie brings with her when she leaves Antigua at seventeen. In the matter of the trunk, as in so much else, Annie's life recalls that of her mother, bringing them as close together in their separation as they were on their island. This is an awareness the adult narrator would have that the child would not, and it is buttressed by the special irony that although the child Annie sees the mother as a heartless despot, the Annie who narrates portrays "no tyrant but a beautiful, loving woman who adores her only child and is wise enough to wish her daughter independent."[15] The act of telling a story of rebellion with such a loving portrait of a mother is, in effect, an act of psychological reconciliation that achieves fulfillment only in the formulation, for there is no indication that Annie ever returns home. On one level, she need not, for what her story reveals is the process by which, in striving for independence, she recapitulates the life of her mother. It is no small point that both the child and the mother share the same name, "Annie John," and both escape home as an act of independence and self-realization.

The turning point for Annie comes when her mother informs her that it is time she had her own clothes, not simply imitations of her mother's dresses. Annie is shocked at this demand for discrete identity: "To say that I felt the earth swept away from under me would not be going too far" (p. 26). Here Annie would seem to be confronting the classic confusion of a girl in her relationship with her mother, desiring the closest possible identification and showing distress when the mother suggests any degree of separation. As Nancy Chodorow suggests, "the child's reaction to its mother in such a situation is not true hate but confusion that is part of the failure to recognize the mother's separateness."[16] This recognition would seem to be part of the awareness of the mature Annie at the time she tells the story.

Although her mother exhibits disgust at Annie's many lies, the precipitating event in their cleavage, from which their relationship never recovers, is the parental sex scene, particularly the image of her mother's hand making a circular motion on her husband's back, an imagistic referent that lends the title for the story, indicating that it is the preeminent event. This image is invested with Annie's confrontation with adult sexuality, a development that will prove more difficult for her than the discovery of death, and with the fact that her mother can love someone other than her daughter. For all her attentions, Annie's mother has never taught her about human sexuality, and the young girl is thrown into turmoil by what she has seen, which inspires a sense of "sin and shame, not joy or pleasure."[17] Annie also discovers that she must share her mother's love with the "other" parent, a fact that inspires not rivalry toward her father but a bitter resentment for her mother: "I was sure I could never let those hands touch me again; I was sure I could never let her kiss me again. All that was finished" (pp. 31–32). In her place Annie proclaims her love for a schoolmate, Gwen, and this and other surrogate alliances sustain her through the break with her mother.

The story concludes with the issue of Annie's move from one school to the other, an event that establishes a context for the following three episodes. There is, however, an important difference between the magazine text and that in the volume. In *The New Yorker* version of "The Circling Hand," she leaves her school because the other children find her arrogant:

> In my old school, all the girls knew me as the bright but frail, much protected Annie. I was very often unable to defend myself against their cruel taunts about my thin legs or against their actual fists. Many days, I had gone home with my clothes in shreds. One day, my mother walked me to school and asked my teacher to please try and protect me, since I was not used to such roughness. That only made things worse between me and the bullying girls. I was not such a bad girl, but I was stuckup and wasn't afraid to show that I knew all the answers. What a good opportunity, then, to wash the slate clean and be someone new. I was sure there was a way that I could still know all the answers, let my teacher know about my abilities, and be loved by my classmates.[18]

Kincaid deleted this passage entirely from the collected volume, where Annie's shift from one school to another is unexplained (p. 29). This is an important issue in that the original story clarifies the motivation for the change of institutions, relates the shift to the identity theme in Annie's desire to "be someone new," and presents yet another dilemma for Annie in her desire to win the admiration of her teachers while retaining the friendship of her classmates. Annie is made a more positive and sympathetic character in the book, although a line of motivation has been lost.

The poles of Annie's ambivalence toward her mother move even further apart in "Gwen" (pp. 34–53), the second story of four devoted to Annie at age twelve, implying that that year was pivotal in her development. Although in the volume this episode is the second with Annie that age, it was the fourth of the group to appear in *The New Yorker*.[19] Although Annie is in a new school, and much of the story is taken with a description of a typical academic day, the salient dimensions of the episode deal with her growing maturity. The emphasis is on the unconditional love she has received throughout her childhood from her mother and on her growing need to move beyond the family to the more expansive social world around her. The key document in the chapter is the autobiographical essay she writes in school, one that describes swimming with her mother and the profound sense of isolation and abandonment she feels when her mother momentarily slips from view.[20]

On one level, this essay presages the very existence of the stories in *Annie John*, for it is here that she begins her life of writing fiction, and the tale she tells is revealing of her preoccupations at the same time it fictionalizes the details of her relationship with her mother. Annie here presents salient themes drawn from her own life presented in terms of invented experience. She makes herself the sympathetic hero of her own tale,[21] but there is also a nostalgic motif in the portrait of her close relationship with her mother, a maternal bond of deep affection and sympathy, and the depth of emptiness Annie feels when she momentarily loses sight of her (p. 43). Annie is not simply puzzled or startled, she experiences a momentary crisis of being: "A huge black space then opened up in front of me and I fell inside it. . . . I couldn't think of anything except that my mother was no longer near me" (p. 43). When her mother sees her crying, she hugs Annie closely and promises never to leave her again, but she is left with the sensation of abandonment.

The depth of Annie's dependence and antipathy here adumbrates the more exaggerated passage she will make through her dark night of the soul in the penultimate story, but even now there are pathological implications to her emotion. This episode predicts Annie's experiences in "The Long Rain," a story about her prolonged mysterious illness, and it suggests that a strong element in Annie's later depression is her contemplation of separation from her mother. In another sense this division has already begun in that Annie reveals that her relationship with her mother, so close in the story she tells her classmates, has in reality already begun to deteriorate: "I placed the old days' version before my classmates because, I thought, I couldn't bear to show my mother in a bad light before people who hardly knew her. But the real truth was that I couldn't bear to have anyone see how deep in disfavor I was with my mother" (p. 45). That these events are juxtaposed with an account of her first menstruation is also telling in that Annie's struggle toward emotional maturity is linked to her biological coming of age (p. 51).

Similarly, the intensification of Annie's love for Gwen is set against the diminution of her love for her mother.[22] In fact, since Annie is beginning to realize that she cannot share her mother's love forever, as her autobiographical essay reveals, she substitutes for it a relationship with Gwen that will compensate for her sense of emotional estrangement from her mother. As Diane Simmons has said, "Annie has succeeded temporarily in recreating a new world to replace the one that has been lost. Once again, she is at the center of an adoring universe."[23] Even thoughts of her mother's death are not as terrifying as they had once been, and Annie says, "since I had met Gwen this didn't matter so much" (p. 51). Annie here exhibits a typical stage in female maturation when in the process of severing dependence on the mother, a young girl often, as Nancy Chodorow explains, transfers her love to "a 'best friend,' whom she loves, with whom she is identified, with whom she shares everything."[24] She envisions moving into a house with Gwen when they mature, a fantasy that would offer solace in the context of Annie's fear of emotional abandonment by her mother. This step in Annie's progress toward individuation is evident in the conclusion in which, returning home following her first menstruation, she reflects that "I could not understand how she could be so beautiful even though I no longer loved her" (p. 53).

It is here, in this third episode, that the intertextual resonance of Kincaid's volume begins to enrich the stories with an increment beyond the events and conflicts contained in each story. Annie's contemplation of her mother's death, for example, reverberates in the context of the young girl's obsession with death in "Figures in the Distance." Her autobiographical essay reveals the construction Annie prefers to give the loving relationship she has had with her mother even as it is beginning to change. Indeed, the items in the family trunk in "The Circling Hand," which presented the artifacts of Annie's prepubescent childhood in counterpoint to her observation of adult sexuality, become even more meaningful as Annie experiences her first menstruation.[25] Another suggestion is that as warm and loving as the mother has been to her daughter as a child, as Annie matures she does so on her own, for "this Caribbean mother is unable to speak about the later stage of the child's development. . . . She does not know how to communicate openly about the girl's development into a sexual being."[26] The progression through the first three stories, in effect, is toward an inevitable conflict between mother and daughter and an even deeper struggle for a redefinition of self as Annie attempts to come to terms with the undeniable changes within her.

Those changes were at the very center of "The Red Girl" when it appeared in *The New Yorker*, in which version Annie is explicit about the meaning of her first menstruation: "I was ashamed to be menstruating. It meant the end of everything. My mother even said so. On giving me my little cloths and the instruction on how to use them, she laughed her triumphant laugh and said, 'You are just like me. I was your age when I started.' "27 When this passage was deleted in the collected volume, the inception of menstruation became less of a transitional event, "the end of everything." It also lessened the sense in which Annie's life recapitulates that of her mother. These revisions are important because the parallels between mother and daughter are implicit throughout Annie's stages of rebellion in such details as the trunk as a vehicle of escape and her departure from home, never to return, following precisely the pattern her mother established. That parallel was lessened in the collected volume.

But even in the assembled book, this moment marks a transition to a new stage of development. From this point onward every episode contains another expression of Annie's continuing rebellion and the substitution of other emotional alliances for the close bond she previously shared with her mother. In "The Red Girl" (pp. 54–71) these ideas take the form of Annie's stealing and lying and playing marbles, all forbidden activities, and of her infatuation with the Red Girl, the personification of familial anarchy, a child who refuses to bathe more than once a week. Gwen, the socially correct young lady who has Annie's mother's full approval, is replaced by the Red Girl, who is free from convention and discipline: "Oh, what an angel she was, and what a heaven she lived in!" (p. 58). The psychological origins of the Red Girl are suggested by the function of the "red-skin woman" in Kincaid's *At the Bottom of the River*, in which Kincaid discusses the desire to marry this woman so that they could "eat bread and milk for breakfast, hide in bushes and throw hardened cow dung at people we don't like. . . ."28 Beyond social iconoclasm, however, there is a softer longing: "This woman I would like to marry knows many things, but to me she will only tell about things that would never dream of making me cry; and every night, over and over, she will tell me something that begins, 'Before you were born.' I will marry a woman like this, and every night, every night, I will be completely happy."29 In the earlier book it is clear that the red-skin girl represents an attempt to cling forever to a woman who will play the role of mother, comforting her every evening with nostalgic bits of family lore. In *Annie John*, however, Annie struggles to replace that dream with an open revolt against the restrictions her mother would impose on her, and the Red Girl is yet another form of that rebellion.

That this expression of betrayal contains portions of both pain and pleasure is expressed in Annie's complex relationship with the Red Girl, who pinches Annie and then kisses the injured spots: "Oh, the sensation was delicious—the combination of pinches and kisses" (p. 63). That all of this activity takes place at a time commensurate with "Gwen" becomes clear when Annie starts to menstruate, the second rendering of that event in the book and once again a cogent episode that coincides with the departure of the Red Girl and the cessation of playing marbles. But through this episode Annie has expanded the terrain of rebellion, embracing forbidden friends, violating the most sacred shibboleths of social behavior, and masking her true nature behind a conventional facade. This double life is revealed to exact its bounty in subsequent stories.

Annie's emotional duality with regard to her mother has its social analogue in the culture of Antigua, an issue of even greater complexity than her familial struggles. What is fundamental in this matter is that in the formation of an independent self, Annie must attempt to understand who she is culturally as well as personally. At the core of her world, inherent in her school and church and governmental structure, is a frame of reference drawn from European intellectual and artistic traditions; beneath the surface is a deeper cultural legacy of slavery and deprivation intertwined with the rich texture of Caribbean life, with its exotic foods, rituals, family histories, and traditions. Daily life in Antigua is carried out in the current of these various cultural streams so that, for example, European Christianity has become interwoven with folk rituals of potions and curses and evil demons.

Indeed, everything in this society has a dual foundation, even the language they speak (an amalgam of English and patois), and it manifests in a double psychological and social identity, a people who live in a world not of their own making. Annie's father distinguishes himself at cricket, decidedly an English game, here played by a descendant of African slaves (p. 88). Annie studies Latin and French and plays a piano, a European instrument (p. 28). Her teachers have English names and present a commonwealth curriculum, with oaths of allegiance to the Union Jack and the celebration of Queen Victoria's birthday (p. 76). The history Annie knows is British, as is her religion, currency, holidays, flag, and name. Her full name is "Annie Victoria John," which suggests that she does not simply live in this society but embodies it, her existence bearing homage to the leader of Britain's enormous colonial empire even as she rebels against its deeply ingrained domination of her life. The most significant changes from *The New Yorker* to the collected volume take place in the most important story, "Columbus in Chains," the episode in which Annie first confronts the legacy of slavery on Antigua. She is brought to consider the extent to which she lives in a British society that exploited people of her race, and she must grapple with the complex cultural duality that informs her sense of identity. As a general rule, the changes from magazine to volume all place extra emphasis on these crucial themes. In the opening of the magazine version, Annie confesses that she was "among the worst-behaved in my class."[30] In the volume, Annie added a further clarification, that she was ill-behaved "and did not at all believe in setting myself up as a good example, the way a prefect was supposed to do."[31] It is not a major revision, but the change further emphasizes her rebelliousness in a story that goes on to broaden the parameters of her protest from family and school to the whole of her island culture. In a related change, in *The New Yorker* version, when Annie reflects on her celebration of Queen Victoria's birthday, she says, "But we knew quite well what had happened . . ." (p. 49). In the volume, that passage is changed by addition: "But we, the descendants of the slaves, knew quite well what had happened . . ." (p. 76).

As the theme of rebellion inspired by the legacy of slavery shifts to the contemplation of the picture of Columbus in chains, Kincaid made other alterations. In the magazine version, Annie simply says, "How I loved this picture!" (p. 49). In the volume, however, she remarks, "How I loved this picture—to see the usually triumphant Columbus, brought so low, seated at the bottom of a boat just watching things go by" (pp. 77–78). In this version there is greater emphasis on Annie's personalization of outrage, her satisfaction in this pictorial revenge, her obvious pleasure in seeing Columbus in the position slaves had occupied in the ships: passive, helpless, at the mercy of a superior power. Annie has here taken a step in her ethnic maturity, one that would have been compromised somewhat by a passage that, in *The New Yorker*, emphasized her childish duplicity:

> Since I had long ago managed to convince my parents that I was the most innocent, most virtuous child who ever lived, they often

felt free to speak frankly to each other in my presence. Whenever I found myself alone with them—and that was quite often—I would get a faraway look on my face, as if to say, I am not really here and you don't interest me with your big thoughts. If that wasn't too successful, I would start to hum a little childish song to myself, while playing with my collar or my shoelaces. My parents would soon start to speak quite openly to each other about many things (p. 50).

Kincaid deleted this passage in *Annie John* so that the young girl does not so blatantly shift from realizations about her culture back to childish tricks on her parents. In the published volume there is a more continuous emphasis on her progressive maturity and transforming awareness.

Another deletion from magazine to volume deals more with family attitudes. In *The New Yorker*, Annie observes her mother's affection for her father and realizes how much her mother loves him: "Until then, I had always thought that she liked him because he was my father; now I could see that she liked him just for himself. I remembered that, the other day, they were sitting outside and when I walked up to them I noticed her hand resting lightly on the nape of his neck. I was taken aback then" (p. 52). That passage was also deleted, lessening Annie's childish narcissism. In the context of the volume, this passage also duplicates thematically the realizations Annie has in "The Circling Hand," when she observes her parents making love. What worked in the isolated story became unnecessary in the volume. The phrase "the other day" would have worked in the magazine version because there is no clear sense of when the story is told; in *Annie John*, however, the context suggests that the telling of all the stories takes place after Annie has left Antigua, not just after the events in each instance, so "the other day" would have been a confusing reference. As revised for the published volume, the retrospective point of view provides temporal unity to the narrative voice.

As revised for the collected volume, the thematic emphasis of "Columbus in Chains" is on Annie's rebellion as she begins to confront the social history of her world, the legacy of slavery and exploitation under British colonialism, the racial implications of the expeditions of Christopher Columbus. Although she does not perceive her society in explicitly racial terms, the figures of authority around her seem to be white:

her doctor, the Methodist minister, her teachers. Peer relations seem to be conducted without racial restriction, as in Annie's friendship with the daughter of the minister: "Ruth I liked, because she was such a dunce and came from England and had yellow hair" (p. 73). But even here there is a powerful sense of the differences between them: "Her ancestors had been the masters, while ours had been the slaves. She had such a lot to be ashamed of. . . ."[32] As she did in *A Small Place* in 1988, Kincaid attributes the moral high ground to the exploited rather than to the powerful.

In reflecting on her personal views of the colonial background of her homeland, Kincaid commented in an interview published in 1990 that "when I was growing up, we still celebrated Queen Victoria's birthday on May 24, and for us England . . . and its glory was at its most theatrical, its most oppressive. Everything seemed divine and good only if it was English." Rather earlier than her character Annie, who is twelve in this story, Kincaid recalls that "when I was nine, I refused to stand up at the refrain of 'God Save Our King.' I hated 'Rule, Britannia,' and I used to say that we weren't Britons, we were slaves."[33] Kincaid herself went to the Princess Margaret School, a detail she leaves out of her stories. For her part, Annie's reaction to the British world around her does not begin to sharpen until her salient realizations regarding the voyages of Columbus.

H. Adlai Murdoch's discussion of the historical background of Antigua is instructive for understanding Annie's attitude toward colonialism. He points out that the islands in the Caribbean were largely slave colonies of Great Britain (Antigua was colonized in 1632), their populations consisting of numerically dominant black populations. In 1708, for example, the slaves numbered 12,943 to a white society of only 2,909. By 1834 the numbers had changed to 29,100 to 2,000.[34] When slavery was terminated in 1834, the slaves on the surrounding islands were given periods of "freedom apprenticeships"[35] that effectively continued their servitude in another form. Unique among the islands, the slaves on Antigua were granted immediate freedom, giving rise to a series of free villages "rejoicing in the resonant symbolism of names such as Freetown, Liberta, and Freeman'sville. . . ."[36] The island of Dominica, where Annie's mother was raised, was a French colony until annexed by the British in 1783. The dialect spoken there is based on French and African languages, and the culture is more closely associated with that of Guadeloupe and Martinique than to those islands under British influence. Since Annie's mother came from Dominica, she would seem, in some respects, quite foreign to Annie, not the perfect model for her to follow in her own formulation of identity.[37] These issues are not unrelated to the psychological and social development of Annie, who envisions her mother as worthy of being a monarch: "But when my eyes rested on my mother, I found her beautiful. Her head looked as if it should be on a sixpence" (p. 18). But the mother's life has been circumscribed by ethnicity, as has Annie's, and in the process of creating an independent self she must attempt to understand who she is ethnically as well as personally. The process of forming a new identity for herself thus involves multiple layers of cultural duality. Annie is a black girl of African descent who has a mother whose background includes French language and tradition. Annie lives in a former British colony, and the overlay of culture is essentially English: she awakens to the ringing of the Anglican church bell and attends the Methodist church presided over by a white minister (p. 100). Her father distinguishes himself at an English game, cricket (p. 88). She studies Latin and French and plays a European instrument, the piano (p. 28). Her teachers have English names and present an English curriculum, with oaths of allegiance to the Union Jack and the celebration of Queen Victoria's birthday (p. 76). Furthermore, since her full name is Annie Victoria John, she does not simply live in this society but embodies it, even as she rebels against its most pernicious aspects.

"Columbus in Chains" is physically in the center of the volume, suggesting its centrality in Annie's development. In school Annie is exposed to such volumes as *Roman Britain* but also *A History of the West Indies*, in which she learns of the discovery of Dominica by Christopher Columbus in 1493. The contemplation of this historical legacy compels her to the realization that her ancestors had been slaves and to a remarkable conception that her English friend Ruth may confront this material with her own series of reflections: "Perhaps she did not want to be in the West Indies at all. Perhaps she wanted to be in England, where no one would remind her constantly of the terrible things her ancestors had done; perhaps she had felt even worse when her father was a missionary in Africa. I could see how Ruth felt from looking at her face" (p. 76). These may well be simply Annie's projections, of course, since there is no confirming evidence of how Ruth felt about things, but Annie is led through these reflections to feel a contempt for Columbus and to write under the picture of him fettered in chains the very words her mother had spoken about her own father: "So the great man can no longer just get up and go. How I would love to see his face now" (p. 78). It is ironically fitting that her punishment should be so English, the copying of Books I and II of *Paradise Lost*. A second dimension of the comment is that Annie repeats an earlier remark by her mother, reinforcing the motif of her progressive identification with her mother even as she moves away from her. The central importance of this story, in short, is that in it Annie moves toward her own realizations about the legacy of slavery and colonialism in Antigua and toward another stage of her individuation in the emotional break from her mother. This is the last of the four stories of Annie at age twelve, and it presents brilliantly the central issues of her conflicts and growth, issues that take unpredictable turns in the remaining three stories.

The first of these is "Somewhere, Belgium" (pp. 85–107), in which Annie appears at age fifteen. There is no attempt anywhere in this story to account for the intervening three years since "Columbus in Chains," a temporal discontinuity prevalent in the cycle form. In terms of publication history, perhaps the most important difference from magazine to volume occurs when Annie begins to feel the depression that will immobilize her throughout "The Long Rain." In *The New Yorker* there is a passage about her father telling stories about himself as a famous batsman in cricket, and Annie knows that he always leaves out an important element of the truth, how he had loved many women on the islands he visited on tour, and how he had fathered many children by these women, children he now refuses to acknowledge. In the magazine version, one of these offspring comes to Antigua and introduces herself to him: "You don't know me, but I'm your daughter Roma. My mother is Christine, from St. Kitts." Annie's father looks into his daughter's face and says, "Oh, yes, I know who you are now." They chat briefly, and Roma leaves. Annie reflects, "We never heard another word from her, and I am sure that my father never sought her out."[38] Kincaid deleted this scene in the volume, leaving the general references to his wandering ways but giving a less severe portrait of him than in the first version.

The title of this story is derived from Annie's fantasy of an escape from the conflicts of Antigua. She has turned fifteen and has entered into a deep depression, the etiology of which would seem to be an emotional schism. Many aspects of her life are warm and protective, as are the stories of her father's youth and the many household objects crafted by his hands. But on another level, Annie's already tenuous circumstances have grown worse. Promoted two grades, she is no longer in the same class with Gwen, and their relationship falters while Annie suffers in the company of older girls well into adolescence. Her own hesitant steps toward courtship all end badly, even the games she plays with neighborhood boys, and in each instance her mother expresses not so much outrage as disgust. When she stops on the way home to flirt with one of the boys, her mother observes the incident and accuses Annie of behaving like a slut, which inspires Annie to say "like mother like daughter." Her mother responds, "until this moment, in my whole life I knew without a doubt that, without any exception, I loved you best" (p. 102). Annie becomes deeply torn: she is filled with a sense of parental love at the same time she wishes her mother were dead. She is arrested at the level of classic philos-aphilos stasis, not really knowing her own feelings: "Something I could not name just came over us, and suddenly I had never loved anyone so or hated anyone so" (p. 88). This duplicitous relationship, outward harmony concealing a deep inner antipathy, is now an obstacle to any integration of self for Annie: "I could not be sure whether for the rest of my life I would be able to tell when it was really my mother and when it was really her shadow standing between me and the rest of the world" (p. 107). Annie needs desperately to be part of the world, independent of her mother, hence her fantasy of escaping to Belgium.

That Annie seeks resolution of this conflict through a daydream about moving to Belgium serves as an adumbration of the conclusion of the volume and as a vehicle for uniting once again the cultural and familial duality of her personal growth. That her full name is first revealed in this story is crucial in suggesting that she can be completely herself only when she is separate from her mother, a point made all the more emphatic by the fact that her parents never call her anything but "Little Miss" (p. 105). It is also significant that, notwithstanding her realizations about British colonialism in "Columbus in Chains," Annie dreams of escape to a European country and eventually moves to England, from where she presumably tells the eight stories that make up the volume.

One suggestion is that however deep her resentment of a legacy of slavery and depravation might be, her revolt against the control of her mother is even deeper. The structure of this story reveals as much in that virtually all of the episodes of youth that Annie recounts within it conclude with some reference to "mother," from the mother that

Annie herself becomes in her game of hanging the young boy Mineu, to the shame her mother expresses when Mineu is nearly hanged for real, to her mother's bitter resentment of the cruel joke Mineu plays on Annie by having her sit naked on an ant nest (pp. 97–100). On a deeper level, the mother's inability to accept Annie's developing sexuality and interest in boys, such as when she calls her daughter a "slut" for flirting, underscores Annie's subliminal realization that her full development to maturity will have to take place outside of familial influence. That is why the story concludes with her request for a trunk of her own, suggesting that she clearly intends to flee her home the way her mother had done before her. That is why the story ends with her obsession with a shadow on the wall that looks like the outline of her mother: "It was a big and solid shadow, and it looked so much like my mother that I became frightened. For I could not be sure whether for the rest of my life I would be able to tell when it was really my mother and when it was really her shadow standing between me and the rest of the world" (p. 107). The final two stories are linked to this one in that they further depict Annie's attempt to move out from under the shadow of her mother.

Within this thematic context, it is significant that in the original publication of this story in *The New Yorker*, Annie was referred to as "Little Ma" rather than "Little Miss" by her parents.[39] It would seem evident that, at least in part, it is this unresolved conflict that leads to Annie's dark night of the soul in "The Long Rain" (pp. 108–29), a literal and figurative downpour that Annie sleeps through for more than three months. Caused by no discoverable physical illness, Annie's sleep is a mechanism to escape emotional irresolution.[40] It is clearly more metaphoric than literal (extended rains of this type are virtually unknown in Antigua), and it serves to demonstrate the depth of Annie's internal struggle, making it clear in the final story that escape is her only viable option.[41] As long as she remains within the sphere of her mother's influence, Annie's formation of self will be circumscribed by familial expectations. It is only in a "free" world that Annie can begin to reconcile and integrate the cultural, sexual, and psychological issues of her life into a coherent matrix.[42] As H. Adlai Murdoch expresses it, "with her mother . . . enveloping Annie's budding personality and giving it no chance to flower, turning Annie into a simple extension of herself, Annie had no opportunity for identity, no possibility of establishing a valid, functioning persona."[43] The narrative method of the stories would suggest that the very telling of the stories, looking back on her childhood from the remove of London, is an attempt to come to terms with the issues of cultural and maternal domination, finding in the narrating of it an avenue toward healthy resolution of the conflicts that caused her dark night of the soul.

Annie's illness in this story also creates the circumstance for one last family summation involving the mysterious appearance of the maternal grandmother, Ma Chess, still dressed in black since the death of her son John decades before, who comes with ritual cures and potions. Annie had first been taken to an English doctor who was unable to find a cure for her ailment. The grandmother's inexplicable appearance and departure suggest that she too is in some dimension metaphoric, an emblem of the residual African *obeah* tradition of healing through potions, and an example of the important positions that women in her culture can play. As Donna Perry has pointed out, within this society "women are often seen as powerful, even awe-inspiring. African tradition featured women as tribal leaders and *obeah* women, trained in witchcraft and knowledgeable about herbal medicine and cures. . . . In short, a woman functioned in other ways than solely in her relationship to men."[44] It is clear, however, that the causative factor of Annie's condition does not lend itself to these cures nor to those of Western medicine: "I looked inside my head. A black thing was lying down there, and it shut out all my memory of the things that had happened to me" (pp. 111–12). This illness resembles in many respects the archetypal pathology in the female *Bildungsroman*: "Sleep and quiescence in female narratives represent a progressive withdrawal into the symbolic landscapes of the innermost self. . . . Excluded from active participation in culture, the fictional heroine is thrown back on herself."[45] In this case, however, Annie's conflict seems less the problem of acculturation than the more fundamental issue of reconciling the life within her to the expectations of her family.

Annie's illness takes her back through the progression of her childhood, linking this story with the previous ones emphasizing her parents' tender solicitations. The complexity of her feelings toward them is stressed when Ma Jolie makes it clear that the cause of the illness may be the curses of the women Annie's father abandoned (p. 117). Other familial artifacts also possess a negative resonance, as is suggested in the photograph of her in the Communion dress wearing shoes her mother had forbidden. It was yet another confrontation that had led Annie to wish her mother dead. Annie's need to break free of the constraints of this heritage is exemplified by her washing the images off the family photographs, all but her own portrait and that of the forbidden shoes. All of this is explored in the theories of Nancy Chodorow, who postulates that "mothers feel ambivalent toward their daughters, and react to their daughters' ambivalence toward them. They desire both to keep daughters close and to push them into adulthood. This ambivalence in turn creates more anxiety in their daughters and provokes attempts by these daughters to break away."[46] The illness does not abate, however, until Annie begins to realize that she never wants to see her mother again, and as soon as she is able to articulate this awareness she suddenly recovers. It has been a transforming respite, one that leads to the final resolution in the last episode.

These two lines of thematic development, Annie's process of individuation and her conception of herself as part of the legacy of British colonialism and slavery, are brought together in the final story, "A Walk to the Jetty" (pp. 129–48). These are the central issues of the book, as Murdoch has indicated: "It is the problematic of establishing a valid identity within this context, subject all the while to pressures of alienation, race, gender, and culture, that makes Annie John's case unique. . . ."[47] Even the temporal structure of the final story suggests its seminal role in Annie's life, for rather than the broad sweep of the earlier stories, it covers a single day hour by hour, moving ever closer to Annie's departure from Antigua. Although there is never any doubt about the psychological need for Annie to leave (she is revolted by nearly everything associated with her mother), at the time of the telling the summation of this day constitutes a revisiting of the scenes of her youth. The objects and places of Antigua are described in great detail in the most sophisticated language of the book, for Annie is now seventeen. Awakened by the bell in the Anglican church, she walks down the road she has trod all her life, past the familiar library and offices and stores she has always known to the jetty and the ship that will carry her to England. Beneath the bitterness that demands her departure at the time of the action, the anterior act of narrating allows for another farewell at the time of the telling to the lush environment of Antigua, to the smell of the sea, the white sand of the beaches, the rich sounds of the voices, for the narrator Annie knows what the young girl cannot, that she will never return.

On the level of action, Annie's final story is one of progressive antagonism and disenchantment that winds inevitably toward her escape; as a narrative act, however, it constitutes an imaginative return to the world of her youth in its full complexity, the pains as well as the pleasures. The submerged implication in the fact that the story is told at all is that the spatial departure from Antigua for Annie did not resolve all of the emotional issues of her childhood, that they still seek resolution through their cathartic reiteration.[48] What is remarkable is that despite the painful realizations that culminate in her leaving Antigua, the narrational implications of Annie's story suggest not pure repudiation of both mother and country but an attempt at emotional and philosophical integration as she synthesizes her heritage into the person she is becoming. That Annie presents an abbreviated summary of her life in this story suggests that it constitutes a personal psychohistory, a retrospective assessment of self at seventeen: "Lying in my bed for the last time, I thought, This is what I add up to" (p. 133).

What she amounts to is much deeper at the time of the telling than at any point in the action she describes, of course, for it is here that she must face what she really is and how close her mature self is to her beleaguered mother. In the process of relating them, she reviews in detail her mother's countless acts of maternal love, "revealing no tyrant but a beautiful, loving woman who adores her only child and is wise enough to wish her daughter independent."[49] It is in this story that the mature Annie reveals that her name is identical to that of her mother, investing the title *Annie John* with referential ambiguity, since in many respects the stories are as much about the mother as they are about the daughter.[50] But it is clear that, for Annie to continue to grow, she needs separation from her mother, who now revolts her even in the mundane ablutions of everyday life: "I especially never wanted to lie in my bed and hear my mother gargling again" (p. 131).

It is important to realize that the mother never speaks of her love for her daughter, never caresses her, never adds herbs to their bathwater except in Annie's memory. The very recitation of these events is itself an act of reconciliation. She cannot be oblivious to the numerous levels on which her life recapitulates that of her mother, from the trunk, to her escape, to the telling of her story. It is an emotional realization, as is the thought that she is leaving her homeland forever. It is not surprising, as the narrator Annie reviews in memory the lush Caribbean scenes of her childhood, that her final description of the short trip in the launch taking her to the ship should linger on details, the smell of the sea, the sounds of the fishermen coming in with a catch, the feel of the hot sun, the glare of the white beach, the texture of her young life.

Similarly, despite her realizations of British colonialism, it is to London, not Africa, that she flees to find her inner self. She writes in English, in England, about coming of age in Antigua, and it is here that she reviews her declaration of independence from British colonialism at the same time she acknowledges how deeply she has inculcated much of its more redeeming values. The telling of the eight stories that constitute *Annie John* is an emotionally powerful narrative act of considerable maturity and courage, and in it she confronts the most painful and meaningful dimensions of her life and comes to terms with them, with her feelings for her mother, her colonial legacy, her severing from the homeland she eagerly left and yet so visibly loves. Annie's deeper feelings are expressed only indirectly in the story she tells, but it is the reflective narrator as well as the liberated adolescent who, on the final page of the book, is preoccupied with "an unexpected sound, as if a vessel filled with liquid had been placed on its side and now was slowly emptying out" (p. 148).

It is a powerful and effective conclusion to the eight stories that Kincaid brought together to form the volume known as *Annie John*, a book that differs in some important ways from the collected texts that appeared in *The New Yorker*. In the book version the stories have been arranged in chronological order to constitute a feminine *Bildungsroman* tracing the growth of Annie from age ten to seventeen, when she leaves home. Her role as protagonist thus provides the strongest element of coherence among the stories, giving them temporal progression, but they are also unified by setting (all of them take place in Antigua) and by a small cast of secondary characters, chief among them Annie's mother. Annie's struggle for independence is in some measure a motif in all of the stories, but there are other issues that give them cohesion as well: death, or the threat of death, a matter prevalent in the first story, is a continuing concern. Her developing sexuality, involving menstruation and flirtation, links the stories about Annie from age twelve to fifteen. The family history, largely on the maternal side, provides a genealogical umbrella from the beginning to the penultimate story, when Ma Jolie comes to treat her in "The Long Rain," a story in which Annie reviews the family photographs. Annie's incremental growth of insight into her racial history and ethnic identity is also a dominant concern, manifesting most dramatically in "Columbus in Chains." All of the stories are unified by a single narrative perspective, the voice of a more mature Annie telling her stories from England. She would seem to be attempting to come to terms with the meaning of the events through narrative iteration, and this act of telling is the single most important aesthetic and thematic thread that binds the eight stories of Annie John into an artistically congruent short-story cycle.

3

Susan Minot's *Monkeys* and the Cycle Paradigm

S usan Minot's brilliant first book, *Monkeys*, which appeared as a volume in 1986, is a classic example of the contemporary short-story cycle. Essentially a chronological sequence of nine independent stories, composed and initially published in a different order than that presented in the book, the volume depicts thirteen years in the lives of the Vincent family of Massachusetts, from the stunning and disheartening opening story, "Hiding," in which the underlying family problems are subtly revealed, to the final distribution of the dead mother's ashes in the concluding "Thorofare." As individual works, the stories are gripping, satisfying, and aesthetically as well as thematically complete. Indeed, they are minimalist masterpieces of understatement in direct descent from the best fiction of Ernest Hemingway. As a collection, the volume resonates with echoes, motivations, and patterns of meaning that the individual stories lacked when originally published in isolation. The stories are dramatically successful in both incarnations. For example, "Thorofare" was chosen for inclusion in *The Best American Short Stories of 1984*, two years before *Monkeys* was published. Later, the complete volume was awarded the Prix Femina Etranger in 1987, an honor Minot received in Paris. By that year, the book was in its third printing, it had appeared as an alternate Book-of-the-Month Club selection, and the movie rights had been sold to United Artists.[1]

From the beginning of the project, there was the usual confusion about the genre of Minot's work. When she sent Seymour Lawrence, her editor at E. P. Dutton, three of her stories, he read them quickly and offered her a contract for a "novel." When she protested that she did not write in that form, the word "novel" was deleted from the contract and "a work of fiction" was substituted.[2] It was a meaningful alteration, and it indicates that there was never any confusion on the part of the author as to the nature of her book.

That was not the case with the reviewers of *Monkeys*, however, who were not at all clear about what they were reading. Despite clear statements on the copyright page that the book contained short stories (the previous publication of seven of them is specifically mentioned), most reviewers, even in prestigious venues, regarded the volume as a novel and judged it according to that assumption. In the *New Statesman*, for example, Sara Maitland commented that "each of the nine incidents in the novel is wonderfully wrought, with vivid observation and lucid prose—each would make a lovely short story actually—but they don't add up to a novel of substance."[3] A. R. Gurney Jr., writing in the *New York Times Book Review*, reviewed *Monkeys* as simply a novel, with no qualifications on the concept,[4] but many other reviewers acknowledged that the book represented some other form, even if they could not articulate precisely what that was. No reviewers mentioned the concept of "short-story cycle." Rosellen Brown, in the *Boston Review*, called the book a "connected series of stories" that develops "in tiny incremental moves, unassertive, understated. *Monkeys* is a small book, all ellipsis, silence and air predominating."[5] Katherine Bucknell, in the *Times Literary Supplement*, was more informed: "Susan Minot's first novel *Monkeys* began as a group of short stories. She has not attempted to disguise this. It is mildly annoying to be told more than once, in so slim a volume written in so spare a style, that there are seven children in the Vincent family, that Sophie is the second eldest between Caitlin and Delilah, that Sherman is the middle brother, or that the Vincent girls 'have parties at the house—huge ones.' But otherwise the short story form gives *Monkeys* sharp focus."[6]

Some reviewers had less problem understanding the nature of the book. Writing in *The New Republic*, Anne Tyler reviewed the volume as a novel but commented that "*Monkeys* is a group of nine stories—each of which could stand alone. . . ."[7] Robert Towers, in the *New York Review of Books*, observed that "though labeled a novel, *Monkeys* is a loose assemblage of nine episodes (most of which were published separately as short stories). . . ."[8] Thomas Hinde complained that "Susan Minot's

Monkeys is another group of short stories described as a novel. There is, however, more justification for the description: the same characters occur in each, and they are arranged in chronological order."[9] And in *Time*, R. Z. Sheppard called *Monkeys* a "novel" but added that "the book is in nine episodes that could be, with minor adjustments, independent stories." He apparently did not know that seven of them had already been published as short stories.[10] The fact that fully competent, professional reviewers of fiction should understand so little about the various subgenres of fiction suggests the importance of clarifying the nature of the short-story cycle.

It makes a good deal of difference in evaluating and understanding *Monkeys* that the form of the book is a cycle and not a novel. Minot wrote "Hiding" for her creative writing class at Columbia and sent it to *The New Yorker*, which rejected it, but Ben Sonnenberg at *Grand Street* published it in 1983.[11] Over the next few years he also accepted "Thanksgiving Day," "The Navigator," and "Wedlock," which appeared under the title "The Silver Box," an alteration not at all uncommon in the story cycle. The people at *The New Yorker* apparently thought better of their ways, for they later published three of the stories: "Allowance," "Accident," and the prize-winning "Thorofare." Two of the stories that make up the volume, "Party Blues" and "Wildflowers," appeared for the first time in book form.

That *Monkeys* is a short-story cycle and not a novel explains much about its basic nature. The nine stories all concern the Vincent family over the period from February of 1966 to May of 1979, and each episode depicts a salient and revealing moment of interaction among them. Many of the stories portray seemingly mundane events, a tea at the yacht club, a family Thanksgiving dinner,[12] but the psychological conflicts, particularly when the stories are read as a group, are riveting and dramatic beneath the understatement. Although they are told in chronological order, there is no attempt to cover the events that occur between the stories, in the interstices of the depicted action, with the result that much of what is important takes place offstage: the death of Mum, the remarriage of Dad, the death of his father, the growth of the children. One reason for this might be that the stories were written and published out of temporal sequence, but another is that a standard feature of the cycle is that there is no attempt to bridge the action between stories, each story being allowed to depict a single episode. In line with

Hemingway's "iceberg theory," what is missing is just as important as what is present, and it can be retrieved only through inference.

There are other discontinuities among the stories. "Hiding" is narrated in first person by one of the children, Sophie; seven of the remaining stories are told in third person from a perspective closely aligned with the point of view of the children; one story, "Accident," is told in third person from a perspective outside the family altogether. The settings of the stories are also disparate: five are set in the family home in Marshport, Massachusetts; two take place at their summer home in Maine; one story is set in Bermuda, where the family has gone on vacation; and the final one involves action at both key locations. In characterization, the key figures are the children, who appear in all of the stories; Mum and Dad are important, but he is sometimes offstage, and Mum dies in the seventh story in the sequence. Some figures of significance, notably the wealthy Kittredge and Dad's second wife, Pat Meyer, appear in only one story. What most strongly unifies the collection is continuity of theme: alienation; emotional longing; the pain of isolation; the progressive maturation of the children; the central issues of socioeconomic conflict. The religious differences between Mum and Dad resonate throughout the stories, uniting them in a pattern of causation and motivation. Since, as a minimalist, Minot works subtly, with much implied and little stated directly, the full significance of these aspects of the book, and the rich artistry of the stories themselves, are apparent only through a detailed examination of each of the stories.

The opening story in *Monkeys* was also the first published, appearing in *Grand Street* in 1983 in essentially the same form as that included in the volume.[13] It is anomalous in that it is the only story in the collected volume that is told in first person, in this case by ten-year-old Sophie. The charm of the narrative stance is that the family is viewed from a child's perspective: hence, much of what she relates in her innocence has deeper implications beyond her awareness, the fundamental method of *Adventures of Huckleberry Finn*. The plot is also simple and straightforward, at least on the surface. One Sunday in February 1966, Mum bundles up the children and takes them to mass; after the services, the family goes skating on the local rink; when they return home, Dad goes off to the store, and Mum hides with the children in a linen closet, waiting to surprise Dad when he comes looking for them. He returns home, calls briefly for his family, and sits down to watch football on television. Mum and the children are humiliated by his lack of concern, and they gather to go down the stairs. Within the temporal progression of this action, there are references to three other episodes: a trip to Castle Hill in Ipswich, during which Mum tells the story of a woman's suicide; family attendance at a football game, during which Mum sees a former beau; and the memory of Dad on the beach with his children. All of this action contains information that is crucial for an understanding of both this story and the subsequent events in *Monkeys*.

"Hiding" is a story not of plot but of character; the events are significant for what they reveal about the backgrounds and fundamental values of Mum, Dad, and the children, especially Sophie. That there are underlying problems in the family is evident from the very first sentence: "Our father doesn't go to church with us but we're all downstairs in the hall at the same time, bumbling, getting ready to go" (p. 1). The most obvious inferences to be drawn from this simple declaration is that there are religious differences between Mum and Dad and that the family functions outside of his sphere. As the story progresses, although the details are never complete, much more becomes evident. Mum is later revealed to be Rose Marie O'Dare (Dad, a gardener, calls her "Rosie"), and she spent her early life somewhere in urban Boston (she used to skate on the Common), most likely in the South End. An Irish Catholic who raises the children in her faith, she seems to have gone to parochial school (p. 61) and then Boston College, where she attended football games (p. 8). Although little is revealed about her parents and her social standing, she is clearly not of the same privileged class as the Vincent family into which she married: in church, she takes back change for five dollars. Mum is warm and nurturing, giving love to her children and needing love from her husband, who is patently remote both emotionally and intellectually. The pain inherent in her unfulfilled longings eventually leads to her death. In this sense, the stories in *Monkeys* constitute an elegy for Mum, a contemplation of her death in the context of a remembrance of the love and charm and vitality that invested her life.[14]

What is implied about Dad suggests a very different background. He grew up a Brahmin New Englander in a family of physicians and bankers, and he went to Harvard, where he was a star hockey player who now has his name on a plaque in the foyer of the rink (p. 9). He is Protestant, most likely Anglican, and he exhibits the emotional reserve of the stereotypical wealthy Bostonian. As Gurney has said, "Gus Vincent, the father, has become an empty man. Fastidiously polite in his behavior, archaically stuffy in his language, he manages to disengage himself from any real involvement with his family until the end of the book."[15] He seems to give nothing to his family, and he gets little in return, despite the fact that in virtually every encounter between them, Mum offers a gesture of closeness and warmth; at no time does he acquiesce. In his solitude, he drinks excessively; rather than respond to the family, he gardens, taking himself outside, away from the need to interact. He has all the formal trappings of genteel society and none of the substance, none of the depth of character that might be expected of an Ivy League banker in his role as husband and father.

The first sentence of the story is thus indicative of the tension in the marriage. That Rose and Gus appear as "Mum" and "Dad" is a function of the narrative technique, since all is told from Sophie's point of view, and part of the charm of her telling is that she speaks in the present tense. Mum is portrayed as the consummate Madonna, bustling about caring for her children, giving some nurturing gesture to each. Revealingly, Dad waits "on the other side of the French doors," separate, cold, remote. He does not help get the children ready to leave, and even young Sophie is sensitive to his remoteness: "When we finally barrel down the hill, he turns and goes back into the house, which is big and empty now and quiet" (p. 3). During mass, a young child, not one of the Vincents, screams out "Dah-Dee," an amusing comment that is also a reminder that Dad is not with his children, not part of the family. What is abundantly evident even in this opening story is that there is pain in the Vincent family: Mum feels it most deeply; Dad is oblivious to it; the children all respond to it, sometimes with devastating consequences.

The first flashback is significant in ways that would not have been evident to the readers of the story in *Grand Street*. There was no way for them to know that a subsequent story would deal with the death of Mum and that the strong indications are that she died as the result of a suicide inspired by the betrayal of her lover. That scenario, however, is the very substance of the initial flashback in "Hiding." In this episode, Sophie is remembering how the family would go to Castle Hill in the autumn and how one time Mum told an intriguing legend about a woman who would surreptitiously meet her lover in the garden; one night he did not come, "and finally when she couldn't stand it any longer, she went crazy and ran off the cliff and killed herself and now her ghost comes back and keeps waiting" (p. 5). That brief tale had little meaning in *Grand Street*; in the collected volume, however, it is an adumbration of what will happen to Mum herself, how she will be rejected by a lover and kill herself. Even her immediate ministrations to Dad suggest such rejection: as they walk along, "she brushes a pine needle from his collar and he jerks his head, thinking of something else, probably that it is a fly" (p. 5).

The resumption of the present action, which moves on to the ice skating scenes, is also subtle in its suggestions: Dad calls his wife "Mum," indicative of her role as mother, not as his lover; she calls him "Uncs," suggesting that he has a family tie but not one as close as that of a husband and father. As they drive along, she flirts with him, and he concentrates on the road (p. 7). The second flashback deepens the sense of Mum as romantic figure, for it deals with a time when, at a football game with Dad, she saw a man she once dated (pp. 8–9). The subsequent skating scene is also suggestive: Dad sweeps across the ice in the style of a hockey player, all power and speed; Mum displays her past as a figure skater, all style and grace; he does not watch her. Back home, when she does her tap dance routine for the children, Dad does not lift his eyes from the book he is reading. In the context of the earlier suggestions, it is not surprising that in the final action of the story, Dad does not look for his family, seems to care nothing about them, and leaves Mum in painful humiliation, yet another overture of love and fun rejected by her husband. Although still a young child, Sophie is not insensitive to the meaning of the rejection: "Though she is turned away, we still can see the wince on her face like when you are waiting to be hit or right after you have been. So we keep standing there, our hearts pounding . . ." (p. 21). The opening story in *Monkeys* ends with this painful moment, a conclusion that is a dramatic and excruciating harbinger of events to follow.

How all of this came to be is suggested by indirection in "Thanksgiving Day," the second story in the chronology but the fourth story published, originally appearing, in somewhat different form, in *Grand Street* in 1984.[16] If "Hiding" is all character definition, a revelation of the basic problems of the current generation of the Vincent family, this story emphasizes the past, offering a historical explanation of the situation, revealing the temporal depth of the issues that divide Mum and Dad. To the extent that there are conflicts in the present action, they are not between Mum and Dad but between his parents; but more important than immediate hostilities are the implications of the socioeconomic status of the family and the legacy of emotional inaccessibility, the impenetrable affective barrier that seems the inheritance of the Vincents. The basic events are straightforward: on Thanksgiving Day of 1967, Mum and Dad take their children to the paternal home in Motley, Massachusetts, for a holiday dinner. Dad's parents host an annual celebration for the family, and the same food, the same conversations, and the same activities take place every year. Dad's brother, Charles, and his family are present, as is their sister, Fran, now married to Thomas Small. The family takes photographs, looks at the pictures from the past, dines on traditional fare, and the story concludes.

Artistically, it differs in important ways from "Hiding," which was told from Sophie's point of view. The perspective in this case is that of a distant omniscient narrator; Mum and Dad are thus called Gus and Rosie Vincent even though the angle of vision is most often identified with that of the children as a collective entity, with Sophie's purview predominating. In the course of the afternoon, the children are often left to their own devices: "There was nothing to do while the grown-ups talked except to look around at each tiny thing" (p. 27). This device is effective in that it allows artifacts to be observed without explanation; conversations can be recorded but not analyzed; the drama can develop through implication, with the children unable to fully comprehend the significance of what is going on around them.

The key issues are not in the action but in the disclosures about the personalities and conflicts that have troubled the family historically, matters persistent in the relationship between Dad and Mum. The central situation is that the Vincent family is well educated, affluent, and genteel, as their photographs reveal: "All the faces in the photographs had straight noses and white eyeballs and hide-gray complexions" (p. 32). Pa, Dad's father, went to prep school and then on to Harvard; his brother was a physician who discovered a cure for a disease; Pa was wealthy enough to work in government as a dollar-a-year man, writing speeches for a senator; the family owns vacation property in North Eden, Maine, where they spend part of every summer. The grandmother, Ma, seems also to have come from a well-heeled family: her father had shot a lion on safari in Africa. That revelation comes in a scene that did not appear in the magazine version, for the entire incident in which Mum takes the children to the attic to pet the lion skin did not appear in *Grand Street*. The scene adds a crucial dimension of family history in that the attic contains meaningful artifacts, "newspaper clippings and tied-up letters and pink-striped hat boxes, and Brooks Brothers boxes with old army uniforms in them. The yellow tweed suitcases looked shellacked" (p. 30). Sophie concludes this scene with an expression of her need for tenderness, as she embraces the lion, putting "her cheek next to the ears, knowing they were the softest part" (p. 31).[17]

The physical environment suggests that there is every reason for the Vincents to be extraordinarily happy, save for the fact that emotional reticence is inherent in the family character. No one can remember ever seeing Pa smile except in the photograph with the senator; he does not greet his children when they arrive; at the dinner table, the Vincents do not look at each other when they converse, speaking instead to the interstices between people. When, after a long interval, Dad saw his sister at a Harvard football game, he did not stop to talk to her, saying simply "Good day to you" as they passed (p. 28). It is significant that when the time comes for a photograph of the family gathering, Dad is taking the picture and is not one of the people in it, not part of the group.

The lack of warmth in the Vincent family comes in sharp contrast to the personality of Mum, a motif subtly interwoven into the activities of the day. Bringing her children to visit her Brahmin in-laws, Mum has dressed them strategically, the girls in plaid skirts, the boys in gray flannels. She is an outsider in a wealthy but emotionally dysfunctional family, and her own family ties seem to have been severed: there are no details anywhere in the book about her family (apart from a brief flashback to a visit with her sister, who lives a glamorous life in New York), no mention of transitional moments in their lives, and no balancing visit to her parents, the O'Dares. Amid the affluence of the Vincent home, Mum takes her children into the kitchen to greet the Irish servant, Livia, who kisses them warmly. When Livia quizzes the children on the "seven blessed sacraments," the cousins wander off, suggesting that they are not Catholic. Throughout the day, Mum is very much the mother, comforting her children, keeping them entertained, attempting to assuage the pain that permeates the day.

That pain is most clearly depicted in the portrait of Ma, whose affective situation predicts what is to come for Mum. It is the always proper Ma who greets her children in the doorway, dressed conservatively in a dark blue pleated dress, her shoes "pale lavender with pink trim and flat bows" (p. 27). A family dispute about whether the front lawn was ever frozen over so that the family could skate on it reveals that Pa is losing his memory, a fact that Ma handles with love and understanding:

> With her perfectly calm face, Ma said, "I do remember it, yes." She looked at Pa and said gently, "It was when you were away." "Nonsense," he said. "I never went anywhere" (p. 33).

She shows similar largesse with regard to the piazza that burned at the Maine house in Cassett Harbor. It is clear, by implication, that some careless act by Pa was responsible for the fire, and he twice insists that the house was torn down, a judgment Ma contravenes. But when asked how it burned down, Ma does not finally answer, protecting her husband's feelings (p. 35).

When Pa becomes recalcitrant, suggesting that Ma shoot herself, he is taken upstairs where he cannot further disrupt the conversation. In his senility, Pa is oblivious to the pain of the moment, but Ma, and Mum, feel it keenly. When Mum attempts to compliment Ma on the dinner, saying that she had arranged it "beautifully," Ma's resigned observation is that "actually, I don't think I've ever arranged anything beautifully in my whole life" (p. 39). Adrift in an emotional vacuum, Ma feels herself a failure, trapped in an empty life. Minot concludes the story with a moving imagistic correlative, as Sherman leaves the rocking chair:

> The chair went on rocking. Ma stared at it. Rocking empty, it meant something to her.
> So she reached out one lavender shoe to still it, and did just that (p. 39).

The kinesthetic image of the moving chair, suddenly stilled, and the implication that this is Pa's chair, one he occupied in happier times, is a brilliant conclusion to a story that is painfully revelatory of the emptiness in the Vincent ancestral home.

The third story in the temporal sequence of events concerning the Vincent family is "Allowance" (pp. 41–57), which was published in *The New Yorker* in 1985.[18] This episode is anomalous in the volume in several respects. It is the only story in the cycle set outside of the United States; it is told from an omniscient perspective that exceeds the knowledge and point of view of the children; the surface action emphasizes ten-year-old Gus rather than the conflict between the parents. The events take place in March of 1969, when the family is vacationing in Bermuda. Since it rains while they are there, a telling metaphor, the family is kept inside, where the fragility of their interactions is dramatically highlighted.

The narrative perspective is also unique. Although the cognitive identification of the narrator is with the children, the parents once again being described as Mum and Dad, there are also independent, expository judgments from another point of view. When the narrator describes the children as being "trapped" in the hotel, it is their feelings that are being projected, but the assessment that "Gus was usually the quietest one" derives solely from the mind of the narrator. In another passage, depicting Dad as drunk at the dinner table, the narrative identification is with his mind and drifts into stream of consciousness: "Perplexed, he saw six children, six hopeful faces looking back at him. Down at the other end was a woman in a pink dress. What did they want? He stood and excused himself" (p. 49). The dominant perspective, however, is with the children.

The central issues in "Allowance" differ depending on whether it is read in the context of the previous stories or in isolation. In context, the crux of the matter is the disintegrating relationship between Mum and Dad; in isolation, the central focus is on Gus. It is he who is strangely agitated at the beginning, an anxiety explained at the end when it is revealed that he has stolen Dad's wallet, suggesting that he steals money habitually. In this dimension, the title refers to the "allowance" of money a parent gives a child, something that Dad, a banker, does not do, which inspires the theft (p. 48). Gus is also the focus of the physical drama when he chokes during dinner and is saved only by the quick action of the waiter. The concluding incident of the missing wallet is significant not simply for the implication that Gus has stolen it but for his calculated attempts at deception, his unconvincing assertion that he found it in the bushes, his feigned nonchalance, his request for confirmation that everything is satisfactory, his final realization that everyone knows the truth:

> Gus tried to smile and, swaggering, turned toward his brothers and sisters. All their eyes were on him, and all watched his expression change, withering into panic, as if he thought that at any moment they would pounce on him.

It wasn't that. They just knew what he'd done (p. 57).

It is a dramatically telling moment and an effective ending. It also suggests that the inherent pathology in the relationship between the parents is having its effect on the children.

In the context of the other stories, the central issue is not so much the awkward revelations about Gus but the continuing deterioration in the relationship between Mum and Dad. The trip to Bermuda was Mum's idea (p. 43), and there is the suggestion that she felt that it was urgent that the family break out of its normal routine. This idea is reinforced when Mum wanders out of the bedroom and bursts into tears, saying that there is a problem with Dad at the bank, a statement she never finishes. Whatever Dad's problem, and he appears as both a paranoid and a malcontent, it is most likely related to his drinking, for he has certainly become an alcoholic by this juncture. Even when he was hospitalized, Mum had to sneak a bottle of bourbon to him (p. 47). In Bermuda he buys whiskey by the gallon (p. 46). Later, at dinner, he is in a stupor that mirrors his father's condition in "Thanksgiving Day," nearly nodding into his soup (p. 51).

It is Mum who bears the emotional weight of the family, and she is brought to tears by Dad: " 'It's okay. It's just things at the bank, and he thinks . . .' This hurt, and she winced" (p. 45). Given her nature, the pain she feels would not seem to be related to financial or occupational problems but to domestic issues. Her attempts to improve the marriage falter on Dad's reticence:

> "I think we should all give Dad a big thank-you for the vacation," Mum said.
>
> They did, in unison. Dad nodded abruptly. Everyone went busily to the plates.
>
> A sound came from Dad.
>
> "You okay?" Mum asked.
>
> Dad pulled at his collar, frowning. A tie was something he wouldn't usually have on for dinner. "Hot in here," he muttered (pp. 50–51).

When he pours his glass of water over his head at the dinner table, Mum again attempts to ameliorate the embarrassment, dabbing water on her neck, emulating the role of Ma in the earlier story. There is more at issue in this scene than Dad's drunkenness, for he displays a pathological inability to communicate warmth and concern or even basic human decency, a matter that, in later stories, has its effects on the children.

It is significant that the two central stories in *Monkeys*, "Wildflowers" and "Party Blues," are the only ones that were not published elsewhere. Much of the substance and motivation of the volume turns on the revelations contained in them. Although the central unifying elements of the collection (the family, the central conflicts) are still in evidence, there are also several innovations: the setting shifts for the first time to the island of North Eden, Maine, where the family summers; although the narrative perspective continues its third-person stance identified with the minds of the children as a collective entity, the formulating intelligence becomes more sophisticated as the children mature; the focus, rather than portraying the interaction between Mum and Dad, is on her affair with the wealthy Wilbur Kittredge and his betrayal of her with another woman.

"Wildflowers" is structured on the model of the previous stories, with a central line of action interrupted by a number of revelatory flashbacks that suggest lines of motivation, give depth to conflicts, and disclose the attitudes of the children toward the dilemmas of their parents. Dad is conveniently tending his garden throughout the present action, which takes place in July of 1970, just after the political protests of the Cambodia incursion that May. The central character is Mum, and the emphasis is on her enormous capacity for love and life, her devotion to her children (she gives birth for the eighth time), and on the crushing discovery of the philandering of her lover. It begins with Mum's squeal of delight at the prospect of seeing her lover at the sailing regatta (Sophie remarks that Mum is "feeling her oats"), to which she brings wildflowers rather than the standard domestic arrangement. The titular flowers metaphorically suggest much of Mum's nature: her spontaneity, her regenerative force, her unaffected beauty. The children are not at all insensitive about the motivation of her enthusiasm: " 'Guess-Who must be racing today,' said Sophie" (p. 60), who is insightful for fourteen.

Mum's romantic enthusiasm is not subtle: "When Mum handed the man a cup of tea, the look was there: thrilled. Wilbur Kittredge had his collar turned up against his tanned skin" (p. 63). It is clear that Mum goes on secretive carriage rides with Kittredge when his wife is away (p. 64); indeed, the children discovered them embracing in the carriage only a few nights before. A flashback to the Kittredge home in Washington depicts their rather indiscreet tryst while Sophie and Caitlin swim in the family pool. Now, at the races, Mum is intensely aware of Kittredge's interest in a tall blond woman, her eyes "lightning quick," searching for hints of clarification. That evening, driving with the children, Mum discovers her lover with the blond in the carriage, the same carriage the two of them had used. She is shocked but puts a good face on the situation: " 'I didn't think we should get any nearer,' said Mum after a while. 'Those are especially spirited horses. They spook.' The crease in her forehead hinted at deeper knowledge" (p. 72). The aftermath is significant: the Vincents do not attend the Labor Day clambake at the Kittredges, signaling the break the indiscretion has wrought. More significantly, the child that Mum bears in the spring, Minnie, could well be sired by Kittredge, a suggestion made all the more strong by Mum's emphatic observation: " 'You see?' she said. 'Her father's hands exactly' " (p. 73).

This central line of action is important in all the remaining stories in that Mum seems unable to escape the deeply disillusioning betrayal by Kittredge, an event that leads directly to her death. The flashbacks are all contributory to the major themes in this action. The remembrance of the time Mum saw a silver fox on Boxed Island resonates with her exuberance for life as her eyes light up with the thrill of the event; on a more subtle level, the silver streak in Kittredge's hair aligns him with the feelings Mum had for the fox. The flashbacks to Mum's affair with Kittredge reveal his furtive courting of her, with unsigned letters and anonymous gifts. The flashback to the death of baby Frances (every story has death in it) also emphasizes flowers and Mum's reverence for children. It is her exaltation at the birth of Minnie that concludes the action, as she revels in the process of embracing and nursing her baby: "The eye was fierce. The baby stayed fast. There is nothing so thrilling as this. Nothing" (p. 73). Thus the story that explains the motivation for Mum's death is also the one that most dramatically affirms life, a poignant irony in a crucial narrative.

"Party Blues" (pp. 75–89) is more a narrative of revelation than event, and its effect is to explain the background of more important action to follow. Thematically, the plot parallels "Wildflowers" in portraying tragic attempts at happiness through romance, the acceptance of sex as love, the empty despair of parties in which everyone is high and low. The basic situation is that in April of 1974, almost four years after "Wildflowers," Mum and Dad are on holiday in Bermuda, a location that recalls the unsettling events of "Allowance." While they are away, their oldest daughters throw parties involving drinking, drugs, sex, and despair, especially for Sophie, the central character.

The narrative method is again third person, with frequent formulations in second person, suggesting that what happens to "you" establishes a normative base for the family situation. The real emphasis, however, is more on Sophie's feelings than on her activities. The action is simple: during the party, Sophie, now a college student at eighteen, discovers that her boyfriend, Duer, is involved with other young women, but her love for him is unconditional and consuming. Deeply depressed, she seeks solace in gin, finally crawls into bed with him, and, in the final scene, ponders a tale her mother used to tell her. The implications of this children's story are significant, for it conflates two tales by Ludwig Bemelmans about a young French girl named Madeline. In *Madeline* (1939), an attentive nun, Miss Clavel,[19] looks in on her charges in the night and discovers that Madeline is ill. She is taken to a hospital for an appendectomy. In *Madeline and the Gypsies*, the children visit a circus, get caught in a rainstorm, and Madeline and her friend Pepito are stranded on the ferris wheel. She runs off with the gypsies who manage the circus, but she is eventually discovered and brought back to the boarding school.[20] In both cases, there is a caring adult who comforts and protects the young girl, a lost child who needs and wants assistance; the implication is that Sophie longs for Mum to protect her, which is why she wanders into Mum's room early in the story: "The only time you came in here was for real emergencies" (p. 76).

The emergency would seem to be Sophie's chronic depression: "It seemed to Sophie that it ought to feel different to be alive" (p. 77). The persistence of this condition is evident in a flashback: "Death was never far from her mind. One evening, Mum asked her to promise she wouldn't commit suicide until she was eighteen" (p. 81). Mum is certain that the depression is a developmental stage, but the obvious suggestion is that Sophie is now eighteen, still depressed, still contemplating ending her own life. One of the motivations might be her relationship with Duer, who leaves the party for a romp with Mimi Vanden. When he returns, embracing Sophie, the electricity is interrupted, and she realizes that it covers the entire area:

"It's all over," said Sophie.
"Soph," said Duer. "Relax."
"No," she said. "I mean, it's everywhere" (p. 85).

The moment of misunderstanding is brilliantly handled, with Duer interpreting Sophie's remark as a response to his indiscretion. The suicide motif, which surfaces in virtually every story, has its greatest resonance not for Sophie but for Mum, and the tangential revelations about her contribute to an understanding of her death. The remembrances of her by the children are of her protective and nurturing affection (p. 76), but the omniscient narrator provides a flashback that exceeds the knowledge of the daughters, one dealing with the earliest stages of the romance between Mum and Dad, with its drinking and flamboyant excesses, Dad dancing on a table at a ball on proper Beacon Hill. Submerged in the gaiety of the courtship is Dad's drinking, an issue that will cause them much pain later in their lives (pp. 79–80). Another flashback, derived from Sophie's memory, depicts the daughter's shocking discovery of the depth of her mother's despair: "She was lying on her side, facing the wall, and her shoulders were shaking up and down, crying. Sophie turned away quietly, her heart loud inside" (p. 86). Even the bedtime stories that Mum used to read contain the element of dread and foreboding, the underlying sense that something is terribly wrong (p. 89). Indeed, both of the previously unpublished stories that Minot inserted into the middle of the volume emphasize incipient family tragedy, which seems progressively more inevitable with each ensuing episode.

Although "The Navigator" (pp. 91–108) was the sixth story to appear in print, coming out in *Grand Street* in 1985, the suggestions are that it was composed first, since Sophie is called "Sidney" in the magazine version.[21] Its importance is that it emphasizes Dad, his personality, responsibilities, and place in the family. That it is set in North Eden in August of 1977 stresses his social and domestic identity in Maine rather than his professional duties at the bank or the swirl of his social set in Marshport. That the events are told from an omniscient perspective, outside the family, allows for a comprehensive frame of reference in describing Dad, rather than the more restricted point of view of the children. That the temporal relationship between telling and action is simultaneity rather than retrospection underscores the dramatic revelation of Dad's character, making the story one of discovery, of fresh and dramatic revelations. Although much about his past is suggested through implication, the central conflicts deal with his present role as father, with the extent to which he gives direction to the family and fulfills his role as "navigator."

The implications of the title, the only one that refers to Dad, relate to the narrator's observations that "when Dad was young he had worked summers on a cattle boat that cruised through the islands. He'd been the navigator. He still had an astronomy book on the bottom shelf of his bedside table" (p. 103). Much is implied. Dad, growing up in a Brahmin family in the suburbs of Boston, spent his youthful summers at the family home in Maine. Despite the wealth of his family, he was employed in the summers consistent with the Yankee tradition of conservatism in financial affairs and the belief that the best way to learn about money is to work for it. A bright student, who goes on to Harvard, he had learned celestial navigation, and he finds a position on a "cattle boat," the local term of condescension for the windjammers that offered cruises to tourists. In the nineteenth century, the windjammers were merchant ships, transporting livestock and produce along the eastern seaboard; now the "cattle boat" reference would apply more to the resentment by the local population of the tourists, whom they are pleased to designate as cattle.[22] That Dad would serve on one, rather than be a passenger on board, aligns him with the local population, a less affluent community that lives closer to nature than do proper, urban Bostonians; his interests in gardening, sailing, and ice hockey strengthen that alliance. In this sense, he is in opposition to the wealthy Kittredge, whom Mom finds so appealing. Dad's preference for a simpler life, closer to common people, would also explain why he was attracted to the Irish Rose Marie O'Dare rather than someone from his own social group. That he still has the astronomy book suggests his lingering interests in sailing, although his drinking has made him progressively less able to navigate.

The suggestion is that Dad's drinking may be related to his unwanted responsibilities and inexorable role as the father of seven children, which would explain his alienation from them. He married a Roman Catholic, who would seem to eschew birth control, given the size of their family. It is Mum who exhibits an interest in maintaining their position in society, in the yacht races, vacations in Bermuda, and swirl of summer people and tourists in Maine. In the social action of this story, it is Mum who arranges for dinner and childish games at the Irvings, giving Dad the choice between that event or the clambake on Sunday at the Kittredges. But Mum is apparently still at odds with Kittredge over his affair with the blond, and Dad would seem to have chosen the lesser of two evils. At the Irvings, Dad gets drunk and reveals his true feelings, as Mum explains to her daughters: "He collapsed on his place mat with his hands over his head. . . . He said, 'This is so *boring*' " (p. 99). This is a social faux pas of considerable magnitude, and his drunken display inspires the children to exact from him the promise that he will quit drinking, which he does, albeit temporarily. It is the trip up the Random River for a family picnic that portrays Dad in the "present" as a navigator. Sober, he is fully capable of steering the boat through tidewater shoals without the usual directions from lookouts. It is his one moment of competence in the book, a triumph that is compromised when he opens a can of beer with a "crack," violating his promise, abdicating once again his role as father. The response of the children to this event is expressed metaphorically in the conclusion, in the flashback to their throwing stones into the ocean, waiting for the splash, and sometimes no sound would come: "It seemed then as if the stone had gone into some further darkness, entered some other dimension where things went on falling and falling" (p. 108).

This theme of disillusionment with Dad links the story to "Hiding" as the motif of drinking links it to "Party Blues" and "Allowance." The strongest intertextual reference to "Thanksgiving Day" is in the portrayal of the situation of Ma, left alone now by the presumed death of Pa sometime over the intervening decade. Isolated within her separate house in Maine, the maid having gone back to Ireland, she drinks "glasses of sherry" and appears for dinner "flushed." The events of "Wildflowers," detailing Mum's break with Kittredge, explain the motivation for the avoidance of his parties. The events of these stories provide thematic juxtaposition to "The Navigator," linking it to a pattern of causation and motivation that comes to tragic results in "Accident."

When Minot's "Accident" appeared in *The New Yorker* in 1983, it was read, quite understandably, as a story about Sherman's car accident, and what seemed important were his drinking, his continuing despair over the death of his mother, and the sympathy his sisters feel for his pain.[23] In the context of the previous stories in *Monkeys*, however, "Accident" has additional meanings: the title refers not to Sherman's mishap with his Volkswagen but instead to Mum's death when she was hit by a train. The strong suggestion is that her death was *not* an accident but a suicide motivated by a complex of emotional conflicts: her need for love and warmth; her husband's cold distance from her and the children; her subsequent affair with Mr. Kittredge and his betrayal of her with the leggy blond from Europe; the birth of Minnie, who is quite likely the daughter of Kittredge, not Dad; and Mum's continuous depression and dark despair that culminate in her tragic death, an event that only Sherman fully understands, that leads to his drinking, that results in his own "accident." Sherman comes to embody the agony of the family, pain no one understood fully when the story appeared in *The New Yorker* with only "Hiding" and "Thorofare" preceding it. Read as part of the cycle, "Accident" involves the central incident of the book, the death of Mum, an event that is clearly motivated, and the collective pain of her loss fully justifies his sisters' fears that Sherman too will commit suicide.

It is indicative of Minot's minimalist methodology that the most important event in the book is never directly portrayed and is revealed only through partial memories obliquely described. The story is set in June of 1978, a few months after Mum died early in the year, and the central focus is on Sherman, on the emotional turmoil that he, at sixteen, has found difficult to express. As a constant reminder of Mum's death, the train that hit her rattles by each day, renewing the familial grief. The only explanation of the event comes in the brief statement that "Sherman has certain theories about the accident, and about the family, and gives them to Chicky late at night, each in his bed— brothers" (pp. 113–14). If her death were simply an accident, there would be no need for theories, and the pattern of references to suicide that begins in the very first story and continues throughout would be a red herring; it is far more likely, and meaningful, that the emotional pathologies inherent in the Vincent family (that cause Sophie and Sherman both to consider suicide), have their manifestation in Mum's death. It is she who has the deepest emotional needs in the family; it is she who reaches out repeatedly to Dad and cries at his rejection; and it is she who is doubly betrayed when the actions of Kittredge reveal that she was simply one of his recreations, unimportant as a person.

The story is told from a third-person point of view with a perspective outside the family but with access to the minds of the Vincent children. Since they are now older, Caitlin being twenty-three, the language reflects their increasing sophistication. This story is the first one in which Dad is described as "Mr. Vincent," reflecting the greater formality and distance of the narrative stance. In *The New Yorker* version, Rose was called "Mrs. Vincent," paralleling Dad; in the collected volume, she is referred to either as the "mother" of the children or as "Mum," suggesting, more strongly than in the magazine, the children's greater affinity for her than for their father. The handling of time is particularly complex, perhaps because so much of what is important is not restricted to the present. The action that is simultaneous to the telling is in present tense (pp. 109–17); the flashback to "the other night," when Sherman said he was going to the West Indies to live, is in past tense (p. 114); the telling of Sherman's car crash, which moves ahead in time into the near future, is also in past tense (pp. 118–26). The effect is to create an immediacy with the pain the children feel in the wake of their mother's death, and to participate in their situations in June of 1978, but also to move back in the intensely emotional scenes in which Sherman becomes drunk and confronts his father.

The surface of Sherman's despair comes out in his direct expression of his father's abdication of responsibility, when he asks him, "Are you my faddah or not?" and follows with "Then you should act like a faddah" (pp. 124–25). As Walter Bede has commented, "that blunted moment is about as close as these characters come to exposing their wounds."[24] In the conversation that ensues, Sherman realizes that his father is oblivious to the family pain, does not share in it, does not perceive any role in Mum's death: "Then from Sherman came a kind of wail, a hollow cry like something heard on a marsh . . ." (p. 125). The other children also finally express what they are feeling, Caitlin sobbing, Chicky feeling that she cannot breathe, Delilah trying to comfort her brother: "Oh, Shermy. Oh, honey" (p. 126). What has been in suspension from the beginning is finally expressed, a deep despair over the death of Mum: "Now the feeling was this: that the Devil had swooped down and had landed and was lingering with them all, hulking in the middle of the kitchen table, settling down to stay" (p. 126). This is the emotional burden that has been building since "Hiding," and it is given its most poetic expression in Sherman's feral wail of despair.

The story now called "Wedlock" (pp. 127–40) originally appeared in *Grand Street* as "The Silver Box," the last of the stories to be published in magazines.[25] The two titles have related but slightly different implications. "The Silver Box" relates to the cigarette case that was a wedding present to the Vincents with the names of the ushers engraved on the lid, and it is resonant with memories of Mum, with family artifacts, and with the inescapable aura of the mother who is missing. The implications are primarily related to the marriage of Mum and Dad, and the silver box is one more reminder for the children of their lost mother. The title "Wedlock," however, would seem to resonate forward rather than backward, to the possible marriage of Dad and Pat Meyer, his romantic interest not quite a year after the death of his wife, and to the marriage prospects of Caitlin, Delilah, and Sophie, all in their twenties. As if to emphasize the negative associations they would have for marriage, Minot added to the book version a comment from the narrator that "none of them would be getting married for a long time" (p. 139).

"Wedlock" is more an account of aftermath than of event, more an evocation of feeling than a description of a series of actions, although what few things do occur are suggestive. The narrative method continues the pattern of progressive distancing, for the third-person omniscient narrator now speaks of the family as the Vincents. Miserable during the first Christmas holiday without Mum, the family attempts to go through the motions. Sophie, "having lost interest in many things," deals with her depression (p. 128). For the rest of the family, "everyone was miserable" (p. 129). The cause of the misery is that "the house was filled with missing things," and the central issue is the absence of Mum. That fact must have mystified the readers of *Grand Street* in 1986, for her death would not make much sense without an understanding of "Accident," published three years earlier in *The New Yorker*. And neither story was fully comprehensible without the information contained in "Wildflowers," not available until the publication of the collected volume. Only then would the "shoebox of postcards from Mr. Kittredge" be meaningful.

Despite her conspicuous absence, the children sense Mum all around them, in the family cats ("It's like they're Mum"), in the memories of how she would watch the lightning, or call the children "monkeys," or say good night. When they trim the tree, the daughters feel they are taking Mum's place, a point that Minot emphasized when she revised the story between magazine and book publication, adding to the scene a telling passage: "Mum had had a certain way of cocking her wrist, with a finger out, dangling the ornament while she decided where it should go. This year, decorating the tree themselves, it was as if they had Mum's hands. The tree was approached by hundreds of Mum's hands" (p. 138). Dad seems overwhelmed by her absence as well, getting drunk and falling in his room, appearing "puffy-eyed" before the children. Sophie understands: "The guy's wife is dead, okay?" (p. 131). In the scene in which he walks naked down the hall, Minot added a sentence to the magazine statement that "without his glasses, he couldn't see a thing." The addition was that "he frowned—a perplexed caveman at the mouth of his cave" (p. 137). Dad is lost without Mum, a primitive in his own family.

If not much happens in "Wedlock," it is closely tied through allusion and thematic resonance to the other stories, linking them to the emotional devastation of Christmas in 1978. The opening church scene relates this story to "Hiding," when Mum takes the children to mass. Young Gus now plays hockey, referring to the skating scene and the flashback to his father's athletic career at Harvard. Sophie's depression relates to her similar condition in "Party Blues," Gus's eating recalls the choking scene in "Allowance," and when his sisters call him "Goatie" they are using Mum's name for him. The drunken father upstairs looks back a year to "The Navigator," when Dad vowed not to drink any more and then broke his promise. "Wedlock" does not drive the action forward; it shows the meaning of the past by revealing the effects of Mum's death on all the members of the family.

When "Thorofare" appeared in *The New Yorker* in 1983, it was a rather different story than in the collected version, and it had a different impact.[26] Narrated in first person by "Sana," clearly the "Sophie" of *Monkeys*, the story presented a highly personal account of the distribution of Mum's ashes in the ocean off the Vincent summer home in Maine. Not only was the formulation of the assertions in first person, but Sana was at the center of the activity, the speaker, the focal point, the principal character in the story. In that version, there was a temporal distance from the action, for Sana spoke in retrospect, at a moment anterior to the action itself, sufficiently later for her to reflect that "I only sort of remember."[27] When the story appeared in *Monkeys* in 1986 it was told by a more sophisticated third-person narrator, at a time closer to the events themselves. The central character is Sophie, retaining access to her sensibility, but the distribution of Mum's ashes is now more of a family event than in the original publication, and the feelings of all of the children are revealed to chilling, cumulative effect.

The version in *The New Yorker* was chosen for inclusion in *The Best American Short Stories of 1984*, even though, as only the second story published, it could not have made complete sense in isolation, lacking the patterns of motivation and meaning that emerge from the total group of nine stories. In the published volume, it is resonant with emotion, with the people and places and family artifacts brought back together for the resolution of the conflicts begun in "Hiding." In this position in the volume, had it remained a first-person story, narrated by Sophie, it would have provided a frame for the collection, with Sophie's voice beginning and ending the volume, the intimacy with her renewed at the end. When Minot changed the story, the narrative structure of the book also changed, with a progressive distancing as a central principle, so that the speaker's voice begins with Sophie, moves to a third-person narrator identified with the minds of the children in the central stories (with the parents still called "Mum" and "Dad"), and then, in the conclusion, to a position outside the family, with the parents addressed as "Mr. and Mrs. Vincent," terms the children never use.

The emotional tone of the stories is increasingly focused on pain, culminating in the excruciating scene in which each child takes a handful of Mum's ashes to cast into the sea, each reaction differentiated from the others. For her part, Delilah had insisted on putting some of the ashes in the garden in Marshport, keeping her close to the family, as near physically as she is emotionally. Out in the thorofare in Maine, young Minnie, eight at the time, does not know how to go about it, tossing a handful right next to the boat; other children are more matter of fact, Gus throwing underhanded for distance; Sophie ponders the ashes, "rounded and porous, like little ruins," thinking about the meaning of what they are doing (p. 157). Dad is characteristically abrupt when his turn comes, suggesting that he wants closure to the event: "Dad took a handful, quickly, gave it a toss, then held the bag upside down over the water and shook it out" (p. 158). As a total event, it is a stunning scene, with nowhere to turn for relief, as when the children return to the cottage in North Eden, "no one with the slightest idea . . . of where to go next" (p. 159).

The story is structured with the same temporal disruptions as the others in the collection. It begins with the "present" action in May of 1979, the family not having retrieved Mum's ashes since the funeral in January of 1978. Dad has married Pat Meyer by this time, and she is in the process of making the family home in Marshport her own, even though the narrator describes her as "Dad's new wife," never as "mother" to the children. In North Eden, she plays very little role, and her emotional conflicts are not an issue. The key flashback is to the day Mum died, the key event in the volume, but the focus is not on the "accident" but on the emotional climate as the family gathers in the television den, not wanting to sit in the living room, so clearly Mum's domain. When Sophie finally enters, she sees the silver box, resonant with implications of Mum's wedding day, a passage that Minot added to the story after its original publication (p. 147). It was in that setting that Sophie revealed Mum's desire to be cremated, indicating that she had anticipated her death, planned for her disposition, underscoring the suicide motif once again. The action then returns to the present, to the distribution of the ashes in the ocean off the summer home in Maine, where Dad had worked on the cattle boats in summer, close to where Mum had carried on her affair with Kittredge. That Pat has not taken Mum's place is clear from her exclusion from the action: "just the family," Delilah emphasizes.

The distribution of Mum's ashes is a powerful conclusion to the volume and a logical extension of the family pathology evident from the beginning. But the book is unified by more than plot development; the continuing characters, the temporal progression of present action from 1966 to 1979, with the growth of the children and the manifestation of the family issues in their own lives, all drive the cumulative themes forward. Much has changed: Mum is dead by the conclusion, but so is Pa, Dad's father, and Ma, since she is not even mentioned during such an important event. The reference to the silver box aligns this story with "Wedlock"; the fact that Gus hitchhikes to North Eden reveals that he has had yet another car accident, as in "Accident." Sherman is in prep school, following his father in the traditional pattern. In characterization, action, setting, and theme, *Monkeys* is a tightly unified short-story cycle in which each episode assumes a significance in context beyond what it had when published as an independent work of fiction.

4

Sandra Cisneros's
Cuentitos Latinos

The House on Mango Street

S andra Cisneros's *The House on Mango Street*, a
collection of forty-four interrelated vignettes,
was published in 1984 by the Arte Público
Press.[1] The following year it was awarded the American Book Award
from the Before Columbus Foundation and Cisneros was given the
Dobie-Paisano Fellowship. In 1995, based in large measure on the success of this volume, she received a MacArthur Fellowship, the most
prestigious and generous grant of its kind for American writers.[2] It was
a heady and conspicuous literary debut for any writer in any period, but
it was all the more remarkable that this sensational success was enjoyed
by a Latina writer recording in fiction the experiences of her own immigrant family. Cisneros has said that she began the book in an Iowa corn-
field in 1977 and finished it on a Greek island in 1982.[3] The more detailed account is that she initiated the book as a graduate student in
creative writing at the University of Iowa, seeking to use material
unique to her Latino background that her fellow classmates could not
duplicate and in which she could find her true voice and subject matter.[4]
As she explains it, "It wasn't until Iowa and the Writers' Workshop that
I began writing in the voice I now write in, and, perhaps if it hadn't
been for Iowa I wouldn't have made the conscious decision to write this
way. It seems crazy, but until Iowa I had never felt my home, family,
and neighborhood unique or worthy of writing about."[5] As her book

well demonstrates, her home and family were richly deserving of fictional portrayal, for she produced a cycle of some of the most powerful and evocative short stories in the American fiction of the 1980s.

The integral family and neighborhood situation portrayed in *The House on Mango Street* is based on Cisneros's personal memories. She was born in Chicago to a Mexican-American mother and a Mexican father, the only daughter among seven children living with their parents in cramped quarters that necessitated having children sleep on the sofa in the living room. Her father had grown up in comfortable circumstances in Mexico City, where his parents maintained a house, and his homesickness required the family to move frequently between their apartment in America, the land of promise for millions of immigrants, and the ancestral residence the father loved in Mexico.[6] The concept of "house" was thus important to the family, and the paternal home was in Mexico, but greater opportunity beckoned in America. As Eduardo F. Elías has explained, "in 1966 her parents borrowed enough money for a down payment on a small, ugly, two-story bungalow in a Puerto Rican neighborhood on the north side of Chicago. This move placed her in a stable environment, providing her with plenty of friends and neighbors who served as inspirations for the eccentric characters in *The House on Mango Street*."[7] Despite the residual attitudes in the Chicago area about Latinos, the family was able to accord opportunity for the children: Sandra went to Loyola University, graduating in 1976 with a B.A. in English, and her older brother graduated from medical school. To some extent they had achieved the promise that their new country held out to them. When Sandra went on to graduate work in the creative writing program at the University of Iowa, she had a rich trove of experiences on which to draw for the substance of her fiction.

As Cisneros has explained about the origin of her most famous book, "when I began *The House on Mango Street*, I thought I was writing a memoir. By the time I finished it, my memoir was no longer memoir, no longer autobiographical. It had evolved into a collective story peopled with several lives from my past and present, placed in one fictional time and neighborhood—Mango Street."[8] Even this casual comment presents a clue to the organizational principle behind the structure of the volume, the use of a progressive chronology for the protagonist, a young girl named Esperanza Cordero, set in a stable and remarkably circumscribed setting, the immediate neighborhood of the Cordero family home on Mango Street. The tight focus on Esperanza's family, as well as on the women and young girls of the neighborhood, not only endows the stories with continuing characters but with developmental themes as well, ethnic and gender motifs derived from the circumstances of a Latino family in contemporary America. Throughout these stories, the recurring issues of religion, sexual conduct, education, and financial aspirations provide an ideological continuity that affords coherence for the brief short stories that constitute the volume.

It is this central idea of coherence, of narrative congruence, that presents greater complexity in the short-story cycle than in the novel, where there is normally a strong narrative thread that provides a framework for the events and episodes of the plot. In the cycle, however, that organizational principle is normally not as pervasive as in the novel. Cisneros has said she was concerned about these issues in the construction of her book:

> I was frightened because I had no idea how these pieces were going to fit together. I was making all of these little *cuentitos*, like little squares of a patchwork quilt, hoping that they would match, that somehow there wouldn't be a big hole in the middle. I said, "I think it's done but, quién sabe!" So when I saw the book complete, when I opened it and read it from front to back for the first time as a cold thing, in the order that it was, I looked and said, "Oh my goodness, qué curioso!"[9]

It seems clear that Cisneros was not cognizant of the tradition of the short-story cycle, even though she well understood its central artistic principles, a situation shared by the reviewers of her impressive volume. Most of them simply called the book a "novel," possibly meaning by the term nothing more formal than a work of extended fiction, but several of the reviewers offered insightful comments about the artistic nature of what they had just read.

Julián Olivares approached the issue of genre in terms of interrogatives, asking, "is *Mango Street* a novel, short stories, prose poems, vignettes?"[10] It is an intelligent question, one that needs a response on which to base a full appreciation of the work Cisneros created. Olivares answered his own query by concluding that the volume is a collection made up of "vignettes, that is, literary sketches, like small illustrations, . . ." which is a good description of the individual units but not of the whole.[11] Most commentators have called *The House on Mango Street* a "novel," including Annie O. Eysturoy in *Daughters of Self-Cre-*

ation: The Contemporary Chicana Novel.[12] María Elena de Valdés, in her useful survey "The Critical Reception of Sandra Cisneros's *The House on Mango Street*," calls the book "a post-modern novel which weaves a tapestry of apparently isolated vignettes into a poetic unity."[13] Yvonne Yarbro-Bejarano also called the book a novel, but she commented perceptively that the individual stories "are marvels of poetic language that capture a young girl's vision of herself and the world she lives in."[14] Perhaps the most extensive and incisive comment on genre is that of Ellen McCracken, who defined the book as

> a collection, a hybrid genre midway between the novel and the short story. . . . Cisneros' collection represents the writer's attempt to achieve both the intensity of the short story and the discursive length of the novel within a single volume. Unlike the chapters of most novels, each story in the collection could stand on its own if it were to be excerpted but each attains additional important meaning when interacting with the other stories in the volume.[15]

Although McCracken seems not to have known the tradition of the short-story cycle, her comment is an excellent description of the norms of that genre.

Within the legacy of the short-story cycle, there are several unifying principles that link the individual stories of *The House on Mango Street* so that they enrich one another. One is a continuing, first-person, narrative voice, approximating the language of a child but capable of selecting meaningful scenes and describing them in poetic language that resonates humanistically, gradually sharpening in perception, deepening in layers of sensibility, conveying, through painful experiences, both compassion and understanding. The stories are arranged chronologically, thus revealing Esperanza's progressive growth, disillusionment, and determination to escape Mango Street to make a better life for herself through her writing. This structural framework constitutes the basic pattern of the traditional *Bildungsroman*, adapted in some ways to portray a Latina protagonist but depicting her developmental stages as the central plot uniting all forty-four of the episodes.

There are, of course, other motifs that inform Esperanza's developmental saga, including her wish for a dignified house in a safe neighborhood, an emblem of her desire to escape the embrace of poverty; her burgeoning craving to be educated and to become a writer; her struggle with restrictive gender roles within the Chicano community, with its stringent tradition of patriarchal domination; the allure and the danger of sexual maturity and the tragedy of the circumscribed lives of married women in her culture; and her family's complex religious heritage, an amalgam of Roman Catholicism, ancient Mexican traditions antedating Christianity, and superstition. Julián Olivares has formulated the issues with impressive insight, saying that Esperanza

> recounts her growth from puberty to adolescence within the socio-political frame of poverty, racial discrimination, and gender subjugation. The book's action is propelled by three major themes: the girl's desire to find a suitable house (essentially a move away from the barrio), to find her identity, and to become a writer. Identity is crucial, for it not only means coming to terms with her Latino ethnicity, but also arriving at a gender consciousness not circumscribed by the gender determinants of her culture.[16]

With a variable emphasis in each of the forty-four stories, all of these factors play a role in Esperanza's life, but all of them, to some extent, are blended into the larger pattern of her progressive development. As María Elena de Valdés formulates it, these stories are "not the day-to-day record of a preadolescent girl, but rather a loose-knit series of lyrical reflections, her struggle with self-identity and the search for self-respect amidst an alienating and often hostile world."[17]

In the opening story, "The House on Mango Street," these concerns are introduced in their full complexity, in the language and speech patterns of Esperanza at the time of the action rather than at the time of the telling, with a surface guilelessness that only suggests the rich issues inherent in the homely events.[18] This vignette constitutes the inception of the developmental theme, for it reveals Esperanza, at her earliest age, largely in terms of household relationships, defining the members of the Cordero family, sketching the history of their impoverished living conditions as they moved from one degraded apartment to another, finally accumulating the means to purchase the simple house on Mango Street. As Annie O. Eysturoy has pointed out, the narration begins with the collective "we," revealing that, at the beginning of the book, Esperanza perceives herself in familial terms, less a discrete individual than part of the collective unit.[19] One dimension of her inner growth will be the separation of her personal life from that of the aggregate family, the differentiation of her personal needs and desires from that of the group, the establishment of the sovereignty and agency she needs in her progress toward maturity.[20]

At an early age she feels disillusionment that the house is not what was promised, not the big white house with trees and grass around it but rather a small red dwelling with only one bedroom, a crowded home that has not relieved Esperanza of her feelings of embarrassment and diminishment about the family residence. That would seem to be the point of the flashback (a rare device in the volume) that recalls her mortification when they lived on Loomis Street and a nun from Esperanza's school walked by and expressed distaste for their building: "The way she said it made me feel like nothing. *There.* I lived *there.* I nodded" (p. 5). What is established in the first story is that the book will elucidate Esperanza's quest to feel like something, to supersede the limitations race, poverty, limited opportunity, and historical accident have placed on her. At a very early age, she desires to establish a future for herself that will allow for self-respect and an acknowledgment of personal substance. That quest will require that she assert her individualized desires and not simply adopt the life of her mother. On another level, that differentiation is also required with reference to the society around her, as she comes to realize that the life she envisions for herself is at odds with the established paradigm of Latino society.

The emphasis on a child's obsession with her family and the immediate environment is particularly evident in the first quarter of the stories in *The House on Mango Street.* The second vignette presents the family in terms of "Hairs," with a special regard for the nurturing role of Esperanza's mother, with her curly locks and protective manner, "holding you and you feel safe" (p. 6). The underlying portrait is of a mother who is beautiful, nurturing, comforting, and reassuring, and it is clear, even indirectly in the sketch she draws of her, that Esperanza loves her. The family is important at this point in the book because it defines the initial parameters of Esperanza's emotional construct, one circumscribed by the values of her parents and culture. That Esperanza longs to exceed the limitations of her family is clear in the next episode, "Boys & Girls," in which she thirsts for a best friend with whom she could share her innermost thoughts and feelings, expressing Esperanza's need for communication and sharing, the essence of the writerly temperament. This brief story also reveals, in innocuous form, the gender differentiation within the Latino community, for "the boys and the girls live in separate worlds," already distinguishing prerogatives and expectations on the basis of sexual identity (pp. 8–9). Esperanza will move toward a rejection of these traditional patterns and begin to assert the freedom to define a life for herself, unshackled by the restrictions of social convention.

These ideas are evident even in "My Name," which presents an underlying theme of self-definition, a quest for an identity she does not yet possess. It is important that she explains that the name "Esperanza" has distinct meanings in English ("hope") and Spanish ("sadness," "waiting"), for it is the English, American side of her self that offers the greatest opportunity for fulfillment, a hope with fewer gender and artistic restrictions. Esperanza has inherited a name and a determination to remain her own person from her great-grandmother, who refused to marry until literally kidnapped and forced into matrimony. Reduced to a circumscribed life, leaning out the window on an elbow, she never forgave her husband. Esperanza craves a richer life, one of her own choosing: "I would like to baptize myself under a new name, a name more like the real me, the one nobody sees" (p. 11). But since her sense of identity remains inchoate, she can only give herself an indeterminate yet unique and imaginative label, "Zeze the X."[21] Even this terse story demonstrates the richness of Cisneros's method, for in barely over a page she presents the issue of Esperanza's "identity," the subordination of women in Latino society, and the concept of the submerged life of the great-grandmother, rich themes on which to build the rest of the book.

Two major points are introduced in "Cathy Queen of Cats," the example of Alicia, who is going to college, and the imminent departure of Cathy, whose family feels the neighborhood has become demeaned. She is disgusted by "Joe the baby-grabber" and "two girls raggedy as rats" across the street, who turn out to be Rachel and Lucy, Esperanza's close friends (pp. 12–13). Cathy does not see the humanity in the new people around her, does not respond to their needs and feelings, possibly because of cultural differences. Esperanza chooses to be friends with people Cathy's family would find unworthy. Still, Esperanza eventually joins Alicia in seeking education as a means to an alternative life and Cathy in craving a clean house in a safe neighborhood away from Mango Street. As Cisneros herself has said, "poor neighborhoods lose their charm after dark, they really do. It's nice to go visit a poor neighborhood, but if you've got to live there every day, and deal with garbage that doesn't get picked up, and kids getting shot in your backyard, and people running through your gangway at night, and rats, and poor housing. . . . It loses its charm real quick!"[22]

"Our Good Day," in which Esperanza and Lucy and Rachel purchase a bicycle, provides a dramatized opportunity to delineate the neighborhood beyond the immediate confines of the Cordero home. All three of them ride down the adjacent street, including a dangerous avenue, and as they pass the local stores, Esperanza feels a sense of joy in her new friends and new possession (p. 16). The economic implications of a jointly owned bicycle are clear but so is the potential for creative approaches to overcoming the socioeconomic limitations of life on Mango Street, a new freedom, both geographic and economic, metaphorically expressed in the mobility of the bicycle. Furthermore, as Juanita Heredia has pointed out, "Esperanza also undergoes a social change because she breaks her relationship with Cathy, Queen of Cats, a girl from a more upwardly mobile social status, in exchange for two working class, Texas Latinas, Rachel and Lucy, who had just migrated north to Chicago."[23] Cathy's family may feel the local society to be irredeemably compromised, but Esperanza, herself part of an immigrant family, displays greater social latitude and a greater capacity for acceptance and cooperation. Yet Esperanza craves a new identity, wishing her name were "Cassandra" or "Maritza," yearning to be anyone but herself (p. 15).

"Gil's Furniture Bought & Sold" illustrates a structural principle of the volume, that the stories do not proceed in linear order, a simple sequential development of themes and issues. The concept of the expanded neighborhood was introduced in "Our Good Day," the memory of Mexico then intruded in "Laughter," and now this story returns to the "junk store" Esperanza passed on her bicycle trip around the area. There is ethnic expansion as well, for Gil is African American, indicating something of the multiracial culture of Mango Street, which includes a Puerto Rican family (p. 23). Esperanza's purchase of a small replica of the Statue of Liberty is symbolically appropriate, for she thus possesses the promise of America to the immigrant poor of the world, the covenant that brought the Cordero family to the United States. The incident of the music box is also instructive, for Gil's refusal to sell it shows Esperanza that even in poverty there are things too precious to trade for money, and art is one of them, even in the humble expression of a wood box (p. 20). It is significant, ethnically, that Esperanza shares an unarticulated but deep appreciation for something artistic with an adult black man. The music box also becomes an emblem of things that are worn or ugly on the outside but inherently valuable on the inside, a metaphor for Mango Street itself, with its abundance of richly felt life. These first eight stories constitute the first unit of *The House on Mango Street*, since they all take place on Mango Street in a limited temporal frame, involving a finite cast of characters, one expanded in the next several stories. The emphasis in this ensemble is on the background of the Corderos' situation on Mango Street, on the family and immediate neighborhood, and on the deeper issue of Esperanza's inchoate identity, her need to establish a sense of self. The next group of stories moves on to issues that are more multifarious, matters involving cultural duality, sexuality, education, and the threshold of puberty.

By "Meme Ortiz," some time has passed, for Cathy's family has now moved from the area, replaced by the Ortiz family. The issues of this second group of stories, however, recapitulate the first, since the prime motif here is multiple identity: Meme is not really "Meme" but Juan; he has a sheepdog with two names, one in English and one in Spanish, suggesting the cultural duality of Latino culture. The children play at Tarzan, the embodiment of cultural dislocation, an especially popular figure in the Chicago area since Edgar Rice Burroughs, the creator of the white king of the African jungle, lived in Oak Park.

"Louie, His Cousin & His Other Cousin" is also pertinent to Esperanza's growth, for it represents an expansion of the ethnic diversity of the neighborhood by introducing a Puerto Rican family who live in Meme's basement. Among them are Louie and Marin, a blatantly sexual young woman who stands in the doorway, singing "apples, peaches, pumpkin pah-ay. You're in love and so am ah-ay" (p. 24). The concept of "love" on Mango Street is always a vaguely threatening idea, for it is linked to sexual aggression, patriarchal domination, and a submerged life, a woman leaning out a window. In this case, love is juxtaposed to crime and violence, for Louie's cousin, driving a yellow Cadillac, is arrested by the police (p. 24). The implication is that the quick, but myopic, way to progress is through crime; in contrast, Esperanza and her friends pool their money to buy wheels of their own, a bicycle. The following story, "Marin," is even richer in its thematic implications, for it presents issues that are central to Esperanza's growth. Among them is Marin's plan to gain employment in "downtown" Chicago, expanding her geographic range and economic opportunities, ideas Esperanza implements in "The First Job," tying the two stories together. There is also a new threat for Esperanza to consider, for "Davey the Baby's sister got pregnant" (p. 27), a development that, on Mango Street, limits hope and opportunity. Esperanza has before her exemplars of this danger, not only in Davey the Baby's sister but two stories later in the situation of Rosa Vargas, in "There Was an Old Woman She Had So Many Children She Didn't Know What to Do," in which a Latino wife has been abandoned by her husband. There is also the example of Marin herself, whose short skirt and made-up eyes suggest her emphasis on sexual allure, oblivious to the future implications of romance.

The conclusion of this brief story is thus of prime importance, for Marin exemplifies the patriarchal paradigm for women in this culture, assuming no agency for herself, no sovereignty over her own life; rather, she dances under a streetlight, "waiting for a car to stop, a star to fall, someone to change her life." Esperanza, following the alternative prototype of Alicia, will decide to change her life by herself. In "Alicia Who Sees Mice," the protagonist takes two trains and a bus in order to get a college education, studying at night (when she sees the mice) because she has had to assume the duties of her deceased mother, making tortillas in the early morning. As Olivares has commented, "here we do not see the tortilla as a symbol of cultural identity but as a symbol of a subjugating ideology, of sexual domination, of the imposition of a role that the young woman must assume."[24] But Alicia does not accept these limitations, rejecting the indications of male power in her household. Instead, she seems determined to develop her own mind free of paternal control and in accord with her own internal desires. In the process, she demonstrates the need for self-discipline and hard work as a means to success, the historic methodology immigrants employed in achieving the American Dream.[25] Alicia affirms an alternative strategy to that of Louie's cousin, who sought wealth in crime.

"Marin" is somewhat anomalous in formal terms because it assumes a retrospective narrative stance for Esperanza. Whereas the point of view in most of these stories implies temporal synchronicity, the events taking place at virtually the same time as the telling, this story, despite the use of present tense, suggests that a significant period of time has elapsed between the events and the telling. Esperanza knows what will happen a year later, when Marin will be sent back to her mother, and enough time has passed so that there are things Esperanza "can't remember now" (p. 27). The implication would be that the telling takes place at least a year after the action, perhaps more, and that Esperanza is the writer she dreams of becoming, telling her story as an act of self-assertion, a confidence dramatically at odds with Marin's passivity. Another anomalous story, "And Some More," relates to this concept in its emphasis on naming and identity. The only narrative in the volume to consist entirely of dialogue, it allows Esperanza to dramatize her intelligence and reading and education, since it is she who has read about the Eskimos, knows the names of the clouds, and has the capacity to narrate a story, even though she calls herself stupid at the end (p. 38).

The issue of progressive maturation and concomitant sexual threat is given new expression in "The Family of Little Feet," in which the descriptions of the feet of a typical Latino family quickly evolves into the game of young girls playing "woman" by wearing high-heeled shoes. Esperanza, Lucy, and Rachel trifle at the game, walking to the corner, "where the men can't take their eyes off us" (p. 40). Mr. Benny, the grocer, articulates what the girls do not comprehend, saying "them are dangerous. . . . You girls too young to be wearing shoes like that" (p. 41). The masculine response, on all chronological levels, is aggressively sexual, from the "boy" who pleads "Ladies, lead me to heaven" to the "Bum man" who offers Rachel a dollar for a kiss (p. 41). The implication is that sexual bellicosity is not only socially acceptable but unencumbered by even the most fundamental restraints regarding children. From the perspective of Esperanza and her friends, they have had the opportunity to play at being older, at wearing shoes that make their legs look longer and give them a sexual presence, and it has been a frightening experience. As Esperanza explains, "we are tired of being beautiful."[26] "Chanclas" stands in juxtaposition, however, portraying a situation in which Esperanza has been given a new dress but not shoes, and she ends up at a party at the Precious Blood Church wearing her mismatched ensemble. She is touchingly self-conscious about her footwear until her uncle asks her to dance, saying "you are the prettiest girl here," and Esperanza forgets herself and dances, and the evening becomes a triumph for her. It is a positive exhibition of familial nurturing, of generosity, of social vindication, as the girl who was ashamed becomes the focal point of the party. Importantly, this story presents nearly the only positive image of a Latino man in the entire volume (pp. 46–48).

"Hips" is a transitional story in the sense that it conjoins the world of childhood (singing nonsense songs while jumping rope) with the adult idea of the sexual allure of a woman's hips. The style reflects the rhythm of the double ropes as Lucy, Esperanza, and her sister, Nenny, take turns in the middle. The theme of the "jumping" songs is courtship:

I like coffee, I like tea.
I like the boys and the boys like me (p. 49).

They discuss the things boys are good for, listing curiously adult functions drawn not from the world of childhood play but from the observed world of adult gender interactions, holding a baby and dancing, for example. In context, these motifs constitute a structural suggestion that Esperanza is leaving the world of childhood and entering a realm of adult concerns that will be increasingly violent and threatening and yet offer new avenues for personal development. The three older girls explore their capacity for invention in their poetry, drawing on their fantasies of the adult world; Nenny is too young for this process, which is why Esperanza is upset with her sister's singing childish verses.

The first group of stories focused on the childhood world of family and play and an incipient sense of self; the second unit on nascent feelings of cultural duality, sexual awareness, and maturation; the third section of stories moves ahead to a set of issues that supersede Esperanza's childhood fantasies to embrace some of the obligations of adult life, among them a consideration of education and writing as a means to personal freedom and the danger to women in Latino culture inherent in marriage and children. Her progressive expansion of individuality and the investment of "self" in the house the family occupies both continue as unifying themes in permutations that reflect her growing awareness that she must take responsibility for her life.

"The First Job" is an excellent transitional story into the next section for in it Esperanza takes a position at the Peter Pan Photo Finishers on North Broadway in Chicago (pp. 53–55). The name "Peter Pan" is an appropriate allusion to the fantasies of childhood, to the never-never land where no one ever grows up; this reference is linked to Esperanza's first major "adult" act, which takes her beyond the geographic and economic limitations of Mango Street, working to earn her tuition for her enrollment in a Roman Catholic high school. She is at a formative age in this story, feeling such pain, so awkward and uncomfortable, in her new environment that she eats her lunch in the bathroom. She ends up getting kissed on the mouth by an Oriental man, an event that reiterates in direct, physical terms the sexual threat that has been present from the beginning. As Juanita Heredia has observed, "even in the workplace, Latina women must be on their guard for any kind of physical harassment. This experience serves as another form of sexual awakening for Esperanza[,] who becomes alert as she crosses new social spaces in the city."[27] Another motif is latent in her work, matching pictures to negatives, since the deepest themes involving her are those of identity formation, and photographs represent a static record of public persona at a given moment, preserving it well into the future. Esperanza, as yet, does not feel she has a personality to preserve.

"Papa Who Wakes Up Tired in the Dark" is a brief but poignant vignette, barely over a page long, and yet it marks a new awareness for the developing consciousness of Esperanza. In this story, her paternal grandfather has died, and Esperanza, for the first time, sees her own father weep. She discovers within herself the capacity for compassion and empathy as she holds her father, comforting him, and imagines her own feelings if he should die. Nowhere in the volume is the love of a child for a parent more touchingly rendered than in this simple story, which stands in counterpoint to the maternal portrait in "Hairs" (pp. 6–7). This story also clarifies that Esperanza is the eldest child in the family, something that was not clear earlier in the volume.

In "Born Bad" Esperanza confronts the concept of moral responsibility, for she and the other children have mocked her aunt Guadalupe in her illness, feigning her paralysis and laughing, not knowing that she was near death, a concept that ties this story to "Papa Who Wakes Up Tired in the Dark." When Guadalupe dies in fact, Esperanza feels the full weight of what she has done, what can never be forgiven: "Most likely I will go to hell and most likely I deserve to be there" (p. 58). Lupe's death transforms her own children into adult roles, washing dishes and ironing shirts, but it also, ironically, contributes to a deepening of Esperanza's ethical sensibility, touching feelings she has never before known. It was Lupe who encouraged Esperanza in her writing, saying that her creativity would keep her free, just after Esperanza read her aunt one of her poems. The poem expresses two major motifs, the desire for freedom of movement ("I want to be / like the waves on the sea / like the clouds in the wind") and for a new identity ("One day I'll jump / out of my skin"). She does not like her current identity, her present skin, and from this point on Esperanza knows that it is her writing that will offer liberation.

Another story that enriches the thematic range of Esperanza's growth is "Elenita, Cards, Palm, Water," which deals with the relationship of the house with religion. As Cisneros herself has explained, "Mexican religion is half western and half pagan; European Catholicism and Precolumbian religion all mixed in. It's a very strange Catholicism like nowhere else on the planet and it does strange things to you. . . ."[28] Thus it is that when Esperanza wants to peer into her future, she contacts the "witch woman" Elenita, who practices an amalgam of witchcraft, astrology, voodoo, and Catholicism, using Tarot cards and the Virgin equally in her ceremonies. The Tarot cards are the most decisive for it is there that the image of the house is introduced. Esperanza desperately wants a house, a new dwelling in which she can have a feeling of decency and self-respect. Elenita tells her she will have a home "in the heart. I see a home in the heart" (p. 64), probably because in this culture, a new house is far beyond practical reach. Esperanza is disillusioned at this immaterial fulfillment, asking "is that *it*?" (p. 64). There is more depth in Elenita's prognostication than is immediately apparent, for it becomes clear that, for Esperanza, the correspondence between the concept of "house" and her emotional well-being grows ever closer. Cisneros has also commented on this point: "I guess as Mexican daughters we're not supposed to have our own house. We have our father's house and then he hands us over to our husband's. . . . The story [of when Esperanza goes to the fortune teller] impressed me very much because it is exactly what I found out, years after I'd written the book, that the house in essence becomes you. You are the house."[29] For the first time in *The House on Mango Street*, the concept of Esperanza's longing for a new identity has merged with her desire for a new dwelling. What is essential for her is that she establish her true personality and live her life according to it, and that, and not simple pecuniary enrichment, is the true quest of the new house.

Thus it is appropriate that this story be juxtaposed to "Geraldo No Last Name," the tale about the young Mexican immigrant who danced with Marin and was later killed in a hit-and-run accident. She did not really know him, having met him just that evening, but he fulfilled the longing she had expressed earlier: someone to dance with, someone to change her life. Perhaps it might have been Geraldo, but now he is dead and there is no one to notify, no one to care. In her rendition, Esperanza either speculates about the normative case or assumes omniscient knowledge of his background for she reveals a wiser, more experienced, perspective in her explanation of what the people who asked about Geraldo did not know: "They never saw the kitchenettes. They never knew about the two-room flats and sleeping rooms he rented, the weekly money orders sent home, the currency exchange" (p. 66). The insensitivity of the local population is at odds with Esperanza's compassionate explanation of the event, a young man reduced to a shirt and a pair of green pants, a young man whose identity was forever erased by a speeding car.

This poignant lament is followed by two stories of broken families, two formulations of one of the dangers awaiting Esperanza, for nothing in her environment can so limit her prerogatives as marriage and children, particularly in an atmosphere in which matrimonial fealty is suspect at best. The account in "Edna's Ruthie" is effective because of Esperanza's innocence about Ruthie's condition, an emotionally disturbed young woman who has left her husband and a house in the suburbs and moved back into her mother's house on Mango Street, sleeping on a sofa in the living room, unable to function in society. It also recapitulates the motif of the house and the concept of writing, since she claims to have once written children's books. Apart from the account of the fortunes of Ruthie, the story perpetuates the resonance of these themes in the context of Esperanza's gradual maturity. Another resident of Edna's house, "The Earl of Tennessee," is also involved in a broken marriage, and he welcomes prostitutes into his apartment, leaving the neighborhood children to misinterpret the events (p. 71). The motif of sexuality is thus given another dimension in Esperanza's world, in which sensual pleasure is something to be purchased, or a danger to be avoided, and never the fulfillment of mutual devotion.

"Sire" is notable in the collection for the introduction of Esperanza's romantic aspirations, which here take the form of a fantasy about a young man in the neighborhood, but she is otherwise explicit about her burgeoning interest in sex: "I want to be all new and shiny. I want to sit out bad at night, a boy around my neck and the wind under my skirt" (p. 73). Despite her mother's admonition about girls "that go into alleys," Esperanza wants her forming identity to have a carnal dimension, a desire related to her need to mold herself. This need for identity is expressed metaphorically in "Four Skinny Trees," a meditation on the trees growing near the street, where they do not belong and yet thrive. The parallels with Esperanza herself are direct, for she is a young woman like Stephen Crane's Maggie, who blossomed in a mud puddle. The trees teach Esperanza endurance and survival in the context of vulnerability, and even though she feels herself out of place, she has learned a key lesson from them. As Annie O. Eysturoy has postulated, "in her longing to escape her present circumstances, Esperanza sees the trees as role models for her own liberation: they grow 'despite concrete,' thus symbolizing Esperanza's own struggle to grow in a hostile environment, her desire to reach beyond the concrete, beyond class and race boundaries, for self-definition."[30]

The stories that follow all explore the matrix of themes already introduced, beginning with the retrograde Mamacita in "No Speak English" who longs for her pink house in Mexico, clinging to her native culture, refusing to speak English. The mother is losing her battle against assimilation into American culture, as is indicated when her infant son sings a Pepsi commercial in English (p. 78). The following story about Rafaela reiterates the idea that marriage involves the loss of opportunity and leads to a submerged life, and Esperanza understands that the young woman would like to go out and dance "before she gets old" (p. 79). The dilemma of a desire for adult sexuality and yet an aversion to its threatening possibilities is heightened in "Sally," in which the beautiful titular character is protected, smothered, by her father, a situation that becomes a destructive obsession in subsequent stories. What is important here is not so much Sally's fate as Esperanza's projection of her own concerns, for in the course of telling about her friend, she expresses her persistent appetite for a new house and escape from Mango Street; less overtly, she betrays her need for romantic fulfillment. At the end, Esperanza explains that "all you wanted, Sally, was to love and to love and to love and to love, and no one could call that crazy" (p. 83). This formulation, of course, is an expression of Esperanza's own inchoate longings.

Part of the maturation process is the recognition that she lives in a complex world of conflicting desires and unfulfilled ambitions. In "Bums in the Attic," which establishes that Esperanza's father is a gardener for wealthy people with a beautiful white house on a hill, she reveals for the first time her sense of disgrace when the family visits her father's place of employment, gawking at what they cannot have: "I don't tell them I am ashamed—all of us staring out the window like the hungry" (p. 86). This experience allows her to state again her longing for a proper house of her own, one in which she would allow "bums" to live in the attic (p. 87). "Beautiful & Cruel" is a story of defiance in which Esperanza resolves not to leave home through pregnancy or marriage but in accord with her own decisions about the direction of her life. She is particularly adamant about escaping marriage: "I have decided not to grow up tame like the others who lay their necks on the threshold waiting for the ball and chain" (p. 88). Within the parameters of her current situation, she can only express her rebellion by defiantly refusing to play the expected role: "I have begun my own quiet war. Simple. Sure. I am one who leaves the table like a man, without putting back the chair or picking up the plate" (p. 89). Her defiant sovereignty, she seems to feel, will compensate for her lack of beauty: "I am an ugly daughter. I am the one nobody comes for" (p. 88). She does not need anyone to come for her, even though, in other stories, she yearns for romance.

Despite her longing for love, she knows the example portrayed in "Minerva Writes Poems" of a girl only slightly older than Esperanza who has two children and a husband who beats and abandons her. The only compensatory satisfaction left to Minerva is the writing of poetry, and she and Esperanza read their verse to each other (p. 84). As Ellen McCracken maintains, "Minerva succeeds in communicating through her art; exchanging poems with Esperanza, she contributes to the latter's artistic development while at the same time offering a lesson in women's domestic oppression and how to begin transcending it."[31] In her endemic circumstances, however, Minerva lacks discretionary mobility; Esperanza, on the other hand, will use her writing as a means of escape.

Esperanza has this feeling reinforced by the example of her own mother, who can sing an opera but is trapped in the house by responsibility and domination. What is most important in "A Smart Cookie" is that the mother stresses education as a means to freedom, reflecting, poignantly, that she lost her chance out of a false sense of shame: "Shame is a bad thing, you know. It keeps you down. You want to know why I quit school? Because I didn't have nice clothes." She adds, ironically, "I was a smart cookie then" (p. 91). This vignette, with its touching portrait of a mother contemplating her lost life, serves as a conclusion to the third group of stories, which have advanced the parameters of Esperanza's quest for identity into new areas. The final group of eight stories depicts a more direct confrontation with adult realities. As a result, the subsequent narratives are more complex thematically, psychologically, and formally, their artistic complexity reflecting Esperanza's passage into a new level of awareness.

"What Sally Said" is, in effect, a continuation of "Sally," in which she defiantly wore makeup and flirted with boys. This story shows the consequences of her defiance, for her father abuses her physically and, perhaps, sexually as well, insisting on a stalwart domination of the women in his family at the same time he feels genuine affection for them. The pathology of the situation is apparent in the lies Sally gives to explain her bruises and in the scene in which she comes to stay with the Corderos to escape the beatings. Her father pleads with her to come home, and she does so, only to be beaten again a few days later. The suggestion of sexual abuse comes at the end of the story:

> Until the way Sally tells it, he just went crazy, he just forgot he was her father between the buckle and the belt
> You're not my daughter, you're not my daughter. And then he broke into his hands (p. 93).

It is an enigmatic conclusion that can be read variously as an indication of continued physical abuse; as the suggestion that the father suspects Sally is the daughter of some other man, which would explain his obsessive concern for his daughter's chastity; or as a revelation of an incestuous transgression. The first possibility is certain and not mutually exclusive with the other two; the second would make Sally's mother promiscuous, the only unfaithful married woman in the volume; the third would establish a level of sexual impropriety beyond anything yet portrayed in the collection. In whatever permutation, the motif of sexual degradation has been introduced, and it is amplified in the final stories.

"The Monkey Garden" is a story of defilement on two levels, natural and sexual. Esperanza recounts how the children used to play in the garden, a rich world of plants and insects, and how this refuge was profaned by abandoned cars. This motif is paralleled in Esperanza's mind by Sally's promiscuous adventures with boys, who taunt her into kissing them. Esperanza attempts to save her, only to be rejected by the adult world and then humiliated by Sally: "But when I got there Sally said go home. Those boys said, leave us alone. I felt stupid with my brick. They all looked at me as if *I* was the one that was crazy and made me feel ashamed" (p. 97). Even though she has longed for love and romance, Esperanza is confused and frightened by sexual intimacy, and she wishes for death. Her sense of the world she lives in has been altered by this experience, and this change is evident as she looks at her feet: "They didn't seem to be my feet anymore. And the garden that had been such a good place to play didn't seem mine either" (p. 98). Esperanza is expelled from Edenic innocence, an emotionally traumatic milestone. Andrea O'Reilly Herrera finds cultural significance in this story, arguing that the garden Esperanza's "family 'took over' is, on one level, a symbol of America as the new Eden; the disillusion and perhaps failure of the Chicano to domesticate or shape the garden—property that is clearly attached to, and an extension of, the father's property (the house)—is signified by the fact that the garden soon grows unkempt."[32] On a personal as well as mythic level, the events in the book are becoming more formidable.

The theme of sexual degradation reaches its apogee in "Red Clowns," a dramatic story in which Esperanza herself is raped. Told in retrospect, after she has lost her innocence, the telling has a bitter tone of recrimination and anguish: "Sally, you lied. It wasn't what you said at all. What he did. Where he touched me. I didn't want it, Sally" (p. 99).[33] In "The Monkey Garden," Esperanza attempted to help Sally; now, she calls for Sally's aid and is once again rejected. Esperanza, who cries out for Sally during the rape, blames her friend for the incident. As María Herrera-Sobek has explained, the logic of culpability would seem to be not so much the failure of direct intervention at the moment of the attack as an antecedent transgression: "The protagonist discovers a conspiracy of two forms of silence: silence in not *denouncing* the 'real' facts of life about sex and its negative aspects in violent sexual encounters, and *complicity* in embroidering a fairy-tale-like mist around sex, and romanticizing and idealizing unrealistic sexual relations."[34] It might also involve a broader social outcry against erotic violence, one with an ethnic component, for the boys who rape her would seem not to be of her own culture, calling her "Spanish girl" (p. 100). It is also important that this violation takes place at a carnival, in a child's world of fantasy and play in which sexual assault is all the more inappropriate.[35] Even at a temporal distance, the telling, the remembering, is deeply painful to Esperanza: "I don't remember. Please don't make me tell it all" (p. 100).

The portrait of Sally, whose story stands in counterpoint to Esperanza's, reaches its logical conclusion in "Linoleum Roses," in which she marries a marshmallow salesman, even though she is not yet in the eighth grade, which helps to establish Esperanza's approximate age. Sally escapes paternal abuse through marriage only to find herself in a relationship as restrictive as her previous life, for her husband does not allow her to use the telephone, or look out the window, or talk to her friends. He is also violent, kicking down the door, threatening her into submission, displaying the worst aspects of Latino male tradition. So, she sits at home, looking at the "linoleum roses" on the floor, a further allusion to the natural beauty of the garden transformed and sullied by human appropriation (pp. 101–02). The lesson of Sally is not lost on Esperanza, who vows never to marry, never to surrender self to cultural expectation.

"The Three Sisters" is pivotal in the volume because in it Esperanza sees death again, echoing the poignant scene when she comforts her father after her grandfather's passing and the vignette involving Lupe's death. In this story, for the first time, she directly conceptualizes her desire to leave Mango Street. The mythic element derives from the three elderly sisters, *las comadres*, who come to visit when Lucy and Rachel's baby sister dies. In the mode of mythological fairy godmothers, they come bearing a gift for Esperanza, but it is an heirloom of knowledge, not material wealth. It is they who articulate Esperanza's desire to leave the neighborhood and they who clarify that her home will always be a part of her: "You will always be Mango Street. You can't erase what you know. You can't forget who you are" (p. 105). Esperanza is shocked that her deepest aspirations are known to others, and she feels ashamed of her "selfish wish." One of the sisters reminds her of another point: "When you leave you must remember always to come back, she said" (p. 105). Here Esperanza receives adult reinforcement of her desire to escape, for a formation of a new identity, for a new life of her own design. María Elena de Valdés has commented on the mythological context of what the sisters bring: "The tradition of the sisters of fate runs deep in Western literature from the most elevated lyric to the popular tale of marriage, birth, and the fate awaiting the hero or heroine. In Cisneros's text, the prophecy of the fates turns to the evocation of self-knowledge."[36] Knowledge of self is the essential ingredient Esperanza needs to make her escape.

The final three stories all focus on Esperanza's desire to flee Mango Street and form an original identity in a fresh context while at the same time acknowledging that her heritage is part of her, a component she must integrate into her forming personality. In "Alicia & I Talking on Edna's Steps" it is clear that the Corderos have lived on Mango Street only a year, so this setting must be viewed as only one locus of her acculturation. Still, it must be said that although Mango Street is degraded in certain respects, there are lives and stories there to be cherished, and they have been internalized by Esperanza, fused to her identity. Alicia repeats the injunction of *las comadres*, that "like it or not you are Mango Street" (p. 107).[37] From this point on, the neighborhood becomes essentially a metaphor of heritage, cultural values, and historical ethnic traditions, elements Esperanza can never leave behind. But she refuses to think of herself in terms of her present house: "I don't belong. I don't ever want to come from here" (p. 106). As is clear in "A House of My Own," she wants to be free from patriarchal control: "Not a man's house. Not a daddy's. A house all my own." There she can have her own books, she says, and there she can write her stories and poems: "Only a house quiet as now, a space for myself to go, clean as paper before the poem" (p. 108).

Esperanza's desire is never actualized in the final story, but it is fantasized in her imaginative evocation of narration at an indeterminate point in the future, after she has left, from which point she can observe "what I remember most is Mango Street, sad red house, the house I belong but do not belong to" (pp. 109–10). She projects the moment, one congruent with Cisneros's own life, at which she has become a writer and can return to Mango Street artistically, imaginatively, living in the world of memory without living there in fact. There, she projects, she will not forget the obligation to return to her friends and neighbors: "They will not know I have gone away to come back. For the ones I left behind. For the ones who cannot out" (p. 110). It is a poignant conclusion to this Latina *Bildungsroman* of a young girl who forms herself, wills herself, into a life more congruent with her inner being despite the degradations of poverty, social approbation, and patriarchal violence.

These factors, especially in the context of the gender roles traditional in Latino society, and the inculcation of a spectrum of cultural values reinforced by church and family, constitute the most menacing threat to Esperanza's quest to become her own person. Julián Olivares's perceptive observation of the Latina situation is that "in their oppressed state, and with its promise of their reward in the hereafter, Catholicism promoted fatalism and resignation to a life of poverty and passivity, and consequently submission to the external elements of oppression."[38] Esperanza's rebellion is thus not a simple matter of the quintessential adolescent rebellion against the strictures of parental control but a deeper and more culturally profound refusal to accept doctrines that diminish the psyche, that limit self-realization and expression for a woman. Annie Eysturoy has explained the narrow boundaries of life for most Latinas: "They are . . . not only confined within their own houses, but also confined by their own minds, by the conditioned limitations of their own self-perception. Their lives and actions, dominated by fathers and husbands, are physically and psychologically entrapped within oppressive patriarchal structures, and they can envision themselves only in the seemingly inescapable roles of future wives and mothers."[39] Within Esperanza's world, almost all the women about her, including her own mother and grandmother, Marin, Rafaela, Mamacita, Ruthie, Minerva, and especially Sally, are subject to a form of gender exploitation that limits their parameters to the immediate domestic sphere.

Although it may be overstating the case to maintain, as does Juanita Heredia, that "this sexual exploitation of her girlfriends leads to the formation of a social and feminist consciousness in Esperanza," it is evident that Esperanza seems determined, at a very early age, to insist on her psychological independence.[40] It must also be acknowledged that *The House on Mango Street* is dedicated "To the Women," a gesture of some interpretive significance. As Reuben Sánchez has said, "Mango Street is a place where Esperanza may have at times felt joy and a sense of belonging, but it is also a place where she realizes that women are locked in their rooms by jealous and insecure husbands, a world in which there is violence, incest, and rape."[41] In the matrix of Esperanza's motivation to escape Mango Street, the negative pole is a desire to avoid the brutality and insensitivity of the world as she has known it; through her reading and education, she has learned to hope for a better society, and her positive aspirations include self-realization in a realm free of gender coercion, the opportunity to write, and the desire to reside in a house more congruent with her inner being.

That is finally the meaning of the house she aspires to own in a clean and peaceful neighborhood, and that explains why the home is the dominant motif of the book. For Esperanza, a house is more than a dwelling; it is an emblem of socioeconomic position, an objectification of the self, a public statement of shame or pride, and, importantly, a place to write.[42] This point is clear from the very beginning of the book, in the flashback in the first story that recalls Esperanza's feelings of humiliation on Loomis Street and her disappointment that the house on Mango Street is not at all what her parents had promised (pp. 4–5). This house, at 4006 Mango Street, is first described primarily from the outside, then in terms of its internal physical features, and then in regard of its meaning for the family. In "Laughter," which comes in the early part of the volume, Esperanza remembers the houses she has seen in Mexico, indicating that the family has been there, since Nenny verifies her sister's remembrance (pp. 17–18). By the end of the book, she has psychologically rejected the home of her parents since it violates her process of self-actualization, and this is an important step in her progress toward maturity.[43]

Cisneros has Esperanza relate her forty-four stories within the aesthetic tradition of the short-story cycle, a genre that always presents problems of structural organization, here exacerbated by the sheer volume of vignettes, awkward in their brevity, challenging in their configuration. If, on the one hand, they are metaphoric *cuentitos*, as Cisneros has said, each piece of the quilt has its own narrative integrity, its own internal drama of sociopsychological circumstance. On the other hand, as a collective entity, they form an aggregate artistic whole, a finely crafted cycle of stories. The central unifying element is, of course, the growth of Esperanza, her progression through painful but liberating experiences, in the same mythos as Huck Finn. In this sense the collection can be seen as being organized roughly into four groups of stories, sections that progress from childhood to her desire to form a new identity, from her interest in education to her early dedication to creative writing, a skill that holds out to Esperanza, as it did to Sandra Cisneros, the promise of personal freedom. Within that structure there are also thematic groupings of stories, recurring issues of the family and the barrio, religion, sexual maturity, and marriage, that provide ideational resonance to Esperanza's temporal progression.[44] As Cisneros has commented, "I collected those stories and I arranged them in an order so they would be clear and cohesive. Because in real life, there's no order."[45] But *The House on Mango Street* exhibits not only a satisfying thematic pattern but a tightly unified narrative strategy, a narrow focus on Esperanza and her immediate family and friends, a consistent voice and tone, and a montage of contributory motifs that further integrate the stories into a single fictional work.

One of those subordinate themes is Esperanza's conception of herself as an author. It is provocative, biographically as well as aesthetically, that Esperanza perceives writing as her means of escape, self-expression, and opportunity. Indeed, Cisneros has explained that in her earliest conceptions of her main character, Esperanza was not going to be a writer:

The book started out as simply memories. Later on—it took me seven years—as I was gaining my class, gender and racial consciousness, the book changed, the direction changed. I didn't intend for her to be a writer, but I had gotten her into this dilemma, and I didn't know how to get her out. I didn't know anything about what it's like to be a doctor or a social scientist. I don't know about those things! So the only way that I could make her escape the trap of the barrio was to make her an artist.[46]

But it is significant in several ways that she is a writer, for it indicates a new prerogative for the Latina in American society, one virtually unknown before the 1980s, but one with increasing moment in American letters. Within the world of *The House on Mango Street*, it is impressive that Esperanza can tell the events of her life with emotional intensity and with artistic grace and organization as well, establishing a voice and a rhythm and a narrative unit, the vignette, congruent with her natural instinct for narrative. In this sense, she fits dramatically into the mythic tradition of the adolescent narrator, one that reaches to the origins of fiction in the United States. Consistent with that historic mode, she tells about the salient moments in the formation of her individual identity, a profoundly American theme within the ideology of liberal democracy, here given fresh application, and renewed vitality, by its emergence in the context of Latino society.

5

The Nightmare
of Resonance

Tim O'Brien's
The Things They Carried

T im O'Brien's *The Things They Carried* appeared in 1990 to a great deal of critical ac-
claim. Roughly half of the twenty-two sto-
ries had been previously published, many of them in the most
prestigious magazines in America. Five of the stories had appeared in
Esquire, three in the *Quarterly*, and single stories in other magazines,
including "On the Rainy River" in *Playboy*. The titular story, "The
Things They Carried," was published in *Esquire* in 1986 and again in
The Best American Short Stories 1987. Both "Speaking of Courage" and
"The Ghost Soldiers" were chosen for *Prize Stories: The O. Henry
Awards*. On the basis of his earlier memoir, *If I Die in a Combat Zone*,
and the novel *Going After Cacciato*, which won the National Book Award
in 1979, O'Brien had clearly established himself as the most prestigious
and innovative American writer of fiction about the Vietnam War, an
impression that was only deepened by his new volume.

Despite the context for the publication of *The Things They Carried*,
reviewers had difficulty in accounting for the genre of the book, inspired in part by the equivocation of the publisher, which apparently
did not know of the genre of the short-story cycle. The title page carries the clarification that the volume is "a work of fiction" with no fur-

ther specification. O'Brien himself once referred to it as "sort of half novel, half group of stories," suggesting that he was unaware of the tradition of the genre.[1] But the most sagacious reviewers understood perfectly well the nature of the book they were reading. Robert R. Harris, writing in the *New York Times Book Review*, observed that *"The Things They Carried* is a collection of interrelated stories. . . . The publisher calls the book 'a work of fiction,' but in no real sense can it be considered a novel. No matter. The stories cohere."[2] Michael Coffey, in *Publisher's Weekly*, observed that the book "is neither a collection of stories nor a novel. Rather, it is a unified narrative, with chapters that stand perfectly on their own (many were award-winning stories) but which together render deeper continuities of character and thought."[3] In *Understanding Tim O'Brien*, Steven Kaplan maintains that "O'Brien tries to make all of his chapters into independent stories, which have their own beginning, middle, and end. This approach to individual chapters reflects his concern with the tightness and compression of his writing. He also strives to give each of his chapters a sense of completeness because he wants them to possess what he calls their own 'internal integrity'."[4] But none of the reviewers, or the scholars who have followed, have examined in detail the implications of genre for the volume, the complex ways in which the stories interrelate, their structural configuration, and the progression of themes, images, and narrative devices that culminate in a unified work of extraordinary thematic power and artistic richness.

The central issue for all short-story cycles is one of unity, the continuing elements from story to story that create thematic resonance, character development, temporal succession, and intertextual coherence among brief narratives, each of which presents a conflict and a resolution within its own domain. Each of O'Brien's previous books had a complex congruence. *If I Die in a Combat Zone* is unified by chronological progression, a central character (always the putatively autobiographical Tim O'Brien), the logical movement of setting from the United States to Vietnam and back, the psychological development from uncertainty and abhorrence of an ill-conceived war to a confrontation with the daily horror of combat, and the final issue of coming to terms with the memory of violence, which necessitates facing the full moral and humane implications of what he has experienced. *Going After Cacciato*, as a novel, has rather different principles of organization involving three planes of action from the "present" night that Paul Berlin spends on guard duty, to his memories of the previous months of combat action and the ultimate fragging of the lieutenant who orders the men into Viet Cong tunnels, to the fantasy he entertains about what might have happened had he pursued the absent Cacciato on a journey out of Vietnam and across two continents to Paris. Throughout this brilliant novel, the interactions of these three levels resonate to deepen the psychological and moral anguish the protagonist faces as he reflects on his war experience and what he has become as a result of it.

The Things They Carried also deals with multiple layers of meaning in the telling of a war story, but its complexity is quite distinct from the method of *Cacciato*. As O'Brien has indicated,

> *The Things They Carried* depends upon the tripartite structure again, with Timmy, the little boy; Tim, the sergeant in the Vietnam War; and Tim, the writer. Yet the mechanics of the two books are quite different. For one thing, the theme in *Cacciato*—of the interpenetration of memory and imagination—is not the subject matter of the new book. Certainly memory plays a big part in the new book, but in this case memory is used to reinvent a war and to reinvent memory itself. In *Cacciato*, the structural tension is between competing *layers* of memory, competing kinds of memory. The new book deals with the imaginative reordering and reinvention of actual events, which is how literature is made. . . . I guess what I'm trying to say is that oftentimes actual occurrence is irrelevant to a higher sort of truth.[5]

As artistic entities, there are distinct differences between the two volumes of fiction. As is often true in the cycle, there is no single protagonist who dominates all of the stories. The emphasis shifts from Jimmy Cross to Lee Strunk and Dave Jensen to Curt Lemon, Henry Dobbins, Norman Bowker, Rat Kiley, and the fictional construct known as Tim O'Brien, a character related to but distinct from the author. If these stories lack a unifying single character, they all focus on the members of Alpha Company, during and after the war, so that there is a continuity of attention to one group of characters.

Unlike the previous books, there is no prevailing narrative strategy that establishes a single perspective from which to view the action. The opening story is told from an omniscient point of view; many of the rest are narrated by the character Tim O'Brien; some are related by Rat Kiley; two are told from a third-person perspective limited to a narrative intelligence that is *not* Tim O'Brien. All of the perspectives, save the first, are unreliable, so that the information presented must be weighed against what is revealed in the other stories, a dimension of interpretation not faced by readers of the individual stories as they appeared in magazines. Nor is there unity of chronology, since many of the stories move backward in time to cover once again events already related by someone else, resulting in a synchronicity that underscores the narrational uncertainties. There is no single theme that dominates the stories, no one psychological progression that can be traced throughout, but rather a coalescence of related ideas, the moral horror of war, the ethical burden of violence, the complex relation of a "true" story compared to "actual" events, the dominance of fear and guilt and responsibility in all the men, and the final sense of moral degradation formulated in the mind of the character Tim O'Brien. Even the setting shifts from Vietnam to the United States and back again, with the final effect of presenting a series of events as disorienting as the experience of war itself.

These matters can be fully appreciated not in generalities but in a detailed examination of the progression of individual stories, a process that is clarifying in interpretive terms and nearly awe-inspiring in confronting the complexity of the book O'Brien has assembled. The first story, "The Things They Carried" (pp. 1–25), is both the most intricate and the most satisfying.[6] As the opening narrative, it has many functions: to introduce the characters and the situation; to establish the setting in Vietnam, where location means everything; to suggest the psychological weight that is carried in a situation of violence and death; and to introduce the issues, especially the death of Ted Lavender and the responsibility born by Lt. Jimmy Cross, that will inform many of the stories to follow.

The central metaphor for the story is the "things" the men of Alpha Company carry, the mundane objects that soldiers "hump" on patrol, with emphasis on what each of these objects weighs. The detail of these items, "pocket knives, heat tabs, wristwatches, dog tags, mosquito repellent, chewing gum, candy, cigarettes, salt tablets," establishes an aura of authenticity, the artifacts of physical realism, the incontestability of experience (p. 4). The weight of each item is given in pounds and ounces. But the men also carry subjective weight, their fears, hopes, and memories of home: "They carried all the emotional baggage of men who might die. Grief, terror, love, longing—these were intangibles, but the intangibles had their own mass and specific gravity, they had tangible weight. . . . They carried the soldier's greatest fear, which was the fear of blushing. Men killed, and died, because they were embarrassed not to" (pp. 20–21). It is a brilliant metaphor, providing insight into individual characters. Jimmy Cross carries the love letters from Martha and his knowledge that she does not reciprocate his affection (p. 3), a matter that links the things they carry to the central event of the first story, the death of Ted Lavender. Lavender died because Lieutenant Cross was thinking about Martha and not paying attention to what his men were doing. Because of Lavender's death, Cross orders the attack on Than Khe, and carnage and destruction follow; because of Lavender's demise, Lieutenant Cross changes as a person and a leader, obsessed with self-recrimination, determined to be a strict disciplinarian as a means to expiation. Everything in this story revolves around the death of Lavender, and it becomes a motivating force for many of the stories that follow.

The Lavender incident owes much to the death of Snowden in Joseph Heller's *Catch-22*, in which the Snowden scene is repeated eight times, each with greater expansion and significance. It begins as a joke, "where are the Snowdens of yesterday," proceeds to more detailed expansions of the situation, as Yossarian crawls back to help his comrade, and ends in the gruesome scene in which Snowden's insides slide out from his opened flight jacket and a horrified Yossarian can think of nothing else to say but "there, there." As a result of this experience, Yossarian sits naked in a tree, divorcing himself from military clothing, eventually deciding to desert. The death of Snowden is the most powerful event in *Catch-22*, the one that forces Yossarian to recognize his humanity and vulnerability, the one that yields the simple and yet profound insight that man is matter, easily destructible, and that the only moral avenue open to him is to choose life.

The Lavender episode proceeds in precisely the same way, recurring a dozen or more times,[7] beginning with the matter-of-fact report that "Ted Lavender, who was scared, carried tranquilizers until he was shot in the head outside the village of Than Khe in mid-April" (p. 4). Unlike the Snowden wounding, however, there is no suspense about the seriousness of the event. Even the conclusion is revealed at the beginning: "In April, for instance, when Ted Lavender was shot, they used his poncho to wrap him up, then to carry him across the paddy, then to lift him into the chopper that took him away" (p. 5). The initial report of the case suggests that the facts are not as important as the psychological significance of the incident, and that matter is revealed incrementally.

Each permutation of the event reveals something not presented earlier: the third time it occurs it contains revealing details about the character of the dead man: "But Ted Lavender, who was scared, carried 34 rounds when he was shot and killed outside Than Khe, and he went down under an exceptional burden, more than 20 pounds of ammunition, plus the flak jacket and helmet and rations and water and toilet paper and tranquilizers and all the rest, plus the unweighed fear" (p. 7). Lieutenant Cross blames himself for thinking of Martha instead of his duties. The matter-of-fact narration of the event, utterly without emotion, reflects the affective insulation of men in combat. The Lavender incident is the central flashback of the first story, the only one given a specific date, April 16, 1968 (p. 11), and the one that suggests, by its repetitions, an obsessive preoccupation.[8]

It leads to the second major issue, the internal transformations of Lieutenant Cross, for

> while Kiowa explained how Lavender died, Lieutenant Cross found himself trembling.
>
> He tried not to cry. . . . He felt shame. He hated himself. He had loved Martha more than his men, and as a consequence Lavender was now dead, and this was something he would have to carry like a stone in his stomach for the rest of the war (p. 16).

The external manifestation of this feeling is the attack on Than Khe: "They burned everything. They shot chickens and dogs, they trashed the village well." But the catharsis is not complete. Cross later burns Martha's letters and his two photographs of her, but he cannot burn his guilt. In the conclusion of the story, the narrative perspective, which has been shifting among the minds of the characters throughout, becomes identified solely with his thinking: "He was now determined to perform his duties firmly and without negligence. It wouldn't help Lavender, he knew that, but from this point on he would comport himself as an officer" (p. 24). Thus Cross emerges as the central character, the one with the internal conflict, the one who is psychologically transformed, and it is in his mind that the central events, and the things they carried, have their most significant expression.

Cross is also the subject of the second story, "Love" (pp. 29–31), one not previously published, perhaps because it would have little meaning without resonance from the preceding narrative. It represents a shift in setting and narration, for it is told by an unnamed writer in the United States who would seem to be the fictional Tim O'Brien. The central issue in this case is Cross's abiding love for Martha, which has persisted more than a decade, for this story takes place some time after 1979, when Jimmy encountered Martha again at a class reunion. He reports to the narrator that he saw Martha, that she had become a Lutheran missionary, and that she still did not love him, did not respond to his affection. But emotions die hard, and he still clings to his love for her, hoping that she will some day feel something for him. The other emotion that persists is his guilt for the death of Ted Lavender: "At one point, I remember, we paused over a snapshot of Ted Lavender, and after a while Jimmy rubbed his eyes and said he'd never forgiven himself for Lavender's death. It was something that would never go away, he said quietly . . ." (p. 29). That would seem to be the matter at hand at the conclusion, when Cross asks the narrator not to write about something from the war, something the narrator understands but does not specify but that would seem to be the Lavender incident. More than a decade after the action, the guilt is still with Cross, linking this story emotionally and thematically to the previous one.

As it appears in *The Things They Carried*, "Spin" (pp. 35–40) is a very brief story that introduces the complex interactions of experiences, memories, storytelling, and reality, how the men put "spin" on the war, give it a grim humor in the midst of horror. As first published in the *Quarterly*, however, it contained other elements, particularly the incident of the girl dancing amid the ruins of her hamlet that now comprises "Style" (pp. 153–54) and the haunting episode later published as "The Man I Killed" (pp. 139–44), Tim O'Brien's obsessive rumination on the Vietnamese soldier he killed on patrol.[9] In the collected volume the story is shorter, more focused, more clearly directed at a cluster of central themes.

"Spin" is a self-reflexive meditation on memory, storytelling, and the nature of reality, on O'Brien's observation that "on occasions the war was like a Ping-Pong ball. You could put fancy spin on it, you could make it dance" (p. 35). Here the emphasis is on comic relief, on how "the war wasn't all terror and violence" (p. 35). Mitchell Sanders mails body lice back to his draft board in Ohio (p. 35), and Kiowa teaches Rat Kiley and Dave Jensen a rain dance (p. 39), but even the "humorous" incidents contain serious issues (such as Norman Bowker's preoccupation with winning a medal in Vietnam to please his father) and horrible events (as when Azar blows apart Lavender's puppy with a Claymore mine). The implication is that even comedy was grim, that these tough memories have a "present" reality, "the remembering is turned into a kind of rehappening" (p. 36). The most difficult of those memories, the death of Kiowa in the shit field and Curt Lemon's death when he was blown into a tree, are presented only in fragments. O'Brien's killing of the enemy soldier is, in the revision, only suggested:

A red clay trail outside the village of My Khe.

A hand grenade.

A slim, dead, dainty young man of about twenty. (p. 40)

The suggestion is that the narrator is not yet capable of dealing with these incidents, has not come to terms with these events sufficiently to integrate them into a coherent narrative, thus the need for spin. Perhaps for this reason, O'Brien added a passage in the volume that was not in the magazine version: "Stories are for joining the past to the future. Stories are for those late hours in the night when you can't remember how you got from where you were to where you are. Stories are for eternity, when memory is erased, when there is nothing to remember except the story" (p. 40). The one other element that is important is the self-revelation of the fictional "Tim O'Brien," who is here a writer of forty-three with a daughter named Kathleen who tells him to forget war stories. The actual O'Brien, of course, has no daughter. The relation of the narrator and character "O'Brien" to the author is as problematic as the relationship of memory to the telling of a story, a theme that is developed as the volume progresses.

"On the Rainy River" (pp. 43–63) further establishes the fictional Tim O'Brien as an entity parallel to but distinct from the author. Many of the biographical details are similar: graduation from Macalester College in 1968; service as president of the student body; Phi Beta Kappa and summa cum laude; a scholarship for graduate study at Harvard. But there are also elements that are clearly fictional: service in Vietnam with the characters of the book; the writer's daughter; and the slim young man the putative Tim O'Brien killed on the trail outside My Khe. The readers who confronted "On the Rainy River" in *Playboy* in 1990 had no way of knowing they were not reading straight autobiography; it is only in the context of *The Things They Carried* that the fictional nature of the story emerges.[10]

In the collected volume the story plays the important role of defining the "O'Brien" character psychologically, philosophically, and personally, since many details of his family and hometown are revealed. It is told by the fictional O'Brien from a distance of two decades: a retrospective narrative, the action takes place in the summer of 1968, when he has received his draft notice but has not yet reported for duty; it is told from the perspective of 1988, long after he has returned from Vietnam, long after the immediate horror of war has ended. The narrator says that "looking back after twenty years, I sometimes wonder if the events of that summer didn't happen in some other dimension, a place where your life exists before you've lived it, and where it goes afterward" (p. 57). In a sense the deepest moral crisis of the book takes place in this story: the central issue is whether he will report for military duty or escape the draft by going to Canada. Everything that follows in the volume is a result of that decision.

O'Brien's moral struggle is intense and given somewhat different form here than in *If I Die in a Combat Zone*, a truly autobiographical account. During the period of his struggle, the summer after graduation from college, O'Brien works as a declotter, spraying water on the slaughtered pigs in an Armour plant. It is a perfect metaphor for his vision of the war to come, from the "trigger" on the water gun, to the blood itself, to the smell of blood and death that never leaves him. But it is his trip north to the Canadian border that precipitates the most intense conflict, as he rents a cabin at a lodge next to the Rainy River separating the two countries. The northern shore offers escape from military service, peace, and moral solace, but the price of flight is high: "I did not want people to think badly of me" (p. 54). When the owner of the lodge, Elroy Berdahl, takes him fishing on the river, he deliberately motors to the Canadian shore, understanding the dilemma. Pretending not to comprehend the conflict O'Brien is facing, Berdahl devotes himself to the business of fishing, while O'Brien bursts into tears, paralyzed by indecision, until he finally accepts his fate: "I would not swim away from my hometown and my country and my life. I would not be brave" (p. 60). That decision in 1968 resolves a key moral conflict, one with profound consequences, one that haunts him throughout his experience in Vietnam and after, even to the time of the telling in 1988.

If the temporal focus of the first four stories shifts from Vietnam in 1968 to some time after 1979 to 1988, and the issues change from a portrait of battle to the moral weight of it, the next group emphasizes individual scenes from the war, sometimes in the omnipresent context of how to tell them "truly." The linked stories "Enemies" (pp. 67–68) and "Friends" (pp. 71–72) deal with the relationship between Lee Strunk and Dave Jensen. In the first story they fight over a stolen knife, with Jensen breaking Strunk's nose. Jensen broods over the possibilities of Strunk's revenge, driving himself to distraction, and finally "he borrowed a pistol, gripped it by the barrel, and used it like a hammer to break his own nose" (p. 68). Apparently this grim business forms a bond between them, for in "Friends" they have become close buddies, even with their deepest fears: "In late August they made a pact that if one of them should ever get totally fucked up—a wheelchair wound—the other guy would automatically find a way to end it" (p. 71). When Strunk's leg is blown off, he is terrified that Jensen will fulfill his promise, a matter darkly ironic: "Later we heard that Strunk died somewhere over Chu Lai, which seemed to relieve Dave Jensen of an enormous weight" (p. 72). Both of these incidents reveal much of the psychological contexts of a war in which Americans are a threat to other Americans. Indeed, throughout the volume, there is very little direct conflict involving the other side. The concept of "enemy" is internalized both nationally and personally; the war is inside, against oneself.

The central issue in "How to Tell a True War Story" (pp. 75–91) is the relationship between actual events and the fictional "truth," between "fact" and what makes a story "real." Although the narrator is not named, it would seem to be the fictional Tim O'Brien speaking once again, and his comments are self-reflexive, metafictional, telling three crucial stories: the death of Curt Lemon; the music at the listening post; and Rat Kiley's killing of the baby water buffalo. In each case the focus is not only on event but on the "truth" of the story, with O'Brien revealing at the end that all of the events are "true" but none of them actually happened. They are true psychologically and morally; they capture the character of the experience; they represent a well-told story that is believable; but none of them represents factual events. O'Brien comments that "in a true war story nothing is ever absolutely true" (p. 88). In *If I Die in a Combat Zone*, O'Brien had reflected on similar ideas: "Can the foot soldier teach anything important about war, merely for having been there? I think not. He can tell war stories."[11]

These three stories are also true within the fictional world of these characters, invented personalities who have no existence outside the literary realm, not even the fictional O'Brien. Thus the opening assertion "this is true" has its verification only within the realm of the fiction in which it is made. The musings of the narrator are instructive, however: "A true war story is never moral. It does not instruct, nor encourage virtue, nor suggest models of proper behavior, nor restrain men from doing the things men have always done. If a story seems moral, do not believe it" (p. 76). Continuing in this negative formulation about what true stories are not, O'Brien later says "true war stories do not generalize. They do not indulge in abstraction or analysis." Finally arriving at an affirmative formulation, he observes that "a true war story, if truly told, makes the stomach believe" (p. 84).

The Curt Lemon episode begins with Rat Kiley writing home to the sister of a friend who had been killed. Kiley, deeply moved, "almost bawls writing it" (p. 75). The story is told in the manner of the death of Ted Lavender: not in chronological order, not in a complete unit, but incrementally, in fragments, beginning with its emotional effect on Kiley. It is not the case, as Kaplan maintains, that "the reader is given six different versions of the death of Kurt Lemon, and each version is so discomforting that it is difficult to come up with a more accurate statement to describe his senseless death than 'there it is.' "[12] Rather, only one story is told, in the midst of other stories, with no fundamental incongruities in the narrative: Rat Kiley writes the letter (pp. 75–76); Lemon and Kiley play in the jungle with smoke grenades (p. 77); Lemon steps on a booby trap and is blown into the branches (p. 85); Kiley's grief and guilt lead him to execute the baby water buffalo (pp. 85–86); Dave Jensen sings "Lemon Tree" while he and O'Brien gather the pieces of Lemon's body from the foliage (p. 89); O'Brien reflects that this is not a war narrative but a love story, implicitly an account of Kiley's love for Lemon (p. 90). It is a powerful and effective device, closely related to the Snowden episode in *Catch-22*.

The listening-post story is more complicated, since the fictional O'Brien heard it from Mitchell Sanders, who did not experience it himself but heard it from other people. Nevertheless, Sanders maintains that "every word is absolutely dead-on true" (p. 81). The story concerns a patrol sent into the mountains to scout for enemy activity. They ascertain little at first, but eventually they start to hear music, the voices of a "big swank gook cocktail party" and a spectrum of other incongruous sounds, including the Haiphong Boys Choir (p. 81). Frightened at the uncertainty of it all, they call in a massive air strike on the area, but later they refuse to explain the incident, even to a superior officer: "Then they salute the fucker and walk away, because certain stories you don't ever tell" (p. 83). The implausibility of the tale gives it a sense of reality, but then Sanders undercut his own veracity by confessing to O'Brien that he invented parts of it but that it is still true (pp. 83–84). O'Brien concurs. Now, in 1988, when he tells it to a woman, he has to explain to her that all of it is true but none of it happened, a passage O'Brien expanded from the magazine version[13] to include the assertion that there was "no trail junction. No baby buffalo. No vines or moss or white blossoms. Beginning to end, you tell her, it's all made up. Every goddamn detail—the mountains and the river and especially that poor dumb baby buffalo. None of it happened. *None* of it" (p. 91). The central issue here, however, is that in the logic of the true war story, it does not matter. The episodes are fictionally true.

These concerns are primary two stories later, in "Sweetheart of the Song Tra Bong" (pp. 101–25), with only a slight story, "The Dentist" (pp. 95–97), intruding. That incident moves backward in time to when Curt Lemon was still alive, trick or treating nude in the village and fainting when he went to the dentist. Later, to conquer his fear, he has a good tooth pulled. But "Sweetheart" is a major story, important for the complex matter of how to tell a story, the relationship of the teller to the tale, the reliability of the telling, and the elusive "truth" of the narrative.[14] It is also important for its focus on gender issues and their relationship to the psychological and moral degradation of warfare. These are weighty matters individually, but they are skillfully interwoven into the narrative in the manner of *Heart of Darkness*.

"Sweetheart" is a study in narrational unreliability, for the story is related by the fictional Tim O'Brien based on information told to him by Rat Kiley, who experienced some of it but heard the rest from others, such as the reports about Mary Anne on patrol with the Green Berets, a matter Eddie Diamond heard from one of the "Greenies" and told to Rat (p. 124). Parts of the telling are dramatized, Rat reciting the tale to his buddies in Alpha Company. They intrude with comments and suggestions. Further, there is not a single telling: Rat has obviously told the story many times, and O'Brien synthesizes the many versions, so that there is a multiplicity of times of the telling set against the retrospective action, which takes place before Rat joined Alpha Company.

No personal verification is possible among the men, and they are skeptical about the authenticity of the events presented. Indeed, O'Brien stresses at the beginning that "Rat had a reputation for exaggeration and overstatement," and he cautions that "he wanted to heat up the truth, to make it burn so hot that you would feel exactly what he felt" (p. 101).

But O'Brien has already established that the "truth" of a story is not as dependent on actual events as on the "feel" of it. The central plot concerns a young American woman named Mary Anne Bell, who is flown into Vietnam by her boyfriend, Mark Fossie. Mary Anne is curious about things, seemingly unafraid: she walks into a Viet Cong village and swims in the Song Tra Bong, also under fire, which inspires Eddie Diamond to observe that she has "D-cup guts, training bra brains" (p. 108). She seems particularly fascinated with the Green Beret unit camped on the periphery, and she goes on patrol with them one night, a night devoted to ambush. When she returns, her conversion is obvious: "She wore a bush hat and filthy green fatigues; she carried the standard M-16 automatic assault rifle; her face was black with charcoal" (p. 113). Not long after that she moves into the Green Beret tent, where there is a stack of bones against a post with the sign "ASSEMBLE YOUR OWN GOOK! FREE SAMPLE KIT!" (p. 119). Mark Fossie then discovers that she has a necklace of human tongues, and he says to Rat:

> "I can't just let her go like that."
> Rat listened for a time, then shook his head.
> "Man, you must be deaf. She's already gone" (p. 121).

The conclusion of her line of action comes quickly, when she disappears into the jungle for good.

The transformation of Mary Anne Bell is obviously a metaphor for innocence corrupted by the moral and psychological degradation of war, which is made more shocking by these changes occurring in a beautiful young woman. The suggestion is that the evil of war is so pervasive that gender is not an inoculation against corruption, as O'Brien indicated in an interview: "I think Rat is essentially trying to say that the young woman in the story, Mary Anne Bell, was in many important respects identical to the young men who went to Vietnam. She went to Vietnam as a naive romantic, full of traditional bourgeois values, and she learned quickly, as the young men did."[15] To the criticism that this episode reflects a misogynist attitude, O'Brien has responded that the story

> seems to me an utterly feminist story. It seems to me to be saying, in part, if women were to serve in combat they would be experiencing precisely what I am, the same conflicts, the same paradoxes, the same terrors, the same guilts, the same seductions of the soul. They would be going to the same dark side of the human hemisphere, the dark side of the moon, the dark side of their own psyches. It seems to me that the story is a fable—that it's meant to make explicit that which I thought was implicit in my work all along.[16]

Nowhere in *The Things They Carried* are the implications of what war can do to the psyche more dramatically presented than in Rat Kiley's tale about the corruption of Mary Anne Bell.

This substantial story is followed by a series of very short ones, each contributing an element to the total picture of the war in Vietnam. "Stockings" (pp. 129–30) relates to "The Things They Carried," showing Henry Dobbins as carrying his girlfriend's pantyhose around his neck, even after she breaks with him. Narrated by the fictional Tim O'Brien, this episode clarifies the retrospective distance between telling and action, for the action would have to be in 1968, the year O'Brien was in country, and the telling two decades later, in 1988: "Even now, twenty years later, I can see him wrapping his girlfriend's pantyhose around his neck before heading out on ambush" (p. 129). The implication is that O'Brien has had a great deal of time to sort out the people and events of the war, to come to terms with his feelings about it, and he still remembers the incident in which Dobbins attempted to hang on to the romantic softness of life by clinging to a pair of pantyhose, believing they would magically protect him in combat.

"Church" (pp. 133–36) is also slight in some respects, but it plays a structural role in its foreboding of tragedy, a feeling most deeply sensed by Kiowa, and it is he who is killed later in "Speaking of Courage." The situation is that the company moves into a pagoda presided over by two monks. There is an uneasy merging of the emblems of war (guns and ammunition) with the artifacts of peace (the pagoda and religious items associated with it). Kiowa is worried, suggesting that the company has violated a sacred place and will have to pay for it: "Kiowa made a noise in his throat. 'This is all wrong,' he said" (p. 136). The irony is that Kiowa is correct in his sense of danger, and it is he who pays the most egregious price. This story is a linking work, making little sense on its own but deriving its significance from "Speaking of Courage," four stories later in the volume, in which Kiowa's ill omen is fulfilled. Perhaps for this reason, "Church" was never published as a separate work.

"The Man I Killed" (pp. 139–44) is a brief but crucial story, one that shifts the central concerns of war in a new direction. The situation is that the fictional Tim O'Brien has killed a Vietnamese soldier on a jungle trail. In this first-person narrative, O'Brien is so traumatized by the sight of the dead body that he, who always stresses his need for expression, is unable to speak. Kiowa, who senses how deeply O'Brien feels, and who tries to protect him, says to him repeatedly, "stop *staring*" and "you okay?" and "come on, man, talk." The focus has shifted from the beginning of the volume, with its concern for O'Brien's personal safety and his responsibility to community, to a moral encounter with the consequences of having fulfilled his duty as a soldier.

It is significant that O'Brien contemplates the enemy soldier in the same terms he earlier reserved for himself and his comrades, describing the things he carried, including "a pouch of rice, a comb, a fingernail clipper, a few soiled piasters, a snapshot of a young woman standing in front of a parked motorcycle" (p. 143). O'Brien is obsessed with the physical description of the young man, which he gives several times, and with his projection of what kind of person he might have been: "He was not a Communist. He was a citizen and a soldier" (p. 140). Tim deals in projection, attributing to the dead man his own attitudes, that "the young man would not have wanted to be a soldier and in his heart would have feared performing badly in battle" (p. 141). He imagines the experience of the dead man as parallel to his own, as including university education, falling in love, and serving, reluctantly, in the army. The final suggestion is that not only does O'Brien see the enemy soldier as a man very much like himself, the story is fundamentally not about the dead man, about whom little is known, but about O'Brien, his moral sensitivity, his humanity, his numbing sense of responsibility that renders him mute. Only in the telling, much later, is he able to articulate the full horror of the experience.

That telling takes another form in "Ambush" (pp. 147–50), in which the fictional O'Brien (the biographical O'Brien does not have a daughter) responds to the suggestion that the nine-year-old Kathleen makes that "you keep writing these war stories . . . so I guess you must've killed somebody" (p. 147). Her insightful comment inspires O'Brien to project what he will tell her at some point in the future, when she is older, when he has sorted it out, when he can confess to her that she was correct about why he keeps writing war stories. The rest of the narration is a formulation of what he will tell her, a statement of the events with an emphasis on how it was not necessary for the young man to die: "There was no real peril. Almost certainly the young man would have passed by" (p. 149). It is clear that the prevailing sentiment is guilt: "Sometimes I forgive myself, other times I don't" (p. 149). Only in fantasy can O'Brien escape culpability, imagining that it has not happened yet, that there is still time to reconsider and let the young man live, let him walk past, fading into the fog as he continues down the trail. Had that happened, it would not be so difficult for O'Brien to live with himself.

In the original magazine publication, "Style" was the opening section of "Spin," providing a dramatic preamble for the reflective considerations that follow.[17] Told in first person, presumably by the fictive Tim O'Brien, the story recounts the effects of the gunship attack on the village of My Khe that Lieutenant Cross ordered in retaliation for the death of Ted Lavender. What is haunting in retrospect is the image of the young Vietnamese girl performing a dance of lamentation in front of her burned hut, where the rest of her family lies dead. The men do not understand her dancing, and Azar calls it a "weird ritual," one he mocks later that night until Henry Dobbins forces him to stop. In the context of the stories on either side of it, "The Man I Killed" and "Speaking of Courage," "Style" is yet another illustration of the human cost of war, the destruction and death and affective devastation that torture O'Brien years later when he tells the story.

"Speaking of Courage" (pp. 157–73) is one of the most complex stories in terms of publication history, congruence, and thematic function. It was originally published in the *Massachusetts Review* in 1976, and in this form it featured Paul Berlin as protagonist, reflecting on the events and characters in *Going After Cacciato*.[18] The thrust of the events, that the principal character is home from Vietnam and ponders what he would tell his father about a friend's death if the opportunity arose (which it does not), is the same, only in the magazine the character who dies is Frenchie Tucker, shot through the neck crawling into a tunnel. In *The Things They Carried* it is Norman Bowker who serves as protagonist, and his memories are about Kiowa, who was killed by enemy mor-

tar fire in a shit field (p. 168). There are other substantial changes between the two versions of the story, so many that they are essentially
separate works, the revision an obvious adaptation to suit the context of
the new book. The central impact of the revision was to put additional
emphasis on Bowker's obsessive memories of the war, his shame at not
having served with extraordinary bravery, his guilt for allowing the
wounded Kiowa to drown in the cesspool in which they have mistakenly
camped, an incident with biographical origins. As O'Brien has explained, "there are certain episodes in *The Things They Carried* where I
drew heavily on personal experience. Kiowa's death is one of them.
This scene has its basis in a piece entitled 'July' in *If I Die*. In this chapter, a bunch of tracks—big, tank-like vehicles—ran over us. A buddy of
mine, named McElhaney, was squashed to death in this mushy red
paddy under one of the tracks. We had to probe for him, trying to find
his body under all the algae and mud. . . . The Kiowa scene is a reimag-
ining of that horrible episode—squashed into the land, joined to the
land, folded in with the waste of the war."[19] O'Brien transformed his
memories into one of the most dramatic stories he ever wrote.

The story abounds with poignant irony. Told from a third-person
perspective, with access to the mind of Norman Bowker, the "present"
action takes place after the war on July 4, 1978. Norman spends the day
driving around the small lake in his hometown thinking about his life
before the war, dwelling on what he has lost: the love of Sally Kramer,
his innocence, his future. He observes two young boys "hiking with
knapsacks and toy rifles and canteens," a projection of his own youthful
idealism that describes the things the boys carried in juxtaposition to
the opening story (p. 159). In the magazine, there is more foreboding
in his view of them: "He watched the boys recede in his rearview mirror. They turned purply colored, like clotted blood, before finally disappearing" (p. 245), the implication being that these are boys destined
for violent death. In the book the description is more benign: "They
turned a soft grayish color, like sand, before finally disappearing" (p.
159).

The core of the action is the episode in which Kiowa is killed, here
rendered not as simple memory but as the narrator's projection of what
Norman Bowker would have told his father had the opportunity arisen,
so that the formulation throughout is on what Norman "would have"
said about the night his platoon camped in a shit field on the Song Tra
Bong. His reflections are interrupted by present action, by descriptions

of sights on his trip around the lake, but the emphasis is persistently on the horror of the attack and the preoccupying guilt he brought back with him. What emerges from the telling is the revelation that psychologically, Norman is still in Vietnam, still combat ready, still in the horror that haunts him, which becomes clear when he orders a hamburger at the local A&W. What blares out from the crude intercom is part actual sound and part imaginative projection: "Affirmative, copy clear. No rootie-tootie?" When he completes his order, what he hears as confirmation is "Roger-dodger. Repeat: one Mama, one fries, one small beer. Fire for effect. Stand by" (p. 170). Norman needs to tell his story, to expiate his demons, but he has never had the chance. On his final pass about the lake, the celebrative fireworks light up the sky, paralleling the sight when the mortars shelled the platoon in the shit field, a setting that suggests the ultimate degradation of death in Vietnam. The same kinds of issues that obsess the fictional O'Brien here haunt Norman Bowker: responsibility, omissions, guilt, and pain.

As it appeared in the *Massachusetts Review*, the story had to be read in isolation, without the related reflections in "Notes" (pp. 177–82), which appeared only in the collected book. This piece has been read as straight autobiographical essay, the truth behind the fictional story it addresses, but that is not the case. Although it contains elements of "reality" (O'Brien was a graduate student at Harvard and he did write both *If I Die in a Combat Zone* and *Going After Cacciato*), there are also important "invented" dimensions to "Notes," so much so that it must be read as another fictional construct, a crypto-story that has a complex relationship to another work. For one thing, "O'Brien" here speaks about Norman Bowker, a fictional construct, recounting his pointlessness after the war, which leads to his suicide in 1978. But there was no Bowker who committed suicide in Worthington, Minnesota, nor was there a Kiowa in O'Brien's platoon who died in a shit field: the only Native American in O'Brien's unit is still very much alive. As a result, "Notes" is an intersection between the universe of fiction and the details of mundane reality, a twilight zone in which beings from another world comment on earthly matters.

Within the world of *The Things They Carried*, however, "Notes" performs several functions. It deepens the impact of "Speaking of Courage" by conveying the information that Norman Bowker killed himself. It does so after establishing a pattern of humanizing comments and letters he wrote to O'Brien. In one he reflects that "that night when

Kiowa got wasted, I sort of sank down into the sewage with him. . . . Feels like I'm still in deep shit" (p. 178). The key figure, however, is not Bowker but O'Brien, for it is he who receives the information, internalizes it, and tells the story, and it is he who reflects that "by telling stories, you objectify your own experience. You separate it from yourself" (p. 179), an outcome devoutly to be wished for his emotional health. That point is made all the more clear in the conclusion, when O'Brien confesses that "Norman Bowker was in no way responsible for what happened to Kiowa. . . . He did not freeze up or lose the Silver Star for valor. That part of the story is my own" (p. 182). Since that guilt is not, in fact, the autobiographical O'Brien's own, it must be read as an increment in the developing themes of the volume, part of the burden, added to the unnecessary death of the young man on the trail, that this character still carries years after the war has ended.

"In the Field" (pp. 183–99) presents the third version of the events in the shit field, a wonderful metaphor for the war in Vietnam, one here related in a series of narrational modulations that present fragments of the episode as seen by various participants.[20] The central action is that the men in the platoon search the shit field for Kiowa's body the morning after the mortar attack. They find it, and Jimmy Cross lays back, floating in the muck. This simple plot suggests that the main emphasis is elsewhere, not on the action but on the perspective of the events from several of the men, their point of view being self-revelatory of their developing values. In each case the narrative stance is third-person limited, with formulations drawn from access to the mind of a single character; as the narrative unfolds, the character chosen for such access changes.

The first center of intelligence is Lt. Jimmy Cross, in effect the protagonist of the story. He has ordered the men to search the field for Kiowa's body, and as they do so he composes in his head the letter he will send home to the parents. The key issue for Cross is that he feels responsible for Kiowa's death because, following orders, he had the men camp in the shit field, where they were vulnerable to enemy fire. Now, during the search, he wrestles with his culpability and the extent to which he should acknowledge it openly: "Lieutenant Jimmy Cross felt something tighten inside him. In the letter to Kiowa's father he would apologize point-blank. Just admit to the blunders" (p. 191). The issues are different for the "young soldier," an epithet for the youthful Henry Fleming in Stephen Crane's *The Red Badge of Courage*. Here the unnamed soldier is later identified as the fictional Tim O'Brien, and the reason for his subsequent guilt is made clear: in the field with Kiowa that night, he turned on a flashlight to show his buddy a photograph of his girlfriend, and the light brought in the enemy fire (p. 192). Kiowa died because of the light, and O'Brien is responsible. That is why he cries, and that is one component of the guilt he must learn to accept in subsequent episodes. The section narrated with access to the mind of Norman Bowker helps explain his psychic anguish in "Speaking of Courage": it is Bowker who finds Kiowa, feels his body in the muck, sees that his shoulder is missing when they get the body to the surface, and it is he who observes that everyone is at fault. The death of Kiowa is thus made a crucial episode through the revelations of what it comes to mean for Cross, O'Brien, and Bowker, and it becomes central to their motivation in the rest of the book.

After a brief metafictional digression in "Good Form" (pp. 203–4) to explore ideas of reality versus fiction, and a reflection on the art of storytelling, the final narrative about the death of Kiowa comes in "Field Trip" (pp. 207–13), in which an older Tim O'Brien takes his young daughter, Kathleen, to Vietnam to visit the scenes of his war experience. The principal conflicts would seem to be dual: the domestic squabble between O'Brien and his impatient daughter, oblivious to the significance of what her father is doing; and the pressing need on the part of O'Brien to bring closure to the experience, to finally have done with the terror in the shit field. Toward that end, he goes back to the scene of Kiowa's death by the Song Tra Bong and buries his friend's moccasins in the mud where he died, an act that brings a cathartic transformation: "I felt something go shut in my heart while something else swung open" (p. 212). Interestingly, in original publication he buried not the moccasins but a tomahawk, leading to the snide observation that he had buried the hatchet. O'Brien has commented that once he realized that the event could be given that formulation, he made the revision.[21] In whatever form, this gesture seems intended to reclaim some of O'Brien's self-respect, "my belief in myself as a man of some small dignity and courage," and to restore normal affect, which had diminished after the Kiowa incident: "There were times in my life when I couldn't feel much, not sadness or pity or passion, and somehow I blamed this place for what I had become, and I blamed it for taking away the person I had once been" (p. 210). O'Brien's return to Vietnam is, in effect, an internal quest to find the wholeness he had enjoyed before the war when it was still bearable to live a fully human life.

"The Ghost Soldiers" (pp. 217–43) is a problematic narrative with a dual plot employing contrasting themes. On the level of physical action, it recounts how the fictional O'Brien was twice wounded in Vietnam: once in the side, when he was ably treated by Rat Kiley; later in the buttocks, at a time when Kiley had been replaced by Bobby Jorgenson, who delayed treatment on O'Brien's wounds, resulting in a severe infection. This sequence of events then becomes a revenge plot, as O'Brien, aided by Azar, schemes to even the score by frightening Jorgenson as he stands guard in the night. The events are darkly comic in tone, even when the joke turns out to be on O'Brien, since Jorgenson is never fooled into thinking that enemy ghosts are attacking him. The second level of concern, however, is more grimly serious. In the process of being wounded and planning revenge, O'Brien discovers a side of himself that is deeply disturbing: "I'd turned mean inside. Even a little cruel at times. . . . I now felt a deep coldness inside me, something dark and beyond reason. It's a hard thing to admit, even to myself, but I was capable of evil" (p. 227). O'Brien desires to hurt Jorgenson psychologically the way he, himself, has been hurt; the revenge is not only for the shot in the rear that nearly became gangrenous but also for the mental damage, the appalling transformation of identity that O'Brien resents. Things progress to the point that he feels invisible in his coldness, a ghost in the night like the Viet Cong enemy he fears. Because of Jorgenson, O'Brien has learned to hate himself.

When this story was originally published in *Esquire* in 1981, only the second of the stories to appear, it was quite different.[22] For one thing, it was not about the fictional Tim O'Brien. The central character, who also serves as narrator, was named Herbie, and he is in Delta Company, not Alpha. Intellectually, he is dramatically distinct from the O'Brien of the book version: Herbie says, "I never went to college, and I wasn't exactly a whiz in high school either. . . ."[23] O'Brien's reflections are that "I'd come to this war a quiet, thoughtful sort of person, a college grad, Phi Beta Kappa and summa cum laude, all the credentials . . ." (p. 227). As part of this alteration, O'Brien is much more self-reflective than Herbie, much more judgmental about the psychic consequences of his attempt at retaliation. On a more mundane level, Herbie's frame of reference is Boston, where he goes to ball games at Fenway Park; O'Brien is from Minnesota, and he follows the Twins at Met Stadium.

In the course of making this story part of a cycle, O'Brien as author had to integrate it into the sequence of stories, making it one step in the protagonist's psychological journey through the war. The time is changed from July in the magazine to December in the book, coordinate with the time scheme of the surrounding stories. Other characters are different as well: the wounded protagonist is first treated by Teddy Thatcher in the magazine and by Rat Kiley in the book. Thatcher is killed in *Esquire*; Kiley is wounded in *Carried*; but Bobby Jorgenson is the replacement in both versions. The guys in the outfit differ as well: Curt Lemon is still alive in *Esquire*, probably because O'Brien had not yet written "How to Tell a True War Story," and he and Herbie are good friends. When Herbie remembers the guys in his company who were killed, he thinks of Teddy, Olson, Ingo, and Becker, none of whom are in the book. O'Brien mentions "all the pale young corpses, Lee Strunk and Kiowa and Curt Lemon . . ." (p. 235). But the central themes are nearly the same, as is the psychological degeneration of the central character. Herbie ends up weeping beyond control; O'Brien's problem is equally emotional: "I was trembling. I kept hugging myself, rocking, but I couldn't make it go away" (p. 241). The most profound alterations of his psychology were added after magazine publication, particularly the loss of self-identity in his obsession for revenge: "And then presently I came unattached from the natural world. . . . Eyes closed, I seemed to rise up out of my own body and float through the dark down to Jorgenson's position. I was invisible; I had no shape, no substance; I weighed less than nothing" (p. 234). In this matter, as in the other important episodes in the volume, it is not O'Brien's wounding that torments him, not his own brush with mortality, but his ethical complicity in bringing harm to others. Just as he dwells on the deaths of Lavender and Lemon and tortures himself with his role in the death of Kiowa, he becomes more concerned with what he has made of himself in seeking revenge than he does with the actual fate of Jorgenson. In *The Things They Carried*, war is internal, personal, and moral, and its battlefield is the terrain of the self.

The following story, "Night Life" (pp. 247–51), takes advantage of the temporal elasticity of the cycle form by going back to action that fits into "The Ghost Soldiers" at a time when O'Brien was recovering from his first wound but before Bobby Jorgenson replaced Rat Kiley. In effect, it explains that the horror of war, and the rumors of an impending enemy attack, broke through Rat's scientific detachment: "He took off his boots and socks, laid out his medical kit, doped himself up, and put a round through his foot" (p. 251). The lack of detail in the narrative is explained by its being reported secondhand, told by O'Brien as he heard it from Mitchell Sanders. O'Brien would have a special interest in it, since Kiley's nervous breakdown now parallels his own, precedes his own, deflecting part of whatever ignominy might be attached to it. O'Brien's embarrassing wound is further paralleled by Rat's self-inflicted injury, his incessant talking and scratching predicting O'Brien's own aberrant behavior before his revenge.

The concluding story, "The Lives of the Dead" (pp. 255–73), takes on the familiar function of recapitulation, summation, and closure, matters more complex in the cycle than in the more tightly unified form of the novel. It does so brilliantly, linking O'Brien's youth with his experience in Vietnam, reviewing the key deaths that haunt him even at the time of the narration in 1990, focusing on the central theme of storytelling as a means to come to terms with experience, to find a way to live, to keep the past alive. The memory of Linda, the girl O'Brien loved, who died of a brain tumor in 1956, is placed in counterpoint with the deaths of Lavender, Kiowa, Curt Lemon, and the young Vietnamese O'Brien killed on the trail, all events too painful to bear, all people who can be kept alive in a story. The resonance of the title, "The Lives of the Dead," is the ironic quest for synthesis within the dichotomy of life and death, with more emphasis on destruction than on vitality, including the grim humor of his shaking hands with the dead man in the village on the Song Tra Bong. O'Brien then reveals, in progressively distressing increments, his memories of Linda beginning with the benign embarrassments of a first date (pp. 258–59). When this story was first published in *Esquire* in 1989, his emotional obsession with her was even deeper than in the book: "I wanted to sleep with her. I wanted to live inside her body so that her body would become mine and there would be no skin between us and we would always be one thing."[24]

The next segment revisits the death of Lavender, adding the details of how O'Brien got the corpse ready to be transported by helicopter, the emotion well transmitted in the correlatives of the items in his pockets and the description of his body, with its missing cheekbone and swollen eye, details that haunt O'Brien two decades later (p. 260). The civilian application of such horror comes in school in 1956, when Nick Veenhof stole Linda's red cap, disclosing the scars of her recent brain surgery. Again, the impact is in the details, the "glossy whiteness of her scalp," the veins on her head, the bandage covering the incision, and, later, the visit to the mortuary to view her body. What unites the two deaths is not only the pain of remembering but the effort to keep people alive in a story, something the men learned in Vietnam, when they would repeat the account of Lemon's trick or treating in the village with his M-16 (p. 268). As long as they could tell it, Lemon was still alive. So O'Brien keeps Linda alive. And so, the final impact suggests, so the adult O'Brien, the storyteller, attempts to keep alive his dead youth, the self he was before his loss of innocence in Vietnam. It is a fitting and dramatic conclusion to the coalescent themes of the book, and it serves to balance the brilliance of "The Things They Carried" that opens the volume, a point O'Brien himself has made: " 'The Lives of the Dead' is necessarily a long story providing a harmonious balance in subject matter, in theme, and in sound to the title story, a balance that is sustained, I think, through the book."[25] The volume opened with the men carrying their civilian lives into the war, and it ends with O'Brien carrying his military life throughout his life back home. It is a heavy weight to bear, and only the art of telling a story makes it possible to sustain the burden.

That theme is one of the ideas that unify the stories in *The Things They Carried*, giving them intertextual coherence, heightening the incremental power of each successive episode. Other motifs also connect the stories, investing them with layers of meaning unavailable when they were separate works in various magazines. No one story could fully convey the psychological weight of what the men of Alpha Company carried in Vietnam: the fear, horror, guilt, and responsibility that were thrust upon these young men resonate more dramatically from the aggregate work than from any one narrative within it. The death of Lavender is a shocking episode in the first story, but the horror of what happened to him is heightened each time the incident is retold, each time Lieutenant Cross struggles with his guilt, even years after the conclusion of the war. Lavender's death takes on new layers of thematic timbre when it is seen in relation to the ghastly episodes in which Curt Lemon is blown into a tree or when Kiowa dies in the shit field. The collective power of these events bears on the suicide of Norman Bowker, the obsessive need of Tim O'Brien to tell stories, the hopeless devotion Jimmy Cross maintains for Martha.

Even with several stories revised for congruence with the others in the volume, they remain, to some extent, twenty-two separate narratives told at varying times by a number of different voices, by Rat Kiley,

Mitchell Sanders, Tim O'Brien, and by a third-person narrator identified with a spectrum of characters. If the collective protagonist is Alpha Company, many of the men within it serve as protagonist of at least one story, including Jimmy Cross, Lee Struck, Dave Jensen, Curt Lemon, Mark Fossie, Henry Dobbins, Azar, Norman Bowker, Rat Kiley, and the dominant central figure, Tim O'Brien. The stories also vary in setting, with most of them placed in the forward areas in Vietnam where Alpha Company was stationed, but some of them take place well behind the lines, and others are set in Iowa, Minnesota, and other locations in the United States. There is also a temporal discontinuity typical of the cycle format, with action taking place out of order from 1956, when O'Brien has a date with Linda, to 1990, when he tells "The Lives of the Dead." Most of the action is in Vietnam from June to December of 1968, but Norman Bowker commits suicide in 1978, Jimmy Cross sees Martha again in 1979, O'Brien narrates "Rainy River" in 1988, his daughter tells him to forget war stories in 1989, O'Brien takes her to Vietnam in 1989 to visit the area where Kiowa was killed, and Tim, at forty-three, shares his thoughts about death in the concluding story in 1990. There is also progression of event, tracing a pattern with flashbacks that show the struggle to decide whether to go to Vietnam, the early deaths of Lavender and Lemon, the retaliation against the village, the death of Kiowa, and O'Brien's attempts to leave the war behind him and get on with a healthy civilian life. O'Brien's skill as a writer of fiction is nowhere more evident than in his ability to preserve these stories as individual aesthetic entities while developing their relational significance as a unified short-story cycle, a fictional aggregate that is aesthetically congruent, thematically powerful, and in many important ways greater than the sum of its component parts.

6

Temporal Inversion and Incremental Insight

Julia Alvarez's *How the García Girls Lost Their Accents*

When *How the García Girls Lost Their Accents* appeared in 1991, Julia Alvarez was heralded as one of the most promising new writers in America, and her volume received the PEN Oakland/ Josephine Miles Book Award and made the *Library Journal* list as one of the best books of the year. In 1992 it was selected as a Notable Book by the American Library Association. Of the fifteen stories in the volume, eight had been previously published as independent works, beginning with "Joe" in 1982. "Snow" had won the PEN Syndicated Fiction Prize in 1987. An essay, "El Doctor," based on Alvarez's experience in emigrating from the Dominican Republic to the United States with her parents and three sisters, provided autobiographical details that directly parallel the fictional situation for the García family, including a physician father who is emotionally guarded, a mother who garbles American clichés, and a family (proudly descended from the conquistadors) that moves to New York in 1960 to escape persecution from the dictator Trujillo.[1] These experiences were quickly given fictional expression in a series of stories about the Garcia sisters before being revised and assembled into a highly organized short-story cycle in 1991.

The basic organization of the volume is the division of the fifteen stories into three groups of five, each story having its own conflict and resolution, each artistically and thematically complete unto itself but enriched in the context of the others. All of the stories concern the García family and attendant servants, and they all concur on the same essential line of action: that the family escaped the island in 1960 after Dr. García was implicated in a failed coup attempt, and the sudden departure for the United States brought about the customary conflicts for immigrants. The four sisters struggle with learning a new language and adjusting to a new set of customs and values, feeling isolated and excluded in a country so different from the Caribbean. What is unique is that Alvarez chose to arrange the book in reverse chronological order, moving backward from 1989 in the opening to 1956 in the conclusion. Telling the stories in this order creates a systematic temporal regression that provides an exploration of causation rather than a drama of consequences. What becomes of these people is known from the beginning; why their lives unfold the way they do becomes the central issue, echoing the methodology of classical tragedy.

Despite the previous publication of eight of the segments as independent stories, the reviewers of *How the García Girls Lost Their Accents* were virtually unanimous in regarding it as a novel, including Ed Morales in the *Village Voice Literary Supplement* and Jason Zappe in the *Americas Review*.[2] Luis Rebaza-Soraluz hedged his bets in the *Hispanic Review*, calling the book a "novel of short stories."[3] Ilan Stavans in *Commonweal* also called the book a novel but went on to remark insightfully that "the volume ought to be read as a collection of interrelated stories. Each segment reads as an independent unit, with the same set of characters recurring time and again in different epochs and places."[4] In the most important initial response to the book, Donna Rifkind concurred in the *New York Times Book Review*, calling the volume a collection of "interwoven stories."[5] None of the reviews placed the book in the context of a long tradition of story cycles, and none of them pointed out the extensive alterations made to the original form of the stories to coordinate them into one unified work. To some degree, *How the García Girls Lost Their Accents* has thus been unappreciated because it is only through an awareness of the normative devices of the cycle tradition that the artistic and thematic subtlety of Alvarez's work can be fully understood. The skill with which she has constructed the volume becomes evident in a detailed examination of the relationships among the fifteen stories that constitute the book.

The five episodes in Section I of *How the García Girls Lost Their Accents* are, in many ways, a disparate assemblage. As is often the case with the stories in a cycle, they were written at various times over a decade, and three of them were published separately in magazines, one of them with different names for the characters. There is no internal evidence, or even suggestion, that they were to be constituent parts of a longer work. On the other hand, as arranged in the volume, there are several levels of unity and resonance among them. All five of them concern the García family, especially the four sisters as a collective protagonist, with an emphasis on Yolanda, the dominant character in three of the five. The stories are arranged in terms of a temporal regression, beginning in 1989 with Yo's return home to the Dominican Republic and moving backward two decades to her undergraduate experience in college in 1969. The most adhesive unity is thematic, and all of the stories focus on the same matrix of familial issues: the immigration to New York; the resultant cultural duality felt by the sisters; an emotional pathology that is, to some extent, culturally based, deriving from paternal domination and a puritanical attitude about feminine sexuality; and Yolanda's obsessive need for romantic love. There are also continuing subordinate motifs: the mother's garbled clichés, the lapsed Catholicism of the sisters, a concern for language and literature, a legacy of family history. The five stories have a good deal of formalistic complexity, with shifting narrative perspectives and temporal layers correlating themes through the transitional events of the family, but there is also a stylistic continuity and a sustained tone that draws them together, coalescing them into an artistic unit.

The opening story of *How the García Girls Lost Their Accents* is "Antojos," a term referring to Yolanda's secret desire for re-culturation into the society of the Dominican Republic, which her family left twenty-nine years ago after a failed revolution against Trujillo.[6] Yolanda has lived in the United States since then, but, as the narrative ultimately reveals, she has never felt fully at home there. Now, on the occasion of her birthday, she has returned, five years after her last visit, hungry for the fruit and life of her homeland. In the book, but not in the earlier magazine version, all of this is told in present tense, with narrational synchronicity with the action, Yolanda's thoughts and actions depicted as they occur by a third-person narrator whose access to information is limited to her mind. Since this, the starting point, is the present, the subsequent stories in the volume are in past tense, constituting the etiology of Yolanda's malaise. Because of the temporal inversion of the entire volume, there is no internal explanation for Yolanda's motivation in "Antojos," her feelings inexplicable except in the stories to follow.

There were, of course, no others to follow when the story first appeared in the *Caribbean Writer* in June of 1990.[7] The magazine text was much shorter than that in the book, and it lacked the present opening concerning Yolanda's return home on her birthday. Told in the past tense, from an indeterminate anterior perspective, it did not contain the suggestion that Yolanda's secret wish is a permanent return home, and there was much less emphasis on the wealth and privilege of women in this society. Only the book edition contains the numerous references to the power of women in the Dominican Republic, to the "authority in their voices," to their control of their families, and this agency is one of the attractions Yolanda seeks in her repatriation (p. 11). The magazine version did not contain her reflections on the turbulence in the lives of the four García sisters, and there was much less detail in her trip north to the coast, during which she gets a flat tire while searching for guavas just outside the village of Altagracia. On the other hand, the original publication sets the action not on Yolanda's birthday but on a commemoration of another sort, on the anniversary of the failed revolution nineteen years before, which would establish the "present" not in 1989, as in the book, but roughly in 1979, since the aborted coup against Trujillo took place in 1960, a year before his assassination in 1961.

The revised time scheme Alvarez created for the collected volume allows "Antojos" to fit into the comprehensive temporal structure of the fifteen stories, which thus recede into the past with each successive episode, revealing not progressive "consequence" but rather antecedent relationships and causation. Despite her initial wealth and privilege as the daughter of a physician, life has not gone well for Yolanda, has not allowed her to sustain a fulfilling romantic relationship, has not left her whole. Her trip home constitutes a quest for the person she was earlier in her life, when she was the beautiful sister, the promising poet, the favorite daughter of her reticent father.

There is thus a good deal of irony when she is called "Miss America" by her cousins, a grimly humorous appellation given what has happened to her since she left her homeland and in the context of her hidden wish to leave the United States altogether. There is also an autobiographical resonance to this comment, since Alvarez has said that as a young woman, she and her sisters were obsessed with the Miss

America pageant for its lessons on beauty in their new country.[8] Compared to the stories to follow, there is much less a sense of internal conflict here, the key decision already having been made before the opening scene. Rather, the emphasis is on character and circumstance, not confrontation. Yolanda has changed since she left the island. She returns looking "shabby" compared to her glamorous cousin Lucinda, and she returns thinking and speaking English but longing to immerse herself in the rich culture of her youth. The metaphor for this desire, her "antojos," is her hunger for guavas, the motivation behind her trip to the country. When she finds them, she eats them ravenously, expressing the depth of her appetite for her native society. In the magazine account, the motivation for her return was more explicit: "She had never felt at home in the States, never, though she knew she was lucky to have a job, so she could afford her own life and not be run by her family. But independence didn't have to be exile. She could come home, home to places like these very hills, and live here on her own terms."[9] In the book, viewing the lives of her female cousins, who control their households, she thinks "let this turn out to be my home" (p. 11).

If the story underlines the authority of women in this culture, it also reveals a spectrum of gender differentiations denoting male preference. Although children of both genders are sent to the United States for prep school, only the young men are allowed to remain for a college education. Men of comfortable standing have mistresses to visit during the drive home from work during the "whore hour" (p. 7). When Yolanda has her flat tire in the country, she is subject to a palpable sexual threat from two men until they discover she is from an important family (p. 20). Although she has returned to familiar surroundings, eaten her guavas, and tasted her culture, her return home is not fully satisfying, for the story ends with the image of the blond woman in the Palmolive advertisement about to cry out for assistance. The terminal point of Yolanda's life in *How the García Girls Lost Their Accents* is thus not a conclusion but a beginning, not a resolution of conflict but a kinetic moment that can be understood only in terms of the subsequent stories.

Although "The Kiss" (pp. 24–39) explains certain elements of motivation for the first story (that Yolanda became a feminist in the wake of her divorce, that Dr. García was obsessed with the sexual purity of his daughters and unable to accept their adult sensuality), it is more important in establishing familial context than in offering linear causation for the psychic circumstances of "Antojos." Indeed, the tangential relationship between the two stories might be accounted for in part because "The Kiss" was initially published three years before the first story,[10] at which point the names of the characters, the age of the father, the nationality of the husband, the number of sisters, and the time of the action were all different from the book version. In the text that appeared in the *Greensboro Review* in 1987, the father is celebrating his seventy-fifth birthday, not his seventieth. There are only three daughters: Mariana, Alma, and the youngest, Felicia, not Sofia. She is married to a man named Otto, but he is Danish in the magazine, not German, which explains the historical error in the book when there is reference to his son as a "new Viking" (Germans were not Vikings, but Danes, along with Norwegians and Swedes, were). In the magazine text, the reference to the infant as "Edward, the Viking" made a sense lost in book publication. Dr. García's name is "Edward" in the first version (using the name of Alvarez's own father, Eduardo), occasioning a series of references to historical figures of that name: "Edward, the Confessor. Edward, the Second. Prince Edward" (p. 21). All of that changed in the book, where the father's name is fictionalized to "Carlos," leading to a different series of allusions to "Charles the Fifth; Charles Dickens; Prince Charles," and, ranging more widely, "Charlemagne" (p. 26). The father is a physician in both editions, but his practice has not yet moved to the wealthier part of New York in the magazine: "He had a very successful practice in a Spanish barrio in Brooklyn that was too dangerous, he said when the girls were growing up, to let them work there summers" (p. 21). Otto is a "world-class physicist" in the magazine but a "world-class chemist" in the book (p. 31), and he and his wife live in Chicago, not in Michigan. But the thematic thrust is the same in the two accounts, emphasizing that the father's prudery drove his youngest daughter away from him, and she is using his birthday as a way of luring him into her home, seeking a reconciliation.

In formal terms, "The Kiss" is a complex narrative, with an omniscient point of view identified predominantly with the mind of Sofia, the central figure, but also with Yolanda, Carlos, and a synthesis of the minds of the four sisters. Structurally, there are three issues of emphasis: the historical celebration of the father's birthdays in the past, on which occasions his daughters momentarily become his children again; the extended flashback to the events leading up to Sofia's break with her father, when she left home for good; and the attempted reconciliation that goes wrong. What is revealed in the glimpses of past birthday celebrations is that the father enjoys being a parent. He is a physician, but very little is made of that fact; rather, he is portrayed in his domestic role as patriarch of a Latino family, benevolent in all but his puritanical insistence on the virginity of his daughters: "I don't want loose women in my family" (p. 28). He is financially generous, handing out envelopes filled with bills, but emotionally penurious when his will is contravened. He exalts in the attention of his family, and he is a devoted father.

The flashback to Sofia's break with him, however, reveals a harsh, judgmental side to his nature, one that erupted when he discovered, rummaging through her personal correspondence, that she had a sexual relationship with Otto. This revelation occasioned not the wise counseling one might expect of a physician but a furious interrogation: "Has he deflowered you? That's what I want to know. Have you gone behind the palm trees?" (p. 30). Sofia's response ("It's none of your fucking business") indicates something of her strength, her capacity to defy even the strongest man in her life, and she leaves her parents' home forever. All of that sets the stage for her attempted reconciliation with her father in the "present" action, and she goes all out in elaborate preparations for the event. He is gratified and deeply moved until the kissing game, in which he is blindfolded and required to guess who has kissed him. Sofia eventually realizes that he never calls her name. Hurt, feeling poorly rewarded for her efforts, she administers an inappropriate kiss to her father, "a wet, open-mouthed kiss in his ear" (p. 39), knowing that he is uncomfortable with sexuality, and he terminates the party. Sofia has sustained her defiance, but she has forfeited the solace of emotional reunion with her father. Since this is the latest temporal moment for Sofia in the book, her relationship with Dr. García concludes as one of distance, tension, and punishment, for she is ultimately no less harsh in her emotional requirements than he, and there is little room for rapprochment between them.

"The Four Girls" (pp. 40–67) is a complex story that provides a partial etiology of familial pathologies in four internal narratives. Not previously published, these dramatized "tellings" offer suggestive childhood vignettes that reveal central character traits, deep longings, and conflicts within the domestic sphere. These matters are predictive of the personalities the young women display as adults. There is thus a temporal duality throughout in dramatized shifts between the adult situation, when the family has gathered in the United States one month before Carla's thirty-first birthday, and the past recounted in the mother's tales of the childhood of each daughter. There are also complex narrational modulations, as the omniscient perspective presents information about the background of the family, then identifies with the mind of the mother during the telling of her four episodes, then indicates reactive attitudes and thoughts on the part of the listeners, and finally pulls back to reveal a "present" circumstance in the lives of each of the four daughters. As is so often the case in a short-story cycle, the concept of "protagonist" is thus diffused to group status, with the mother and the four daughters occupying the center stage and the father and the daughters' husbands or lovers relegated to "flat" roles, important only in the ways in which they affect the women in the family.

The opening comments by the omniscient narrator reveal that, in their early childhood, the four girls were dressed alike, defined only by the color of their clothing. As an adult, Carla became a child psychologist and published a paper postulating that "the color system had weakened the four girls' identity differentiation abilities and made them forever unclear about personality boundaries" (p. 41), a dubious contention in that the personalities of the four sisters are quite distinct from one another, even in childhood. The mother was wounded by a vague sense of having been criticized in her daughter's article, and there is a maudlin scene of reassurance by the daughters that their mother had been a superb parent. This activity leads into the mother's first anecdote, an account of Carla and the red sneakers, which is related as having been told by the mother not simply in the present but also on the occasion of Carla's wedding celebration years before, thus linking three temporal settings. There is a cathartic function in the act of telling for the mother, who is still recovering from having been wounded by Carla's paper, and she revisits the poverty of the early years before the father's medical practice was well established. But the tale about her eldest daughter contains a theme of longing for not simply new sneakers but "red" ones, distinct in color from the shoes of any of her sisters.

As the eldest, Carla would naturally be resentful of the displacement each succeeding sibling represented, and the sneakers signify an early quest for "separateness" that remains a theme in her life even as an adult psychologist. The "family" inherent in this episode also resonates, the recounting of the "rise" from poverty to social respectability, the task of raising four girls, the father's soft heart for his daughter as he and young Carla use red nail polish to paint the white sneakers. The dramatized reactions of the family in the present are also revealing, the father saving his pride by editorializing about his financial status but remaining emotionally uninvolved in the tale, entertaining Yo by puffing out his cheeks, and Carla's second husband rubbing her neck sensuously, more concerned with the present than with the revelatory dimensions of a family episode he has heard before.

The story the mother tells about Yolanda (pp. 46–50) is similarly suggestive, with psychological and thematic interactions between present and past. At the moment of the telling, the mother is speaking to Clive, her daughter's lover, sitting in the audience before one of Yolanda's poetry readings. Yolanda, survivor of several failed marriages, is an instructor of comparative literature who is dating the head of the department. In this case, the mother's rendition of how Yolanda, as a child, was left on a bus and enthralled the passengers by reciting poetry presages Yo's interest in literature. That she was in New York to be treated for "nerves," causing her hair to fall out, adumbrates her adult emotional problems, suggested by her fastidiousness in personal matters: "An immediate bathrobe after her bath. Lights out when they made love" (p. 48). The suggestion of the past moment of poetic triumph resonates in the dramatic present, when Yolanda appears onstage to recite her poems, an event related with narrative objectivity: "At the podium, the poet had been introduced and was waiting for the white-haired woman in the first row to finish talking" (p. 50). There is submerged humor in the subject of the poem, dedicated "To Clive" and entitled "Bedroom Sestina," for Yolanda's parents both find it difficult to deal with the adult sexuality of their daughters, but here the mother beams at her daughter, oblivious to the implications of the poem that is about to be read.

The story that is told about Sandra (pp. 50–56) is especially complex because the mother finds it painful to think about it, so she does not recount the tale in the present. Rather, the narrator reaches into the past to the time the mother told Dr. Tandlemann about why they were committing Sandi to a mental hospital. The temporal intricacy is that there is thus the time of the present, the past time of the action in the hospital, and the antecedent past time of the events that are related. The act of "telling" in the hospital is dramatized in that the father's responses to the story his wife is relating reveal much of his emotional involvement with his daughter. What the mother explains is that at first Sandi seemed to be anorexic, seeking to emulate "those twiggy models." Dr. Tandlemann, quite erroneously, believes that Sandi is free of psychosis, suffering a simple breakdown. Apparently the inner turmoil in her life derives from the fact that she is of fairer complexion than her sisters, there being a Swedish ancestor in her maternal lineage. As the mother recounts shock at how Sandi refused to eat when she was a graduate student, the father's memories well up in him, and as he looks out the window at the gardener mowing the lawn, "the father's view of the lawn was blurring," his emotion overtaking him even in memory (p. 54). Just as the mother's tale relates Sandi's psychotic belief that she is becoming a monkey, the father sees his daughter walking with a nurse on the hospital grounds, and he jumps to his feet. Sandi, however, misinterprets the lawn mower for a "roaring animal on a leash" and runs off in panic. It is a disturbing but intense narrative, despite the temporal layers ingrained in its rendition. Inherent in the narrative are the explicit pathological expression of family relationships; the deeply felt involvement of both father and mother in the lives of their daughters, despite his feigned detachment; the suggestion that the parents do not understand each other; and the dramatized realization of how deeply disturbed Sandra has become.

The episode involving Sofia is also a formal composite of narrative elements, with an omniscient narrator telling about the mother in the hospital when Fifi's daughter was born and the mother talking to a young man, relating a burglary incident the night of Fifi's birth (pp. 56–59). The references to the hospital and to the mother making a "monkey face" link this episode to Sandi's tale, to family tragedy. This story, which hints at the cruelly judgmental attitude of the father when he discovered Fifi was having an affair with Otto, also presents positive reassurances of familial regeneration, of the recovery of things lost, of the continuity of life. Those ideas are present in the birth of the granddaughter and in the antecedent incident of the burglary the night Fifi was born, when all the stolen things were recovered.

The final section shifts the present time to a week after the birth of Fifi's child, seven days after the preceding episode. The family has gathered at Sofia's home to celebrate Christmas, and the four sisters talk in the early morning: "The four girls lounge in their nightgowns and tell each other the true story of how their lives are going" (p. 60). What they relate provides a gloss on the earlier narratives, sometimes contrasting facts and interpretations, sometimes extending the sequence of events. The narrator reveals that Sandi was released from Mt. Hope

Hospital a month earlier, but she cries easily and carries antidepressants in her purse. A study in emotional fragility, she is nonetheless dating again, seeing another mental patient she met in the hospital. Yolanda, who has had failed romances with John, Brad, Steven, and Rudy, has, in the last week, been rejected by Clive, which explains her motivation in returning to the Dominican Republic in "Antojos." Fifi corrects her mother's account of how she met Otto, saying they did not meet in Peru but in Colombia, a point that calls into question the reliability of all of the mother's narratives.

The more serious background issue is not Fifi's romance but her father's intrusion into her personal letters and his harsh judgment that she had gone behind the palms. He is in Fifi's home in the "present" time, but, the narrator reveals, he has not spoken for the two days he has been there (p. 65). He apparently does not reconcile with her until the birth of her next child, Carlos, in "The Kiss," although the intervening period is not covered. The story, so dominated by the mother's telling the four accounts of her daughters, ends just as she begins another episode, about the time they were living on a farm: "The room is hushed with sleepiness. Everyone listens to the mother," but what she says is not recorded (p. 67). Even this humorous conclusion is resonant with references to the father's frequent assertion that "good bulls sire cows," to the four Garcia girls, the only offspring of that generation, and to the fact that it is the birth of a grandson, not a granddaughter, that brings about the father's reconciliation with Fifi.

"Joe," as the title suggests, is devoted to Yolanda, to the relationship between her name and her sense of identity, and to her emotional breakdown when her first marriage collapses (pp. 68–85). It was first published in the *Syracuse Scholar* in a rather different version, with the central character named "Io," with other characters who do not appear in the book, with long expository passages that were deleted, and with a number of issues, homosexuality among them, that were excised before book publication.[11] In both versions, however, the central focus is on the intensity of Yolanda's yearning for romantic love, her vulnerable sense of identity, and her obsession with language and poetry. The narration is not linear; instead, there is a frame in the present, when Yo is being treated by Dr. Dennis Payne in a mental hospital (which the magazine version indicates is in Vermont), and a long interior flashback to her romance and failed marriage to John. In the present, there has been a transference of her affections to her psychiatrist, and she is obsessed with his every movement and gesture. In each case, the narrative perspective is in third person, including not only the frame but the interior flashback as well, so that Yolanda's comments to Dr. Payne are mediated through the narrative intelligence, creating a distance from her own story, from her own life, that relates to her pathology.

As is typical of a cycle, when the story was first published in 1982, it appeared without the context of the other fourteen, without its causative history, particularly significant in matters of psychological illness, and without its predictive role of Yolanda's status in "The Kiss" and "Antojos." "Joe" resonates forward and backward within the volume, but in the magazine its conflicts and significance were limited, so there was no indication of the other three sisters, the problems within the family, the prehistory of Yolanda's instability. In place of the family there were two friends, Vickie and Vaughn, who play important roles in the magazine but are totally absent in the book. Vaughn, once an English major at Core College, plays the role of confidant, allowing direct articulation of concepts that remain abstract in the book. In a discussion of Yolanda's problems understanding the function of language, Vaughn explains that "language is personal and impersonal, capable of affirming self . . . and communicating to another. Terrific, no?" (p. 66). Later, it is John's derisive references to Vaughn as a homosexual that lead to Yolanda's emotional break with her husband, whom she finds not only insensitive but obtuse: " 'We just don't talk the same language,' Io said" (p. 68). Another important change is that Yolanda's parents do not appear in the magazine, so the etiology of her condition is limited to her romantic relationships. In the book there is more suggestion of a parental origin for some of her problems, for her father is emotionally distant even while visiting his daughter in a mental hospital, not hearing what is said to him (p. 82).

The frame in the present develops themes that resonate within the interior narrative. The concept of "naming" and its relation to identity is important in both areas: the first sentence reveals that Yolanda is called "Yo" in Spanish, suggesting one cultural personality, and "Joey" in America when she selects a key chain, suggesting an alternative sense of self. In the interior story, it is significant that when she leaves her husband, she signs her note "Joe," using his name for her, her own sense of being having been destroyed (p. 79). Another point of timbre is "love": in the frame Yolanda has fallen in love with her psychiatrist;

in the interior story she falls in love with John. Her new amour in the opening gives her a renewed sense of beginning: "The world is sweetly new and just created" (p. 69). There are only two beings in it, the "first man," an Adam figure, and herself, projected in mythic terms: "Eve is lovely, a valentine hairline, white gossamer panties" (p. 69). In the concluding half of the frame, her love has proved to be therapeutic, for her deep feelings have restored her sense of identity, "the real Yolanda resurrecting on an August afternoon above the kempt green lawns of this private facility" (p. 83). But when, in the conclusion, Dr. Payne (whose name is suggestive of this ending) uses the name "Joe" for her, not her own name, she is again wounded: "Inside her ribs, her heart is an empty nest," a trope that concludes the bird imagery used for her throughout the story (p. 85).

What she tells her psychiatrist is similarly painful, recounting her early lovemaking with John and her uncertainty about whether she truly loved him (p. 70). Although it is told in third person, with Yolanda emotionally insulated from its implications, the narrative is clearly the account of her marriage that Yolanda is telling as part of her therapy, including formulations of self-justification for leaving her husband: "Because his pencils were always sharpened, his clothes always folded before lovemaking" (p. 73). John is so compulsively organized that he had constructed a "for" and "against" list for marrying her. But the central weakness in their relationship is the failure of language, since they use distinct lexicons drawn from differing conceptions of reality: "He spoke kindly, but in a language she had never heard before" (p. 77). When she explains the divorce to her parents, her formulation is that "we just didn't speak the same language," she being poetic, he being, as is more clear in the magazine version, an accountant. Indeed, all of this is more directly developed in the *Syracuse Scholar*, where her thoughts of separation are cast in terms of language: "He can have half of the words: words having to do with business, capitalism, pain, sorrow, fear, disgust, terror, loathing" (p. 60). It is a telling sequence. Within the stories in *How the García Girls Lost Their Accents*, however, this account of Yolanda's collapse and psychic resurrection is essential for understanding the opening of the volume, in which her vulnerability is otherwise unexplained.

The antecedent events for Yolanda's breakdown are in "The Rudy Elmenhurst Story" (pp. 86–103), which focuses on the central pathological elements of her vulnerability, a deep-seated need for romantic involvement coupled with an uneasy ambivalence about sexual purity, a concern for language, and an awareness of her cultural alienation in American society. Not previously published, this retrospective narrative is told by an adult Yolanda looking back at two periods in her life when she had interaction with Rudy Elmenhurst. The first was in 1969, when she transferred to a coeducational college and met Rudy in a creative writing class. The history of their romance is a seduction melodrama, with Rudy proffering the clichés of the genre in an unsuccessful assault on Yolanda's virginity. He finally rejects her as a lover and begins an affair with a more willing partner. Of interest is not so much the theatrics of the bedroom but what it reveals about Yolanda's self-definition as a young adult. A lapsed Catholic, on whose crucifix Jesus has become unglued, Yolanda has few religious qualms about sex, and she is obviously obsessed with a need for affection, writing a sonnet on "the nature of love" (p. 92). Her reluctance to engage in sex is quite clearly motivated by a fear of pregnancy, not ethereal retribution (p. 96).

Always the poet, sensitive to connotations, she is also offended by Rudy's crude language in discussing sexual experience. When his poem, filled with innuendoes, is a favorite of the class, Yolanda blames not her poetic limitations but her cultural background: "For the hundredth time, I cursed my immigrant origins. If only I too had been born in Connecticut or Virginia, I too would understand the jokes everyone was making on the last two digits of the year, 1969 . . ." (p. 95). A college undergraduate, she is still formulating her sense of self: "I saw what a cold, lonely life awaited me in this country. I would never find someone who would understand my peculiar mix of Catholicism and agnosticism, Hispanic and American styles." Such understanding obviously does not come from Rudy, who says to her, by way of dismissal, "I thought you'd be hot-blooded, being Spanish and all . . . but Jesus, you're worse than a fucking Puritan" (p. 99). The second retrospective period is in 1974, when Yolanda, now a graduate student, rejects Rudy, who has resumed his aborted seduction campaign of five years earlier. In one sense this is not a story of great moment, the themes and technical manipulations being rather simple in comparison to the others in the first section, but it is precisely her driving need for love, her sensitivity for language, and her fragile sense of identity that lead to her mental breakdown in "Joe."

The first section of five stories thus deals with the adult lives of the four sisters and their parents, with the outcomes of the immigration to

America, and with the fruits of assimilation and adjustment to the new language and new land. The dominant themes are those of pain and pathology, failed romances and collapsed marriages, and of tension and resentment between the parents and their children. Both Yolanda and Carla spend time in mental institutions, Sofia remains estranged from her father, and Sandra has problems adjusting to a new society. Despite their comparative wealth and privilege, despite servants and private schools and the finest colleges, the four daughters have found it difficult to find happiness in America. Perhaps for that reason, these stories are told largely from the outside, in third person, with only "The Rudy Elmenhurst Story" related in first person. Significantly, the imagery associated with the Dominican Republic is that of verdant vegetation, of fecundity, and of growth, and it is this country that ultimately holds out the promise of fulfillment to Yolanda in "Antojos." In the opening section, America has become a place of disappointment and conflict, of emotional betrayal, the failure of language, the breakdown of family. Three of the stories deal with birthdays, but there is little rejoicing. The events in the remaining two sections explain why.

The five stories in Section II cover the decade from 1970 back to 1960, from the time Dr. García becomes a citizen of the United States and Fifi is sent to spend a year with relatives in the Dominican Republic back to three months after the Garcias immigrated to America. The decade of the 1960s is a period of transition for the family, and it is not without stress and conflict. This group contains two "original" stories plus three works published previously before becoming part of the assembled book, and the independent nature of their original composition is evident despite revisions to coordinate the names and dates with the other episodes. In one instance, "Snow," the dates simply do not fit. In most instances, however, Alvarez made revisions to create a unified fictional sequence, moving backward in time, linking five stories into one narrative whole.

"A Regular Revolution" (pp. 107–32) is a family narrative, told from the point of view of the collective consciousness of the four sisters, covering events concerning the Garcías over an extended period. The perspective is plural and retrospective, reflecting on the salient events that "we" remember. Many of the details explain motivations and implications not clear in the other stories: that the parents had green cards when they first arrived in the United States and did not apply for citizenship until after a failed revolution in the Dominican Republic; that the girls were sent to a preparatory school in Boston; that they spent summers on the island so as not to lose touch with their heritage and extended family; and that the family brought a maid, Primitiva, with them to New York. But the heart of the story, as the title suggests, deals with revolutions, with multiple variations of the attempt to overthrow established authority.

The most literal of these, and the least important, is the attempted political revolution in the Dominican Republic, which inspires Dr. García to take out American citizenship, feeling the political situation on the island too unstable for the raising of four daughters (p. 107). Earlier, he had been involved more directly in a revolution when he plotted against Trujillo (p. 110). His experience is metaphoric of the atmosphere of change and turmoil that envelops the entire family, and it may explain why he is so remote from the emotional lives of his daughters, his emphasis being elsewhere, on national political concerns. The mother has her own transition, taking adult education courses in business and planning a new career for herself, a modest endorsement of the feminist ideas that her daughters grow to embrace (p. 110). Children of comparative wealth and privilege, the four sisters are sent to preparatory school and then to college, becoming Americanized in the process: ". . . Island was old hat, man. Island was the hair-and-nails crowd, chaperones, and icky boys with all their macho strutting and unbuttoned shirts and hairy chests with gold chains and teensy gold crucifixes" (pp. 108–09). Even though they spend their summers quite happily in the Dominican Republic, the sisters are revolting against their island heritage, albeit their rebellions are essentially innocuous: smoking in the bathroom, using hair removal cream, reading *Our Bodies, Our Selves*, and spending all night out on a date. But it is the mother's discovery of marijuana that leads to Sofía's banishment to the island for a year, a sentence that evokes other levels of revolution, the most significant of which is her sexual romance with Manuel Gustavo.[12] This affair, with a cousin who has been educated in the United States but reverts to macho domination in his homeland, inspires a feminist revolution on the part of the sisters, who conspire to expose the situation to save their sister from getting pregnant. Their interference, interpreted as betrayal by Sofía, brings about the final revolution, the break the youngest sister makes with her siblings, which explains her eagerness for the romance with Otto and her subsequent alienation from the rest of the family. These events thus have special resonance for Sofía in "The Kiss," when she attempts to reconcile with her parents on the birth of her son. This is a family that has experienced more than its fair share of stressful confrontations, and the multiplicity of "revolutions" suggests the many levels of reconciliation required to fully heal the family.

When "Daughter of Invention" first appeared in *Unholy Alliances* in 1988, it was narrated by Yolanda in first person and Dr. García's name was "Eduardo," as it had been in the initial publication of "The Kiss," suggesting that they were written at roughly the same time, from an autobiographical origin, and before the final planning of *How the García Girls Lost Their Accents*. The story was revised later to coordinate with the others in the volume, not an uncommon aspect of the construction of a story cycle. In first publication, Yolanda was clearly the dominant character, the focus of the reflections and action, and her poetic aspirations and the speech she gives in school were the central issue.[13] In the revised version (pp. 133–49), the story is told in third person from a retrospective stance at some temporal remove from the action and some psychic distance from Yolanda, and the central focus is very much on the mother, Laura, with her daughter's crisis as a conclusion. It is also explicit as to the time of the action, indicating that the central event, Yolanda's ninth-grade speech, comes just after the fall of Trujillo in 1961 and just before the first free elections in the Dominican Republic for three decades in 1962. Yolanda would then seem to have been born about 1948, allowing for the dating of other stories as well. There is some ambiguity as to the identity of the "daughter" of the title, since both mother and daughter are "inventors" of sorts, and both of them are, in important ways, daughters of note.

Laura García, a proper and proud "de la Torre" who descends from the conquistadors, is an "inventor" in several senses. The most literal is her attempt to create some new practical item for the household, "time-released water capsules for your potted plants when you were away," and other notions on that level (p. 137). A more important permutation is that she is attempting to reinvent herself, to create, in a new country, a viable economic and social self, a motif that runs throughout the action that takes place in America. She is also, amusingly, the creator of variations on the clichés of middle America: "When in Rome, do unto the Romans" and "It takes two to tangle" (p. 135).[14] She is the inventor of the heralded speech that Yolanda gives before the school assembly, one for which Yolanda receives credit but, as the narrator makes clear,

"Yoyo thinks of the speech her mother wrote as her last invention" (p. 149).

As a writer, Yolanda is also an inventor, having developed a sufficient lexicon in English to allow for the creation of verse and stories and essays. Perhaps her most significant production is the paper she writes for the Teacher's Day address at her school, a talk based on Walt Whitman's sentiments in "Song of Myself." This speech, deeply admired by her mother, is Yolanda's breakthrough to her own voice in a new language, but it is destroyed by Dr. García as being insubordinate to the nuns at the school, and that is when Laura helps her daughter write a replacement address. A good deal is revealed about the father, however, how he had lost brothers and friends in the Dominican Republic, executed on orders from Trujillo. This fact explains Dr. García's persistent preoccupation and distance from his daughters, and even his wife thinks of him as "an unhappy, haunted man" (p. 146). The original text made explicit a concept missing from the final volume, Yolanda's reflection on problems in the marriage: "Ever since they had come to this country, their life together was a constant war" (p. 24).

This motif is greatly reduced in *García Girls*. Yolanda's speech, in some respects, echoes her father's valedictory address of some decades ago. He is still engaged in a financially unrewarding "Centro de Medicina in the Bronx," before his practice on Long Island, and his humble status in America is humiliating after the wealth he enjoyed on the island. He is humbled again when Yolanda calls him "Chapita," Trujillo's nickname, protesting her father's tyrannical destruction of her original speech. His declaration of love for her, embodied in the gift of an electric typewriter, reveals again his emotional investment in his daughter, adumbrating his sentiments in "Joe" after Yolanda's emotional collapse.

As is often the case with the titles within the volume, which have a literal and a figurative significance, "Trespass" is enriched by ambiguity (pp. 150–65). The most prosaic application of the term is to the sign "Private, No Trespassing" posted by the vacant lot Carla passes on her way to school. The second reference is to the religious concept of trespassing in the Lord's Prayer, Carla's only previous awareness of the term. But the most salient definition applies to the psychological and sexual violation by the exhibitionist who exposes himself to young Carla, only in the seventh grade, just beginning to deal with her own emerging puberty. When the stranger exposes his erect sexual organ, and then masturbates, he has committed a significant trespass on her innocence, and it is clear that the emotional consequences for her will be significant. Although all of the details of Carla's development are not provided, there is certainly the suggestion that this event precipitates an emotional pathology that subsequently requires analysis, and that experience leads to Carla's interest in psychology and in choosing an analyst for a husband.

That line of thematic development is central, but there are contributory motifs that also resonate throughout the volume. The time would seem to be 1961, since it is one year after the Garcías arrived in the United States in 1960. Carla, the oldest sister, and thus the one most firmly inculcated into the culture of the Dominican Republic, has difficulty adjusting to her new society, and she prays to return home (p. 150). Her adjustment is complicated by the family's move to Long Island a month after their arrival and by her commute to school. It is also significant that the sisters are all held back one grade in school, probably to allow time for language acquisition, and the upshot is that they are a year older than their classmates in America. As a result, Carla is entering puberty earlier than her friends, and she has no peers going through the same experience. The young boys in her class tease her and taunt her, and they account for the final trespass, for it is their faces who haunt her dreams, disturbing her sleep (p. 164).

"Snow" (pp. 166–67), a very brief story of only five paragraphs, first appeared in the *Northwest Review* in 1984 and won the PEN Syndicated Fiction Prize in 1987 before appearing in *How the García Girls Lost Their Accents* in 1991. As is often the case when stories are published independently before being assembled into a cycle, the original text had to be adjusted to fit into the volume, and there were some insolvable problems in doing so. The heart of the matter is temporal. In the story as originally published, the motivation for the García family's move to America was made explicit, as was the time: "In the summer of 1960 my family emigrated to the United States, fleeing the tyrant Trujillo."[15] The book publication establishes the time as simply "Our first year in New York . . ." (p. 166). Neither formulation is consistent with American history, for the central event is the Cuban Missile Crisis during the presidency of John F. Kennedy, and he did not take office until 1961 and the confrontation over Cuba took place the following year. The only resolution of the problem is to accept the date of emigration as 1960, primarily because it establishes a fixed point in the time line, and to adjust history to allow for international events two years before they actually happened.

In the original version, the young girl who narrates was not named; in the book she is "Yolanda." She has sisters in the book who were not mentioned in the magazine. But beyond these revisions, the heart of the story remained the same. The young Yolanda, attending fourth grade at a Roman Catholic school in New York, becomes aware of the Russian missiles in Cuba and is taught about nuclear bombs and radioactive fallout. Shortly thereafter, upon seeing snow for the first time, she assumes it to be "the dusty fallout that would kill us all" but is informed that it is only snow. Even as a child, Yolanda lives in a threatening and confusing world that contains mechanized destruction and the grandmotherly attentions of the kindly Sister Zoe, who teaches her that snowflakes are unique, like people, "irreplaceable and beautiful." Yolanda is clearly designated as protagonist, and it is her psychic history that most dramatically dominates the collected volume.

Other issues dominate "Floor Show," which was first published in *Story Magazine* in 1991, the same year as *How the García Girls Lost Their Accents*.[16] Perhaps because the composition of the story was so close to the publication of the volume, "Floor Show" made the transition from magazine to book without substantial change. The last chronological step backward in Section II, it deals with the García family three months after their arrival in the United States in 1960 (pp. 168–91). Embedded in the action is a good deal of information about the circumstances of Dr. García: that Dr. Fanning had arranged a fellowship that allowed Carlos to move his family to America (p. 172) and how the family narrowly escaped the secret police the night before they left. These events, the omniscient narrator reveals, occupy Carlos's mind, making him seem distant: "Mostly he worried about *la situación* back home. Some uncles were in trouble. Tío Mundo had been jailed, and Tío Fidelio was maybe dead" (pp. 171–72). It is clear that he does not yet have a license to practice medicine in the United States and that Dr. Fanning is arranging an interim position for him as a hotel physician. An aristocrat in the Dominican Republic, living in a walled compound with chauffeurs and servants, in America Carlos has been reduced in stature, taking money each month from his father-in-law, accepting generosity from the Fannings. Conversely, Laura has gained in authority: "Mami was the leader now that they lived in the States. *She* had gone to school in the States. *She* spoke English without a heavy accent" (p. 176).

There is also a spectrum of issues for other members of the family. Since the point of view is omniscient, the narrator provides access to the thinking of many of the characters, providing elements of psychic history crucial for a full reading of the book. This is the first revelation that Laura was emotionally distressed after the narrow escape from the island: "At the least provocation, she would burst out crying, lose her temper, or threaten to end up in Bellevue, the place, she had learned, where crazy people were sent in this country" (p. 169). On the other hand, the dinner out with the Fannings gives the sisters an opportunity to see their mother not as "parent" but as an attractive young woman: "She wore a black dress with a scoop back and wide shoulders so her long neck had the appearance of a swan gliding on a lake" (p. 173). When the family first arrived in New York, they lived in a multiethnic apartment building, with an Irish doorman and a Puerto Rican superintendent, where they were nevertheless subjected to the enmity of their neighbor: "Spics! Go back to where you came from" (p. 171). If they had not brought the theme of alienation with them to America, it would have been provided for them.

Although the parents are haunted by their narrow escape from the island, it seems to have made less impact on the sisters, whose lives have been limited to island culture. It is natural that they would be interested in the Spanish dancers at the club, for "they had all been enthralled by the folk dancers from Madrid at the Dominican World's Fair last year," and their night out is a celebration of their native culture (p. 170). Sandi has her own moment of self-discovery when she looks in a mirror that evening: "She was surprised to find a pretty girl looking back at her. It was a girl who could pass as American, with soft blue eyes and fair skin, looks that were traced back to a great-great grandmother from Sweden at every family gathering" (p. 181).

The villain of the situation is an archetypal ugly American, Mrs. Fanning, who reveals herself to be a drunken, loud, and sexually aggressive woman, dancing provocatively onstage and kissing Dr. García in front of Sandi, which causes her some confusion but also arms her with leverage. The heart of the action thus belongs to Sandi, the predominant consciousness, and the central event is the floor show at the El Flamenco, when Mrs. Fanning becomes drunk and takes the stage with the Spanish dancers. Sandi's prime focus is on the "Barbie dolls dressed like Spanish señoritas" being offered for sale, dolls that constitute an expression of the advantage Sandi holds over her father. They are also an embodiment of her beloved island culture, an implication voiced at the end when she expresses her gratitude for the doll by saying "gracias." The second section thus ends with a confrontation of cultures, precisely where it had begun thematically in "A Regular Revolution." The five stories are patently independent units, employing different narrative perspectives, time schemes, and a spectrum of conflicts and resolutions involving all four sisters and their parents. They are here given congruence through thematic resonance and character motivation. Given the inversion of time, these stories about the 1960s help explain the characters from 1972 to 1989 in the first section. In the second group of five stories, the preoccupations of Dr. García in protecting his daughters, the mother's desire for acceptance in the new country, Yolanda's triumph in giving a speech in her new language, Carla's confrontation with the exhibitionist, and Sandi's experience at El Flamenco all provide insight into the psychic history of the family and the meaning of the malaise with which the book begins. Part of the consummate skill of Julia Alvarez is in bringing together separate stories and crafting thematic patterns of cultural duality, of assimilation, and of personal growth and familial accommodation that unify them into an artistic whole. Given the temporal inversion of the entire volume, however, the motivation and significance of this group cannot be fully established without a consideration of the stories in Section III.

The first two sections of stories take place in the United States from 1960 to 1989, and they concern a spectrum of issues that are the result of immigration to America. The third section, however, takes place in the Dominican Republic from 1956 to 1960 and deals with issues that antedate those that come later, matters of Spanish heritage for the de la Torres, the influence of the grandparents and aunts and uncles on the four sisters, the consequences of the aborted plot to overthrow Trujillo, the backgrounds of the servants who are employed by the family, and, especially, the world of the García children in the Dominican Republic. It is a world of toys and play conjoined with the adult concerns of sex, death, and life-threatening politics. In many respects, the childhood issues in these five stories serve as adumbrations of the more mature concerns of the first two sections of the volume.

What is fascinating about "The Blood of the Conquistadors" is not just its dramatic plot but the method of its narration. Although Alvarez employs a variety of narrative techniques, including shifting perspectives from one character to another, nowhere is that device used with more telling effect than in this story, in which several characters serve as the center of consciousness for an omniscient point of view and two of them, Sofia and Chucha (a Haitian servant in the García household), relate substantial parts of the action in first person. The device is essentially that of narrative parallax, a shifting of the angle from which events are comprehended and told so as to reveal disparities in the meaning of experience when viewed from differing perspectives.[17] Alvarez here uses that mode effectively by portraying the seminal event in the lives of the García family not only from their vantage point but from the purviews of one of their servants, an embassy official, and the secret police as well.

All of these perspectives describe the same basic plot; the disparity is in the meaning of what took place, the information available to the focalizing agent, the motivation for actions as perceived from that perspective, and the impressionistic data of experience for that character. The basic action is simple: Carlos García was involved with the American CIA in a plot to overthrow Trujillo. At the last moment, support for the coup was withdrawn, and the assassination attempt failed. The secret police came to the García de la Torre family compound to interrogate and probably arrest Carlos, who hid in a closet in the house. Laura sent for Victor Hubbard, an official at the American Embassy, and he arranged for the family to immigrate to the United States. There was little time to prepare for departure, and the children could pack only a few clothes and one toy to be brought with them. Stated so baldly, these events are melodramatic and psychologically "flat." The brilliance of the narrative is in the method of its telling, as brief sections of these events are related from shifting perspectives, revealing the psychological preoccupations and underlying values of the characters.

As is true throughout the entire volume, "The Blood of the Conquistadors" has a domestic setting; even when the central character is Dr. García, the focus is on his role at home, not at the office, not at the hospital, not in interaction with other men in the social life of the Dominican Republic. The story is broken into twelve narrative units, quite different from one another, each advancing the central events. The first is a third-person perspective, in present tense (which heightens the aura of immediate danger), with access to the mind of Dr. García but with sufficient fictive "distance" to refer to him as "Carlos." When he sees the two members of the secret police approaching the house, he retreats to a cubicle behind a back panel in a closet, a hideaway equipped with water and food and a revolver. The implication is

175

that the Trujillo government has established an intrusive, totalitarian regime of sufficient threat that Dr. García has taken precautions, prepared for the moment when the secret police come to get him. The second narrative unit sustains the present tense but shifts to Yolanda's point of view in duplicative time, covering again the activities from the moment the police arrived and her father fled to the closet. This device is common in narrative parallax because it allows experience to be seen from another vantage point, two or more perceptions of the same temporal event, and here it permits the presentation of a child's perspective to counter that of the father. Yolanda's preoccupation is on past events, not the immediate danger, and at first she misinterprets the action, thinking her father is playing one of his games. When she realizes that the strangers at the door are the secret police, she recalls an ordeal when she was only five, which would seem to be about eight years earlier, when she disingenuously told a general about her father's gun, and he was placed in danger. She was beaten for that indiscretion, and she feels sufficient guilt in the present to be preoccupied with it.

The point of view then shifts to that of the mother, Laura, as she arrives home to find the police in the compound. Before she enters her home, she sends a servant for Victor Hubbard, a family friend who is an undercover CIA man involved in the plot against Trujillo. When she enters the house, Chucha indicates where Carlos is hiding, and Laura's concern is in misdirection through lavish courtesy, delaying the police long enough for Hubbard to arrive: "The grand manner will usually disarm these poor lackeys from the countryside, who have joined the SIM [secret police], most of them, in order to put money in their pockets, food and rum in their stomachs, and guns at their hips" (pp. 201–02). Since the arrival of Hubbard is of crucial importance, the next two sections deal with him. The first is from the point of view of Doña Tatica, who rents cabins, and young ladies, in which Hubbard has a regular tryst. She is reluctant to disturb him, but the secretary's insistence of urgency prompts her to do so. That leads to Hubbard's own perspective as his lovemaking is interrupted: "A goddamn bang comes at the goddamn door" (p. 205). His emphasis is on sex, and he habitually assesses women on that basis, even Carmen: "A sweetheart, this little lady, not bad legs either" (p. 206). He implements the plan to get the Garcías out of the country.

The manifestation of that strategy comes from the shared perspective of Carla and Sandi as a dual center of consciousness, yet another device employed by Alvarez. Their brief section covers Hubbard's arrival at Carmen's home in the family compound and the background information that the García sisters' maternal grandfather, Papito, has resigned his post as a representative to the United Nations but remained in the United States with his wife. This passage also establishes the time of the present action as August of 1960. Hubbard's entrance to the García home is covered by Laura's point of view, which indicates that thirty minutes have passed since the arrival of the police. It also reveals that Laura and her husband have sexual problems related to the violent atmosphere of the island (p. 211). Victor Hubbard arrives and relates the crucial news that Dr. García has a fellowship at an American hospital and will leave the next day.

The next section is told by another center of consciousness, that of Pupo, one of the two secret policemen who come to the García home. It also moves backward in time to begin in the morning, when they were given their assignment for the day: to report on Dr. García's activities. It is clear that the intrusion into the home exceeds their authorization, and this makes them vulnerable to Hubbard's manipulations. He calls the supervisor of the two men and announces that the Garcías will shortly be leaving the country. The emphasis is on Pupo's awkward situation as he "sits among these strange white people, ashamed and cornered" (p. 214). He is clearly one of the peasant class of police Laura was accustomed to seeing, free from malice, earning a living working for a corrupt regime. The following segment is equally innocent, for the concentration is on Sandi, still a child although the oldest of the sisters, and the key event for her is the instruction to go to the bedroom and choose her best clothes along with a single toy, and she feels an emptiness because she does not have a favorite object to embrace on the trip. That revelation explains her motivation in "Floor Show," in which she is given a doll that is a Spanish dancer that reminds her of her native culture.

All of this activity is taking place within the compound while Dr. García is hiding in the dark cubicle, and the next section shifts to his perspective, recording his thoughts and his auditory impressions, since he can see so little. He hears the conversations and activity as the police leave and Laura comes into the bedroom to get him from his hiding place. This section, as do virtually all of the narrative units, also contains a narrational intrusion providing background information, in this case that Dr. García "is the youngest of his father's thirty-five children, twenty-five legitimate, fifteen from his own mother, the second wife; he has no past of his own" (p. 216). The crisis is over, the Garcías are to leave the island the next morning, and the rapidly shifting perspectives on the action now give way to two final narrative units.

The first is an entirely new narrative method, a first-person retrospective episode told by Sofia about her memories of her last day in the Dominican Republic. The implication is that the telling takes place a good while after leaving home but before her extended stay on the island in "A Regular Revolution." Fifi's preoccupation, however, is not the national politics and grand issues of emigration but rather with her memories of the Haitian servant, Chucha, who had served the family for two generations but who was left behind when the Garcías emigrated. Many years ago Trujillo had decreed the execution of all black Haitians in the Dominican Republic, and Chucha had fled to the de la Torres for assistance. She was taken into the household, trained as a servant, and remained with them the rest of her life. On the night before the departure, Chucha came to the sisters to present them with a statue she had carved for their good luck, and it is this moment that has emotional resonance for Fifi years later, remembering that "we all started to cry as if Chucha had finally released her own tears in each of us" (p. 221). Sophia does not tell about her father coming out of hiding, the preparations for the trip, or the flight to America; rather, she remembers this emotional scene with a simple servant.

It is extraordinary that the concluding section of the richest and most complex story in *How the García Girls Lost Their Accents* is told in first person by Chucha, who remained in the house after the family had left: "They are gone, left in cars that came for them, driven by pale Americans in white uniforms with gold braids on their shoulders and on their caps" (p. 221). Chucha has lost her only sense of familial belonging, and she is sensitive to the "deep and empty silence of the deserted house," but her concerns are not so much for herself as for Laura and the girls and the adjustment they will have to make in the new country, a change not unlike Chucha's own experience in leaving Haiti. She looks forward, rather than backward, and she sees the inevitable raiding of the family residence and the desecration of the compound by Trujillo's minions. The story ends with her ritual cleansing before preparing to sleep in her coffin, her life having ended with the departure of the García family. By reverting to these rituals, Chucha's actions also recall her origins in Haitian culture, with its amalgam of voodoo and Christianity, as Elizabeth Starcevic has pointed out: "The portrayal of Chucha, the ancient Haitian servant, who is feared for her temper, her voodoo spells, and her practice of sleeping in a coffin, offers a glimpse into the historical complexity of the relationships of the two countries that share the island of Hispaniola."[18] It is also a dramatic end to the most complex and intriguing narrative in the volume, one that features the central event in the lives of the Garcías, their leaving the Dominican Republic for America, and tells it from a multiplicity of perspectives, giving thematic depth and psychological penetration to action that could have been melodramatic. Everything that is told in the first two sections of the book is the result of the events in this story.

"The Human Body" (pp. 225–38) is slight in comparison, but it provides a good deal of family background. It is a unique feature of the cycle genre that an individual narrative might be more significant for its thematic resonance than for the drama inherent in its own action. The narrator in this case is Yolanda speaking as an adult about things that happened in her early childhood, a time "back then" when "we all lived side by side in adjoining houses on a piece of property which belonged to my grandparents" (p. 225). The ancestors in question are the de la Torre clan, of course, for the Garcías were poor, with over thirty children, and they seem not to have owned anything. Yolanda offers, in largely expository observations, a good deal of background about Papito and Mamita, that they live in a huge home and have the entire family over for Sunday dinner when they are in residence, and that grandfather has a post with the United Nations representing the Dominican Republic, a position he resigns in "The Blood of the Conquistadors." He is a deeply respected man, so good "he pees holy water," and he hesitated to represent the Trujillo regime, but his wife's health required attention and New York offered the best possible services. The key disclosure about Mamita is that she "had been a very beautiful young woman, and she had never fully recovered from losing her looks" (p. 227). This is obviously a judgment made from the time of the telling, with a mature Yolanda reflecting on the mutability of feminine beauty, and not the youthful understanding of a child.

The emphasis is on the world of children, especially the friendships of each of the sisters, particularly Yolanda and her cousin Mundín. The titular concern is for the transparent, anatomical "Human Body doll" that Mundín receives as a gift, acknowledging his early interest in medicine, following Dr. Garcia's profession. He and Yolanda play with the doll, examining its internal parts, and that interest leads to "playing doctor," when Yoyo and Fifi take down their underwear to show their cousin that they are girls. He is disappointed, saying they look just like dolls (p. 235). It is an innocent adumbration of the more serious issues of sexuality and indiscretion that will play an important role in the lives of both of these sisters, leading to Sofía's controversial marriage in "The Kiss" and Yolanda's emotional pathology in "Joe," her failed marriage in "The Kiss," and her return to the island in search of a new life in "Antojos."

A number of subordinate motifs are also significant, including the totalitarian political world of an island on which "God and Trujillo are taking care of you" (p. 227), the appearance of Mimi, the intellectual but still unmarried aunt whose experience reinforces the concept that university degrees render young women unfit for matrimony, and Yolanda's fascination for the telling of stories, particularly the legend of Scheherazade. This allusion to the woman who could forestall execution only as long as she could continue telling a tale suggests why Yolanda is such a dominant narrator: it is her capacity to tell the story of her life that keeps her alive. That is what she is doing as an adult in "The Human Body," telling her life, coming to terms with the meaning of her experience.

As is often the case in the short-story cycle, the next tale presents a different narrative perspective and a new set of thematic concerns, although related to the contiguous stories. In this case, Sandi has an opportunity to review a salient event in "Still Lives" (pp. 239–55), which was previously published in the *Caribbean Writer* in 1987.[19] The title is suggestive of three planes of meaning: the still lives painted by the German Doña Charito; the enormous wood sculptures crafted by her husband, Don José; and the portraits painted in words by Sandi in the telling of the narrative. It is also a useful episode for the clarification of some aspects of the de la Torre household, particularly the full names of Sandi (Sandra Isabel García de la Torre) and her maternal grandparents: Don Edmundo Antonio de la Torre and Doña Yolanda Laura María Rochet de la Torre. It is clear here, and nowhere else in the book, that Yolanda was named for her maternal grandmother, as was Laura García. There were no grandsons to carry on the lineage, so the maternal ancestry is preserved in names. Significantly, in the original form of the story, the grandparents were "Don Erasmo and Doña Emilia Maria de Jesus Castillo," a direct reference to a province in Spain and a reminder, one of many, that the de la Torre clan descends not from the native peoples of the island but from the Spanish conquistadors.[20] On the authorial level, there is also the suggestion that Alvarez had not yet reconciled the details of her stories for publication as a coordinated work.

"Still Lives" is anomalous in *How the García Girls Lost Their Accents* for its predominantly comic tone and for the detailed attention it gives to two people outside the family, artists who do not play a role elsewhere in the volume. Narrated by an older Sandi, looking back on events in her eighth year, the action presents a humorous portrait of Doña Charito, an absurdly Wagnerian figure in Dominican culture whose paintings are all of European subjects, "no tarantulas, no mangoes, no lizards, no spirits, no flesh-and-blood people" (p. 245). Indeed, one of Sandi's concerns in studying painting with the German woman is her fear that "I would never get to draw the brilliant and lush and wild world brimming over inside me" for the García experience of the world is decidedly Caribbean, and their Latin perspective clashes with the artist's Teutonic manner (p. 247). Her influence destroys Sandi's artistic inclinations and her sense of confidence, which contributes to her later need for psychological therapy: "It seemed like everything I enjoyed in the world was turning out to be wrong" (p. 248). She turns inward, bereft of her ability to reproduce the lush nature around her: "I could no longer draw. My hand had lost its art" (p. 254). At the same time, the mad Don José captures her face in the visage of the Virgin he sculpts for the National Cathedral, an innocuous reference within this single story that is ironic in the context of the others, with the lapsed Catholicism of the sisters and their failed marriages.

"An American Surprise" (pp. 256–74) shifts the narrative perspective yet again, to Carla's purview, although in the original publication of the story it was related from a third-person point of view.[21] By making this change, Alvarez has created a progression of perspectives in the last section from that of the aggregate family, to Yolanda, to Sandi, and to Carla. Sofia cannot, of course, relate the final story in the section, although that would have had the virtue of symmetry, because she has not yet been born. As the previous episodes all explored aspects of the domestic household in the Dominican Republic, "An American Surprise" depicts the lives of the servants, particularly the new pantry maid, Gladys. In the process, it also supplies critical details that relate to the stories that have come before but that follow in chronology.

The situation is that Dr. García (called Dr. Bermudez in the first version) has come home from New York with gifts for his young daughters. In the original publication there were only three of them (Ana, Lydia, and Marie), and there was no infant Sophia. In *How the García Girls Lost Their Accents* the details have been coordinated with the other stories, changing the names of the sisters and adding Fifi, born only recently and thus not a factor in the events. The shift of point of view, however, changes the impact, for the original text was an objective, third-person portrait that described the action from the outside with as much attention to the father as to the daughter. Now it is more an interior narrative detailing Carla's view of the servants and stressing her sense of guilt when Gladys is fired at the end, feelings exacerbated by the fact that Carla had given Gladys the bank and her parents interpret it as having been stolen. This version thus contributes to Carla's psychological baggage as an adult, the same effect as virtually all of the substantive revisions from original appearance to the final collected volume.

There are other details of significance, notably the fascination of the sisters with the snow their father reports having seen in New York, a motif reiterated by Yolanda in "Snow." In the course of her description of the García home, she also sketches the full contingent of servants, Chucha, the cook (who here sleeps on a cot and not in her coffin, a detail not reconciled with "The Blood of the Conquistadors"); Milagros, the nursemaid; Mario, the chauffeur; Nivea, the laundry maid; Pila, another laundry maid (needed in a large family with a young baby); and the new pantry maid, Gladys. Part of the implication of all these servants is the wealth and privilege of the García family; another aspect is the racial division of life in the Dominican Republic, where the servants are often "black-black" and the de la Torres pride themselves on having white, European heritage. That Dr. García brings home three mechanical banks for his daughters suggests obliquely the capitalistic system of America, to which they all immigrate in the first story in this section, and the fact that Carla gets a baby doll for Christmas helps explain Sandi's intense desire later for a toy in "Floor Show."

"The Drum" (pp. 275–90) is a closely related story, containing many of the same elements, although it is narrated in retrospect by the adult Yolanda. Once again the precipitating situation involves a gift brought home from F. A. O. Schwarz in New York, this time a drum for the very young Yolanda by her maternal grandmother, Mamita. Once again there is the issue of a servant suspected of being a thief and leaving the household, in this case Pila. Also of interest is the promise Mamita makes to take Yolanda to New York, where she can see F. A. O. Schwarz's toy store and witness snow for the first time, a promise that instills expectations that explain the events in "Snow." It also gives the volume the ironic structure of beginning and ending with Yolanda's perspective, with her desire to go to the United States in the last story and her desperate, pathological return to the Dominican Republic in the first. Yo thus becomes the dominant figure in the book, the teller of the envelope, the unifying, normative personality, which is perhaps why her full name is given here and nowhere else, Yolanda Altagracia.

The ancillary details are once again as important as the central action, which has Yolanda receiving the gift of a drum, finding a litter of young kittens, and throwing one of them out her window to stop it from meowing. Other matters of the household date it as the earliest action, the fact that Tía Isa is still married to an American being one of them, for she is divorced throughout the rest of the volume. As was true in "An American Surprise," much attention is paid to the servants, particularly to Pila, the old laundry maid. In describing her, Alvarez went back to recover a passage deleted after the original publication of "An American Surprise," where she had written that "Pila, the laundry maid, was a curious looking woman: she had splotches of white on her black arms and legs and one blind eye and one good eye, but no one ever knew which was which."[22] Alvarez changed the text of the book publication to have these general comments refer to Nivea, and she deleted this specific description entirely, moving it to "The Drum," where, somewhat revised, it once again describes Pila: "That old laundry maid, Pila, was the strangest maid we had ever had, for it seemed everything that could go wrong with her had gone wrong. She had lost an eye, her left, let's see, or was it her right? You never knew. . . . She had splashes of pinkish white all up and down her dark brown arms and legs" (p. 279). The suggestion is that the children have the time and opportunity to observe the servants in some detail, since they are the adults with whom the sisters most frequently interact, including this old Haitian woman.

In its conclusion, this story gives an overview of the ensuing action: that the family moves to the United States, that Yolanda went away to school and saw snow, that she continued her interest in literature, that she became a writer, that what she is telling is what she has written: "You understand I am collapsing all time now so that it fits in what's left in the hollow of my story? I began to write, the story of Pila, the story of my grandmother" (p. 289). As an adult, the implication is, she writes out of a desire to create art, to palliate her loneliness, to expiate her guilt for actions in the past, including her treatment of the kitten: "There are still times I wake up at three o'clock in the morning and peer into the darkness. At that hour and in that loneliness, I hear her, a black furred thing lurking in the corners of my life, her magenta mouth opening, wailing over some violation that lies at the center of my art" (p. 290). In a sense, these comments give meaning and motivation to the entire volume, especially to all of the stories narrated in first person by Yolanda as well as to those told in third person from a perspective identified with her mind. It is her voice and her concerns that dominate the narration and the action of *How the García Girls Lost Their Accents* and that provide its most penetrating psychological portrait.

Beyond the continuing depiction of the García family in the Dominican Republic and their subsequent immigration to America, the intellectual, linguistic, and psychological growth of Yolanda is especially important in unifying the disparate stories into one coherent narrative. The arc of her development begins and ends the volume, creating a regressive *Bildungsroman*, moving backward from Yolanda at age thirty-nine, a university instructor of Comparative Literature returning to the Dominican Republic in search of her inner self, through her earlier failed romances, mental breakdown, educational success, childhood adventures, and ending with her at age six playing with a new drum. Throughout all of these stories, as Ilan Stavans has said,

> a secondary leitmotif also colors the plot—that of the coming of age of a candid female writer and her indomitable need to describe, in literary terms, her feelings and immediate milieu. . . . Although its content is told by shifting narrators, she is the soul inside the text. She contrasts and ponders. She is puzzled and flabbergasted by the circumstances around her. The world gains and loses its coherence in her mind.[23]

As the central figure, Yolanda's need for storytelling explains why she is so frequently the first-person narrator or, conversely, the central intelligence, the focalizing agent, with whom the omniscient narrator identifies. Her portrait thus develops a depth beyond that of the other characters, for it is she who is driven by a need for art, for language, for romantic love, and for an integrated personality based on self-respect.

That is something she is never able to achieve, her identity remaining inchoate, struggling for formation.

There are other elements as well that lend coherence to what were originally separate stories. *How the García Girls Lost Their Accents* is essentially about the world of women, primarily the four sisters and their mother but also the female servants in the household; men play decidedly secondary roles even when it is they who give impetus to a series of events. The feminine world of the book is depicted in conditions of stress, conflicts exacerbated by domestic and national tyranny and conditioned by the cultural heritage and language of the Dominican Republic. As Mary Batts Estrada maintains, "Alvarez treats the subjects of immigration, exile, Hispanic culture and the American Dream with a sensitive and often irreverent touch, giving special attention to the aspirations of female Hispanic immigrants."[24] Alvarez has commented that this aspect of her fiction, feminist concerns in the context of Latina gender restrictions, has an autobiographical basis, for she recalls, with regard to herself and her sisters, "we were being groomed to go from being dutiful daughters to being dutiful wives with hymens intact. No stops along the way that might endanger the latter: no careers, no colleges, no shared apartments with girlfriends, no boyfriends and social lives. . . . Girls were to have no aspirations beyond being good wives and mothers."[25] This is a motif never directly articulated in any of the stories, not by a narrator and not by any of the characters, but it is inherent in the psychological dynamic nevertheless.

In this sense the book presents, in reverse temporal order, the salient affective matrix of each of the sisters followed by suggestions about the origins of their personalities, the central events that helped shape their early development. This is a feature of the volume absent from the independent publication of the stories, in which conflicts in the "present" could be analyzed but which would remain unexplained without the events in other stories. Thus, for example, Sandra's fascination for psychology, and her marriage to an analyst, can be seen as related to her nervous breakdown, to her sense of exclusion within the family, to her cultural dislocation during a crucial formative period in her life. It is no small aspect of the artistic skill of Julia Alvarez that this line of development is made compelling in each episode and yet cuts across six of the fifteen stories.

It is the fictional artistry of *How the García Girls Lost Their Accents* that constitutes its most dramatic achievement, for it is, as a literary work, a tour de force of narrative method, of complex variations on the technique of storytelling, of the handling of time, the interweaving of themes and motifs, and the incremental development of character and psychological depth. In this sense "The Blood of the Conquistadors" is certainly the richest and most complex of the fifteen stories, building an undercurrent of danger and suspense through narrative parallax as the events are seen from the vantage point of eight differing perspectives. As a whole, the volume itself is similarly diverse in viewpoint: Yolanda narrates "The Drum," "The Human Body," "Snow," and "The Rudy Elmenhurst Story" in first person and her point of view is revealed in third person in "Antojos," "Joe," and "Daughter of Invention." Carla narrates "An American Surprise" in first person and serves as the central intelligence in "Trespass." It is Sandra's perspective that informs the telling of "Floor Show," and it is she who directly narrates "Still Lives." As the youngest daughter, Sofia is too young to tell the earliest stories, but her point of view emerges as the most significant in "The Kiss." Within this aesthetic context, there are more complex narrational patterns, the synthesis of third-person perspectives in "The Kiss," for example, and the conflated, pluralized first-person telling of "A Regular Revolution." This spectrum of narrative methods is more common to the short-story cycle than to the novel since each episode often has its own strategy of "telling." It is also more common in the cycle format to shift protagonists in each narrative unit, allowing various members of the Garcia family to be the dominant focus in respective stories, broadening the center of interest to embrace their concerns.

The handling of time is similarly complex, and narratives frequently contain not only the temporal duality of the time of the telling set against the time of the action but multiple flashbacks and duplicative periods as well. If the continual move backward in time gives shape to the collected stories, the temporal shifts within each story add thematic intensity as related scenes are juxtaposed and highlighted. Despite shifting narrators, there is a persistent Hispanic "voice" and tone of gentle irony throughout the volume, even though the dominant theme is the cultural assimilation of the four sisters, the titular issue of losing their accent.[26] But the culture of the Dominican Republic is never entirely absent, even in the scenes set in America, for the ethnically differentiated gender roles of the island, as well as its folkways of sexual behavior, political expectations, and educational prerogatives, influence the assumptions of the four sisters and their parents throughout their lives.

That is why it is appropriate, structurally, thematically, and ethnically, that the opening story be "Antojos," about Yolanda's return to her homeland. But issues of ethnic origin notwithstanding, Alvarez's consummate skill in handling the interrelationships among the fifteen stories, the structural integrity of the volume, and the progressive development of thematic depth all demonstrate the essential importance of reading *How the García Girls Lost Their Accents* as part of the tradition of the American short-story cycle.

7

Generational Identity and Form

Amy Tan's *The Joy Luck Club*

A my Tan once remarked that she read Louise Erdrich's *Love Medicine* in 1985, and it changed her life. Although Erdrich's stories are about Native American characters, a tradition remote from Tan's own Chinese background, she found in them an artistic design that would allow expression for some of the salient issues of her life, especially the events surrounding the emigration of her mother from China to America in 1949 during the Communist revolution, leaving behind three infant daughters by the roadside.[1] At the beginning of the project Tan was a free-lance writer employed by major corporations, as she has explained: "I wrote everything from manuals for AT&T salespeople on how to sell 'Reach Out America' plans to business proposals for companies doing consulting for Fortune 500 businesses. . . . One of the last things I wrote was a book for IBM called *Telecommunications and You*, which is twenty-six chapters on telecommunications geared to systems engineers and CEOs of major corporations."[2] Although she continued to write business manuals of various kinds, she also began working on three short narratives based on the background of her family, stories that would eventually become part of one of the most celebrated books in contemporary American literature.

The material she drew from was close at hand. Her mother's life had been dramatic and intriguing; she had formed a social organization in China called the "Joy Luck Club" that focused on dining, storytelling, and mah jong; in the midst of a war she had left daughters behind in China and had no knowledge of what had become of them.[3] There were also other aspects of her mother's life that lent themselves to fictional representation, as Tan has indicated: "She was the little girl watching her mother cut a piece of flesh from her arm to make soup, and she was the little girl watching her mother die when she took opium because she had become a third concubine. . . . And then the other part, of course, is that my mother is still alive—I'm not like June Woo."[4] As this comment suggests, Tan worked from autobiographical details but quickly began to add invented material to them. She did not live in Chinatown in San Francisco, nor did she become a chess champion, as does her character Waverly Jong. Tan's mother came from a wealthy Shanghai family and worked as a nurse in the United States. Her father was a Baptist minister. After both her father and brother died of brain tumors, her mother suffered a heart attack, prompting Tan to fear that her mother would die before they had a chance to truly know each other.[5] The unifying experience in the relationship was a joint trip to Shanghai and Beijing in 1987 for the reunion with the girls who had been abandoned nearly four decades earlier. In that rich family experience, Tan found the energy and invention to begin her life as a writer of fiction.[6]

According to Elaine Woo, in 1985 Tan joined the Squaw Valley Community of Writers, where she was taught creative writing by Molley Giles, who eventually introduced her to an agent, Sandra Dihkstra, who was instrumental in securing a contract for what eventually became *The Joy Luck Club*.[7] The first story Tan wrote was entitled "End Game," later changed to "Rules of the Game," the episode in which Waverly Jong, drawing on the invisible strength she has inherited from her mother, becomes a chess champion. When she had written three stories, the first plus "Waiting Between the Trees" (Ying-Ying St. Clair's reflections on her early marriage in China to a man who left her for an opera star) and "Scar" (An-Mei Hsu's poignant tale about the ancestor who cut flesh from her arm to feed her dying mother), Tan's agent asked her to write a proposal for the entire book, so she wrote abbreviated summaries of the planned episodes that would complete the volume.[8] As she has outlined the process, "I quickly wrote a proposal, briefly describing sixteen stories for what was then to be a first collection. I had in mind a set of stories, divided into five sections, each related to one of the Chinese elements that make up one's nature and fate: wood, earth, fire, water, and metal. In it would be separate vignettes told by women, young and old, who lacked one element, had too much of another."[9] It is significant for the study of the short-story cycle that even at this early stage Tan was working on a structural design for the volume, albeit not the one that ultimately emerged. In any event, in what has become a legend of contemporary publishing, Putnam's purchased the book on the basis of these slender materials, and Amy Tan's career as a serious writer of fiction was officially launched.

It did not come easily. Tan has said that she wrote 7,000 pages in the composition process to get the 350 pages that went into the book.[10] As she has explained, "when the book was sold, I went back and started with the very first story. I didn't go in the same order that I had outlined them; I just went with the story that seemed to want to be told next, and it seemed to alternate between mother and daughter. I'd write a mother's story, and then I'd hear the daughter saying, 'Well, let me tell my side of it.' And the very last story I wrote was the one that's last in the book."[11] At this stage she seems to have envisioned two structural elements: the concept of alternating stories by mothers and daughters, which was to give the volume its essential design; and the notion of "sections," which was preserved, but not in the way she initially planned. Part of that development is indicated even in the "entitling" of the book, which Tan originally intended to call "Wind and Water," indicating the elements related to harmony with nature in the Chinese tradition of *feng shui*. Then, Tan's agent suggested using the title of the first story, "The Joy Luck Club," drawn from the social organization her family had belonged to for years. As she explains it, "after my agent suggested the title change, I could see the stories revolving around a community of women who were more intimately related to one another than what I had originally proposed to write. I changed the title, figuring if it didn't sound right by the time I finished writing the book— which, by my estimate, would be years later—I could change it then."[12] But she did not need to change the title because the mah jong club, involving four families, with four mothers and four daughters, provided precisely the structural design for the entire book, one that allowed for eight speakers and eight protagonists in sixteen stories united by a common matrix of themes of Chinese heritage and cultural duality in America.

This design is quintessentially that of the short-story cycle, not that of the traditional novel, a point that Tan was cognizant of from the very beginning: "The book was actually written as a collection of short stories, not a novel, and I still think of them as stories. . . . They're connected by theme or emotion or community." When the first reviews of the book appeared, calling the book a "novel," the misattribution of genre demanded Tan's consideration: "Putnam's said to me, 'You know, everybody is calling this a novel.' And I said, 'But that's not what I wrote.' So we compromised; on the jacket flap it's called a 'first work of fiction.' The only place you see the word 'novel' on the hardcover is in the *Publisher Weekly* review blurb."[13] The concept of form was clearly important to Amy Tan even if the initial reviewers were oblivious to the idea that separate stories can be organized in such a way so as to gain thematic resonance from one another even though there are multiple narrators, protagonists, and lines of action. In a sense, what Tan ultimately constructed is a much more intricate volume than is traditional in the novel, a short-story cycle of tight artistic unity and thematic coherence that achieves its final impact through juxtaposition, counterpoint, and incremental accretion.

The basic configuration of *The Joy Luck Club* is that there are four sections, each with four stories, one from each family. Each group is introduced by a brief vignette that establishes thematic unity to the episodes that follow. The vignette that opens the first cluster, "Feathers from a Thousand Li Away," introduces many of the central issues of the book.[14] In four brief paragraphs, the vignette portrays the longings of an archetypal Chinese woman to tell her story to her daughter, a tale about longings and aspirations. Even the swan in the tale has its own ambitions, for it is said to have been a duck that desired to become a goose, so it stretched its neck and inadvertently became a swan, too beautiful to eat. At the time she leaves China for the United States, the old woman brings her swan with her as a gift for the daughter she expects to have, confident that the child will understand that the bird was "a creature that became more than what was hoped for," an obvious lesson for the girl herself (p. 17). But the swan was confiscated in the immigration process, and the mother was left with a single feather as a memory, waiting for the right time to tell this story to her thoroughly Americanized daughter.

This brief tale contains the essential elements of the four stories that follow. The old woman's desire to tell about her journey from China presages this group in which the mothers tell of their hardship in China and immigration to America. The central impulse in the vignette is that of rendition; the secondary motivation is for the mother to convey her intentions for the successful assimilation of her daughter, to express her desire that the daughter be respected, and to present to her an emblem of her Chinese heritage, a single feather that gives form to the mother's hopes and aspirations. The tone of patient desire, of waiting for the moment to share her innermost feelings with her daughter, establishes a narrative context in which the four mothers can now relate their own heartfelt memories.

The first story in the collection, "The Joy Luck Club," first appeared in March of 1989 in the *Ladies' Home Journal* in a truncated version that is missing many important elements of the final text.[15] The magazine edition is without Suyuan Woo's expression of pleasure that she is to host the next meeting of the Joy Luck Club, an important reference in that she dies before the event and her daughter feels incapable of taking her place (p. 19). The magazine is missing some of the mother's reflections on Kweilin, where she had abandoned her infant daughters during the Japanese advance in World War II, a matter with biographical significance in that Tan's own mother had left daughters behind during the later onslaught of the Communist Revolution in China (p. 21). Tan has not explained why she changed the historical facts, an alteration that makes implausible some aspects of the chronology by setting the "past" events back a decade, but it may have been out of a desire to avoid offending the current regime on the mainland, whose cooperation was necessary for the Tans to visit members of their family. Also missing is Suyuan's hatred of American Air Force officers, which would underscore her desire that her daughter not become fully assimilated into the society of the United States (p. 22). It is without the detail that at the dinners of the club the hostess invariably serves "boiled peanuts for conceiving sons," which is ironic for the Woo family, which has produced nothing but daughters (p. 23). There is more emphasis in the published book on the background of the club and on the misery the members faced in China; thus the function of the social organization was to offer solace so that "each week, we could hope to be lucky. That hope was our only joy. And that's how we came to call our little parties Joy Luck" (p. 25). Also missing in the magazine is the mother's instruction to her daughter that each person is made of five elements and the "organic chemistry" of each, too much fire resulting in a bad temper, for example (p. 31). This comment originally lent itself to the unifying structure of the volume, before Tan embraced the idea of using the Joy Luck Club itself as the framework for the integration of the stories. The magazine text did not include various suggestions about the lives of the other three families, perhaps since those episodes could not be even suggested in the reduced space of a magazine.

In its final form in the book, the function of "The Joy Luck Club" is in many ways the most complex of the sixteen stories since it must set the tone for those to follow, introduce the situation and strategy of narration, define the mothers and daughters who are the central players in the "present" action, and relate a conflict and motivational pattern that unifies and gives shape to the entire collection. It does so brilliantly. Since the stories in the first group are to be related by the mothers, there is a fundamental problem in the narration of this initial episode, since this mother, Suyuan Woo, has been dead for two months and thus cannot take her place at the mah jong table. At the urging of her father, Canning Woo, June (Jing-Mei) takes her mother's place, a psychologically complex substitution since June and her mother never understood each other. Far from meeting her mother's aspirations in America, it is clear that June feels herself very much a failure, lost in the new world, alienated from the old, adrift without an identity. She will have an opportunity to find herself in the chronicle of her mother, in the rich events and feelings Suyuan wanted to share with her daughter but, as was the case in the opening vignette, waited for the perfect moment for rendition.

She waited too long, until 1987, when her death prevents her from telling her own saga, so June tells it out of fragments of the tale her mother shared with her over the years. June speaks in English in the present tense when she tells about the meeting of the Joy Luck Club and in past tense when she recalls what her mother told her in Chinese. The situation is tragic: Suyuan died of a cerebral aneurysm eight weeks before, just as she was about to host the next meeting of the club, the group she had established in China to create a sense of good fortune when everything seemed hopeless. Now, in America, the meetings continue, and June has just become a key player. Suyuan's death is the first for the group, and it has delayed their meeting for two months. Significantly, however, June does not host the meeting in her mother's stead but relinquishes that role to An-Mei Hsu. June apparently feels incapable of managing the complexities of even such a routine social event.

Since the Joy Luck Club is the central motif of the volume, the occasion for the telling of the stories, and the structural principle for their organization, one of the first memories June relates is how her mother initiated the current version of the club in San Francisco in 1949, after all of the members had fled to the United States. What is clear is that the club has become an extended family for the sharing of their American lives and, perhaps more important, the means of preservation, through storytelling, of their tragic past in China. The parents have become surrogate aunts and uncles for all the daughters, and the families share the common generational and cultural problem of communication between parents and children from two different worlds. The central issue for the mothers is the desire to pass on their heritage to their daughters, to transmit their "accumulated wisdom and experience,"[16] to aid in establishing a sense of identity. As Carolyn See indicated in a particularly insightful review, the mothers' "deepest wish is to pass their knowledge, their tales, on to their children, especially to their daughters, but those young women are undergoing a slow death of their own, drowning in American culture at the same time they starve for a past they can never fully understand."[17] Thus the opening story contains two narrative threads: what June reveals about her relationship with her deceased mother; and the mother's story about the abandonment of babies in Kweilin. It is the tension between these two lines of action that is of greatest moment, for any hope of retrospective reconciliation between mother and daughter depends on June's capacity for insight and compassion, qualities she did not have at the time of her mother's death.

June tells the story in the way she had heard it, as a repeated tale that related only the beginning, that her husband was an army officer in the Kuomintang attempting to repel the Japanese invasion, and how, in the hardship of the war, she had formed the Joy Luck Club. When her mother told the account it always ended obliquely with pleasure in her skill at mah jong. June is skeptical about the veracity of the family legend: "I never thought my mother's Kweilin story was anything but a Chinese fairy tale" (p. 25). But then one evening her mother shared the rest of it, how she had abandoned two daughters by the road during the retreat. It is a powerful narrative, and it haunts June, calling for a resolution that comes only in the final pages of the book.

In that resolution rests the potential for June's psychological coherence, for some comprehension of her mother's loss, of why she so wanted June to excel, of why they do not understand each other. June's description of the meeting of the Joy Luck Club contains the foreshadowing of the ending. She recalls her mother's saying " 'you don't even know little percent of me!' " (p. 27), and yet June must now take her mother's place at the mah jong table, *be* her mother for an evening. June's grasp of her mother's identity will require a trip on two levels, a journey to China and a quest into herself, into her capacity to understand and empathize. As it turns out, both the Jongs and the Hsu family have made the trip back to China, and these journeys generate the necessity of June's passage to meet her Chinese sisters, financed in part by the generosity of the Joy Luck Club. This is the event that gives coherence to the entire volume and shape to June's psychological development.

The self-revelation that emerges from June's opening story reveals her sense of futility and lack of identity, for she has been a failure in her mother's eyes as well as in her own, not a "prodigy" to rival Waverly Jong, not the sensation on the piano her mother had wanted. In fact, she is awkwardly self-conscious when she arrives at the Hsus' for the evening: "They look up and laugh at me, always tardy, a child still at thirty six" (p. 27). Sitting at the mah jong table, she thinks about how she is a "college drop-off" with "half a degree in biology," a partial degree in art, and a mundane career as a copywriter. Her mother once told her she was "lazy to get up. You never rise to expectations," a failure to emulate the aspirations of the swan of the vignette (p. 31). On an elemental level, she knows she cannot play mah jong as well as her mother, which suggests metaphorically that she is not worthy of her mother in a larger sense. Still, within the narrative she relates there are indications of her inherent virtues, her sensitivity to others, as when she realizes that "Auntie Len is oblivious to Auntie An-mei's pain" (p. 36). She is aware of her own lack of understanding: "We translated each other's meanings and I seemed to hear less than what was said, while my mother heard more" (p. 37). She knows what she means to the other women in the club: "In me, they see their own daughters, just as ignorant, just as unmindful of all the truths and hopes they have brought to America. . . . They see daughters who will bear grandchildren born without any connecting hope passed from generation to generation" (pp. 40–41). In her expository comments, as much as in the narrative she tells, June reveals her redeeming awareness and sensitivity, qualities not fully realized at this point in the volume.

"The Scar" (pp. 42–48) is the first episode to be narrated directly by one of the mothers, An-Mei Hsu. Originally published in virtually the same form in the *San Francisco Focus* in 1988,[18] the story addresses not the mother-daughter issues of the Hsu family in America but the antecedent drama of an earlier generation, An-Mei's development of *shou*, respect for family, regard for her mother. The title refers to two scars: the one An-Mei got from boiling soup in 1918, and the more significant scar her mother lived with after cutting flesh from her own arm in a futile attempt to save her dying mother's life. There are thus three generations of mothers and scars and a fourth by implication, since there are many unresolved concerns between An-Mei and Rose in the present that parallel the Chinese events.

As was the case in the double story of "The Joy Luck Club," the two lines of action in "The Scar" resonate with thematic implications. The tale of a disgraced mother who demonstrates the utmost respect for a mother who has shunned her reverberates against the account of how An-Mei learned *shou* for her own mother. The irony is that An-Mei's mother was not shunned because of anything she did but rather because her first husband died and, in Chinese culture of the early twentieth century, she had no alternative but to become the third concubine of Wu Tsing, subordinate to his wife and two superior concubines. An-Mei is told that her mother is a ghost, a person so disgraced that the family is forbidden even to mention her name. As the Auntie tells An-Mei's brother, "you are the son of a mother who has so little respect she has become *ni*, a traitor to our ancestors. She is so beneath others that even the devil must look down to see her" (p. 44). This is the judgment that An-Mei's narration refutes, since it depicts the beauty of her mother, "this pretty woman with her white skin and oval face," the tenderness with which she caresses her daughter, the resolve with which she cuts the flesh from her arm to make a magic soup that will cure the grandmother.

As An-Mei says even in 1987, at the time of the telling, "I could see the pain of the flesh and the worth of the pain" (p. 48). The secondary implication is that it was this event that transformed An-Mei's attitude toward her mother, that taught her the true meaning of respect: "This is how a daughter honors her mother. It is *shou* so deep it is in your bones." An-Mei's account of the events of 1918, incidents that all of the mothers would clearly understand, has direct implications for the daughters of the Joy Luck Club in 1918: "Here is how I came to love my mother. How I saw in her my own true nature. What was beneath my skin. Inside my bones" (p. 48). The search for a sense of identity, the implications are, must begin with the relationship between mother and daughter.

The story that Lindo Jong tells, "The Red Candle" (pp. 49–66), is the first to be presented as an explicit statement from mother to daughter, with an agenda directly related to issues in 1987. Lindo would not seem to be speaking at the same Joy Luck Club meeting as in "The Joy Luck Club" because there is no indication that the daughter, Waverly, is present on that occasion. Lindo speaks at an unknown point, during Waverly's pregnancy, a propitious moment for a tale of marriage and woe, resourcefulness and inner strength. Since the Jongs have recently been to China and show their photographs at the club meeting, these memories would be particularly strong at the time of the telling.

The story begins "I once sacrificed my life to keep my parents' promise. This means nothing to you, because to you promises mean nothing" (p. 49). The development of the latter conflict, the bitterness, the sense of neglect, awaits subsequent stories. Instead, "The Red Candle" explores the first idea, sacrifice for the honor of the family. The time of the action is in the distant past in China. Born in 1918, Lindo was betrothed through the intercession of the village matchmaker when she was only two, an event that occasions a sense of distance within the family. Her own mother begins to treat her as though she is the daughter of her prospective mother-in-law, Huang Taitai. Since Lindo rebels against the arranged marriage, she is never emotionally part of either family and must find her identity within herself rather than in a preexisting structure. All of this becomes evident in 1930, when Lindo is sent to live with the Huangs, to begin an apprenticeship to become the wife of Tyan-yu. She leaves home with only a key artifact, a necklace of red jade, which assumes an important value later in the book.

The central theme that emerges as Lindo turns sixteen and marries is her strong sense of personal identity, her resolve to escape her circumstances without violating the promises between the two families, her resourcefulness in anticipating the motives of others, and her ability to manipulate the situation to her own advantage, qualities she passed on to her daughter, a prodigy in chess. In the background is the Japanese invasion of 1934, an event that more directly affects Suyuan Woo in the first story but here simply prevents the wedding guests from attending. It is clear from the beginning that the Huangs will be no match for the strength of Lindo: "I was strong. I was pure. I had genuine thoughts inside that no one could see, that no one could ever take away from me." It is this quality that sustains her in the wedding ceremony, when she would seem to have sealed her fate forever: "I still knew who I was. I made a promise to myself: I would always remember my parents' wishes, but I would never forget myself" (p. 58). The unifying conflict thus centers on the logistical strategy of manipulation, of discovering a way to escape the marriage without violating the promise her family had made. She finds that opportunity in the desire of the Huangs for an heir and in their belief in the providential power of dreams. Lindo invents a dream that uses the prevailing circumstances of a pregnant servant girl, a mole on the back of Tyan-yu, and her own desire to escape to convince the Huang family to free her and marry their son to the servant, which they do. As Lindo explains, "I got my clothes, a rail ticket to Peking, and enough money to go to America" (p. 66). Lindo was true to her major quest: "I promised not to forget myself." Her comment, in one dimension, is a message to her daughter.

Lindo's revelation of a strong identity is juxtaposed to Ying-Ying St. Clair's tale of the submerged self in "The Moon Lady" (pp. 67–89), a haunting story of passivity and ineffability that explains something of the enigmatic comment by June Woo in the opening story that "auntie Ying has always been the weird auntie, someone lost in her own world" (p. 35). She tells about how she became lost in China, an unknown child plucked from a surrealistic lake during the moon festival. This tale is not about a conflict with her mother, nor even precisely about the "loss" of self, since the issue seems to be that she had never established a sense of her own being. Even before the events of the Moon Festival, when she falls off a party boat into Tai Lake, she longs for a firm personality and seeks to ask the legendary Moon Lady how she came to lose herself (p. 83). These events happened in 1918, when Ying-Ying was only four, but they dominate her life even at the time of the telling in 1987, and they invest the life of her daughter, Lena, as well: "We are lost, she and I, unseen and not seeing, unheard and not hearing, unknown by others" (p. 67). On one level, the rendition itself is a quest for identity, for expression and understanding, for connection with a daughter who lives in an incomprehensible world of Sony Walkmans and cordless phones.

It is ironic that it is Ying-Ying who has the deepest problems of the mothers, for she is by far the most affluent of the four, born into a family with a handsome house, with a scholarly father who keeps several concubines, with nursemaids to tend the children from his various wives. Living in Wushi, near Shanghai in the south of China, the family has the resources to enjoy handsome clothes and good food. Ying-Ying's weak ego may derive from their very affluence, for instead of a close relationship with her mother, who has little to do with her, she is tended by her Amah, a nursemaid whose widowhood required her to abandon her own son to survive (p. 73). Ying-Ying is a child obsessed with finding herself, playing with her shadow, attempting to explore her forbidden willfulness and selfish desires: "I loved my shadow, this dark side of me that had my same restless nature" (p. 72).

But the key incident takes place the evening of the Moon Festival when, startled by firecrackers, Ying-Ying falls into the lake. Lost in the darkness, her absence not noticed amid the celebrations, she realizes her insignificance: "I had seen nobody who cared that I was missing. . . . And I now felt I was lost forever" (p. 79). After she is rescued by fishermen, she wanders the shore and observes a surrealistic play depicting a Moon Lady who is doomed to "stay lost on the moon, forever seeking her own selfish wishes" (p. 81). In the highly gendered values of Chinese society, there is a sharp distinction between the roles of men and women: "For woman is yin, . . . the darkness within, where untempered passions lie. And man is yang, bright truth lighting our minds" (p. 81). Even when she is found by her family, she says her deepest feeling is that "I never believed my family found the same girl" (p. 82). Ying-Ying internalizes the thought that she is living someone else's life, that she is not herself, that her true being was somehow lost in the lake.

The first section of *The Joy Luck Club* is thus a study of contrasting character types and social levels in episodes that focus on the central issue of identity and on the mothers' desire to communicate with their daughters. Suyuan Woo's account of being forced to abandon her daughters on the rode to Kweilin contrasts sharply with An-Mei Hsu's tale of a familial loyalty so strong that her mother cut her own flesh in an attempt to save her mother. Lindo Wong's narrative of cleverness and manipulation, her strong personality, resonates against Ying-Ying's story of the loss of self. But all of the stories reveal the mothers' purposes in speaking for the edification of their daughters, conveying the Chinese wisdom they need to survive in the new world, needs not fully outlined until the daughters begin to tell about their own lives.

The central narrative "logic" of the four stories differs, however. The structural principle of the book would imply that the tales are related at the Joy Luck Club, but in only the first of these episodes would that seem to be the case, and then only in part, in the information that Jing-Mei is given by the other mothers. Her rendition of her mother's background is essentially an internal reminiscence rather than a dramatic expression at the mah jong table. Lindo Jong's "The Red Candle" seems spoken directly to her daughter, Waverly, whereas the other two narratives would seem to constitute what the mothers would say if only their daughters would listen. But all of the stories serve the dual purpose of the mothers' expression of self and the attempt to inform and assist the daughters in their struggle for identity and assimilation in the new world.

The second set of four stories, united under the title "The Twenty-Six Malignant Gates," are all told by the daughters in narrative counterpoint to the first group. The vignette that introduces the stories once again suggests some of the themes to follow. On the literal level, it recounts a mother who warns her young daughter not to ride her bicycle far from the house. When questioned, the mother says that a book written in Chinese entitled *The Twenty-Six Malignant Gates* contains a warning about all of the bad things that can happen to the daughter beyond familial protection. The young girl scoffs, rides away, and falls before she reaches the first corner (p. 86). Taken more broadly, that it contains not only a warning from mother to daughter but a caution based on Chinese lore, written in Chinese, a language the daughter does not understand, and that it is ignored by the girl, foreshadows the conflicts in the stories that follow. The persistence of Chinese philosophy in the lives of the mothers in America and the rejection of ancient values by the Americanized daughters constitute the foundation for the central dilemma of the entire volume.

During the early stages of composition, "Rules of the Game" (pp. 89–101) was entitled "End Game," a term with references both to the final stage of a chess match, when a player's superior strategy has maneuvered the opponent into an inescapable and indefensible position, and to the final stage of any human interaction, such as that between a mother and a daughter. The story was first published as "End Game" in *FM Five* in the spring of 1986 with the proud notation that "Amy Tan lives in San Francisco. This is her first published story."[19] There were only minor differences between this version and that in the final volume. Significantly, when the story appeared in *Seventeen* magazine in November of that year, three years before book publication, the text was in somewhat dissimilar form, with many word changes, with paragraphs in a different order, and with two fairly substantial sections of the final version missing in the magazine.[20] The first dealt with the Chinatown neighborhood in San Francisco, with its fish markets and playgrounds, both notable in the lives of the local children, and with the related issue that Lindo took her daughter's name from the street they lived on, Waverly Place. Thus she became Waverly Place Jong, an identity with American significance, but at home she was called "Meimei," Chinese for "little sister," since she was the youngest child (pp. 90–91). The second section missing in the magazine relates to how Waverly became obsessed with chess and how she would spend hours in imaginary battles, contemplating her moves with mythical opponents. Her brothers, on the other hand, seem to have become thoroughly Westernized, as their names suggest: "Winston and Vincent decided they were more interested in roaming the streets after school in their Hopalong Cassidy cowboy hats" (p. 95). But the fundamental elements of the plot were essentially the same as in the book.

The story concerns the inception of Waverly Jong's career as a chess champion, how she began to play and how she inherited a capacity for calculation and an indomitable will from her mother, which allowed the girl to become a tournament winner at a very young age. As Waverly explains about herself, "I learned why it is essential in the endgame to have foresight, a mathematical understanding of all possible moves, and patience; all weaknesses and advantages become evident to a strong adversary and are obscured to a tiring opponent" (p. 94). The secondary level, which becomes more important than the first, is how she came to engage in a battle of will with her mother, something Waverly began without knowing the endgame, without seeing the consequences of her actions. Both of these implications are also present in the title "Rules of the Game," albeit with less emphasis on calculation, on being able to perceive the final resolution of the conflict. Instead, there is somewhat more relevance of the title to the theme of immigration, as when Lindo Jong comments on the book of chess regulations that her daughter has been studying: " 'This American rules,' she concluded at last. 'Every time people come out from foreign country, must know rules' " (p. 94). Chess becomes the metaphor for how mother and daughter relate to each other and how an immigrant from China will make a place in American society: "It is a game of secrets in which one must show and never tell" (p. 95).

"Rules of the Game," the first story that Waverly Jong narrates, is doubly enriched by juxtaposition, since it must be compared not only to the other stories told by the daughters but to her mother's story in "The Red Candle" as well. Lindo's complex tale of calculation and manipulation, revealing her strong sense of identity, is a perfect prelude to Waverly's account of becoming a chess champion. She does so on the basis of the "invisible strength" her mother gave her, powers of commitment, concentration, determination, and pride. Despite their home in an alley in a grubby section of San Francisco's Chinatown, Waverly possesses the confidence to aspire to superiority in chess, and she wins all of the local tournaments on the way to the national championship. Born on March 17, 1951, by her ninth birthday in 1960 she has her photograph in *Life* magazine, and her life would seem to be one of unqualified success.

In a relationship involving two such strong personalities, the inevitable struggle is that of control and resentment. Lindo takes pride in her daughter's success, attending every contest, freeing Waverly from household duties to concentrate on her chess. With the perversity of childhood perception, however, Waverly resents the pride that her mother takes in all this success, saying " 'Why do you have to use me to show off?' " (p. 99). At that point Waverly runs away from her mother, literally and metaphorically, leaving her isolated at the end of the story: "I closed my eyes and pondered my next move" (p. 101).

What enriches the conflict is the haunting resonance of Lindo's struggle against domineering forces in "The Red Candle" and her ability to maneuver her way to victory, a skill Waverly possesses in chess but not in family life, where she chooses direct confrontation. She does not transfer the wisdom of the calculated position from chess to her own life, the awareness that "for the whole game one must gather invisible strengths and see the endgame before the game begins" (p. 94). In the language of her narrative, Waverly seems to acknowledge that much of her power in chess derives from her cultural legacy, and she uses the language of mah jong to describe her approach to the new game, describing the movement of pieces in terms of the "winds" that blow in mah jong. At the same time, her mother's pride violates the etiquette of chess that Waverly learns so painfully, particularly the proscription against hubris: "Never announce 'Check' with vanity, lest someone with an unseen sword slit your throat" (p. 95). But the direct confrontation with her mother produces only ostracism: Lindo says to the other members of the family, " 'we not concerning this girl. This girl not have concerning for us' " (p. 100). They have reached a stalemate of familial dissent, and Waverly's only thought is the dream of escape that concludes the story.

Lena St. Clair's "The Voice from the Wall" (pp. 102–15) illustrates the intertextual resonance of the short-story cycle in that it can be fully understood only in the context of her mother's tale in "The Moon Lady." Ying-Ying's weak identity and loss of self when she falls into Tai Lake during the Moon Festival has developed into chronic psychological pathology by the time Lena is five. In contrast to Waverly Jong's intense assertion of her own strong will, Lena's narrative is largely about her mother in America, about her paranoia and destructive passivity.

Even as a young child, Lena reveals, she thought of her mother as lacking an identity, as a woman chased by "unspoken terrors" that "devoured her, piece by piece, until she disappeared and became a ghost" (p. 103). The world conspires to deny identity to Ying-Ying, from the designation of "displaced person" given to her at the Angel Island Immigration Station to the change of her name on the official papers from Gu Ying-Ying to Betty St. Clair. Ying-Ying is displaced even within the Chinese American community since she speaks Mandarin and everyone else Cantonese. But beyond dialect, her ineffability requires her husband to speak for her, articulating what he thinks she might want to say, denying her the expression of self once again (p. 106). That she marries a white American and moves to an Italian neighborhood further compounds her confusion of self. The destructiveness of her pathology is nowhere more evident than in her obsession with sex and pregnancy. When Lena was five her mother told her a horrifying tale about a bad man in the basement, one who "would have planted five babies in me and then eaten us all in a six-course meal, tossing our bones on the dirty floor" (p. 103). Now the mother is obsessed with her own pregnancy and her attempts to destroy her unborn baby: "My mother began to bump into things, into table edges as if she forgot her stomach contained a baby . . ." (p. 109). It is not surprising, at least metaphorically, that her infant is born without a brain, with no capacity for self-awareness, and it does not survive. The guilt and shock from this event drive the mother insane, and that status, predictable from the beginning, remains the dominant fact about her.

But the story is Lena's to narrate, and, in the course of telling about her mother, she reveals a good deal about herself, about her own problems with "identity." The child of a Chinese-American mother and an English-Irish-American father, Lena has a culturally split heritage, although she primarily sees life with "Chinese eyes" (p. 103). The move into an Italian section of San Francisco when she is ten enriches her exposure to other ethnic groups at the same time it causes confusion. Unaccustomed to the emotional exuberance of Italian families, she construes their loud exchanges as murderous violence, only to be stunned when she overhears their loving reconciliations: "I could almost see them hugging and kissing one another. I was crying for joy with them, because I had been wrong" (p. 115). As the previous stories often conclude with a dream or vision, so does Lena's, a fantasy that reveals her central obsession: "I saw a girl complaining that the pain of not being seen was unbearable" (p. 115). But beyond her own need for identity, she imagines herself saving her mother, showing her the worst that can happen, killing her with a thousand cuts and pulling her back from the other side free from fear. But these are only the imaginings of a young girl who loves her mother.

The episode told by Rose Hsu Jordan, "Half and Half" (pp. 116–31), is a confessional of indecisiveness and guilt that is ironic when compared to her mother's memory of the enormous determination of the grandmother, who cut flesh from her arm to make soup. "Half and Half" is a double narrative of how her mother lost her faith in God and how Rose lost her faith in herself, in her ability to make decisions. Her indecisiveness is responsible for the collapse of her marriage to Ted and, at least in part, for the death of her younger brother, Bing.

Rose's story is essentially a series of reminiscences told from the narrative present in 1987, a specific moment in the present that she identifies as "tonight" (p. 116). She is not at the Joy Luck Club, however, but at her mother's apartment, where she has come to inform her family about her impending divorce, something she does not finally disclose to them. Rather, the pain of this situation allows her to recall an even greater loss when she was fourteen and in charge of tending young Bing on the beach. Distracted for an instant, Rose allows Bing to fall from a dangerous reef, where he disappears forever. Her indecisiveness prevents her from shouting while there is still time to rescue him, and he is swept under the waves (p. 126). Attempting to sustain hope, her mother recalls a miracle in China of a boy who had his hand restored after an accident, and she is certain that her Christian faith, embodied in a white Bible, will wrest her child from the sea. When it does not, she consigns the book to the floor, supporting the leg of a table.

The other half of the story belongs to Rose, who feels herself to be American, not Chinese. But her reticence is at least in part a cultural variation, strongly at odds with her husband's self-assurance and assertiveness. He comes to resent her passivity, snapping at one point "How the hell did we ever get married? Did you just say 'I do' because the minister said 'repeat after me'?" (p. 120). Rose feels guilt over her role in the death of her brother and for the loss of her marriage: "I know now that I had never expected to find Bing, just as I know now I will never find a way to save my marriage" (p. 130). Once again the daughter's weak personality is a major factor in causing pain in her life.

"Two Kinds" (pp. 132–44), the story that Jing-Mei Woo tells to end the second section, resonates against Rose's rendition of indecisiveness as well as Suyuan Woo's opening account of the abandonment of her daughters.[21] What Jing-Mei loses is her relationship with her mother, and her mother loses the dream of having a prodigy for a daughter, an aspiration born of the idea that in America anything is possible. There is a good deal of humor in the mother's attempts to make her daughter into first a Chinese Shirley Temple with a bad haircut and then a virtuoso taught by a deaf piano teacher. At the disastrous recital, attended by all the members of the Joy Luck Club, Jing-Mei first sees the depth of disappointment in her mother: ". . . My mother's expression was what devastated me: a quiet, blank look that said she had lost everything" (p. 140). But there is further loss for Suyuan as Jing-Mei shouts at her "I wish I wasn't your daughter. I wish you weren't my mother," and then, to move past what can never be taken back, she adds that she wishes she were dead like the abandoned babies in China (p. 142).

The rich drama of this encounter is heightened by an awareness that at the time Jing-Mei relates her story in 1987, her mother is already dead. The daughter is thus dealing with her remorse at having disappointed her mother: "I failed her so many times" (p. 142). In the relating of her narrative, however, Jing-Mei expresses her point of view in the conflict, that she had come to accept her limitations when her mother could not, that she was determined to sustain her own sense of identity: "I won't let her change me, I promised myself. I won't be what I'm not" (p. 134). At the beginning of the piano lessons she pleads her case with her mother: " 'Why don't you like me the way I am? I'm *not* a genius!" (p. 136). It is only through reference to "The Joy Luck Club" that she can find an answer, that perhaps if she is exceptional it will fill the void left by the abandoned daughters. Jing-Mei has not yet come to this understanding, but it offers her the only opportunity of reconciliation with her mother's desires and her own sense of personal wholeness.

The four stories by the daughters in "The Twenty-Six Malignant Gates" do not constitute a direct answer to those by the mothers in the opening section. Rather, they suggest thematic counterpoint: American stories to offset the tales of China; struggles to establish a personal identity set against the acceptance of cultural norms; will against obedience. The aspirations of the mothers in the opening vignette are countered by the rejection of ancient values in the second one, just as the two groups of four stories show the differing perspectives of mothers and daughters. But these episodes also establish other significant points, particularly that the time of the telling in 1987 is a progressive present, so that not all the events of the book have taken place as these four stories are told: Rose has not yet divorced Ted; June has not yet left for China. The retrospective scenes reach back in time, but almost entirely into the American past in these four stories, unlike the opening group. Within the section there are psychological variations of being a Chinese daughter in America, with Lena feeling the loss of her mother and Rose aware of her weak sense of self, while Jing-Mei and Waverly exhibit defiance of their mothers and a fierce determination to express their will. The next set of four stories deepens these conflicts.

The third section of stories, grouped under the title "American Translation," is introduced by a vignette that unites Chinese folklore with predictive powers and a concern for generational continuity. A Chinese-American mother is concerned by the mirror at the foot of the bed of her daughter because "all your marriage happiness will bounce back and turn the opposite way" (p. 147). The mother solves the problem by placing another mirror at the head of the bed that allows her to see the future and to bring the "peach-blossom luck" that will assure a child the next year. These central issues, the desires of the mother, Chinese folklore, marital relations, children, and the sustaining concept of "luck" constitute the unifying themes of this section of the book, a group of four episodes narrated by the daughters.

The close connection between vignette and story is evident in the first sentence of "Rice Husband" (pp. 149–65), the second tale told by Lena St. Clair: "To this day, I believe my mother has the mysterious ability to see things before they happen" (p. 149). The temporal moment referred to in "this day" is the time of the telling in the progressive present: Lena tells only "memories" in retrospect; the "current action" is related as the events unfold. This device is particularly meaningful in that the mother is purported to see the future, although what she actually sees is the turmoil at the base of her daughter's marriage, discontent that predictably disrupts the stability of the union. That Lena reiterates an idea from Chinese folklore suggests the extent to which Oriental values from the past play a role in the "present" American action.

That concept functions even in the title in that the meaning of "Rice Husband" emerges only in the context of a flashback to when Lena was eight and her mother peered into her rice bowl and said that her daughter would marry a bad man (p. 151). Although the point at that moment would seem to be the familiar strategy of a parent attempting to get a daughter to eat all of her food, the power of the prediction raises complex issues of causation, whether tragedy is a personal responsibility, generated by a pattern of mistakes freely chosen, or whether it is somehow determined by external forces, Fate or Luck or the Gods. These alternatives, which invest classical tragedy in the Western tradition, also seem inherent in the philosophical matrix of the East.

What Lena chose, with such character as she had, was her marriage to Harold Livotny, an architect who is obsessed with money, a somewhat hyperbolic expression of American merchantilism. That the preservation of capital will be one of his main themes is clear even in the wedding ceremonies, in which they marry at city hall (no rental fees to pay), have photographs taken by a friend (rather than a professional photographer), and hold the reception at their apartment (BYOB). Predictably, they sign a prenuptial agreement that gives Harold the advantage, a detail that suggests that even in romance his obsession is with money, while her interest is in the relationship.

This flashback leads to the conflict of the present, the visit of Ying-Ying to her daughter and the discovery of the accounting documents on the refrigerator door, listing expenditures on various household items. Ying-Ying objects to the entire scheme, but even within the financial plan she can see the injustice of his listing "ice cream" as an item of his purchase since Lena does not eat it, which her mother points out: " 'She become so thin now you cannot see her,' says my mother. 'She like a ghost, disappear' " (p. 163). Several things are significant about this observation: the literal financial application; the metaphoric suggestions that Lena's identity is submerged in this relationship; the intertextual reference to "The Voice from the Wall" in which this precise language was used to describe Ying-Ying's paranoia with the threat of imagined terrors that "devoured her, piece by piece, until she disappeared and became a ghost" (p. 103). The referential suggestion is that Lena's life is beginning to recapitulate that of her mother.

The concluding metaphor, not fully explained until Ying-Ying tells her final story in the last section, deals with the marble end table Harold made when he was young: it appears valuable, with its marble top, but it is vulnerable, standing on rickety legs. The mother is upstairs, in the bedroom with the table, while her daughter is downstairs, just beginning the fight that will eventually dissolve her marriage, when the table crashes to the floor, interrupting the argument. The strong suggestion of the context is that the mother, hesitating to intervene in her daughter's marriage, has something she wishes to say. She says it, by implication, in the demonstration of how unstable Harold's prize table really is. " 'I knew it would happen,' " Lena says of the broken furniture. " 'Then why you don't stop it?' " the mother asks, the meaning clear. Once again the superior wisdom of the mother has been brought to bear on the life of a daughter, who knows more about the ways of America but not as much about how to live.

The title of Waverly Jong's story in this group, "Four Directions" (pp. 166–84), resonates from the central metaphor of the collection, the four directions employed in the game of mah jong, the four directions in Chinese culture that Waverly used to steel her concentration in chess, the four directions the mothers took in their approach to Chinese society, the four directions taken by the daughters in attempting to survive in modern American society while sustaining an honorable relationship with their mothers. It is also a specific reference to the Four Directions Restaurant where Waverly and her mother meet for lunch in the opening scene. In the background of the interaction of mother and daughter is the intertextual allusion to Lindo's manipulation and strong sense of identity in "The Red Candle" and Waverly's calculation in chess and family life and subsequent war of wills with her mother in "Rules of the Game."

To spite her mother, Waverly had quit chess at fourteen, misinterpreting the strategy her mother would employ to encourage her to resume playing. Throughout their conversation it continues to be evident that Lindo is the stronger of the two personalities and that her capacity to manipulate has not abated, although Waverly has scored some points. Rather than a continuous narrative beginning with the disastrous lunch, the story consists primarily of a series of reflections on previous events, all of which have a bearing on Waverly's decisions in the present. The mother's displeasure with the food at the lunch has its corollary in her distaste for the key decisions Waverly has made over the years, including the time when Waverly quit playing chess, failed to force her mother to beg her to resume playing, and then went back to the game only to discover that she had lost her supreme concentration and her desire to win, at which point she stopped for good (p. 173).

The "new" experiences she recounts fill in some of the key events of her life in the intervening years, how she eloped with her high school sweetheart, Marvin Chen, when she was only eighteen (p. 174). Now, in the "present" of the story in 1987, her daughter, Shoshana, is four, and Waverly is contemplating marriage to Rich Schields. It is significant that her marriage within the Chinese-American community was not a success and that she has a strong emotional bond with an "American" who is not only generally obtuse but woefully oblivious to the values and traditions of Chinese culture. This point is made in two painfully comic scenes. The first is when Waverly attempts to introduce the subject of her relationship with Rich through the rather obvious strategy of giving her mother a tour of their apartment, with his possessions much in evidence. The results are unsatisfactory: Lindo even questions the quality of the mink coat Rich has given her daughter: " 'This is not so good,' she said at last. 'It is just leftover strips. And the fur is too short, no long hairs' " (p. 169). Waverly's attempt to seize the emotional advantage does not work: " 'He gave me this from his heart,' " she objects, only to have her mother observe " 'That is why I worry' " (p. 169). Lindo has outmaneuvered her daughter once again.

The second scene, the dinner episode, is more purely comic, although with somber implications. To bring together mother and future husband, Waverly concocts a scheme to get Rich invited to lunch at Suyuan Woo's home, a fact that clarifies that the "present" action precedes that of "The Joy Luck Club," in which Suyuan has been dead for two months. After the lunch, Waverly, always calculating, writes to Suyuan to thank her for her hospitality and includes the information that " 'Rich said it was the best Chinese food he has ever tasted,' " knowing that this comment would get passed on to Lindo in the never-ending culinary competition of the members of the Joy Luck Club. The gambit works, and Waverly and Rich are invited to dinner, a comic disaster in which Rich exhibits a fertile imagination for the faux pas, from bringing French wine to a Chinese banquet, to calling the parents by their first names, to putting soy sauce on Lindo's celebrated pork and vegetable dish. In the ensuing psychological negotiations, as Waverly seeks approval of her plan to marry Rich, she comes to see her relationship with her mother as a chess match in which her mother always has the advantage: "In her hands, I always became the pawn. I could only run away. And she was the queen, able to move in all directions, relentless in her pursuit, always able to find my weakest spots" (p. 180). This battle inspires two realizations for Waverly: that from the beginning she has been fighting for her individuality, some expression of her own prerogatives; and that, despite her mother's formidable weapons, she has also become simply "an old woman, a wok for her armor, a knitting needle for her sword, getting a little crabby as she waited patiently for her daughter to invite her in" (pp. 183–84). The story thus ends in indecision, the wedding postponed, the mother maneuvering for an invitation to join them on a honeymoon to China, Waverly looking forward to her new marriage but also seeking reconciliation, wholeness, in her relationship with her mother (p. 184).

The opening line of "Without Wood" (pp. 185–96), told by Rose Hsu Jordan, echoes that of "Rice Husband." It begins, "I used to believe everything my mother said, even when I didn't know what she meant" (p. 185). In contrast to Waverly's turbulent struggle for control with her mother, Rose's weak personality presents other difficulties. Rose initially tells about her youth, when her fears made it difficult to sleep, to enter into the realm of the mythical Mr. Chou, the guardian of dreams. But Rose does sleep, and she dreams of independence from her mother, choosing, in her fantasy, a doll different from the one predicted by her mother. At the time of the telling this struggle for an independent will is not over, and its application involves Rose's divorce from her husband, Ted.

It is significant that in the rendition she chooses to tell, one of independence from her mother's domineering will, Rose portrays her mother in prescient terms. When Rose reveals that Ted sends her a check every month, An-Mei says "He is doing monkey business with someone else" (p. 188), which turns out to be true. In contrast, what she reveals about herself is that she still lacks substance. When she tells

Waverly of her enduring love for Ted, Waverly says "You want my opinion, you're better off without him" (p. 189). She then tells Lena that she is better off without Ted, having adopted Waverly's attitude, and Lena advises her to hire an attorney and sue for everything she can get, which she does. When she relates all of this to her psychiatrist (An-Mei calls him a "psyche-atricks"), he is bored and suggests that they talk about it next week (p. 189).

Nowhere in all of this does she express her own desires, her own judgment about the course of her life. Significantly, she dislikes American freedom of opinion because "there were too many choices, so it was easy to get confused and pick the wrong thing" (p. 191). The dissolution of a marriage of fifteen years is a significant development, but Rose needs the encouragement of her mother to speak for herself. But it is not until she discovers her husband's infidelity, that he *was* doing monkey business with someone else, that she can assert herself for the first time, declaring that she, not he, will get their house in the divorce settlement. This time her assertiveness leaves him confused, "the power of my words was that strong" (p. 196). This plot is the most linear in the book in that it consists simply of the rendition of past action, revealing her childhood weakness, and then picks up the current action involving the divorce and her final assertion of herself, with only a few brief interruptions of remembered conversations. The energy is directed toward the revelation of self, the first significant moment of strength Rose has experienced, and that expression is the focal point toward which the narrative moves.

The story that concludes this section is "Best Quality" (pp. 197–209), told by Jing-Mei Woo five months after the Chinese New Year, three months after the death of her mother, and a month after she tells "The Joy Luck Club." Jing-Mei is thirty-six at the time of the telling, still in the process of finding herself, still searching for her "life's importance," the term her mother used for the jade pendant she gave her daughter at the New Year celebration. It is significant that Jing-Mei still ponders the meaning of the pendant, as though within its inscriptions and carvings could be found the meaning of her existence. It is also important that what she tells is as much about her mother as it is about her; in a sense, the deceased mother is kept alive in narrative, still cooking dinner, holding forth with her opinions, reviewing the events of her life, although this account does not address the key issue of her past, the abandoned daughters in China.

Instead, Jing-Mei chooses to depict the events surrounding the New Year celebration five months before the telling, a dinner held in the apartment building owned by the Woo family. Much of what is related is, in a sense, mundane, the routine squabbles between tenants and landlady, the mysterious disappearance of a troublesome cat, the perception that tenants use too much hot water. But these details become meaningful at the end when Jing-Mei, making dinner for her father, experiences many of the same annoyances as her mother, thinking of the tenants what her mother expressed as " 'even you don't want them, you stuck.' And now I know what she meant" (p. 209). When the cat the mother allegedly had poisoned appears once again at the window, Jing-Mei feels her mother has been vindicated. In taking her place, sharing her role and her feelings, Jing-Mei begins the process of emotional reconciliation that was prevented by her mother's death.

But the heart of the story deals with Jing-Mei's self-revelation, a confession of character weaknesses and disappointments that must be very painful to disclose. The key scene is the New Year celebration when Suyuan invites the Jongs over for crab dinner, a group that includes not only Lindo and Tin but Waverly and her daughter, Shoshana, Waverly's fiancé, Rich Schields, and old Mr. Chong, the deaf piano teacher so crucial in "Two Kinds." There is thus much present at the table: the unspoken abandoned daughters; the role of Waverly as prodigy in chess; Jing-Mei's disastrous piano recital; the calamity among the Jongs at Rich's performance at the family dinner; and Jing-Mei's general sense that she is a failure and a disappointment to her mother.

The daughter's disenchantment is well illustrated in the incident of choosing a crab for dinner and in her attempt to settle a score with Waverly about an outstanding bill for some advertising copy Jing-Mei had done. In the matter of the crab, Jing-Mei watches as Waverly chooses the best ones from the serving bowl for her party, and then Jing-Mei picks the worst one for herself, the crab missing a leg. Her mother switches with her, so that her daughter can have a proper dinner. The significance of this incident is that it is revelatory of Jing-Mei's sense of her own worth, a matter not lost on Suyuan: " 'Only *you* pick that crab. Nobody else take it. I already know this. Everybody else want best quality. You thinking different' " (p. 208). The mother's sense of values apparently does not include the idea of self-sacrifice for the benefit of others.

The attempt to settle scores with Waverly fares no better. Even the seemingly innocent discussion of hairdressers becomes a struggle between the two, as when Waverly suggests that Jing-Mei is taking a risk in going to a gay hairdresser (p. 204). That idea segues into the issue of professional success when Waverly says " 'you should go see my guy . . . although he probably charges more than you're used to' " (p. 204). Jing-Mei's attempt at revenge is to humiliate Waverly about the unpaid bill, but even that backfires when Waverly reveals that the firm was dissatisfied with the quality of the ad, that Jing-Mei lacks inventiveness in her copy. The final humiliation is when Shoshana begins banging on the piano, the one Jing-Mei was supposed to use to become a prodigy, and old Mr. Chong praises her, bringing back all the old issues of the competition between Waverly and Jing-Mei. All of this leads her to an epiphany: "That was the night, in the kitchen, that I realized I was no better than who I was. I was a copywriter," and one who can handle only routine cases (p. 207). Jing-Mei's narration ends in dissatisfaction, with her resignation to her inferior status, with her sense of failure to fulfill her mother's ambitions.

These four stories told by the daughters thus provide resolution to the issue of parental guidance, with all of the young women failing to succeed in the ways the mothers had envisioned. Lena and Rose are perched on the edge of divorce in unsatisfactory marriages, while in the background their mothers hover with counsel from Chinese tradition about the importance of permanence, the depth of familial obligation. Waverly, on the other hand, is about to embark on a new marriage with a grossly unsuitable young man, at least from Lindo's perspective. June, the most introspective but always the least sure of herself, receives her "life's importance" from her mother in the form of a jade pendant, but she still feels unworthy, inadequate to take her place in the world. These episodes are unified by the narrative perspectives of the four daughters, by the themes of failure within family responsibilities, and by the final statements by the daughters about the direction of their lives.

The final section provides the concluding observations of their mothers and offers not so much a resolution of these themes as an enrichment of them, events that suggest not closure but the opening of possibilities. The vignette that precedes the stories suggests two important ideas, the fulfillment of the desire of the mother for a grandchild, made explicit in the vignette for "American Translation" (p. 147), and the most important lesson the mother has to offer her daughter: "How to lose your innocence but not your hope" (p. 213). Involved in these ideas are the collateral matters of the importance of self-knowledge, particularly an awareness that one shares in human weaknesses, a concept important in American literature since the fiction of Nathaniel Hawthorne, and the mystical notion of the transmigration of souls, that the infant is actually "Syi Wang Mu, Queen Mother of the Western Skies, now come back to give me the answer!" The humanistic expression of these themes might be that mother and daughter have much to teach each other, as becomes clear in the stories that follow, three of them told by the mothers, with Suyuan Woo's concluding episode related by Jing-Mei.

What is immediately apparent about "Magpies," told by An-Mei Hsu, is that its central focus is not about her relationship with her daughter. The main conflict for Rose, her indecisiveness, her weak sense of self, her struggle with the husband she is divorcing, is resolved in her declaration that she is going to keep the house despite the fact that Ted wants it (p. 196). Although the story begins with Rose, with her grief, her visits to a psychiatrist, An-Mei's primary interest is in the continuity of past and present. An-Mei realizes that she is much like her mother, as Rose is much like her: "All of us are like stairs, one step after another, going up and down, but all going the same way" (p. 215). An-Mei's ruminations about the past thus bring together four generations: Rose, An-Mei, her mother, and Popo, whose illness prompted her daughter to put her own flesh in the soup in a vain attempt to save her. Nearing the end of her life, concerned about her daughter, An-Mei reviews the familial history, searching for answers.

What she finds is that her own mother faced problems and humiliations far greater than those that drive Rose to her psychiatrist; even in her despair, there was much love in the mother, love for the grandmother, love for An-Mei. It is clear that the cultural norms of Chinese society present obstacles for the mother, since she had once been the honored first wife of a scholar, but his death, and the restriction on remarriage for a widow, force her to become a concubine. The fact that she is third concubine, and fourth wife, to Wu Tsing, and that he in turn takes a fifth wife, brings such pain to the mother that she commits suicide. That is the key event in the family history, not Rose's divorce, and it suggests a legacy of humiliation and ineffectuality that is finally resolved in Rose's declaration about the house.

In narrative terms, what is significant about the plot is that it is not a single act of reiteration and action but an assemblage of smaller units, originally recited by a variety of tellers. An-Mei addresses the "present" in the opening segment about Rose, recalling the conversation between them that took place "yesterday" (p. 215). But the focus quickly shifts from 1987 to 1927, when An-Mei's mother returned home for the death of Popo, when she cut her arm for the soup, the subject of "Scar." Within this memory are other tales, those of the magic turtle who eats their tears and knows of their sorrows and of the magpies who emerge from the turtle to drink the water from the pond. The myth is clearly an attempt on the part of the mother to instruct An-Mei in the value of stoicism: " 'Your tears do not wash away your sorrows. They feed some-one else's joy' " (p. 217).

The subsequent line of action, An-Mei's decision to reject her un-cle's demands and accompany her mother in her disgrace, is an act of loyalty and love roughly equivalent to the extraordinary gesture of "Scar." The long segment depicting the opulence of the house of Wu Tsing contains the lessons that material wealth does not compensate for psychological humiliation and that people attempt to manipulate others with false generosity, the implication of the episode of the false pearls given An-Mei by the second wife.

Within this narrative is another told by her mother's servant, Yan Chang, whose wisdom and insight are extraordinary, and whose com-ments foreshadow the mother's death: "And everybody knows that sui-cide is the only way a woman can escape a marriage and gain revenge . . ." (p. 234). Yan Chang is crucial in that she provides An-Mei with the central events of the mother's life: how Wu Tsing forced him-self on her; how she was rejected by her mother and brother because of this dishonor; how her only alternative was the role of third concubine; and how she bore a son taken from her by the second wife. The depth of suffering by her mother begins to come clear to the young An-Mei: "After Yan Chang told me this story, I saw everything. I heard things I had never understood before" (p. 237). This epiphany for An-Mei con-nects "Magpies" to the opening vignette in its loss of innocence and its recognition of pain and humiliation. That is the awareness An-Mei needs to understand her mother's death, that the suicide was not simply an escape but that her mother "would rather kill her own weak spirit so she could give me a stronger one" (p. 240). And the gesture works, for An-Mei becomes defiant of the second wife, expressive of her feelings, confident of her resilience: "I can see the truth, too. I am strong, too" (p. 240).

It is only in the brief concluding segment that An-Mei returns to the concerns of her daughter, Rose, whose problems pale in comparison to those of her grandmother. An-Mei expresses not compassion but a call for Rose to "wake up and try to understand what has already happened" (p. 240). It also becomes clear in the conclusion, as it is not earlier, that An-Mei is speaking directly to her daughter, admonishing her for her weakness: "You do not need a psychiatrist to do this. A psychiatrist does not want you to wake up. . . . He is just another bird drinking from your misery" (p. 241). Her contempt for those who feed on the misery of others is expressed in her final comments about how the people of her region in China frightened the parasitic birds into the air and kept them there until they died, the magpies that drank the tears in the beginning of the story.

In "Waiting Between the Trees" (pp. 242–52), Ying-Ying St. Clair talks more about herself than she does about her daughter, although the reiteration of her episode has a direct application for Lena. The "time" of the telling is also important in that it is just before the end of "Rice Husband," before the breaking of the end table that brings Lena rushing upstairs. What has happened is that Ying-Ying has broken a table to save her daughter, the same motivation she has in telling her story, an internal narrative not spoken directly to Lena but "rehearsed" to be told for her benefit. As Ying-Ying reflects, "now I must tell her everything about my past. It is the only way to penetrate her skin and pull her to where she can be saved" (p. 242).

Ying-Ying's tale has a relatively simple structure: an envelope in the present moment, with the mother sitting upstairs listening to her daughter and Harold argue down below, and the internal reflection that takes her back to Wushi, China, and the events that followed the Moon Festival in Tai Lake, the subject of "The Moon Lady." Her account also emphasizes how a parent lives on in her daughter, for Ying-Ying is much like her mother: "She loved me too much to get angry. I was like her. That was why she named me Ying-Ying, Clear Reflection" (p. 243). Her account of the wealth of her youth, her first marriage to an older man, and of his abandonment of her for an opera singer are only the prelude for the dark secret she has kept from Lena, that she had an abortion, killing her baby out of hatred for her husband. That shame is the burden Ying-Ying has carried all these years through her work as a sales clerk and her marriage to Clifford St. Clair, an unfulfilling union because she always thought herself a ghost (p. 251).

Part of her sense of alienation derives from cultural dislocation, an issue even in her relationship with Lena. Ying-Ying says, "I raised a daughter, watching her from another shore. I accepted her American ways" (p. 251). But at the end, in the resumed present action, her daughter downstairs needing her help, she realizes that she must pass on some strength to Lena, give her some spirit, and that is why she breaks the vase and the table. Through this act she hopes to give strength to her daughter, to pass on some of the spirit of the tiger, which explains the metaphor that concludes the story: "She will come up the stairs and into my room. Her eyes will see nothing in the darkness, where I am waiting between the trees" (p. 252). The conclusion of the story of the St. Clair family thus hangs suspended on that moment, an instant anterior to the final action of "Rice Husband," when Lena says she knew the table would be broken, and Ying-Ying asks why she did not stop it (p. 165). The implication of "Waiting Between the Trees" is that Lena's problems are not as severe as those faced by her mother in her youth and that she now needs the strength to assert herself in her marriage, a strength she can obtain only from Ying-Ying.

Lindo Jong's "Double Face" (pp. 253–66) is another double story, with the recollection of her struggles in China encapsulated within the account of Waverly's impending marriage to Rich Schields and a planned honeymoon in China, the issue that concludes "Four Directions" (p. 184). The central theme again concerns identity, the mother's sense of being Chinese in a foreign culture and having an American daughter who does not understand her heritage. She is oblivious to what her mother wanted for her: "American circumstances and Chinese character" (p. 254). The structure is a progressive envelope, with a concern for Waverly and her situation in the "present" at the beginning and end; inside this narrative is the episode at the hairdresser, at which Mr. Rory (the hairdresser of contention in "Best Quality" [p. 204]) prepares Lindo for her daughter's wedding. During the treatment Lindo recalls her early years in China, particularly her relationship with her mother. The three levels of narrative interact thematically around mother-daughter relationships, ethnic identity, marriage, and family.

The first level, Waverly's imminent wedding, does not "progress" in Lindo's telling so much as it clarifies the mother's disappointment that her daughter does not respect her in the Chinese tradition and that

Waverly is so deeply Americanized that everyone in China will know she is a foreigner (p. 253). As Lindo suggests, her daughter is Chinese on the outside but American on the inside, and the Chinese know how to see inside (p. 254). The action on this level is not resolved at the end: Lindo's account of Waverly still leaves her about to be married, undecided as to whether she and Rich will bring the mother along to China, still struggling with cultural duality.

Within this story is the painfully comic situation at the hairdresser, with Mr. Rory speaking only to Waverly, who reveals her dissatisfaction with Lindo's appearance. She is unaware of the depth of her mother's feelings: "I am ashamed she is ashamed. Because she is my daughter and I am proud of her, and I am her mother but she is not proud of me" (p. 255). But what Lindo sees in her daughter's face is deeper than surface appearance: she sees herself, the recapitulation of her life in her daughter, the realization that leads to the internal flashback to the China of her youth.

Lindo's tale of China actually precedes in action that of "The Red Candle," the earlier episode that centered on her manipulations to escape her first marriage to Tyan-Yu at the age of twelve. This action occurs when she is ten, when her primary relationship was still with her own mother. Her attitudes toward her mother contrast sharply with Waverly's feelings about Lindo: Waverly is clearly displeased with the comparison of her face with that of her mother (p. 256), whereas Lindo wanted nothing so much as to look just like her mother (p. 257). But beyond this early incident, she goes on to recount how she survived after she left her first marriage, her migration to America, her struggles to survive in an alien culture. The meaning of her life is inherent in these events, and she wants Waverly to grasp it, which is why she speaks directly to her daughter: "You must understand my real circumstances, how I arrived, how I married, how I lost my Chinese face, why you are the way you are" (p. 259). So her recounting of all these events, how she met and married Tin Jong, the early life of the family in America, has a didactic function, to teach Waverly who she is, to help her understand the Chinese part of herself, to see how her mother's life still lives in her.

The last story in the volume, "A Pair of Tickets" (pp. 267–88), cannot be told by Suyuan Woo in the present, in October of 1987, because she died some months earlier, but she is much the subject of what is told. Amy Tan has commented on the inception of the end of her book:

"For the last chapter, 'A Pair of Tickets,' I wrote, 'A woman goes to China to meet her sisters with expectations and discovers something else.' That's all I knew about that one. What they all had in common is that I knew these characters would discover something about themselves but I didn't know what it was."[22] The plot involves the interaction of two temporal episodes: the present action of Jing-Mei's trip to China with her father; and the memory of the past, told by the father, Canning Woo, the only part of the book narrated by a man. The tension between the two stories is intense, since the meaning of the present depends on an understanding of the past, as is suggested by the frequent shifts between the two times, the juxtaposition of Suyuan's struggles with war and flight from the Japanese with two infant daughters set against Jing-Mei's feelings of inadequacy, of never having fulfilled her mother's dreams. Jing-Mei learns much on this trip that she did not know before.

One of the things she learns is the meaning of her name, "best quality little sister," concepts that unite the present concerns of "Best Quality" with the abandoned older sisters of the past. She also comes to understand the meaning of her mother's name, "Suyuan," which can be interpreted as "Long-Cherished Wish," the desire of the mother for reunification with her Chinese daughters, a wish fulfilled by Jing-Mei. But she cannot understand the situation fully until she hears the account of her mother's background from her father.

That narrative is enclosed in an envelope of present action, the largely comic incident of Canning's visit to his relatives in Canton, in which Jing-Mei sees four generations of one side of her family. The experience further juxtaposes past and present, since what she sees in Canton is not the old China of her mother's memory but a modern culture in a city that looks like an American metropolis, with an elegant hotel and the technical artifacts of contemporary life. It is a fitting irony that when they all have dinner together they dine not on Chinese food but on "hamburgers, french fries, and apple pie à la mode" (p. 278).

It is on the flight to Shanghai that Canning Woo finally tells the full story of Suyuan to his daughter, how and why she abandoned the babies, how she worked to find them, how they were adopted by a peasant family, how her deepest wish was to return to China and embrace them. It is in this recitation that Jing-Mei finds the feelings that allow for emotional reconciliation with her mother, "realizing how much I have never known about her, grieving that my sisters and I had both lost her" (p. 286). In her embrace of her sisters she not only fulfills her mother's most cherished wish, she finds herself, the Chinese part of her identity: "It is so obvious. It is my family. It is in our blood. After all these years, it can finally be let go" (p. 288). It is a poignant and unifying conclusion to a rich series of events.

The *Joy Luck Club* is an excellent example of the structural possibilities of the short-story cycle. In subject and narrative method, it presents a clear arrangement of sixteen stories, four by the mothers, two sets of four by the daughters, and then a narrative quartet by the mothers once again, giving closure and design to the volume. Within this pattern there is also thematic progression from the hardship and psychological devastation the mothers endured in China to a second section in America in which each daughter falls short of her mother's expectations: June by failing to become a prodigy on the piano, Rose by getting a divorce, Waverly by giving up chess, and Lena by being unable to establish any solid identity for herself. The third group, once again focused on the daughters, depicts psychological resolution for all of them save June. Rose is getting a divorce from Ted and asserts herself by insisting on keeping the house; Waverly becomes a tax attorney and is reestablishing a family by marrying Rich Schields; and Lena, still enduring marriage problems, is given strength by her mother when she breaks the end table. It is only June who feels utterly inadequate, even though her mother gives her a jade pendant that represents her "life's importance." The concluding quartet of stories shifts back to the mothers in episodes that illustrate how the past influences the present, indeed, how "the past holds the only keys to the meaning in every life examined" in the book.[23] These stories provide thematic resolution to the narratives about each of the four families: Ying-Ying St. Clair is determined to give her daughter spirit; Lindo Jong completes her saga of the trip to the United States; An-Mei Hsu displays her defiance when she stamps on the pearls the second wife had given her; and June fulfills her mother's ultimate wish as she returns to China and is united with the abandoned daughters.

As these events suggest, *The Joy Luck Club* is very much a woman's book, with men drawn primarily as villains out of central casting or as spear carriers in a feminine drama. Despite the cultural and psychological depth given the eight women, there is no richness to any of the portraits of husbands and fathers and suitors, who, with the exception of Canning Woo, are either long dead or best forgotten, a point endorsed

even by Amy Tan, who commented in an interview that the diminishment of men "is a flaw in the book, but for me to correct the flaw would
have thrown the book in another direction, and I couldn't do it at that
point. The men are in there almost as pawns for bringing up the conflicts between the mothers and daughters; that's sort of unfortunate."[24]
Tan may apologize too much. Her volume does not suffer from a want
of conflict or interest, even though it has its gender limitations. There
is no prerequisite for proportional representation in the writing of fiction, only that the characters depicted come alive as personalities employed in meaningful engagement with the world about them.

Within these stories, the conflicts are essentially between mother
and daughter and, to a lesser extent, among the daughters themselves.
Dorothy Stein may have stated the case too strongly when she observed
that

> the women who crossed the ocean to escape the ravages of the Japa-
> nese invasion, the hardships of a feudal society, the cruelties of a
> tyrannical family system, never considered that their children
> should be free to absorb any wisdom but that dictated by their own
> experience and beliefs. The result is that a book meant, I think, as
> a tribute to their strength and devotion comes off unintentionally
> as a study of well-meaning despotisms that poison with competi-
> tiveness not only the friendship of the mothers' generation, but the
> relationships among their daughters.[25]

The most dramatic exception to this pattern is in the conclusion, in
which June's return to China, and her meeting with the lost sisters, fulfills not only her mother's dream but provides a way out of her pervasive sense of inadequacy. In the opening story, June says that she wishes
she were dead, like the babies in China (p. 29). The conclusion suggests
that despite the fact that June did not become a prodigy on the piano,
did not finish college, and proved to be a failure as a copywriter, in the
restoration of her family, in the integration of her Chinese heritage into
her American sense of identity, she can begin to find wholeness and fulfillment. In that the volume begins and ends with these concerns, suggesting that they are not only the envelope for the book but its central
focus, "A Pair of Tickets" provides both conclusion and coherence to
the sixteen stories that make up the volume.

The Joy Luck Club, from its composition and publication history, to
its structure, diversified protagonists, multiple narrators, and complex

thematic development, is an exemplum of the rich possibilities within the tradition of the short-story cycle. Since its publication, it has become celebrated as a major work of Asian-American literature, a status it certainly deserves, but it is also much more than that, a book that can take its place in any library as a work of art that transcends ethnic limitations. It should not be forgotten that it was inspired by a volume of Native-American stories, and it derives from an international tradition of linked tales that has played an essential role in the development of the fiction of the United States since Washington Irving. Amy Tan is a writer of brilliance and consummate aesthetic grace, an artist rather than a social propagandist, who will take her place as one of the most gifted American writers of the twentieth century.

8

Vietnam Redux

Robert Olen Butler's *A Good
Scent from a Strange Mountain*

Robert Olen Butler's *A Good Scent from a
Strange Mountain* (1992), fifteen stories about
Vietnamese immigrants living in the United
States after the war, presents a counterpoint to *The Things They Carried*.
O'Brien's book deals with Americans in Vietnam, Butler's with Vietnamese in America. O'Brien's stories are all told by Americans, Butler's
by Vietnamese. To some extent the issue of cultural conflict plays a role
in each book but from a contrasting perspective, since the historical, religious, ethnic, and sexual values of the narrators of Butler's stories are
indigenous to Southeast Asia. These people are, in a sense, aliens in
America, situational displaced persons who look to the past for meaning
and for the direction their lives should take in their adopted country, a
society they know only on the surface. Butler conveys this point of view
with consummate skill, using the language and frame of reference of the
narrators of each episode, drafting characters who embody cultural duality in contemporary America. It is all the more remarkable that this
volume, for which Butler was awarded the Pulitzer Prize in 1993, is his
first collection of short stories.[1]

Butler's previous fiction, much of it based on his army experience
in military intelligence during the Vietnam War, had been in the form
of the novel. *The Alleys of Eden* concerns an American deserter who lives
with a prostitute in the back streets of Saigon until the conclusion of

the war, at which point they escape to the United States. The emphasis throughout focuses on the cultural differences between the two lovers. *Sun Dogs* is also about Vietnam, about a former prisoner of war who gropes for an understanding of his experience, for the meaning of the horror of battle and the suicide of his wife. Butler has emphasized this point in explaining his motivation for writing: "I write novels to explore for myself—and to reveal to others—my vision of the fundamental patterns inherent in the flux of experience. These patterns concern man's search for love, kinship, connection, God; man's capacity for desertion, violence, and self-betrayal. But I also write novels to tell stories, a primal human impulse since cave-mouth campfires."[2] But his achievement would seem to transcend the simple recitation of individual tales, for what he has accomplished in *A Good Scent from a Strange Mountain* is the more complex matter of a collection of interrelated stories, parallel to the "cycles of plays with the same characters" he wrote while a graduate student in creative writing at the University of Iowa.[3] Indeed, Butler has said that he conceived of the fifteen stories all at once as a group of interrelated narratives set to reinforce or balance one another.[4]

Butler's short-story cycle does not use the continuity of character of *The Things They Carried*, since the people depicted are restricted to one work each, but it features a continuing dual setting in Vietnam as remembered from the bayou country of Louisiana, the locus of the telling for nearly the entire book. The stories are unified by a common narrative technique in that they are told in first person by fifteen different characters; in each instance, the tale that is told, the action that is described, is subordinate to the personal revelations and self-discovery taking place by the teller. Further, these narrators all share a Vietnamese perspective and a rich and intriguing lexicon based on their own linguistic tradition.[5] As Robert Towers has indicated, Butler "gives to all his narrators, whatever their background, a fairly educated, slightly stilted English with a few idiomatic uncertainties."[6] But whatever the accuracy of the rendering of their dialect, having these narratives about Vietnamese characters told from their cultural perspective in their own language is congruent with the human conflicts in the stories they tell, dramatic situations in which it is the Vietnamese who matter, who have agency and responsibility and guilt and moral stature, and it is they who ultimately come to terms with the meaning of their lives.

Butler has been explicit about this dimension of his objectives: "I don't think the fiction about Vietnam has dealt adequately with the

Vietnamese people; it has not found their humanity. . . . I think this is at least partly due to the fact that the vast majority of the books about the war deal with the fighting soldier, who related to the Vietnamese primarily through the barrel of a gun."[7] Certainly part of the achievement of this remarkable book is that it succeeds in presenting a new perspective on the war in Vietnam, one so obvious as to seem ideologically axiomatic but one that had not been realized in American fiction until the publication of this volume in 1992. The reviewers of the book, almost universally celebrative in their responses to the stories, were not oblivious to this point. George Packer's assessment was typical:

> *A Good Scent from a Strange Mountain* goes a long way toward making the Vietnamese real, and its method is bold: each of the 15 stories is told in the first person from the viewpoint of a Vietnamese transplanted from the Mekong Delta to the Louisiana bayou. The Americans have become foils; it's the Vietnamese who are now at the center, haunted by the past, ambivalent about their hosts, suffering sexual torments, seeking a truce in their various wars.[8]

There is little difference in Butler's depictions of characters from the north or the south of Vietnam, little sense of who was ally and who was "enemy." The deep cultural background of both parts of Vietnam is identical, as are the conflicts and problems all the Vietnamese face in the contemporary world of the United States.[9]

The individual stories in the book are related not only in setting and narrative technique but by a matrix of thematic elements as well, all deriving in some measure from the trauma of the Vietnam War in the background and the process of immigration and assimilation as more immediate issues. In broader terms, although the characters appear in a single story only, the central issues faced by a person in one instance continue into other episodes, the way assimilation unites "The Trip Back," "Crickets," and "The American Couple," for example. The motif of cultural duality that is introduced in "The Trip Back" resonates in "A Ghost Story," "Snow," "Relic," and "A Good Scent from a Strange Mountain," joining those works into thematic patterns. The concept of romance links "Snow" and "Preparation" in the hope for the fulfillment of love just as "Mid-Autumn," which features a mother speaking to her daughter, is juxtaposed to "In the Clearing," in which a father speaks to a son. These ideas permeate the stories, binding them together in intricate and resonant patterns entirely absent from their individual appearances in magazines, and they are much of the reason why *A Good Scent from a Strange Mountain* has had such a dramatic impact on readers throughout the world.

The initial story in the volume, "Open Arms" (pp. 1–15), originally appeared in the *Missouri Review* in 1990 in virtually identical form.[10] One level of meaning for the title derives from the military policy in the south of Vietnam to accept "with open arms" defectors from the other side, a policy of receptivity that has resonance for the rest of the action, particularly for the attitude of the narrator. Told in first person by an unnamed Vietnamese Buddhist who has immigrated to Gretna, Louisiana, "Open Arms" is a double narrative revealing the values and conflicts of the narrator at the same time he tells about his tragic encounter with Thâp, a memory that still haunts him two decades after the events.

To some extent the story belongs to the narrator: it is he who offers self revelation, who reveals internal struggle, who is actively in the process of self-evaluation. Even his initial assertion, "I have no hatred in me," is open to question given his deep sense of loss, for he has lost family, country, a sense of "personal purity," and, to some extent, self-respect. Because of the Vietnam War, he lost his wife to another man, his country to the Communists from the north, and his religious devotion to cultural dislocation: "I'm not that good a Buddhist. I live in America and things just don't look the way my mother and my grandmother explained them to me" (p. 8). His act of "telling" is thus a means of appraisal of the transitional moments in his life, all of which would seem to have been in Vietnam and to bear some relation to the narrator's brief encounter with Thâp. He realizes, even at the time, that this man has a strange power: "I knew that Thâp was no ghost but a man and he loved his wife and desired her as I loved and desired mine and that was within the bounds of his purity. He was a man, but I wished from then on only to stay far away from him" (p. 8). The narrator's sense of foreboding is quickly justified in the events that follow.

The account the narrator gives of Thâp is a deeply humane one, one that manifests the narrator's sense of decency, his political philosophy, his stance on the war, his standing as a man of honor. Thâp appeared at an Australian base in South Vietnam, where he was interviewed by the narrator, an interpreter with military intelligence. Originally a devoted Viet Cong, Thâp expressed his political philosophy: "I believe in the government caring for all the people, the poor before the rich. I believe in the state of personal purity that makes this possible" (p. 7). He insists that he has not changed his views in shifting sides in the war; rather, he has reversed allegiance because the Viet Cong burned his village and murdered his wife and two children. It is a deeply personal decision for him, as Richard Eder has suggested: "He is a man of tragedy; his wife and children were killed in a Viet Cong raid on a village. His personal devastation contrasts with the sleek South Vietnamese major who takes part in his interrogation."[11] The narrator is sensitive to Thập's perspective, one that the two of them share: "The communists were full of right views, right intentions, right speech, and all that. And Buddha's second Truth, about the thirst of the passions being the big trap, the communists were real strict about that, real prudes" (p. 7). It is these issues, not the broad objectives of the war, that precipitate the central crisis of the story.

The crucial event comes when the Australians show a pornographic movie during which they make crude suggestions and behave boorishly. The narrator is offended but intrigued, and he is cognizant of how the film will be received by Thập: "They just didn't understand what sort of man he was" (pp. 9–10). Thập is deeply ashamed of what he is witnessing, the *sexual* "open arms" of the title, and he is angered by this breach of decorum by his new political allies, this corruption of civilized values: "That night he went to a tent and killed one of the two infantry officers, the one, no doubt, who had insisted on his coming to the club. Then Thập killed himself, a bullet in his brain" (p. 14). His death inspires devastating realizations for the narrator, which he now formulates in retrospect: "Thập was a true believer, and that night he felt that he had suddenly understood the democracies he was trying to believe in. He felt that the communists whom he had rightly broken with, who had killed his wife and shown him their own fatal flaw, nevertheless had been right about all the rest of us" (p. 14). This comment is a profound statement of the moral corruption in the West presented by the narrator when he is living in Louisiana but reflecting on his memories of Thập. More than two decades after the events, it is still this man who provides lessons to be pondered. More than the narrator himself, more than his own family, it is Thập who occupies the center of attention in the narrator's retrospective musings, and it is in these events that he seeks the definition of his life.

"Mr. Green" (pp. 17–28) provides yet another dislocation of perspective, a counterpoint to the opening narrative, since it is told by a

Catholic woman, born in North Vietnam, now living in Versailles, Louisiana, an enclave for refugees from that region. First published in the *Hudson Review* in 1991, the story is told in the United States with action primarily in Vietnam.[12] The titular Mr. Green is a parrot that belonged to the narrator's grandfather and that speaks with the grandfather's voice. In auditory terms, the bird keeps the grandfather alive, although the narrator expresses her skepticism about the transmigration of souls, the Buddhist idea that her ancestor now lives in the bird. Another level of religious conflict is the grandfather's belief that "the souls of our ancestors continue to need love and attention and devotion," and that by moving from Hanoi to Saigon the family would allow the ancestors to become lost, wandering spirits with no one to care for them. When, as a young girl of seven, the narrator reassured her grandfather that she would always make offerings for him, he told her that her sentiments do not count: "Only a son can oversee the worship of his ancestors" (p. 19). She felt the gender insult keenly, and it plays a role decades later, at the time of the telling. In coming to America, by implication, the narrator has shown disrespect for the souls of her forebears, although the bird is clearly the embodiment of her grandfather: "There are times when he seems to hold the spirit of my grandfather and all his knowledge" (p. 20). Recalling the time when her mother killed sparrows for dinner by twisting their necks, and wishing to preserve the dignity of the aged bird who has grown ill, the narrator wrings the neck of the parrot. It is a gesture with elements of hatred, love for the grandfather, revenge, kindness in ending the misery of the bird, and cultural dislocation, since the bird still seems to represent the grandfather himself. It is not insignificant that the narrator begins and ends her story with a definition of self, outlining her values and beliefs, at once justifying and explaining her actions.

"The Trip Back" (pp. 29–43) was originally published in the *Southern Review* with only one substantial difference from the collected text: the name of Mai's mother in the magazine is "Diem," and in the book it is "Chim."[13] Butler has not explained his rationale for changing the name, but it could be that "Diem" still has associations with a South Vietnamese regime that resonates with inappropriate layers of reference. Whatever the case, this story offers yet another permutation on the varieties of narrative perspective since it is told by a thoroughly acculturated Vietnamese Catholic named Khánh, who is now a businessman living in Lake Charles, Louisiana. The situation is that his wife,

Mai, has a grandfather, Mr. Chinh, who has finally been allowed to leave Vietnam and immigrate to America, and the narrator drives to the airport in Houston to meet him. Mai loves her grandfather and has worked hard for years to win his release, but it is not she who speaks; indeed, she does not even appear in the present action. She is there only in the recollections of her husband as he drives to and from the airport.

The narrator is a locus of normative values: he is a very successful businessman in a free enterprise society, and he admires hard work and a disciplined life. At the same time, he shares a loving relationship with his wife; he understands her extraordinary love for her grandfather, who became a surrogate father when Mai's true father was drowned; he is sensitive to her desire to be a granddaughter again, riding on the back of her grandfather in the manner of a small girl (p. 32). The narrator's mission to bring home the grandfather is thus a gesture of love. Once the grandfather appears in the story, however, the events take on a comic tone: the old man comes off the plane wearing "a red-and-black-plaid sport shirt and chino pants," not the traditional clothes the narrator anticipated. Once in the car, the old man is unimpressed with the narrator's Acura, expecting a Citroën, a reference to the French legacy in Vietnam. The narrator finds that it is not easy to make conversation with his guest, allowing opportunity for self-reflection during the long drive. His experience with the old man brings Khánh to the realization that he has been transformed since he left Vietnam, that he has participated in the vast American experience of immigration, dislocation, cultural duality, and gradual assimilation:

> I found that I myself was no longer comfortable with the old ways. Like the extended family. Like other things, too. The Vietnamese indirectness, for instance. The superstition. I was a good American now, and though I wished I could do more for this old man next to me, at least for my wife's sake, it was not an unpleasant thought that I had finally left Vietnam behind (p. 36).

These kinds of ideas lead to serious overtones, especially the realization that the grandfather has lost his memory and has no recollection whatever of a granddaughter.

That situation inspires the narrator to lament the effect it will have on Mai, who has so longed to see her beloved grandfather. It also leads Khánh to the sensitive realization that it could be he who had grown old and lost his memory. When they arrive home, and Mai embraces an unresponsive grandfather, the narrator is deeply affected: "Perhaps I should have stayed at my wife's side as the old man went on to explain to her that she didn't exist. But I could not" (p. 41). He thinks about his own experience with loss: "I'd lost a whole country and I didn't give it a thought" (p. 42). But he is especially empathetic when Mai comes weeping to him in the yard, having discovered her grandfather's mental state, and he picks her up on his back, becoming the grandfather she remembered from Vietnam, and he carries her about the yard, allowing her to experience the joys of her youth once more. In its deepest levels, however, the focus is not on Mai or the grandfather but on the transformation of values of the narrator, whose act of telling involves both self-discovery and self-revelation.

If "The Trip Back" is about life lost, "Fairy Tale" (pp. 45–57) is about life reclaimed, for Miss Noi finds domestic peace and security at last in Thibodoux, Louisiana after a tragic beginning in Vietnam. First published in the *Virginia Quarterly Review* in 1990,[14] the story recounts the life of a barroom dancer in Saigon who falls in love with an American diplomat who, speaking Vietnamese, says "The sunburnt duck is lying down" when he intends to say "May Vietnam live for ten thousand years." He does not realize the importance of pitch and tone in establishing meaning in the language.[15] But that romance is short-lived, ruining her dream of becoming a housewife, although it brings Miss Noi to the United States, where she becomes a dancer on Bourbon Street in New Orleans. The role of the Vietnam War in her life is suggested only tangentially, but she was a dancer and a prostitute in Saigon during the war, bore a son by an American who abandoned her, is forsaken in Atlanta by the diplomat who brought her to America, and ends up in Louisiana dancing and selling sex for money.

The fairy tale aspect of the plot is the happy ending, the appearance of Fontenot as a man who does not wish to degrade her but cares for her sincerely and marries her. His tenderness is evident from the first, when he cries after they make love, an emotion paralleled by her own weeping in the scene in which he proposes. It is sentimental romance at its clichéd best, but the crux of the story is not so much plot as narrative perspective, the language and values of Miss Noi. For all her amusement at the American's twisted Vietnamese, she speaks English with a charming lack of guile. She says "I can shake it baby, and soon I am a dancer in a bar on Bourbon Street" (p. 47) and, later, "I am not sexy bitch, wiggle it baby, oh boy oh boy it's hot, it feels good" (p. 51). Nor is she ever evasive or apologetic for her years of prostitution, even though, at the time of the telling, she is a housewife in a small town. She reveals herself to be a person of substance who made calculated choices about the best way to make a living for herself, the best way to care for her son (allowing him to grow up under the care of her mother), and the best life she can hope for, marriage to Fontenot. The war destroyed traditional roles for her, but she established a new, satisfying life in America, a "fairy tale" come true.

The next tale is ultimately one of Vietnamese culture lost in America, a theme that links it to "The Trip Back" earlier in the volume and to many stories to follow, including "Mid-Autumn," "In the Clearing," and the concluding "A Good Scent from a Strange Mountain." Ted, the narrator of "Crickets" (pp. 59–64), is a chemical engineer in Louisiana and, like Miss Noi, a Roman Catholic. Only eighteen when Saigon fell to the north, he and his wife immigrated to the United States and settled in Lake Charles, Louisiana, in the bayou area that reminds them of the Mekong Delta. Attempting to entertain his ten-year-old son, he recalls the fighting crickets that fascinated him in his childhood, but the American insects are the wrong species and his son is quickly bored. The father cannot find the small but ferocious fire crickets, only the lethargic charcoal variety, who are reluctant combatants. Ted, a small man in a country of giants, identifies with the fire crickets, "a very precious and admirable thing" (p. 64), for he has not assimilated and his child knows and cares nothing for the old country: "He doesn't speak Vietnamese at all and my wife says not to worry about that. He's an American" (p. 60). The center of the story, the psychological conflict at the heart of it, is the narrator's realization that his wife is correct.

"Letters from My Father" (pp. 65–72), which originally appeared in the *Cimarron Review* in 1991,[16] is a delicate tale in which action is subordinated to indirect self-revelation by the narrator and central character. The plot is simply that during the war an American serviceman married a Vietnamese woman and they had a child, Francine, who narrates the story from Louisiana. Separated by the confusion of the fall of Saigon, Fran lived with her mother in Vietnam for many years until her father finally secured clearance for them to join him in the United States, where they settled in the Vietnamese community of Lake Charles. This level of action recapitulates the positive theme of the reclaimed life in "Fairy Tale," but there is a more subtle dimension to "Letters from My Father" in the theme of Fran's quest for an understanding of her inner nature. That is the endeavor that leads her to read her father's letter repeatedly, searching for clues to her true self. She finds it not in the letters but in the act of telling her life, articulating, at the age of seventeen, the people and events that have been important for her.

What is clear is that after the war, during the "lost" years in Saigon, she had no strong sense of herself. A "child of the dust," born of an absent American father, she felt herself invisible, undefined, a pariah in her native country. Even the implications of "naming" suggest her lack of stable identity: her name is "Francine," a name that recalls the years of French presence in Indochina; her father calls her by the diminutive "Fran," a more American formulation; she calls herself by the Vietnamese name "Trán," short for "Hôn Trán," which means "a kiss on the forehead," a domestic, familial act. The city she lives in changes names, from Saigon to Ho Chi Minh City. Identity is in flux for both her and the community she lives in; there is no stability to her life. She feels herself to be American and Vietnamese but apart from both cultures, a "Saigon girl" with no future. Perhaps that is why she is obsessed with the cemetery, especially with the memorials displaying the French names of the young people who died in the battles of 1968 (p. 68). Now, at the time of the telling, she lives in a French section of the United States.

Fran remembers an account a girl told her back in Saigon, an internal episode with resonance for the story Fran is relating. The girl's tale is highly unreliable, having been relayed through several hands, but its thematic vibrations touch issues of identity and reality. The girl's tale of an absent father and a mother who projects shadow images on the wall, pretending that those are a protective father, allowing her daughter to sleep easily, comes to a tragic conclusion of misunderstandings. The father misconstrues the daughter's comments about the shadow father, thinking him the mother's lover; when the father leaves, silently slipping away, the mother drowns herself in the Saigon River. When the father learns the truth, he too commits suicide in the river, a Vietnamese manifestation of the Romeo and Juliet plot. This tale is in contrast to Fran's story, which ends with her father greeting her and her mother at the airport and establishing a new American family. It is here that Fran finds herself, in the assertive articulations of her father, revealed in the letters he wrote to the American government as well as those he wrote to Fran's mother. That is why, at the time of the telling, she sits in the storage shack in Louisiana, reading her father's letters, reviewing her life, and forming herself in the events she relates. It is a delicate narrative of "coming into being" despite cultural duality, geographical displacement, and a shattered sense of self.

The resonance of "Love" (pp. 73–93) is not so much to the preceding story as it is to "Fairy Tale" in its ironic treatment of romantic commitment. Originally published in *Writer's Forum* in 1991,[17] "Love" presents an unnamed narrator who was once a powerful spy during the war but now realizes that he is a "wimp," a nondescript, small man with no remarkable qualities other than his resourcefulness in manipulating others. Since he has lost the power of the American military, which he once enjoyed in Vietnam, he now resorts to consulting a voodoo priest for assistance in dealing with an unfaithful wife. It is the absurd consequence of this effort that casts the story in the genre of "a contemporary version of a comic medieval fable" with its scatology and slapstick antics, including the narrator's falling out of a tree.[18] The war, normally a motivating entity in Butler's fiction, is present as memory, but it is not a precipitating cause of the conflict, which is more a matter of matrimonial constancy than of international political turmoil.

There is no fundamental quest for identity in this story, and cultural duality is a factor only in the accessibility to the black conjure man, Doctor Joseph. Rather, the narrator knows who and what he is; his problem is not self-discovery but self-assertion, the instigation of subtle events that sever his wife from her current lover, since she copulates seriatim with a progression of Vietnamese men. The narrator does not seek confrontation with these men; he does not even wish for them to know he has wreaked vengeance upon them, as when, in Vietnam, he called air strikes on the homes of his wife's lovers. Now he is reduced to filling a hog bladder with goat droppings and flinging it over a house in mystical reprisal on the offending couple, and he is inept even in this poor attempt at revenge. As the narrator climbs a tree to free the tangled bladder from a branch, he observes that "the man who once could bring fire from heaven now could only bring shit from the trees" (p. 92). The final ironic indignity is that the narrator catches his wife in the midst of her affair just as he falls from the tree and breaks both of his legs. But even in her unfaithfulness, she does not abandon him; rather, she is affectionately solicitous in her attentions to his needs in convalescence. It is a sweetly comic development, one that lends a light tone to a volume depicting darkly tragic events.

If the thematic values of "Love" involve the transformation from betrayal to dutiful attendance, those of "Mid-Autumn" (pp. 95–101) are more subdued, emanating from lost romance and resignation to a diminished life. First published in the *Hawaii Review* in 1991,[19] this episode is unique in the volume as the English translation of the putative story a Vietnamese mother living in Louisiana relates to her unborn daughter. The tale, in fact a double story, is one of the fulfillment of the deepest self, one cast in Vietnamese cultural terms, since there is no tradition of speaking to the unborn in American society. The mother tells of her childhood in a misogynist community in which her birth, as a female, was a disappointment to her parents. By implication, the mother is saying that this will not be the case with the birth of her daughter, whom she is attempting to instruct to pay attention to her deepest self. She tells about her love in Vietnam for Bao, whom she met and fell in love with at the Mid-Autumn Festival.

This narrative is interrupted by the insertion of an explanation of the origin of the festival, which derives from a Chinese celebration of a poet emperor who rode a horse on a rainbow to the moon, where fairies danced with him while he sang his poems and had the most wonderful time of his life, feeling that "his deepest self belonged in this place" (p. 99). But when he returned to earth he discovered that there was no way back, no returning to the fulfillment he had known, and this lament is observed in the Mid-Autumn Festival. The implications for the mother's story are clear, that she, too, found fulfillment in her love for Bao, but when he was killed in the war in Vietnam, she would never again find full satisfaction of her deepest self. Now, at the time of the telling, the mother is married to an American soldier who adores her as he will love their daughter, but the mother will never care for him the way she did Bao. All that is left is resignation to the diminished present and the annual commemoration of lost love as the mother lights a lantern and looks into the night sky.

"In the Clearing" (pp. 103–10) is a companion piece in the collected volume, a function it did not have when it was originally published separately in *Icarus* in 1991.[20] In "Mid-Autumn" a Vietnamese mother speaks to her daughter; conversely, "In the Clearing" features a Vietnamese father speaking to his son, whom he has never known, seeking to assume the instructive functions of a father. In each instance there is an ancient legend that conveys a defining mythological structure for Vietnamese life, in this case the myth of a gentle dragon and a fairy princess who began the country of Vietnam. In each story an un-named character expresses parental affection for a child, reveals a deep lament for a lost romantic love, and assumes a tone of resignation for opportunities irredeemably destroyed because of the war. It is a signifi-cant pairing of stories that deeply enriches the two tales in the final book in ways that were totally invisible in magazine publication.

The speaker of this epistolary episode, a Vietnamese man living in New Orleans at the time of the telling, is a former soldier who was un-wittingly spirited out of the country just before the fall of Saigon. He left behind a pregnant sweetheart who has since married someone else; he now writes to his son seeking to explain how to deal with fear and courage, to instruct him on the origin and temperament of his country, and to describe the desirable attributes of Vietnamese children. The first objective involves an explanation of the father's experience in the war, how he became a teenage soldier fighting against the invasion from the north, how he barely escaped death when his patrol stopped to rest in a clearing and was attacked from positions in the jungle. Only the lieutenant and the speaker survived, and they fled the country just ahead of the advancing forces from the north. The motif of the virtues of Vietnamese young resonates from the myth of the dragon and the prin-cess, who give birth to a hundred children: "The children were very wonderful, inheriting bravery and gentleness from their father and beauty and charm and delicacy of feeling from their mother" (p. 109).

These children are the founders of Vietnam, "the ancestors of all of us," and, by implication, they give the country its true character, temporarily distorted by war. The most serious message the father con-veys is in this internal digression, since it will help the son form his in-nermost character consistent with the mythological spirit of his people. The final wish of the father for his son is that "you save your life. Tell this story that I have told you. Try to think of it as true" (p. 110). This is a legend that the speaker's father told him; its reiteration in a letter to his son places the narrator in a similar parental role, somewhat amel-iorating his estrangement from a child he has never seen. The telling is an act of conciliation, a connection between father and son on a mytho-logical level that transcends the specific circumstances of their estrange-ment. In this sense it is fully coherent as an individual story but, within the volume, it complements the situation in "Mid-Autumn" at the same time it resonates from, and is congruent with, "Letters from My Father."

"A Ghost Story" (pp. 111–23) was originally published in the *Colorado Review* in 1991, in which publication it lacked the resonance of the previous episodes in the volume, especially those containing supernatural legends derived from Vietnamese culture.[21] In this case the focal myth functions on two levels, as the titular gothic tale and as a metaphoric expression of the tragedy of a country torn by danger and enigmatic violence. The action also suggests a dual application, since the unnamed narrator has his own story to tell, one complementary to the internal event involving Major Trung. The narrator describes himself as a "late-middle-aged sort of shabby Oriental man, a little frayed at the collar and cuffs, . . . hair a little shaggy over the ears" (p. 111), hardly an auspicious depiction. The tale he tells, however, is riveting. In 1971, Major Trung, of the Army of the Republic of Vietnam, is returning to base after a visit to his mistress in An Khê. He must pass in the dark through a stretch of road controlled at night by Communist forces. Rounding a turn, he is startled by a beautiful young woman, dressed in a white *aó dài*, whom he narrowly avoids hitting. A moment later, impossibly, she is before the car again, and this time she becomes transformed as her mouth gapes open and a giant tongue flicks out, "and the monstrous tongue licked at the car and the car lifted up, and the major's eyes and his head were filled with a vision of the tongue and then all was darkness" (p. 114). But the major is not injured, and the woman again appears before him, saying, "there is an ambush ahead. I am Nguyêm thi Linh of the street called Lotus in An Khê. You will see me again. I wish for you to be alive" (p. 115). As he continues to the base he passes the bodies of his comrades, killed in a raid a few moments before. The mysterious woman has saved his life. Later, visiting her mother in An Khê, he learns that Linh has been dead for four years, killed in the war. Later, again driving in the night, he encounters Linh on the same road and greets her with eagerness; she becomes transformed into a monster and devours him; as the narrator says, "the major died horribly in the jaws of this enticing woman" (p. 121).

The narrator swears that this tale is true and, as verification, he adds his own coda to the mysterious events. During the fall of Saigon in 1975, he was working for the American Embassy when they were evacuating by helicopter. Delayed in traffic, unable to break through the crowds around the embassy, the narrator was in danger of being left behind when Linh suddenly appeared, stopped an official staff car, and the narrator was saved and immigrated to America. As the limousine pulled away, he looked back and saw "Miss Linh's tongue slip from her mouth and lick her lips, as if she had just eaten me up. And indeed she has" (p. 123). It is an enigmatic conclusion to a strange tale, but it ends with the confession of the narrator's continuing obsession with the memory of a beautiful young woman who is also dangerous, deadly, and unforgettable. On the literal level, the narrator is sharing his fascination with the mysterious death of Major Trung and his own momentary encounter with the agent of Trung's death, at once savior and assassin. The narrator is also sharing the most significant thing that ever happened to him, the transforming moment that cannot be forgotten. On the metaphoric level, Linh seems the embodiment of Vietnam itself, beautiful but violent, capable of sustaining and protecting life and yet proficient in inflicting horrible death. In this sense, the narrator's obsession with her takes on the cultural implication of the internalization of national identity, the embracing of the country of origin even as one seeks assimilation into the new nation of choice. On this level, it is the narrator, rather than Major Trung, who emerges as the central figure, for it is he who contemplates the internal effect of the strange encounter, and it is he who is psychologically transformed by it.

"Snow" (pp. 125–35) was also published in 1991, and it repeats some of the standard structural elements of Butler's stories, particularly the narrative frame with a retrospective narrative within the present action.[22] In this case the narrator is a thirty-four-year-old Vietnamese woman living with her mother in Lake Charles, Louisiana. At the time of the narrational present, she is waiting for a date for dinner with a Jewish lawyer, and the preceding exposition explains the significance of this forthcoming event, how it happened, and what forces led to a romantic sympathy between two people of very different backgrounds.

As the narrator, Miss Giàu, recounts her background during the war in Vietnam and her adjustments to a new culture when she immigrated to America, she establishes a pattern of values that is repeated in Mr. Cohen's story. Miss Giàu lost her true love in the war, although she knows he is now a taxi driver in Ho Chi Minh City and married to someone else; Cohen is a widower. Both of them have deceased fathers, Cohen's having been killed in the holocaust in Poland, where the family lived until 1939. Both of them associate snow with death, hence the resonance of the title: Miss Giàu saw snow for the first time in St. Louis when she awakened and saw a white blanket covering everything, and she was afraid that the earth had died (p. 134). Cohen remembers seeing his father, a professor in Warsaw, for the last time during a snowfall, which suggested to Cohen that his father would be killed, which was correct. Both of them are immigrants who live with their mothers, but both are lonely and long for a loving companionship. Despite the vast cultural differences between them, this union between a Vietnamese Buddhist and a Polish Jew seems to promise fulfillment and happiness for them, and the parallels between their lives establish a basis for understanding and sympathy and, given the maturity of both of them, continuity.

"Relic" (pp. 137–42), previously published in the *Gettysburg Review* and then in *New Stories from the South: The Year's Best, 1991*, is a meditation by a wealthy Vietnamese immigrant on his life in Vietnam, the wife and children he left there, the shoe worn by John Lennon that sits on the desk before him, and, most important, his longing for assimilation into American society.[23] Much of the narrative is essentially an attempt at self-definition revealing his habits of mind, his orientation to experience, his abiding values in a new country. That he is a Roman Catholic from North Vietnam who became dislocated in the disruption of the war places him in a particular subset of Vietnamese society in Versailles, Louisiana. His religion causes him to think about life in theological terms, seeing a mark on the shoe Lennon was wearing when he died as "the stigmata of the shoe, the sign of his martyrdom" (p. 142). As he puts on the shoe, he longs for community, his sense of cultural dislocation overwhelming the satisfaction of his material success. He reflects on the rapid acquisition of his wealth in the food industry, supplemented by a video parlor, but it is clear that fulfillment for him does not rest in the accumulation of wealth alone. He fears that psychologically, he still lives in Vietnam: as he looks out his window at the gardens of his neighbors, he expects to see a water buffalo or a sampan, and he concludes, "I am living in the past" (p. 140). He laments the absence of his family, but he expresses no desire to return to them; rather, his preoccupation is with the American Dream, the land of opportunity, and his desire to establish an identity within his adopted country, to be accepted by it.

The titular implications of "Preparation" (pp. 143–54) are dual, referring both to the immediate task the narrator faces of preparing her friend for burial and to the long-term issue of her life having been a preparation for a romance, which would seem in the offing, with her deceased friend's husband. This story, which originally appeared in the

Sewanee Review in 1992, follows the repeated design for Butler's stories of a narrative frame in the present with explanatory flashbacks that establish the thematic significance of the current situation.[24] In this case, the narrational moment is provocative, as the narrator, a Vietnamese Catholic widow now living in Versailles, Louisiana, sits before the body of her friend Thuy preparing to groom her for funeral ceremonies. The physical action of the present is the simple act of brushing Thuy's hair and applying makeup; the psychic action is a review of their friendship and their mutual attraction to Le Van Ly, the man Thuy married but whom the narrator has always loved. This activity, which forms the heart of the story, is presented in a series of disconnected flashbacks that constitute a chronological history of this complex set of relationships.

The narrator's reflections on the meaning of the past also involve acts of self-definition, as though the narrator, her original desires having been thwarted, has waited for this moment to form herself, to actualize the person she aspired to become. She has always been humbled by the greater beauty of her good friend, and she thinks of herself as a mere "expert pair of hands" (p. 144), a plain woman who can perform tasks well but who lacks the feminine allure Thuy had possessed: "I am nearly fifty and I am no beauty at all," the narrator says (p. 147). Although she married in Vietnam, her husband died in the war, and she thinks very little about him; nor does she dwell on her relationship with her sons, who also live in America. She thinks instead about herself, Thuy, and Ly and how she lost him. She reflects on how they met during tennis at the Cirque Sportif in Saigon when the young women were sixteen (pp. 145–46), how Ly was drawn to Thuy by her sensuality and beauty, and how two years later Thuy and Ly declared their love for each other (p. 150). The narrator's husband was killed in the war, leaving her to bring her sons to America alone, but Thuy and Ly soon came as well, and the three of them continue to be friends with no open revelation on the part of the narrator of her continuing love for her friend's husband.

The conclusion is saved from predictability by the discovery the narrator makes of the mastectomy Thuy endured during a brief interlude in California many years before, leaving her with only one breast. The significance is that the narrator has assumed all along that Ly was drawn to Thuy by physical beauty alone, particularly by her sensual breasts. Now, it becomes clear that she has been wrong, that there must have been other qualities that bound them, other dimensions of their affection. If Ly is the kind of man who can venerate for reasons other than physical beauty, then he might be able to love the narrator, hence her optimism in the conclusion that Thuy "would understand if I did all I could to make Le Van Ly happy" (p. 154). It is a sensitive narrative of self-exploration, confession, sympathy, and generosity.

"The American Couple" (pp. 155–234) is the longest story in *A Good Scent from a Strange Mountain* and, because of length, the only one not previously published.[25] It is told by a Vietnamese American woman, Gabrielle Tran, who is on holiday in Mexico with her husband, Vinh, having won a free trip on a television game show. There, in Puerto Vallarta, they meet other couples on a similar vacation, and their interaction, the extent to which these American couples, in Mexico, constitute a definition of what it means to be American, compels the action of the story, with many levels of irony. Gabrielle is Vietnamese with a French name, for her parents in Saigon had always admired the French "for their food and for their riding club in Saigon, mostly" (p. 159). She and Vinh, even though they are immigrants, are the "American Couple," embracing the fundamental values of the country more than any of the other people in the story. At various points, Gabrielle, who narrates, explains features of her new nation: "This is what's good about America. There is always some improvisation, something new, and when things get strained, you don't fall back on tradition but you make up something new" (p. 158). In this sense, "The American Couple" serves as a unifying story for those around it in that it develops the themes of assimilation, acculturation, and identity more emphatically than have any of the previous stories.[26]

Part of the definition of America that Gabrielle proffers derives from popular culture, particularly from game shows and soap operas on television, which not only provide entertainment in her life but inform her very sense of identity, her fundamental habits of mind. As she explains, "you'd think I would've had enough of daily disaster, but the soaps remind me that somewhere somebody knows what life can really be. It makes me enjoy even more all of this wonderful lightness before my eyes in America" (p. 157). She perceives the other women in the hotel in terms of what roles they might have played on the game shows, which show they probably attended, how they would have dressed and behaved. These issues unify the women, create a bond among them, link them in common concerns. That Puerto Vallarta was the set for

The Night of the Iguana is another dimension of the fascination for popular culture, and there is a local obsession with the romance between Elizabeth Taylor and Richard Burton during the shooting of the movie.

What links the two most important men in the story is the war in Vietnam, for Vinh was a major in South Vietnamese airborne and Frank was a mechanic, an enlisted man; both men have yet to resolve their feelings about their experience. Ironically, Vinh dresses as an American on vacation, in Bermuda shorts, while Frank follows Vietnamese tradition, wearing all black, further indicating that it is Gabrielle and Vinh who are the "American couple." Almost from the beginning, the two men spar over their roles in the war, Frank baiting Vinh over his superior rank in the army, Vinh stressing his more direct involvement in combat (p. 195). As the action progresses through a visit to the movie set, it becomes clear that the men are fixated on the war, and they enter into combat in a surrogate Vietnam, disappearing into the heavy woods of Mexico. They engage in a war game of their own design, arguing, stalking, throwing stones, finally wrestling on the ground, at once clinging to the dramatic turbulence of their war experience and yet purging unresolved emotions.[27] Gabrielle offers her own explanation: "They had shared something once, something important—rage, fear, the urge to violence, just causes, life and death. They'd both felt those things in service of the same war. And neither of them wanted to let go of all that" (p. 230). Gabrielle also develops the insight into Vinh's life that "from all of this purging of the war, he was now free to do something special" (p. 232). The future is opening out for him, and it is significant that this idea leads directly to an epiphany for Gabrielle, the realization that in her marriage to Vinh it is she who withdrew, who embraced American culture so intensely that she removed herself from her husband.

The final action of the story, when Vinh rides the parasail (as Gabrielle has earlier), is filled with possibilities of reconciliation, some rapprochement between the two men, some closer union between Vinh and Gabrielle. In the aftermath of the fighting, the parasailing returns him to his former glory in the airborne, and he seems to find cathartic rejuvenation in it. As Gabrielle explains, as Vinh floated by the hotel on the parasail, "he turned his face to the Fiesta Vallarta Hotel and he saw me on the balcony and he smiled. I could see the smile very clearly, and when I waved at him, he raised his hand and threw me a kiss" (p. 234). She seems confident in the portent of these events, that they constitute

a new basis for an acceptance of American society and a new relationship with each other: "Night was coming on and my husband was about
to return to earth. And so was I" (p. 234). She has moved beyond soap
opera insights into the feelings of her husband and the potentialities of
America; on the most ephemeral of occasions, a vacation in a world of
kitch and artifice, she has found something real and genuinely valuable
in her marriage.

The concluding story, "A Good Scent from a Strange Mountain"
(pp. 235–49), was first published in the *New England Review* in 1991,
before the appearance of "Preparation," so it was not originally the cap-
stone it is in the volume, where central themes coalesce around the
deathbed of the central figure.[28] The telling is highly personalized, a
retrospective meditation by Dao, a Vietnamese Buddhist who narrates
on his deathbed, preoccupied with surveying the central issues in his
life. He is nearly a hundred years old at the time, residing physically in
New Orleans but living psychically in the world of his youth, when in
1917 he and Ho Chi Minh worked together in the kitchen at the Carl-
ton Hotel in London, Ho as a pastry chef and Dao as a dishwasher. Dao
dwells not on grand international issues but on the personalized and
mundane, far more concerned about the fantasized appearance of Ho at
his bedside than about his own offspring gathered about him. Through
indirection and progressive iteration, other vital issues emerge as well.

The narrational situation is that Dao is dying, and, consistent with
Vietnamese tradition, he has gathered his family about him, "a formal
leave taking," as he explains (p. 236). There should be a close familial
bond among them, and there is not: "But these people who come to
visit me have been in America for a long time and there are very strange
things going on that I can see in their faces" (p. 237). He is sensitive to
the cultural estrangement that distances him from his own children and
to the new "war" going on in America within the expatriated Vietnamese community, a conflict that involves his family. In direct action, the
war in Vietnam is not present: there are no flashbacks to tragic scenes,
no horrifying memories that haunt the narrator. His son Thang was a
colonel in the Army of the Republic of Vietnam, and his grandson Loi
was a lieutenant, but their experience in the war is not at issue. What
matters is the killing of Nguyen Bich Le, a newspaperman who had
advocated the opening of diplomatic conversations with the Communist government in Vietnam. As Dao can perceive, Thang and Loi
would seem to have been involved, for Thang reassures his son that no

murder weapon will be found, he emphasizes that Loi has proven himself not to be a coward, and Dao's daughter Lam stresses, unconvincingly, the "terrible" tragedy of the murder. The war continues, brought home to America, and it has not ended.

But even that issue is not the central focus of Dao's last thoughts, which dwell on Ho, a mythic figure for the Vietnamese people, and the implication is that if he can come to terms with his earlier friendship with him, Dao can find peace in his dying. Dao, a Hoa Hao Buddhist, needs harmony in his final moments, especially within the family, and somehow his search for quietude involves Ho, who attempted to meet with Woodrow Wilson in Paris in 1918 to press for basic rights for Vietnam, principles consistent with Wilson's Fourteen Points then being negotiated in the failed attempt to establish a League of Nations. Ho advocated "equal rights, freedom of assembly, freedom of the press" (p. 240), ideas Wilson certainly would have endorsed, but they never met, and Vietnam went on its colonial course toward external occupation, three major wars, and deep internal tragedy. This was a transitional moment, in other words, a time when Dao was friends with Ho and when Ho's proposal could have changed the course of history, but it never happened. So Dao seeks peace in his religion, in which happiness is expressed as "Bao Son Ky Huong," "a good scent from a strange mountain" (p. 242). In his fantasy, Ho says that he is not at peace in the spirit world, even though there are no countries there (p. 245). His lack of contentment would seem a projection of Dao's own unresolved conflicts, the distress in his family, his dismay at the killing. As Pat C. Hoy III has pointed out, at its core this story is about "a man's enlightening 'visitation' from his old friend Ho Chi Minh[,] who helps him clarify his own obligation to establish harmony in the Vietnamese family before he dies."[29] Dao also seeks to reconcile with Ho, thinking that upon his death, "he and I will be together again and perhaps we can help each other" (p. 249). Here, in this union of a South Vietnamese immigrant with the spirit of Ho Chi Minh, there is the promise of fulfillment and peace. Richard Eder was certainly just in his review of the book maintaining that "in a collection so delicate and so strong, the title story stands out as close to magical."[30]

As the final story explains, the definition of the title of the volume is "happiness," and positive values permeate the collection of fifteen stories, giving it a life-affirming, celebrative tone uncommon in contemporary fiction. "Fairy Tale," for example, portrays not only a fulfilled romance but a reclaimed life in a new land, themes echoed in "Snow" and "Preparation." Other stories emphasize more complex ideas, particularly the irreducible sense of cultural duality on the part of recent immigrants, Vietnamese refugees from a destructive war that left them with haunting memories of family tragedies. As a general rule, the stories explore domestic themes, not international diplomacy, and it is issues of lineage and obligation that drive most of the works, including "Mr. Green," "The Trip Back," "Letters from My Father," "Mid-Autumn," and "In the Clearing." The last three of these stories all feature familial letters, manifest bonds of parent to child, traditions with deep roots in Vietnamese culture.

Some of the stories explore problems of assimilation and cultural loss, a painful severing from what was historically sacred, as when, in "The Trip Back," Khanh has accepted the values of the United States at the loss of his Vietnamese identity, or when the child in "Crickets" shows no interest in the childhood games of his father, or when, in "Relic," the central character lives in the past, in the Vietnam of memory. No one does this more movingly that Dao in "A Good Scent from a Strange Mountain," whose dying moments center on antecedent events from several decades earlier. In each case, however, the stories deal with sensitive issues that humanize the characters for a Western audience. As George Packer has said, "*A Good Scent from a Strange Mountain* is remarkable not for its flaws, but for how beautifully it achieves its daring project of making the Vietnamese real."[31]

These fifteen stories all have their own independent artistic and thematic integrity, and yet, combined into thematic patterns, they resonate off one another, gaining layers of significance denied to the individual works. All of them are told in America, and all relate in some degree to the Vietnam War, the past living in the present, motivating events, modifying the telling of the tales. Nearly all of them involve immigration and resultant issues of social confusion, language acquisition, cultural loss, the sense of ethnic and religious dislocation, and assimilation into a new society. In some instances, more specific matters link stories together, as in the settings in Lake Charles or Versailles, Louisiana, or the epistles at the heart of "Letters from My Father," "Mid-Autumn," and "In the Clearing." Intergenerational conflicts, complicated by varying degrees of commitment to cultural heritage, unite "Mr. Green," "Crickets," and "Relic," although in different ways. If romance binds together "Preparation" and "Snow," the loss of love sits in counterpoint in "Mid-Autumn" and "Open Arms." Although the motif of the acquisition of English and integration into American society is at the heart of most of the stories, the reverse theme of the loss of Vietnamese values informs "The Trip Back," "Crickets," "In the Clearing," and the concluding "A Good Scent from a Strange Mountain." Throughout, the most dominant thematic thread is the search for identity, the definition of self, the exploration of the new life possible in America, an issue inherent from the opening to the concluding story. These are rich themes, at the heart of the multicultural society of the United States, and Butler presents them with impressive sensitivity and insight.

Indeed, it is remarkable that this deeply personal book about Vietnamese characters should have been written by a white American. Perhaps, as Kathleen Kilgore maintains, "it's too soon for the Vietnamese themselves to tell their stories. Like all immigrants, the first generation is preoccupied with survival. The next generation of Vietnamese-Americans will produce anthropologists, sociologists, and journalists with a foot in both cultures."[32] It is also significant that the volume was planned from the beginning as a short-story cycle and executed directly according to the original conception. The stories thus resonate from one another, the concept of death in "Open Arms" serving as a point of reference for "A Ghost Story" and "Preparation" before the conclusion on the point of death in "A Good Scent from a Strange Mountain." If the most dramatic point of aesthetic unification for the stories in the volume is the Vietnamese characters and narrators, the thematic emphasis on family and heritage provides a tight ideological bond as well. In initial conception, artistic expression, and thematic development, *A Good Scent from a Strange Mountain* is a classic short-story cycle, richly deserving of the Pulitzer Prize that followed its publication as a volume of interrelated short fiction.

Conclusion

The short-story cycle is the most neglected and the least well understood of the major genres in American literature. From the beginning, it has been without a place in literary history, and the individual works within the form have been greeted with misunderstanding and misinterpretation for well over a century. Even in modern times, Edmund Wilson's suggestion that in *in our time* Ernest Hemingway "has almost invented a form of his own" and Malcolm Cowley's remark that in *Knight's Gambit* William Faulkner developed a genre "peculiarly his own" illustrate that even the most sagacious of reviewers were innocent of the long tradition of interrelated short stories that could be arranged to form volumes with structural integrity and artistic congruence.[1]

Beyond the glib commentary of initial reviewers, more serious readers, similarly innocent of the internal resonance of the cycle format, have been led to misinterpret individual stories within a volume, not knowing that they depended on intertextual context for the full development of character motivation and theme. A case in point is Hemingway's "Big Two-Hearted River," the concluding story of *in our time*. F. Scott Fitzgerald, indicative of the initial readers, understood it in highly literal terms ("It is the account of a boy on a fishing trip—he hikes, pitches his tent, cooks dinner, sleeps, and next morning casts for trout. Nothing more"), thus ignoring the fact that the preceding episodes establish a pattern for Nick Adams of observing violence and cruelty in America as well as war and brutality abroad in World War I.[2] Had Kenneth Lynn been more sensitive to this point he would not have objected so strenuously to the idea that Nick is on a fishing trip as a therapeutic attempt to expiate the trauma he has just experienced in battle, where he has been severely wounded.[3]

Indeed, even the most perfunctory reading of the volume could not miss the fact that the previous stories and vignettes make it clear that Nick has been in Europe during World War I, for he was wounded on the Italian front in "Chapter VI" (in which he and Rinaldi make their separate peace) and in "Cross Country Snow" he is still affected by a wound to his leg, for he snowplows down the mountain while his friend George telemarks, a more elegant and sophisticated turn. The background of the war is central in the non-Nick episodes as well, for it is the setting for "Chapter 1," "Chapter III," "Chapter IV," "A Very Short Story," "Chapter VII," and "Soldier's Home," in all of which military conflict is the occasion for disillusionment, wounding, death, and psychic pain.

Even the biographical evidence points to this assessment. Throughout his life Hemingway was consistent in commenting that "Big Two-Hearted River" was "about coming back from the war but there was no mention of the war in it," as he wrote in *A Moveable Feast*.[4] Earlier, in 1953, he wrote to Charles Poore to say that "I suppose you know it ["Big Two-Hearted River"]; but it is a story about a boy who has come back from the war. The war is never mentioned though as far as I can remember. This may be one of the things that helps it."[5] The ultimate justification for an interpretation must rest within literary data itself, but here, given the nature of the short-story cycle, the basic notion that Nick is back from the war, seeking solace in an activity he loves and finds therapeutic, that he has been wounded, that he still suffers psychological effects from his exposure to violence and death, and that his fishing trip in the Michigan woods is salutary if not curative, is well justified by the events in preceding stories. Those readers, from Fitzgerald to Lynn, who could find nothing of war or wounding in the conclusion, failed to recognize the interpretive implications of genre.

So it has been with regard to the contemporary short-story cycle. Had Sara Maitland better understood the form when she reviewed *Monkeys* for the *New Statesman*, she would not have concluded that "each of the nine incidents in the novel is wonderfully wrought, with vivid observation and lucid prose—each would make a lovely short story actually—but they don't add up to a novel of substance."[6] Robert Towers was similarly uninformed when he criticized the "structural problems" of *Love Medicine* in the *New York Review of Books*, not comprehending that the stories had been previously published in magazines and had subsequently been organized into a pattern that folds and unfolds in a thematically symmetrical design. With few exceptions, literary scholars, even those who have written on the tradition of the short-story cycle, have neglected to investigate the dual nature of the stories, comparing the magazine texts with those in the assembled volume and considering the revisions and modifications that were made in establishing synergy for the entire work.

There are also distinctions that can be made about a story as it stood isolated in comparison to its significance in the context of other stories. In some instances the interpretive consequences can be substantial, as in the case of O'Brien's "On the Rainy River." When it appeared in *Playboy* in 1990, with no explanatory notations, it gave every indication of being straight autobiography, the "O'Brien" of the fiction equating to the author without qualification. In the context of *The Things They Carried*, with the presentation of clearly fictional elements for the "O'Brien" character, including an invented daughter and a spectrum of war buddies who never existed in reality, the more complex nature of the "fiction" emerges, changing its very essence.[7] Kincaid's stories, appearing in *The New Yorker*, did not have the character, nor the sequentiality, of a *Bildungsroman* until they were assembled in the book. The ten previously published stories that went into the first edition of *Love Medicine* appeared singly with no suggestion that the death of June would provide the thematic linkage that brought all of the episodes together. When the first three stories of *The Joy Luck Club* were initially published, there was no hint of the complex structural organization that ultimately gave the volume unity, the pattern of alternating mother-and-daughter narratives representing each of the four mah jong families.

Fundamentally, the stories in a cycle have a dual existence that the chapters of a novel seldom have, even in the serial world of nineteenth-century publication, and for this reason the study of composition and publication history becomes all the more essential. Such an investigation reveals two material interpretive dimensions: the textual variants between magazine and book versions and the organizational structure that gives disparate stories an integrated form. Although it is true that in given instances stories move from serial to book publication without substantial modification, sometimes the alterations are dramatic and need to be considered in any serious study of the work.

No one should write about *How the García Girls Lost Their Accents* without taking into account the fact that when "The Kiss" initially appeared it contained a different time scheme for the action, gave variant names for the characters, and had fewer sisters in the Garcia family, all of which have consequences for close reading.[8] "The Red Convertible" is often taken as the crucial story in *Love Medicine*, and it is frequently anthologized in short-story collections, but even the most energetic interpretations have missed the fact that when it was first published it was told by a character named "Marty," not by Lyman Lamartine, and the older brother who returns home was named "Stephen," not Henry Jr. The alteration of names and narrators was necessitated by the need to coordinate this story with the others in the volume. In the process, the story placed in the context of the others gives the events layers of significance missing from the magazine version, including the fact that Henry Jr.'s suicide was antedated by his father's, that Henry Jr. was the product of a union between his mother and his uncle, and that Henry Jr. has returned from the war consumed with pathological violence, much of which he internalizes. These issues, missing in the magazine version, motivate his suicide and make the events comprehensible.[9]

Individual stories appearing in a magazine may have a high degree of internal unity, but they of necessity lack the structural organization that accrues to the collected volume, a key issue in integrating separate short works of fiction into an aesthetically congruent book. Kincaid, Minot, Cisneros, and Tan all arranged their events in chronological sequence, even though the individual stories had been published in a different order and, in some cases, had anomalous temporal references in first publication. In each case, even though the "present" action progresses in succeeding episodes, there are important flashbacks that shift the time to salient moments in the life of the central character or family, to life in Mexico or the earlier house on Loomis Street in *The House on Mango Street*, to scenes in China when the mothers underwent the dramas that led them to immigrate to the United States in *The Joy Luck Club*, to depictions of Annie's early childhood in *Annie John*, to memories of the courtship of Mum and Dad in *Monkeys*. These flashbacks all resonate in the present, suggesting motivations and meanings for the events that occur years later, but they do not compromise the progressive movement of plot and action that give the volume a sense of unification.

The Things They Carried not only moves backward and forward in time but uses one of the unique features of the cycle format, duplicative time, with some stories regressing to cover again, from a contrasting visage point, events already related by someone else, as in the multiple representations of Kiowa's death in the shit field. Although a novel can present synchronicity of this kind, it is especially common in the cycle format. *How the García Girls Lost Their Accents* achieves unity in reverse chronological order, moving backward to the causation of action rather than forward to the effects. Similarly, although it starts in 1981 with the death of June, *Love Medicine* moves quickly back into the 1930s, tracing the historical developments and family events that lead to death in the opening story before going on to episodes that follow the tragedy. In whatever arrangement, the individual stories are brought together into meaningful patterns of action, character development, and thematic progression.

The traditional means of unifying a collection has been to place all of the action in a single setting, the method of *Winesburg, Ohio*, Crane's *Whilomville Tales*, Naylor's *The Women of Brewster Place*. *The House on Mango Street* and *Annie John* both employ that technique, although those volumes are unified by continuing family groups as well. *The Joy Luck Club* has a unified setting in a more expanded sense; most of the action of the present (save for that of the concluding story, which involves a journey back to China) takes place in California, while all of the flashbacks are set on the Chinese mainland. *A Good Scent from a Strange Mountain* has a similar pattern, with the present in Louisiana and the past in Vietnam at the time of the war, and all fourteen stories in *Love Medicine* have scenes within driving distance of the Turtle Mountain Reservation in North Dakota. *Monkeys* takes place either in the north-shore region of Massachusetts or at the Vincent summer home in Maine, with the exception of one story set in Bermuda when the family is on vacation. Some of the events of *The Things They Carried* are set against the American landscape of Iowa and Minnesota, but the more dramatic scenes take place in Vietnam, the two locations sometimes vibrating against each other, the possibilities of one having been lost in the other. *García Girls* has a similarly expanded dual setting, the events in the United States having their inception in the Dominican Republic, with that island serving as the location for the opening and closing stories, despite their distance in time.

Another means of introducing linkage among stories published separately is to give all of them the same narrative stance, the same perspective, from the same time and place, joining the episodes together in voice and tone and sensibility. *Annie John* functions in this way, the older Annie speaking from England about her childhood in Antigua. *The House on Mango Street*, a decidedly more disjointed work in action and theme, nevertheless is united by the voice of Esperanza speaking about her life in the course of a year. In *A Good Scent from a Strange Mountain*, Butler uses a variation on the device in that all of the fifteen stories are told in first person, in America, but there is a different narrator in each case.

The short-story cycle can function in this way, with tight narrative integrity, but more often the tendency is to introduce a spectrum of voices, with contrasting sensibilities and values, who are in some way related or involved in the same setting or plot. The eight speakers of *The Joy Luck Club* (in a sense there are seven, with June recalling the family tales her mother told her, giving her mother voice even though she is dead) are a case in point, with separate agendas for each family and contrasting issues for the mothers and the daughters. There is also the implication, in their multiplicity, that in some sense the conglomerate voices in the book represent the concerns of the Chinese-American community, an effect the multivocal narrative stance facilitates.[10] This concept works in more complex ways in *Love Medicine* and *How the García Girls Lost Their Accents* in that there are, in part, third-person narrators who use a main character as a center of intelligence, as the focalizing agent, without presenting direct formulations from that mind. It becomes even more intricate when such third-person presentations are juxtaposed by first-person episodes using the same character, the mediation of the narrational intelligence in one instance necessarily modifying the sensibility presented directly in first-person segments.

In narrative multiplicity of this kind, the short-story cycle mitigates away from the unifying presence of the omniscient narrator customary in the novel, emphasizing instead what Gerald Kennedy has called "a variety of voices or perspectives reflective of the radical subjectivity of modern experience."[11] *The Things They Carried* is especially problematic in narrative terms because the first story is told from an omniscient perspective but all the rest are related from more limited, and unreliable, points of view, some by Rat Kiley, some by the fictional entity known as Tim O'Brien. In interpretative terms, all information presented must be weighed against the special interests of the teller. This situation also pertains in *Love Medicine*. Two stories employ an omniscient technique, at least in part; the other twelve have more complicated methodologies, with five of them being related in first person, several with third-person perspectives limited to the mind of a single character, and many of the rest using multiple techniques within one story, including, in the case of "Lulu's Boys," a synthesized community voice. Sophie tells one story in *Monkeys*, but seven are told from a third-person perspective identified with the mind of one of the children, and one, "Accident," is related from outside the family. In nearly every case, however, narrative method is yet another element lending not only a point of view but structural unity to a series of independent short stories.

Beyond setting and narrative perspective, the richest element of intertextual unity in a cycle is theme, the coalescence of ideas and implications that resonate throughout the volume. This matter may involve both motifs (subordinate concepts that play a role in only part of the volume) and major themes (ideas that run throughout the book, linking virtually all of the stories together). In *How the García Girls Lost Their Accents*, for example, the motif of corruption and violence in the Dominican Republic plays an increasingly significant role as the stories regress in time; conversely, the concept of assimilation and its linguistic consequences becomes less important as the volume develops. But the theme of Yolanda's psychological growth from age six to thirty-nine, her romances and failed marriage, her struggles with adjustment to a new culture, her development of a new emotional construct, draws together the entire volume, providing a focus and a direction to the assembled stories, even though they move backward in time. Internally, each group of stories presents its own unifying theme. A painful adjustment to America, family pathologies, and generational tension draw together the first five stories, for example. Similar thematic patterns unite the other sections of the book.

It is fundamentally the growth of Esperanza that unifies the stories in *The House on Mango Street*, giving the book psychological as well as temporal progression. Her developing maturity and self-assurance, her explorations, however painful, of early sexual awareness, and her ultimate determination to escape Mango Street to pursue her writing provide an overarching set of concerns to forty-four stories. If the tradition of the *Bildungsroman* is obvious in *Annie John*, with its chronological growth of the first-person narrator, it is more subtly presented in *Mango Street* and in those volumes with group protagonists, such as *Monkeys*, which offers nine stories about various members of the same family, all of them, to some extent, presenting variations on the consequences of the fundamental pathology inherent in Dad's obtuse insensitivity and Mum's agonizing need for emotional fulfillment. *Love Medicine* similarly presents a spectrum of characters as protagonists in various stories, but the uniting themes are those of cultural duality, the loss of traditions, alienation, and self-destruction, suicide being the dominant form of violence. In contrast, the stories in *A Good Scent from a Strange Mountain*, despite the background of war, presents positive, life-affirming values (the title means "happiness"), and cultural duality involves not only lost traditions but the embracing of new ones, forming new relationships, new families, new lives. These themes run throughout the fifteen stories, even when there is death and destruction in the flashbacks to Vietnam. The stories in *The Things They Carried* are more complex in their treatment of Vietnam, focusing on the horror of war, its ethical nightmares, its collision of fear and responsibility, and the self-reflexive issue of what is "true" about a war story.

If the stories in *The Joy Luck Club* do not present a fulfillment of each mother's wishes for her daughter, they are unified by those desires and by the psychic growth of the daughters in each case, a maturing that allows them to reach back and embrace parts of a lost Chinese heritage. Indeed, in broader terms, what emerges from a consideration of the contemporary short-story cycle is that not only is there thematic coherence within the volumes but as a genre they represent an articulation of a spectrum of American issues at the end of the twentieth century. One of these, as in the stories by Amy Tan, is the theme of immigration with its matrix of attendant concerns for the American Dream, assimilation, cultural duality, language acquisition and loss, religious conflict, and intergenerational conflict over familial respect and the preservation of traditional values. Although these issues are as old as the United States, they emerged as major literary concerns in the late nineteenth century during the burgeoning of immigration, as waves of Europeans swept across the continent, doubling the population of the country and giving rise to a tradition in fiction. It is perhaps uniquely American that a century later these concepts are still of the moment in fiction, still providing the familial and psychological conflicts that generate great works of art.

The Joy Luck Club is perhaps the richest of the recent short-story cycles in these terms for it presents compelling glimpses of life in the country of origin in scenes that implicitly suggest the motivation for emigration from China, the struggles of the immigrants in contending with the linguistic and cultural challenges of a new society, and the generational confrontations that come with children who move more easily into the American mainstream, slightly embarrassed by their parents and their old-fashioned ways. Tan's book offers both a dramatization of this situation and a resolution, in the journey of June Woo back to China, for synthesis and reconciliation within American families. *How the García Girls Lost Their Accents* presents many of the same issues, manifested in characters with more socio-economic privilege and, ironically, more personal pathology, but the familial story ends (and the book begins) with Yolanda back in the Dominican Republic, back with the extended family and the culture she more clearly understands. This retrograde immigration plot is the contemporary equivalent of the "backtrailer" novels of a century earlier, those books such as Hamlin Garland's *Back-Trailers from the Middle Border* that portrayed disillusionment with the frontier and the relentless westward movement and a return to and a reaffirmation of life in the more cultivated eastern seaboard. Although this idea works for Yolanda, the rest of the family is more jaded about the island, more determined to make their lives, and fulfill their dreams, in America.

The situation in *The House on Mango Street* is more complex as well in that it involves a more pronounced sense of ethnic exclusion even as the American Dream looms large for Esperanza in her aspiration to become a writer. Here, as in the earlier books, cultural duality is a central issue, and the exploration of a sense of identity, the construction of self, is complicated by language and racial "markers" that suggest exclusion and by the gender dominance traditional within Latino society, perhaps the most intransigent of the problems faced by the women in the neighborhood. It is this issue, along with the sexual threat Esperanza faces every day, with its attendant prospect of children and a place leaning out the window, that drives her desire for escape. Unlike Yolanda, however, Esperanza longs to flee not back to the homeland but outward into American society and a respectable house in a safe area. The Vietnamese immigrants in *A Good Scent from a Strange Mountain* represent an even more positive attitude toward movement into American society despite the fact that they have lost much in war. They left behind not only their families and language and ethnic tradition but often their conception of themselves, yet they prevail in their attempt to establish a meaningful new life in Louisiana. Immigration is not an issue for the Native American families in *Love Medicine*, of course, but cultural duality, the loss of tradition and religion, and assimilation play as large a role in these stories as in those about people from another country. Erdrich's book is less optimistic than the others, however, and there is little commitment to the American Dream, little hope of cultural synthesis, personal fulfillment, or deeply rooted happiness. In the case of each of these books, the cycle format lends itself to the dramatization of conflict within a single character or social group, the aggregate volume representing the situation of the ethnic community as a whole. It is a genre that works well for the portrayal of the immigrant experience at the heart of American society, for the dramatization of the cultural dislocation within a family, and for the revelation of the psychic alienation of a central character.

Perhaps that is part of the reason why the story cycle has found such appeal for contemporary writers across a spectrum of ethnic traditions. Indeed, the proliferation of volumes of stories from virtually every racial and nationality group in the United States suggests that there is something transcendent in its literary essence, something that lends itself easily to adaptation and implementation. Rocío G. Davis has postulated that "a survey of ethnic fiction in the United States demonstrates a proliferation of the short story cycle, a hybrid form with roots in the western tradition, which many of the principal ethnic writers have adapted and perfected as a tool through which they enact their dramas."[12] Davis is certainly correct in his observation of the prominence of the form, but nearly every term of the rest of his formulation would seem to require qualification. The cycle is not so much a "hybrid" form of long fiction as an original, "antecedent" construction that anticipates the novel by centuries. Nor is it limited to the "western tradition," linked stories being known worldwide, in the East as well as the West, among people of disparate ethnic, class, and linguistic backgrounds.

What would seem to be a unifying generic force is the legacy of the oral tradition, reaching back through time and across national boundaries to bind together legions of tellers of tales. Secondary to that impulse would have been the desire to link stories to others, to make a coherent narrative of smaller units, as Erdrich indicated when she observed that the "storytelling cycle is in [the] oral traditions of all cultures."[13] On the social level, there is the effort to create a community of tellers and listeners who share a nucleus of concerns and values inherent in the tales of the culture. Ian Reid has considered this issue and suggested that "the impulse to combine individual tales into larger wholes has its origin in the very nature of imagination itself, a 'coadunating' power as Coleridge described it. Certainly many old story-clusters show that the impulse goes far back into oral tradition. . . ."[14] Forrest Ingram has speculated that "the fact that the original stories arose from folk imagination, from the collective effort of many people, gave each a separate identity, a uniqueness, and an independence which then was subsumed and integrated into a whole by a single author who modified and retold the stories as he fitted them into his own design."[15] This formulation of the evolution of a cycle has been supported by the comments of Louise Erdrich on the historic method of Chippewa storytelling, a tradition with a more recent access to the oral tradition than any of the European forms imported into America. She reflects that her ancestors favored "cycles" of stories unified by a common, often mythological, subject: "Night after night, or day after day, it's a storytelling cycle."[16] Far from being a modern "hybrid" form, a compromise between the story and the novel, the cycle is an ancient construction that Native Americans, and many other racial groups, found consistent with their fundamental need to tell stories.

In contemporary American literature, the prevalence of the cycle might be attributed to another coalescence of factors, among them the difficulty of placing novels for young writers in publishing houses now owned by giant conglomerates and run according to corporate objectives. The result has been that beginning writers initiate a career by publishing stories in "little magazines" such as the *Georgia Review*, organs owned by universities and dedicated to the objective of promoting literature of quality regardless of its lack of mass marketability. Another outlet has been the "popular" magazines, such as the *New Yorker*, that allot space in each issue to a very small number of stories of high quality. The writer of a series of such stories, all focused on some salient subject, might subsequently modify them to constitute a volume in the cycle tradition, as did Jamaica Kincaid with *Annie John* and Susan Minot with *Monkeys*. The literary situation at the end of the twentieth century was ripe for the production of short-story cycles, and they were rapidly becoming a dominant form.

That the cycle format has appealed to writers across ethnic lines has been both an enrichment of the national literature and, in at least one sense, a diversion. It has been a valuable contribution to American fiction because of the quality of the volumes involved and because of its educative function, the distribution to a mass audience of a literature

256

that directly illustrates the sensibilities of people from a given ethnic background, expressing their unique concerns and aspirations as well as their more generalized participation in the human condition. No one could read *Love Medicine, Annie John, The House on Mango Street, How the García Girls Lost Their Accents,* or *The Joy Luck Club* without some enlargement of sensibility. Indeed, the power of these stories is profoundly moving, and that is true as well for *Monkeys* and *The Things They Carried,* which involve their own dramatization of human interactions, albeit on a different set of issues.

The ethnic consideration of the contemporary cycle is a diversion only to the extent that it subordinates literary concerns to the transient political issues of a given era, however compelling those concerns might be. The force of literature considered as an aesthetic form is for consolidation, for the construction of an inclusive social community unified by the power of artistic expression. This is the essence of what Erdrich was promoting when she commented that Native-American literature should not be considered as a sui generis expression but as part of the literary richness of the United States: "Setting it apart and saying that people with special interest might read this literature sets Indians apart too."[17] She is even more forceful in her consideration of the separation of literary traditions within society: "All of the ethnic writing done in the United States is American writing, and should be called American writing."[18] In this sense, the short-story cycle, in addition to providing a contemporary medium of expression compatible with ancient narrative methodologies, can also serve as a socially unifying medium, a community of readers willing to understand and empathize with a spectrum of characters from ethnic groups unlike their own. But this concept notwithstanding, as Susan Pérez Castillo has argued, contemporary writers from minority traditions should be judged as literary artists and held to the same rigorous standards as "majority" writers, and "anything else is patronizing and demeaning to the texts in question. Surely it is more productive, in the evaluation of so-called 'ethnic' texts, to view ethnicity not as a static entity but rather as a dynamic, historically constructed process."[19] The consideration of the contemporary American short-story cycle is enhanced by the impressive quality of the genre, a richness beyond measure or full articulation, and that aesthetic character has transcended any limitation by ethnic category. For example, *The Joy Luck Club,* as a best-selling book and a widely popular movie, has permeated all dimensions of American cultural life, and that book had its inception when Amy Tan read a Native-American short-story cycle, Louise Erdrich's *Love Medicine*.[20]

Gerald Kennedy has attempted to postulate a correspondence between individual stories in a collected cycle to individuals in a larger society, suggesting that there is a parallel in the "paradoxical semblance of community in its structural dynamic of connection and disconnection. The simultaneous independence and interdependence of stories in a sequence fosters a corresponding awareness of both the autonomy of individual stories and the elements that conjoin them."[21] The American experience, is, after all, the process of making one out of many. If this analogy were to be pushed a step further, there could be said to be an equivalence between an analysis of the themes that unite the stories in contemporary cycles and the ideas that consolidate American society. In this sense, the literary themes of immigration, ethnic diversity, the American Dream, cultural duality, language acquisition and loss, individual responsibility, the dynamic role of the past in the present, and intergenerational conflict over the preservation of cultural values might be said to mirror the issues that are very much of the moment in American society. Literature is no small social force, in the sense that it provides a window into the soul of a nation, reveling both its anguish and its bliss, its promise and its ongoing internal struggle. The study of the contemporary short-story cycle, as represented by the extraordinary books by Louise Erdrich, Jamaica Kincaid, Susan Minot, Sandra Cisneros, Tim O'Brien, Julia Alvarez, Amy Tan, and Robert Olen Butler, can illuminate both the literary enrichment and the powerful social critique expressed in this important genre. It is an area of intellectual inquiry that has only just begun.

Notes

INTRODUCTION

1. Edmund Wilson, "Mr. Hemingway's Dry-Points" [Review of *in our time*], *The Dial*, 77 (October 1924): 340–41.

2. Malcolm Cowley, "Faulkner Stories, in Amiable Mood," *New York Herald Tribune Books* (November 6, 1949): 7. I am indebted to Susan Garland Mann for bringing the reviews by Wilson and Cowley to my attention. See her book *The Short Story Cycle: A Genre Companion and Reference Guide* (Westport: Greenwood, 1989), ix–x.

3. Forrest L. Ingram, *Representative Short Story Cycles of the Twentieth Century* (The Hague: Mouton, 1971), 17.

4. Arnold Williams, *The Drama of Medieval England* (East Lansing: Michigan State University Press, 1961), 130–31.

5. Rosemary Woolf, *The English Mystery Plays* (London: Routledge & Kegan Paul, 1972), 304.

6. I am indebted here to Mann, *The Short Story Cycle*, 1–5.

7. For a more detailed assessment of the categories of short fiction, see Ian Reid, *The Short Story* (New York: Barnes & Noble, 1977), 30–33. Reid also discusses the "yarn," with its stress on the oral nature of the telling, with colloquial language and comic interruptions; the "fable," with the anthropomorphizing of animals; and the "parable," and its tendency for symbolic treatment of setting and character.

8. I am indebted to Maggie Dunn and Ann Morris, in *The Composite Novel: The Short Story Cycle in Transition* (New York: Twayne, 1995), 159–82, and to Mann, *The Short Story Cycle*, 187–208, for their annotated bibliographies of the role of the short-story cycle in American literature.

9. See Ingram, *Representative Short Story Cycles*, 19. Ingram set his definition in italics, which I have removed.

10. See Mann, *The Short Story Cycle*, 187–208.

11. Mann, *The Short Story Cycle*, xii.

12. Mann, *The Short Story Cycle*, 15.

13. J. Gerald Kennedy, ed., *Modern American Short Story Sequences* (New York: Cambridge, 1995).

14. Reid, *Short Story*, 46.

15. Norman Friedman, "Recent Short Story Theories: Problems in Definition," in *Short Story Theory at a Crossroads*, ed. Susan Lohafer and Jo Ellyn Clarey (Baton Rouge: Louisiana State University Press, 1989), 29.

16. My ideas here are consistent with those of Austin M. Wright in "On Defining the Short Story: The Genre Question," *Short Story Theory at a Crossroads*, 50–51.

17. See Helen Mustard, *The Lyric Cycle in German Literature* (Morningside Heights: King's Crown Press, 1946), 20.

18. In my introduction to the most recent edition of this important volume, I offer an extended analysis of the role of setting and character as linking devices. See James Nagel, "Introduction," John Steinbeck, *The Pastures of Heaven* (New York: Penguin, 1995), vii–xxix.

19. Robert M. Luscher, "The Short Story Sequence: An Open Book," in *Short Story Theory at a Crossroads*, 153.

20. Ingram, *Representative Short Story Cycles*, 200.

21. See Ingram, *Representative Short Story Cycles*, 22.

22. Mann, *The Short Story Cycle*, xii.

23. See Mann, *The Short Story Cycle*, 13, for a similar comment.

24. Kennedy would concur (*Modern American Short Story Sequences*, x).

CHAPTER 1

1. See D. J. R. Bruckner, "Books of The Times," *New York Times* (December 20, 1984): 21; Marco Portales, "People with Holes in Their Lives," *New York Times Book Review* (December 23, 1984): 6; Linda Taylor, "On- and off-reservation," *[London] Times Literary Supplement* (February 22, 1985): 196; and Harriett Gilbert, "Mixed Feelings," *New Statesman* (February 8, 1985): 31.

2. Robert Towers, "Uprooted," *New York Review of Books* (April 11, 1985): 36.

3. Gene Lyons, "In Indian Territory," *Newsweek* (February 11, 1985): 70.

4. Catherine Rainwater, "Reading Between Worlds: Narrativity in the Fiction of Louise Erdrich," *American Literature*, 62 (1990): 415.

5. Andrew O. Wiget, "Contemporary Native American Literature," *Choice* (June 1986): 1508.

6. Joseph Bruchac, [Review of *Love Medicine*] *North Dakota Quarterly*, 53, No. 2 (Spring 1985): 255–56.

7. Jay Parini, "*Love Medicine* by Louise Erdrich," *Saturday Review* (November/December 1984): 83.

8. Thomas L. Kilpatrick, [Review of *Love Medicine*] *Library Journal* (October 1, 1984): 1860.

9. See Louise Erdrich, "The World's Greatest Fisherman," *Chicago*, 31, No. 10 (October 1982): 159–68; "The Red Convertible," *Mississippi Valley Review*, 11, No. 2 (1982): 10–17; "Scales," *North American Review*, 267, No. 1 (March 1982): 22–27.

10. See Kay Bonetti, "An Interview with Louise Erdrich and Michael Dorris," *Missouri Review*, 11, No. 2 (1988): 84–85.

11. See Erdrich's comments in *Conversations with Louise Erdrich and Michael Dorris*, ed. Allan Chavkin and Nancy Feyl Chavkin (Jackson: University Press of Mississippi, 1994), 6.

12. See Bonetti, "An Interview with Louise Erdrich and Michael Dorris," 89.

13. See Erdrich's comments in *Conversations with Louise Erdrich and Michael Dorris*, 4.

14. See Dorris's comments, in *Conversations with Louise Erdrich and Michael Dorris*, 22.

15. Frederick Baraga, *Chippewa Indians: As Recorded by Rev. Frederick Baraga in 1847* (New York: League of Slovenian Americans, 1976), 14.

16. Baraga, *Chippewa Indians*, 43.

17. I am indebted here to Hertha D. Wong, "Louise Erdrich's *Love Medicine*: Narrative Communities and the Short Story Sequence," in *Modern American Short Story Sequences*, ed. J. Gerald Kennedy (New York: Cambridge, 1995), 174; and Kathleen M. Sands, [Commentary on *Love Medicine*] *Studies in American Indian Literatures*, 9, No. 1 (1985): 14–15. See also Susan Pérez Castillo, "Postmodernism, Native American Literature and the Real: The Silko-Erdrich Controversy," *Massachusetts Review*, 32, No. 2 (Summer 1991): 286.

18. Hertha Wong's assessment is that "in general, the work is organized as the juxtaposed stories of eight narrators: Albertine Johnson, Marie (Lazarre) Kashpaw, Nector Kashpaw, Lulu Lamartine, Lipsha Morrissey, Lyman Lamartine, Howard Kashpaw, and a third-person narrator" ("Louise Erdrich's *Love Medicine*," 175). My argument is that there are many more narrators than that because the third-person perspectives are identified with the minds of eight different characters, relating only the perspective of that one individual, in addition to five first-person narrators and one omniscient voice. In terms of stating the facts of the case and interpreting the events, there are, in effect, fifteen narrative perspectives.

19. Wong has commented perceptively that the "native use of multiple narrators often has little to do with alienation and loss and much more to do with the coherent multiplicity of community" (174).

20. Sands, [Commentary on *Love Medicine*], 15.

21. All page references in the text to the fourteen stories in the first edition refer to Louise Erdrich, *Love Medicine* (New York: Holt, Rinehart and Winston, 1984).

22. See "The World's Greatest Fisherman," *Chicago*, 160.

23. Wiget commented on this point in his review ("Contemporary Native American Literature," 1508). See also the perceptive comments of Hertha D. Wong in "Louise Erdrich's *Love Medicine*," 183.

24. Rainwater, "Reading Between Worlds," 407–08.

25. See Baraga, *Chippewa Indians*, 65.

26. Edmund Jefferson Danziger Jr., *The Chippewas of Lake Superior* (Norman: University of Oklahoma Press, 1979), 8–9.

27. I am indebted, in my discussion of these matters, to Ronald Takaki, *A*

Different Mirror: A History of Multicultural America (Boston: Little, Brown, 1993), 231–37.

28. Louise Erdrich, "Where I Ought to Be: A Writer's Sense of Place," *New York Times Book Review* (July 28, 1985): 23.

29. For the original publication of the story, see Louise Erdrich, "Saint Marie," *Atlantic Monthly*, 253 (March 1984): 78–84.

30. Erdrich has indicated that an early version of this story was told in third person; other versions were told by minor characters; only the final magazine text, and that contained in *Love Medicine*, are told by Marie. See Erdrich's comments in *Conversations with Louise Erdrich and Michael Dorris*, 251.

31. For the first publication of the story, see Louise Erdrich, "Wild Geese," *Mother Jones*, 9 (October 1984): 21–22. Except for the direct assertion of the year, 1934, and the narrator, Nector Kapshaw, the text in the volume is identical to that in the magazine.

32. For the first publication of the story, see Louise Erdrich, "The Beads," *North Dakota Quarterly*, 52 (Spring 1984): 54–61.

33. Catherine Rainwater seems to assume that the beads have greatest significance for Marie, not June, when she says that "if they are Cree beads, they should speak to the shamanic dimension of Marie (who is a sorcerer and healer), and if they are a rosary, they should speak to her Catholic dimension." See Rainwater, "Reading Between Worlds," 412. My thinking is more congruent with that of David Mitchell, who contends that "much of June's past is tempered by her association with 'the woods.' The black beads that she comes out of the woods wearing are a symbol of the Cree Indian tribe which first discovers June after her mother has died (possibly from exposure?). A reminder of her connection to a past that is rapidly shrinking away for most characters in the novel, the beads are symbols of survival that the tribe offers to the young girl when she appears seemingly out of nowhere, a child of the forest manitous." See David Mitchell, "A Bridge to the Past: Cultural Hegemony and the Native American Past in Louise Erdrich's *Love Medicine*," in *Entering the 90s: The North American Experience*, ed. Thomas E. Schirer (Sault Ste. Marie: Lake Superior University Press, 1991), 167.

34. For the original publication of the story, see Louise Erdrich, "Lulu's Boys," *Kenyon Review*, 6, No. 3 (Summer 1984): 1–10. The clarification about the seven-year time difference, deleted in book publication (87), is on page 9 of the magazine.

35. For the first publication of the story, see Louise Erdrich, "The Plunge of the Brave," *New England Review*, 7, No. 1 (Fall 1984): 120–36. There are no substantial differences between magazine and book publication of the story.

36. For my understanding of Native American conceptions of time, I am indebted to Debra C. Holt, "Transformation and Continuance: Native American Tradition in the Novels of Louise Erdrich," in *Entering the 90s*, 150.

37. Rainwater, "Reading Between Worlds," 414.

38. In "The Beads" the suggestion is that Nector's brother Eli is Cree, since he sings their songs (69). In this story and elsewhere, however, it is clear that both of them are Chippewa.

39. See Marie's reference to "this morning" (113).

40. For the original publication of "Flesh and Blood," see Louise Erdrich, "Love Medicine," *Ms.*, 13 (November 1984): 74–84, 150. In *Love Medicine* the title of the story has been changed and the year and narrator specified, but there are no other substantial changes.

41. For the original publication of the story, see Louise Erdrich, "The Red Convertible," *Mississippi Valley Review*, 11, No. 2 (1982): 10–17. In the magazine, the title assertion contains the notation "for Earl Livermore."

42. There are other details as well that were altered in the book text. The younger brother, Marty, was twenty in the magazine; Lyman is sixteen in the volume (144). His restaurant is destroyed by a tornado in the magazine and by a fire in the book, a tornado perhaps seeming a low-probability disaster. In the magazine version, it is 1968 when "Stephen" goes to Vietnam, and he is stationed specifically in Khe Sanh; in *Love Medicine*, Henry is more vaguely located in "the northern hill country" in 1970 (147).

43. See Erdrich's comments in Bonetti, "An Interview with Louise Erdrich and Michael Dorris," 91–92.

44. For the first publication of the story, see Louise Erdrich, "Scales," *The North American Review*, 267, No. 1 (March 1982): 22–27.

45. I am indebted to Wong for her comments on the alterations from the magazine text. Comparing the revisions in "Scales" to those made in the other stories, she maintains that "in 'Scales' the editing was more extensive, but still not substantial. In addition to minor alterations in word choice, phrasing, and punctuation, Dot's five-month pregnancy became a six-month pregnancy, and her baby boy was transformed into a baby girl. Although the gender switch is dramatic, it does nothing to unify the narratives in *Love Medicine*." See Wong, "Louise Erdrich's *Love Medicine*," 170–71. The modifications have somewhat greater significance than Wong indicates, but her general point is well taken.

46. See Erdrich's comment in *Conversations with Louise Erdrich and Michael Dorris*, 252.

47. I am indebted here to the observations by Margie Towery in "Continuity and Connection: Characters in Louise Erdrich's Fiction," *American Indian Culture and Research Journal*, 16, No. 4 (1992): 104–05. She goes on to describe the supernatural powers of Gerry: "Gerry personifies the trickster in two important ways. First, he is able to change forms, to escape despite his enormous size, thus acting out the trickster's escape and recapture cycle. . . . Gerry is also able to make Dot pregnant, even though he is in jail." My contention is that there is nothing necessarily magical about his escaping. His impregnation of Dot is clearly explained in the text as a physical event in the corner of the visiting room, not as a supernormal aberration. See *Love Medicine*, 160.

48. For the first publication of the story, see Louise Erdrich, "Crown of Thorns," *Chicago*, 33, No. 9 (September 1984): 206–09, 238, 240.

49. For Erdrich's comments, see Joseph Bruchac, "Whatever Is Really Yours: An Interview with Louise Erdrich," *Survival This Way: Interviews with American Indian Poets*, ed. Joseph Bruchac (Tucson: University of Arizona Press, 1987), 81.

50. See Louise Flavin, "Louise Erdrich's *Love Medicine*: Loving Over Time and Distance," *Critique*, 31, No. 1 (Fall 1989): 63–64.

51. Hertha Wong has given the organization of *Love Medicine* careful attention, pointing out that "the structure of *Love Medicine* (in its original form) is somewhat chiasmic, the first and last stories thematically mirroring each other, the second and thirteenth echoing each other, and so on. Specifically, the first and final stories focus on homecomings, one failed, one successful. Stories two and thirteen both address Marie's spiritual condition: her early desire to be a martyred saint contrasted with her truly saintly behavior in forgiving and helping to heal her life-long rival, Lulu. The third and twelfth stories deal with Nector and Marie's relationship: its beginning when they meet on the hillside and its end as Nector chokes on Lipsha's love medicine meant to restore Nector's love for his wife. Stories four and eleven focus on memories of June: Marie muses about taking in June and Gordie hallucinates about June's return. The fifth and tenth stories share the vaguest connection, but both focus on Lulu's boys. The first introduces them and the latter develops the character of one son, Gerry. Stories six and nine mirror each other more clearly as Nector poses for the painting 'The Plunge of the Brave' in one and Henry Jr. literally plunges to his death in the other. Finally the seventh and eighth stories seem linked by an explosive combination of love and violence. In the first, Marie returns to the convent to see the crazed, would-be saint, Leopolda, and in the second, Albertine leaves home for the big city" ("Louise Erdrich's *Love Medicine*," 179–80). My assessment adopts the structural organization of her plan but on the basis of somewhat different thematic linkages among the stories.

52. See Erdrich's comments in *Conversations with Louise Erdrich and Michael Dorris*, 16.

53. See Robert Silberman, "Opening the Text: *Love Medicine* and the Return of the Native American Woman," in *Narrative Chance: Postmodern Discourse on Native American Literatures*, ed. Gerald Vizenor (Albuquerque: University of New Mexico Press, 1989), 105.

54. See Kilpatrick, [Review of *Love Medicine*], 1860. He describes "mother love," "sibling love," and "passion." I see the concept in broader terms.

55. I am indebted here to Hans Bak's perceptive observations in "Toward a Native American 'Realism': The Amphibious Fiction of Louise Erdrich," *Neo-Realism in Contemporary American Fiction*, ed. Kristiaan Versluys, Postmodern Studies 5 (Amsterdam: Rodopi, 1992), 146.

56. See Erdrich's comments in *Conversations with Louise Erdrich and Michael Dorris*, 240–41.

57. See Erdrich's remarks in *Winged Words: American Indian Writers Speak*, ed. Laura Coltelli (Lincoln: University of Nebraska Press, 1990), 47.

58. See Bonetti, "An Interview with Louise Erdrich and Michael Dorris," 95.

59. See *Conversations with Louise Erdrich and Michael Dorris*, 175.

CHAPTER 2

1. The dates of first publication of the stories in *The New Yorker*, in chronological order, are as follows: "Figures in the Distance" (May 9, 1983): 40–42;

"The Red Girl" (August 8, 1983): 54–71; "Columbus in Chains" (October 10, 1983): 48–52; "The Circling Hand" (November 21, 1983): 50–57; "Gwen" (April 16, 1984): 34–53; "Somewhere, Belgium" (May 14, 1984): 44–51; "The Long Rain" (July 30, 1984): 28–36; and "A Walk to the Jetty" (November 5, 1984): 45–51.

2. Jamaica Kincaid, *Annie John* (New York: Farrar, Straus & Giroux, 1985). Subsequent references are to this edition and will appear in the text.

3. Patricia Ismond has commented on the style of *Annie John*, observing that "Kincaid remains close to the child's modes of perception and language in these renderings. The roots of her style . . . lie in the child's instinct for fantasy; the free play between its imaginings and the world of fact; its spontaneous connections between widely different spheres and categories; and the natural simplicity with which it does all this." See "Jamaica Kincaid: 'First They Must Be Children'," *World Literature Written in English*, 28, No. 2 (1988), 336–41. My own reading differs in that I stress that it is the mature Annie who narrates *all* the stories, not the child of the time of the action, and that the language becomes progressively more sophisticated as Annie matures, the language matching her developing maturity.

4. See Jamaica Kincaid, "Figures in the Distance," *The New Yorker* (May 9, 1983): 40–42.

5. "Figures in the Distance," *The New Yorker*, 42; *Annie John*, 12.

6. "The Circling Hand," 51; *Annie John*, 18.

7. Ike Onward, "Wising Up," *Times Literary Supplement* (November 29, 1985): 1374.

8. Moira Ferguson, *Jamaica Kincaid: Where the Land Meets the Body* (Charlottesville: University Press of Virginia, 1994), 41–44.

9. A similar point is made in H. Adlai Murdoch, "Severing the (M)other Connection: The Representation of Cultural Identity in Jamaica Kincaid's *Annie John*," *Calloloo*, 13, No. 2 (1990): 339. This article contains a valuable discussion of the cultural history of Antigua.

10. Diane Cole, in "The Pick of the Crop: Five First Novels," *Ms.* (April 1985): 14, comes to a similar conclusion.

11. See Jamaica Kincaid, "The Circling Hand," *The New Yorker* (November 21, 1998): 50–57.

12. See Charlotte H. Bruner, "Antigua," *World Literature Today*, 59 (1985): 644.

13. Wendy Dutton discusses this point in "Merge and Separate: Jamaica Kincaid's Fiction," *World Literature Today*, 63, No. 3 (1989): 408.

14. Ferguson sees the father as a dominant patriarchal presence, one who arranges "family power relationships that directly favor the sons" (*Jamaica Kincaid*, 49). But aside from the fact that Annie does not have brothers, as Ferguson erroneously concludes, the father is barely present in these stories, drifting on the edge of family life. Annie's mother is clearly the dominant factor in the young girl's daily activities.

15. Bruner, "Antigua," 644.

16. See Nancy Chodorow, *The Reproduction of Mothering: Psychoanalysis and the Sociology of Gender* (Berkeley: University of California Press, 1978), 79–80.

17. Helen Pyne Timothy, "Adolescent Rebellion and Gender Relations in *At the Bottom of the River* and *Annie John*," *Carribean Women Writers: Essays from the First International Conference*, ed. Selwyn R. Cudjoe (Wellesley: Calaloux, 1990), 238.

18. Kincaid, "The Circling Hand," *The New Yorker*, 56.

19. See Kincaid, "Gwen," *The New Yorker*, 34–53.

20. Annie's autobiographical essay is on pp. 41–45.

21. Donna Perry discusses this aspect of the Annie's autobiography in "Initiation in Jamaica Kincaid's *Annie John*," *Caribbean Women Writers*, 248–49.

22. Nancy Chodorow has posited that in becoming independent, a young girl often becomes critical of her mother and seeks an emotional bond with a best friend, with whom she shares her innermost self. See *The Reproduction of Mothering*, 137.

23. Diane Simmons, *Jamaica Kincaid* (New York: Twayne, 1994), 109.

24. Chodorow, *The Reproduction of Mothering*, 137.

25. Helen Pyne Timothy, in "Adolescent Rebellion and Gender Relations," in *At the Bottom of the River* and *Annie John*," 236–37, discusses the contrast of the items in the trunk with Annie's developing sexuality.

26. Timothy, "Adolescent Rebellion," 236.

27. Kincaid, "The Red Girl," *New Yorker*, 38; see *Annie John*, 70.

28. I am indebted here to Dutton, "Merge and Separate," 406.

29. Jamaica Kincaid, *At the Bottom of the River* (New York: Vintage, 1985), 12.

30. Jamaica Kincaid, "Columbus in Chains," *New Yorker*, 54.

31. "Columbus in Chains," *The New Yorker*, 48; *Annie John*, 73.

32. Jamaica Kincaid has given a more direct expression of her feelings about racism and colonialism in Antigua in her Philippic *A Small Place* (New York: Farrar, Straus & Giroux, 1988).

33. See Selwyn R. Cudjoe, "Jamaica Kincaid and the Modernist Project: An Interview," *Caribbean Women Writers*, 215–32.

34. See Murdoch, "Severing the (M)other Connection," 326.

35. The term is Murdoch's, "Severing the (M)other Connection," 326.

36. Murdoch, "Severing the M(other) Connection," 326–27.

37. See Murdoch, "Severing the M(other) Connection," 327, for an extended discussion of this point.

38. Kincaid, "Somewhere, Belgium," *The New Yorker*, 44–45.

39. Kincaid, "The Long Rain," *The New Yorker*, 30. There are no substantial changes in the two versions of the story, although the Brownie leader is "Miss George" in the magazine and "Miss Herbert" in the book. "George" carries with it yet another reference to a British sovereign, but perhaps Annie's middle name, "Victoria," was sufficient for that purpose.

40. John Bemrose gives this chapter a similar interpretation, saying that "Annie suffers a nervous breakdown from the strain of being a good girl in pub-

lic and a rebel in secret." See "Growing Pains of Girlhood," *MacLean's* (May 20, 1985): 61.

41. I am indebted here to Roni Natov, "Mothers and Daughters: Jamaica Kincaid's Pre-Oedipal Narrative," *Children's Literature*, 18 (1990): 11. Natov feels that Annie emerges from her sleep with a "fragmented vision and a deep sense of loss."

42. Timothy explores Annie's conflict in terms of her African heritage and its conflict with the essentially European world in which she lives ("Severing the M(other) Connection," 241); in "Growing Pains of Girlhood," 61, John Bemrose maintains that "Annie suffers a nervous breakdown from the strain of being a good girl in public and a rebel in secret"; on the other hand, Wendy Dutton, in "Merge and Separate," 409, reads the breakdown as Annie's severing from tradition and her mother.

43. Murdoch, "Severing the M(other) Connection," 339.

44. Perry, "Initiation in Jamaica Kincaid's *Annie John*," 247.

45. See Marianne Hirsch, "Spiritual *Bildung*: The Beautiful Soul as Paradigm," *The Voyage In: Fictions of Female Development*, ed. Elizabeth Abel, Marianne Hirsch, and Elizabeth Langland (Hanover: University Press of New England, 1983), 23.

46. See Chodorow, *The Reproduction of Mothering*, 135.

47. Murdoch, "Severing the M(other) Connection," 326.

48. Pamela Marsh even suggests that Annie's affection finally overcomes her resentment. See "Ambivalence in Antigua: Leaving Childhood Behind," *Christian Science Monitor* (April 5, 1985): B2.

49. Bruner, "Antigua," 644.

50. The original magazine publication of the story was quite explicit about this point. Annie there says, "My mother's name is Annie also; I am named after her, and that is why my parents call me Little Miss." See Kincaid, "A Walk to the Jetty," *The New Yorker*, 45. The full text of the story is on pp. 45–51. The magazine version is more negative than the book about the portrait of the father. For example, in *The New Yorker* he has false teeth that clop like the sound of a horse (47).

CHAPTER 3

1. See Kelli Pryor, "The Story of Her Life: Writer Susan Minot Begins a New Chapter," *New York* (June 12, 1989): 52, 54. Minot comments on the reception of her book in Anne O'Malley, "An Interview with Susan Minot," *Poets & Writers Magazine*, 15, No. 3 (1987): 11–15.

2. See O'Malley, "Interview," 14.

3. Sara Maitland, "Small Worlds," *New Statesman* (August 29, 1986): 25.

4. A. R. Gurney Jr., "Men, Women and Children First," *New York Times Book Review* (April 27, 1986): 1, 27.

5. Rosellen Brown, "The Emperor's New Fiction," *Boston Review* (August 1986): 7–8.

6. Katherine Bucknell, "The Children of Charm," *Times Literary Supplement* (September 5, 1986): 978.

7. Anne Tyler, "The Art of Omission," *New Republic* (June 23, 1986): 34.

8. Robert Towers, "Good News," *New York Review of Books* (June 26, 1986): 33.

9. Thomas Hinde, "Bursts of Lucidity," *Books and Bookmen* (September 1986): 37.

10. R. Z. Sheppard, "Really Rosie," *Time* (June 9, 1986): 71.

11. See O'Malley, "Interview," 13.

12. See Tyler, "Art of Omission," 34.

13. Unless otherwise indicated, all of my citations to "Hiding" are from Susan Minot, *Monkeys* (New York: E. P. Dutton, 1986), 1–22. All subsequent references to the other stories in this collection are from this volume and are given in the text, unless periodical publication is specifically indicated. The first publication of "Hiding" was in *Grand Street*, 2, No. 2 (1983): 19–32. With the exception of occasional alterations of accidentals, such as the introduction of quotation marks for certain expressions, the story was identical to that included in the volume.

14. For the concept of the book as elegy, I am indebted to Bucknell, "Children of Charm," 978.

15. Gurney, "Men, Women and Children First," 27.

16. The first appearance of the story was in *Grand Street*, 3, No. 3 (1984): 44–53.

17. In the *Grand Street* version of the story, Sophie was said to be ten years old (44); however, since she was born in 1956, that is one year off, and Minot made her eleven in *Monkeys* (24).

18. For the original publication of the story, see Susan Minot, "Allowance," *The New Yorker* (April 29, 1985): 37–41. My parenthetic citations are from *Monkeys*.

19. Minot, probably working from memory, misspells the name "Clavel" from Bemelmans as "Clavell" (89).

20. I am indebted here to an unpublished paper by Karen Weekes entitled " 'Party Blues': Allusion in Susan Minot."

21. The first appearance of the story was in Susan Minot, "The Navigator," *Grand Street*, 4, No. 2 (1985): 90–100. Among the other changes, Minnie is said to be seven in the magazine, which would be too old, since she was born in 1971; she is six in the volume. In the magazine version, Dad calls Mum "Rosie" after the character in *The African Queen* who pours out the "whisky" of her companion. That statement is inaccurate, in that the Humphrey Bogart character drinks gin; in the volume, the drink is changed to gin.

22. For information about the background of the cattle boats, I am indebted to an unpublished paper by Patricia L. Watson entitled "Cattle Boats and Navigation in Susan Minot's *Monkeys*."

23. The first publication of the story was in Susan Minot, "Accident," *The New Yorker* (November 7, 1983): 50–54. Since it was only the third story published, with only "Hiding" containing preceding action, there was little motiva-

tional explanation of the meaning of her death and no indication that Mum's affair with Kittredge was in any way involved. This story thus changed substantially when published as part of the collection.

24. Walter Bede, "Pall in the Family," *Village Voice* (August 5, 1986): 46.

25. Susan Minot, "The Silver Box," *Grand Street*, 5, No. 2 (1986): 26–33.

26. See Susan Minot, "Thorofare," *The New Yorker* (June 27, 1983): 32–37.

27. Minot, "Thorofare," *The New Yorker*, 37.

CHAPTER 4

1. Although *The House on Mango Street* was first published in Houston by the Arte Público Press in 1984, I am using the revised version of 1989 for all citations because it is more readily available and because Cisneros objected to some of the alterations made to her manuscript in the first edition. See Sandra Cisneros, *The House on Mango Street* (New York: Vintage, 1991). For comments on the revision of the book, please consult María Elena de Valdés, "In Search of Identity in Cisneros's *The House on Mango Street*," *Canadian Review of American Studies*, 23, No. 1 (Fall 1992): 69.

2. Sandra Cisneros, "Guadalupe: The Sex Goddess," *Ms.*, 7, No. 1 (July/August 1996): 46.

3. Her efforts were supported by a National Endowment for the Arts grant, which also assisted in its initial publication.

4. Sandra Cisneros, "Do You Know Me?: I Wrote *The House on Mango Street*," *Americas Review*, 15 (Spring 1987): 77–78.

5. Sandra Cisneros, "Ghosts and Voices: Writing from Obsession," *Americas Review*, 15 (Spring 1987): 72.

6. Cisneros, "Ghosts and Voices," 69–73.

7. Eduardo F. Elías, "Sandra Cisneros," *Dictionary of Literary Biography: Chicano Writers, Second Series*, ed. Francisco A. Lomelí and Carl R. Shirley (Detroit: Gale, 1992), 77–81.

8. Sandra Cisneros, "Introduction," *The House on Mango Street* (New York: Knopf, 1994), xii.

9. Pilar E. Rodríguez Aranda, "On the Solitary Fate of Being Mexican, Female, Wicked and Thirty-Three: An Interview with Writer Sandra Cisneros," *Americas Review*, 18, No. 1 (Spring 1990): 74–75.

10. Julián Olivares, "Sandra Cisneros' *The House on Mango Street* and the Poetics of Space," *Chicana Creativity and Criticism: Charting New Frontiers in American Literature*, ed. Maria Herrera-Sobek and Helena-Maria Viramontes (Houston: Arte Público, 1988), 160.

11. Olivares, "Sandra Cisneros' *The House on Mango Street* and the Poetics of Space," 161.

12. Annie O. Eysturoy, *Daughters of Self-Creation: The Contemporary Chicana Novel* (Albuquerque: University of New Mexico Press, 1996), 89.

13. María Elena de Valdés, "The Critical Reception of Sandra Cisneros's

The House on Mango Street," *Gender, Self, and Society,* ed. Renate von Bardeleben (Frankfort: Peter Lang, 1993), 287.

14. Yvonne Yarbro-Bejarano, "Chicana Literature from a Chicana Feminist Perspective," *Chicana Creativity and Criticism: Charting New Frontiers in American Literature,* ed. María Herrera-Sobek and Helena María Viramontes (Houston: Arte Público Press, 1988), 142.

15. Ellen McCracken, "Sandra Cisneros's *The House on Mango Street*: Community-Oriented Introspection and the Demystification of Patriarchal Violence," *Breaking Boundaries: Latina Writing and Critical Readings,* ed. Asunción Horno-Delgado, Eliana Ortega, and Nina M. Scott (Amherst: University of Massachusetts Press, 1989), 64.

16. Julián Olivares, "Entering *The House on Mango Street* (Sandra Cisneros)," *Teaching American Ethnic Literatures: Nineteen Essays,* ed. John R. Maitino and David R. Peck (Albuquerque: University of New Mexico Press, 1996), 209.

17. Valdés, "In Search of Identity," 55.

18. Cisneros has commented that "the language in *Mango Street* is based on speech. It's very much an antiacademic voice—a child's voice, a girl's voice, a poor girl's voice, a spoken voice, the voice of an American-Mexican." See Cisneros, "Introduction," xvi.

19. See Eysturoy, *Daughters of Self-Creation,* 91.

20. Juan Daniel Busch has commented perceptively that "Esperanza gains agency as she better understands her personal relationships to social and cultural meanings." See "Self-Baptizing the Wicked Esperanza: Chicana Feminism and Cultural Contact in *The House on Mango Street,*" *Mester,* 22, No. 2 (Fall 1993) and 23, No. 1 (Spring 1994): 126.

21. I am indebted here to Olivares, "Entering *The House on Mango Street,*" 216–17.

22. See Cisneros's comments in Aranda, "On the Solitary Fate of Being Mexican," 69.

23. Juanita Heredia, "Down These City Streets: Exploring Urban Space in *El Bronx Remembered* and *The House on Mango Street,*" *Mester,* 22 (Fall 1993) and 23 (Spring 1994): 98.

24. Olivares, "Sandra Cisneros' *The House on Mango Street* and the Poetics of Space," 164.

25. In a similar vein, Juanita Heredia maintains that "Alicia attempts to define her own space by developing her mind. Cisneros demonstrates this progression of Latina consciousness because now she explores the intellectual role of a Latina who has a right to think for herself and dictate the direction of her life" ("Down These City Streets," 102).

26. Ellen McCracken maintains that "Cisneros proscribes a romantic or exotic reading of the dress-up episode, focusing instead on the girls' discovery of the threatening nature of male sexual power that is frequently disguised as desirable male attention and positive validation of women, through what is, in fact, sexual reification" ("Sandra Cisneros's *The House on Mango Street,*" 67).

27. Heredia, "Down These City Streets," 102.

28. See Cisneros's comments in Aranda, "On the Solitary Fate of Being Mexican," 67.

29. Cisneros comments in Aranda, "On the Solitary Fate of Being Mexican," 73.

30. See Eysturoy, *Daughters of Self-Creation*, 94–95. Julián Olivares, in "Entering *The House on Mango Street*," maintains a similar point: "The image of the four skinny trees serves to express Esperanza's character development and the will to assert her identity. Against the many odds of her harsh environment and dominating culture, she must struggle, like the trees, to grow and to survive. Like the trees, she must be tenacious in her aspiration to greatness" (222).

31. McCracken, "Sandra Cisneros's *The House on Mango Street*," 69.

32. Andrea O'Reilly Herrera, " 'Chambers of Consciousness': Sandra Cisneros and the Development of the Self in the BIG House on Mango Street," *Bucknell Review*, 39, No. 1 (1995): 198.

33. I am indebted, for this point, to María Herrera-Sobek's insightful discussion in "The Politics of Rape: Sexual Transgression in Chicana Fiction," *Chicana Creativity and Criticism*, 171–81.

34. See Herrera-Sobek, "Politics of Rape," 178.

35. Juanita Heredia makes a similar point in her study of *The House on Mango Street* and *El Bronx Remembered* (101).

36. See Valdés, "In Search of Identity," 65.

37. I am indebted here to Reuben Sánchez, "Remembering Always to Come Back: The Child's Wished-For Escape and the Adult's Self-Empowered Return in Sandra Cisneros's *House on Mango Street*," *Children's Literature 23*, ed. Francelia Butler, R. H. W. Dillard, and Elizabeth Lennox Keyser (New Haven: Yale University Press, 1995), 226.

38. See Olivares, "Entering *The House on Mango Street*," 229.

39. Eysturoy, *Daughters of Self-Creation*, 102.

40. Heredia, "Down These City Streets," 101.

41. Sánchez, "Remembering Always to Come Back," 238.

42. Eysturoy argues that "Esperanza sees the house as a symbol of the shame that threatens her own self-perception. To Esperanza the house on Mango Street is an emblem of the oppressive socio-economic situation that circumscribes her life and is the source of her feelings of alienation" (*Daughters of Self-Creation*, 920).

43. Eysturoy makes a similar point (93).

44. Olivares, in "Entering *The House on Mango Street*," charts the stories into five thematic groups (217).

45. See Aranda, "On the Solitary Fate of Being Mexican," 64.

46. See Cisneros's comments in Aranda, "On the Solitary Fate of Being Mexican," 69.

CHAPTER 5

1. See O'Brien's comment in Martin Naparsteck, "An Interview with Tim O'Brien," *Contemporary Literature*, 32 (1991): 7.

2. Robert R. Harris, "Too Embarrassed Not to Kill," *New York Times Book Review* (March 11, 1990): 8.

3. Michael Coffey, "Tim O'Brien," *Publisher's Weekly*, 237 (February 16, 1990): 60–61.

4. See Steven Kaplan, *Understanding Tim O'Brien* (Columbia: University of South Carolina Press, 1995), 12. I am uneasy about Kaplan's formulation of this concept, since it implies that he knows O'Brien's intentions, always an elusive matter, but the general point is well taken.

5. See O'Brien's comments in Ronald Baughman, "Interview with Tim O'Brien," *Dictionary of Literary Biography Documentary Series*, ed. Ronald Baughman, Vol. 9 (Detroit: Bruccoli-Clark-Layman-Gale, 1991), 205.

6. Tim O'Brien, *The Things They Carried* (New York: Penguin, 1990). All subsequent references are given in the text and are to this volume unless otherwise noted. The story first appeared in *Esquire* (August 1986): 76–81, in essentially the same form as in the collected volume. Beyond changes in accidentals, O'Brien deleted the comment that "the war came at them in 3–D" (*Esquire*, 80) and made other minor alterations, but nothing of substance was added or eliminated.

7. The variable of the number of times the Lavender scene recurs depends upon what is considered a scene. On at least a dozen occasions there is mention that Lavender is dead, shot while coming back from urinating in the brush.

8. The Lavender flashback lasts eight pages, 9–17.

9. For the complete magazine version of the story, see Tim O'Brien, "Spin," *Quarterly*, 13 (1990): 3–13.

10. See Tim O'Brien, "On the Rainy River," *Playboy*, 37 (January 1990): 97–98, 100, 108, 194–96. The two versions are virtually identical, although O'Brien changed some formulations, so that in *Playboy* the character remembers, "I was a seven-year-old in a white cowboy hat," and in *The Things They Carried*, "I saw a seven-year-old boy in a white cowboy hat" (60). There are several changes of this type.

11. Tim O'Brien, *If I Die in a Combat Zone: Box Me Up and Ship Me Home* (New York: Laurel, 1969), 32.

12. Kaplan, *Understanding Tim O'Brien*, 48.

13. See Tim O'Brien, "How to Tell a True War Story," *Esquire* (October 1987): 214. Other than a few changes in phrasing, the story is otherwise identical to the book publication, save for this crucial addition in the conclusion.

14. The first publication of "Sweetheart of the Song Tra Bong" was in *Esquire* (July 1989): 94–103. The two versions of the story are very similar, with some word choices changed for the volume. O'Brien altered somewhat the final portrait of Mary Anne Bell by adding the clarification to the conclusion that "she was lost inside herself" (124) and deleting from the magazine text the statement that "she was dangerous, she was ready for the kill" (*Esquire*, 103).

15. See Baughman, "Interview with Tim O'Brien," 205.

16. See Brian C. McNerney, "Responsibly Inventing History: An Interview with Tim O'Brien," *War, Literature, & the Arts*, 6, No. 2 (1994): 21.

17. See Tim O'Brien, "Spin," *Quarterly*, 13 (1990): 3–4. No substantial changes were made in the incorporation of the "Style" section into the book.

18. See Tim O'Brien, "Speaking of Courage," *Massachusetts Review*, 17 (1976): 243–53.

19. O'Brien is quoted in Baughman, "Interview with Tim O'Brien," 211.

20. For the original publication of the story, see Tim O'Brien, "In the Field," *Gentleman's Quarterly* (December 1989): 217, 220–22, 224, 227. There are only stylistic differences between the magazine and book versions.

21. See David Streitfeld, "Never Done," *Washington Post Book World* (May 19, 1991): 15.

22. Tim O'Brien, "The Ghost Soldiers," *Esquire* (March 1981): 90–93, 95–96, 98, 100.

23. "The Ghost Soldiers," *Esquire*, 95.

24. See Tim O'Brien, "The Lives of the Dead," *Esquire*, 111 (January 1989): 134, 136–39, 142. The quotation is from p. 136.

25. See Baughman, "Interview with Tim O'Brien," 211.

CHAPTER 6

1. See Julia Alvarez, "El Doctor," *Outlooks and Insights: A Reader for Writers*, ed. Paul Eschholz and Alfred Rosa (New York: St. Martin's Press, 1983), 123–32.

2. See Ed Morales, "Madam Butterfly: How Julia Alvarez Found Her Accent," *Village Voice Literary Supplement* (November 1994): 13, and Jason Zappe, [Review of *How the García Girls Lost Their Accents*,] *Americas Review*, 19 (Winter 1991): 150–52.

3. Luis Rebaza-Soraluz, [Review of *How the García Girls Lost Their Accents*,] *Hispanic Journal*, 14 (Spring 1993): 173–75.

4. Ilan Stavans, "Daughters of Invention," *Commonweal*, 119 (April 10, 1992): 23–25.

5. Donna Rifkind, "Speaking American," *New York Times Book Review*, 96 (October 6, 1991): 14.

6. All references, unless otherwise noted, are given in the text and are to Julia Alvarez, *How the García Girls Lost Their Accents* (Chapel Hill: Algonquin, 1991). The subsequent Plume/Penguin edition uses the same pagination. "Antojos" covers pp. 3–23.

7. For the original magazine version of the story, see Julia Alvarez, "Antojos," *Caribbean Writer*, 4 (June 1990): 68–73.

8. See Julia Alvarez, "Translating a Look," *Allure* (March 1995): 148, 150, 159.

9. Alvarez, "Antojos," *Caribbean Writer*, 71.

10. For the original publication of the story, see Julia Alvarez, "The Kiss," *Greensboro Review*, 42 (Summer 1987): 20–31.

11. For the first publication of the story, see Julia Alvarez, "Joe," *Syracuse Scholar*, 3, No. 2 (Fall 1982): 58–74.

12. Alvarez has commented that, in her own experience, she and her sis-

ters were held to similarly restrictive codes of sexual behavior: "We were being groomed to go from being dutiful daughters to being dutiful wives with hymens intact. No stops along the way that might endanger the latter: no careers, no colleges, no shared apartments with girlfriends, no boyfriends and social lives. . . . Girls were to have no aspirations beyond being good wives and mothers." See "Translating a Look," 159.

13. For the original version of the story, see Julia Alvarez, "Daughter of Invention," *Unholy Alliances*, ed. Louise Rafkin (San Francisco: Cleis Press, 1988), 15–27.

14. In mixing clichés, Laura Garcia exhibits a trait that Alvarez described about her own mother, who advised her daughter to "save for a snowy day." See "El Doctor," 126.

15. For the first publication of the story, see Julia Alvarez, "Snow," *Northwest Review*, 22, No. 1 (1984): 21–22.

16. For first publication of the story, see Julia Alvarez, "Floor Show," *Story Magazine* (Spring 1991): 12–25.

17. For a more extensive discussion of narrative parallax, see James Nagel, *Stephen Crane and Literary Impressionism* (University Park: Pennsylvania State University Press, 1980), 68–77.

18. Elizabeth Starcevic, "Talking About Language," *American Book Review*, 14 (August/September 1992): 15.

19. For the original publication of the story, see Julia Alvarez, "Still Lives," *Caribbean Writer*, 1, No. 1 (Spring 1987): 62–69.

20. See "Still Lives," *Caribbean Writer*, 1, No. 1 (Spring 1987): 63.

21. See Julia Alvarez, "An American Surprise," *An American Christmas: A Sampler of Contemporary Stories and Poems*, ed. Jane B. Hill (Atlanta: Peachtree Publishers, 1986), 39–56.

22. "An American Surprise," *An American Christmas: A Sampler of Contemporary Stories and Poems*, 43.

23. Stavans, "Daughters of Invention," 24.

24. Mary Batts Estrada, "Four Sisters and a World of Difference," *Bookworld*, 21 (June 16, 1991): D11.

25. Alvarez, "Translating a Look," 159.

26. Ilan Stavans maintains that "the idea of 'losing' one's accent is nothing but a metaphor: a symbol of cultural abandonment" ("Daughters of Invention," 24). My view is that, for immigrants of whatever nationality, the significance of losing an accent is that of assimilation, integrating the values of ethnic origin into those of the chosen culture of emigration.

CHAPTER 7

1. For Amy Tan's comments on the inspiration of Louise Erdrich's *Love Medicine*, see Dorothy Wang, "A Game of Show Not Tell," *Newsweek*, 113 (April 17, 1989): 69.

2. Barbara Somogyi and David Stanton, "Amy Tan: An Interview." *Poets & Writers*, 19, No. 5 (1991): 27.

3. Carole Angier, "Chinese Customs," *New Statesman and Society*, 2 (June 30, 1989): 35.

4. See Tan's remarks in Somogyi and Stanton, "Amy Tan," 28.

5. Elaine Woo, "Striking Cultural Sparks," *Los Angeles Times* (March 12, 1989): Section 6, pp. 1, 14.

6. See Woo, "Striking Cultural Sparks," 14, and Somogyi and Stanton, "Amy Tan," 25.

7. Woo, "Striking Cultural Sparks," 1, 14.

8. See Somogyi and Stanton, "Amy Tan," 26.

9. Amy Tan, [On the Writing of *The Joy Luck Club*] *Literary Outtakes*, ed. Larry Dark (New York: Fawcett Columbine, 1990), 319.

10. *Literary Outtakes*, 319.

11. Somogyi and Stanton, "Amy Tan," 26.

12. *Literary Outtakes*, 319–20.

13. Somogyi and Stanton, "Amy Tan," 26.

14. Amy Tan, *The Joy Luck Club* (New York: G. P. Putnam's Sons, 1989), 17. Subsequent references are to this edition and will be made parenthetically by page number in the text.

15. Amy Tan, "The Joy Luck Club," *Ladies' Home Journal*, 106 (March 1989): 98, 100, 102–6.

16. Merle Rubin, "Chinese-American 'Bridge Club,' " *Christian Science Monitor*, 81 (April 21, 1989): 13.

17. Carolyn See, "Drowning in America, Starving for China," *Los Angeles Times Book Review* (March 12, 1989): 3, 11.

18. See Amy Tan, "Scar," *San Francisco Focus*, 35 (December 1988): 129, 170–74.

19. Amy Tan, "End Game," *FM Five* (Spring 1986): 7–9, 12. There are only minor stylistic differences between this version and "The Rules of the Game" in the book.

20. See Amy Tan, "Rules of the Game," *Seventeen*, 45 (November 1986): 160–61, 177–79.

21. For the original publication of the story, see Amy Tan, "Two Kinds," *Atlantic Monthly*, 263 (February 1989): 53–57. This text is nearly identical to that in *The Joy Luck Club*. The magazine version clarifies that Suyuan Woo came from China to San Francisco, a detail deleted in the book, perhaps because it is made evident in the preceding stories. The other alterations made to incorporate the story into the volume are essentially minor.

22. See Tan's comments in Somogyi and Stanton, "Amy Tan," 26.

23. See, "Drowning in America, Starving for China," 3, 11.

24. Somogyi and Stanton, "Amy Tan," 29.

25. Dorothy Stein, "Pieces of China," *Listener*, 122 (September 14, 1989): 25.

CHAPTER 8

1. Robert Olen Butler, *A Good Scent from a Strange Mountain* (New York: Henry Holt, 1992). Subsequent references refer to this edition and will be made parenthetically in the text.

2. Jean W. Ross, [Interview with Robert Olen Butler Jr.] *Contemporary Authors*, 112 (Detroit: Gale, 1985): 90.

3. Ross, interview, 90.

4. Robert Olen Butler, in a telephone conversation with James Nagel, May 20, 1997.

5. Richard Eder has said of Butler, "it is the Vietnamese voice that he seeks and that, in these stories, he has so remarkably and movingly found. What it means for these expatriates to come to a new country and function in it is more the setting than the theme." See "Seeing the Vietnamese," *Los Angeles Times Book Review* (March 29, 1992): 3.

6. Robert Towers, "Far from Saigon," *New York Review of Books* (August 12, 1993): 41.

7. See the interview with Ross, 91.

8. George Packer, "From the Mekong to the Bayous," *New York Times Book Review* (June 7, 1992): 24.

9. Pat C. Hoy II has commented that Butler's stories "bring us face to face with the people we fought for and the people we fought. In that strange war in Vietnam it was hard to tell the difference. Through them we experience the effects of war, effects continuing long past the putative end of hostilities." See Hoy, "Suffering and Desire," *Sewanee Review*, 100 (1992): cxvi–cxviii.

10. See Robert Olen Butler, "Open Arms," *Missouri Review*, 13, No. 1 (1990): 7–18. As is true for all the magazine versions of Butler's stories, the text is virtually the same as in *A Good Scent from a Strange Mountain* except that it does not use accent marks for the Vietnamese names. Because of keyboard limitations, I will follow the practice of the magazine in the representation of the names while otherwise citing the text of the collected volume.

11. Eder, "Seeing the Vietnamese," 3.

12. See Robert Olen Butler, "Mr. Green," *Hudson Review*, 43 (Winter 1991): 607–16.

13. Robert Olen Butler, "The Trip Back," *Southern Review*, 26 (Autumn 1990): 856–67.

14. See Robert Olen Butler, "Fairy Tale," *Virginia Quarterly Review*, 66 (Autumn 1990): 601–12. There are no differences of substance between magazine and book publication.

15. Madison Smartt Bell, in his review of the book, observed that " 'Fairy Tale,' the story of a Saigon bargirl who comes to America as the wife of an American diplomatic functionary, turns on subtleties of language. As in many Oriental languages, a shift of tone in Vietnamese can change meaning altogether, a factor that leads to many strange utterances from the mouths of maladroit foreigners." See "At a Cultural Crossroads," *Chicago Tribune Books* (February 23, 1992): Section 14, p. 3.

16. See Robert Olen Butler, "Letters from My Father," *Cimarron Review* (October 1991): 14–18. The magazine version of the story differs only slightly from book publication, with a few word changes but no alteration of substance.

17. See Robert Olen Butler, "Love," *Writer's Forum*, 17 (1991): 18–31.

18. See Towers, "Far from Saigon," 40–41.

19. See Robert Olen Butler, "Mid-Autumn," *Hawaii Review*, 33 (Fall 1991): 118–22. Except for some changes in paragraph breaks, the two versions of the story are identical.

20. Robert Olen Butler, "In the Clearing," *Icarus*, 1 (Winter 1991): 17–26.

21. Robert Olen Butler, "A Ghost Story," *Colorado Review* (Spring–Summer 1991): 16–26.

22. For the original magazine version, see Robert Olen Butler, "Snow," *New Orleans Review*, 18, No. 3 (1991): 28–32. There were no substantial revisions from magazine to book publication.

23. See Robert Olen Butler, "Relic," *New Stories from the South: The Year's Best, 1991*, ed. Shannon Ravenel (Chapel Hill: Algonquin Books, 1991), 78–83. There are no substantial differences in the three publications of the story.

24. See Robert Olen Butler, "Preparation," *Sewanee Review*, 100 (Winter 1992): 42–52.

25. Robert Olen Butler, in a telephone conversation with James Nagel, May 20, 1997.

26. Madison Smartt Bell maintains that this story "takes up the issue of assimilation more directly than some of the other stories and also reveals its own doubleness more plainly. Butler's achievement is not only to reveal the inner lives of the Vietnamese but also to show, through their eyes, how the rest of us appear from an outside perspective, one more objective than our own." See Bell, "At a Cultural Crossroads," Section 14, p. 3.

27. Bell maintains that "the bitterness of the mock combat forces both Vinh and his wife to consider just how far, and to what effect, they've been absorbed by the culture into which they've immigrated." See Bell, "At a Cultural Crossroads," 3.

28. Except for the use of Vietnamese accents on names, the magazine version is identical to that in the volume. See Robert Olen Butler, "A Good Scent from a Strange Mountain," *New England Review*, 13, Nos. 3–4 (1991): 35–43.

29. Hoy, "Suffering and Desire," cxvi–cxviii.

30. Eder, "Seeing the Vietnamese," 3.

31. Packer, "From the Mekong to the Bayous," 24.

32. Kathleen Kilgore, "How Others View Vietnam," *Christian Science Monitor* (September 4, 1992): 12.

CONCLUSION

1. See Edmund Wilson, "Mr. Hemingway's Dry-Points," *Dial*, 77 (October 1924): 340–41, and Malcolm Cowley, "Faulkner Stories, in Amiable Mood," *New York Herald Tribune Books* (November 6, 1949): 7.

2. F. Scott Fitzgerald, [Review of *In Our Time*,] *Bookman*, 63 (May 1926): 264.

3. Kenneth S. Lynn, "Hemingway's Private War," *Commentary*, 72, No. 1 (1981): 24.

4. Ernest Hemingway, *A Moveable Feast* (New York: Scribner's, 1964), 76.

5. Carlos Baker, ed., *Ernest Hemingway: Selected Letters, 1917–1961* (New York: Scribner's, 1981), 798.

6. Sara Maitland, "Small Worlds," *New Statesman* (August 29, 1986): 25.

7. See Tim O'Brien, "On the Rainy River," *Playboy*, 37 (January 1990): 97–98, 100, 108, 194–96.

8. See Julia Alvarez, "The Kiss," *Greensboro Review*, 42 (Summer 1987): 20–31.

9. See Louise Erdrich, "The Red Convertible," *Mississippi Valley Review*, 11, No. 2 (1982): 10–17.

10. Rocío G. Davis makes a similar point in "Identity in Community in Ethnic Short Story Cycles: Amy Tan's *The Joy Luck Club*, Louise Erdrich's *Love Medicine*, Gloria Naylor's *The Women of Brewster Place*," *Ethnicity and the American Short Story*, ed. Julie Brown (New York: Garland, 1997), 14.

11. See Kennedy, ed., *Modern American Short Story Sequences*, x.

12. Davis, "Identity in Community," 3.

13. See *Conversations with Louise Erdrich and Michael Dorris*, 175.

14. Reid, *Short Story*, 46.

15. Ingram, *Representative Short Story Cycles*, 17.

16. See Erdrich's comments in *Conversations with Louise Erdrich and Michael Dorris*, 4.

17. See Erdrich's comments in Coltelli, *Winged Words*, 47.

18. See Erdrich's comments in Bonetti, "An Interview with Louise Erdrich and Michael Dorris," 95.

19. See Castillo, "Postmodernism, Native American Literature and the Real," 289.

20. For Amy Tan's comments on the inspiration of Louise Erdrich's *Love Medicine*, see Wang, "A Game of Show Not Tell," 69.

21. J. Gerald Kennedy, "From Anderson's *Winesburg* to Carver's *Cathedral*: The Short Story Sequence and the Semblance of Community," in Kennedy, ed., *Modern American Short Story Sequences*, 195.

List of Works Consulted

Abel, Elizabeth, Marianne Hirsch, and Elizabeth Langland, eds. *The Voyage In: Fictions of Female Development*. Hanover: University Press of New England, 1983.

Alvarez, Julia. "An American Surprise." *An American Christmas: A Sampler of Contemporary Stories & Poems*, ed. Jane B. Hill. Atlanta: Peachtree Publishers, 1986, pp. 39–56.

———. "Antojos." *The Caribbean Writer*, 4 (June 1990): 68–73.

———. "Daughter of Invention." *Unholy Alliances*, ed. Louise Rafkin. San Francisco: Cleis Press, 1988, pp. 15–27.

———. "El Doctor." *Outlooks and Insights: A Reader for Writers*, ed. Paul Eschholz and Alfred Rosa. New York: St. Martin's Press, 1983, pp. 123–32.

———. "Floor Show." *Story Magazine* (Spring 1991): 12–25.

———. *How the García Girls Lost Their Accents*. Chapel Hill: Algonquin, 1991.

———. "Joe." *Syracuse Scholar*, 3, No. 2 (Fall 1982): 58–74.

———. "The Kiss." *Greensboro Review*, 42 (Summer 1987): 20–31.

———. "Snow." *Northwest Review*, 22, No. 1 (1984): 21–22.

———. "Still Lives." *Caribbean Writer*, 1, No. 1 (Spring 1987): 62–69.

———. "Translating a Look." *Allure* (March 1995): 148–49, 159.

Angier, Carole. "Chinese Customs." *New Statesman and Society*, 2 (June 30, 1989): 35.

Anon. "Briefly Noted." *The New Yorker* (January 7, 1985): 76.

Aranda, Pilar E. Rodríguez. "On the Solitary Fate of Being Mexican, Female, Wicked and Thirty-Three: An Interview with Writer Sandra Cisneros." *Americas Review*, 18, No. 1 (Spring 1990): 64–80.

Bak, Hans. "Toward a Native American 'Realism': The Amphibious Fiction of Louise Erdrich." *Neo-Realism in Contemporary American Fiction*, ed. Kristiaan Versluys. Postmodern Studies 5. Amsterdam: Rodopi, 1992, pp. 146–70.

Baker, Carlos, ed. *Ernest Hemingway: Selected Letters, 1917–1961*. New York: Scribner's, 1981.

Baraga, Frederick. *Chippewa Indians: As Recorded by Rev. Frederick Baraga in 1847*. New York: League of Slovenian Americans, 1976.

Baughman, Ronald. "Interview with Tim O'Brien." *Dictionary of Literary Biography Documentary Series*, ed. Ronald Baughman. Vol. 9. Detroit: Bruccoli-Clark-Layman-Gale, 1991, pp. 204–14.

Bede, Walter. "Pall in the Family." *Village Voice* (August 5, 1986): 46.

Bell, Madison Smartt. "At a Cultural Crossroads." *Chicago Tribune Books* (February 23, 1992): Section 14, p. 3.

Bemrose, John. "Growing Pains of Girlhood." *MacLean's* (May 20, 1985): 61.

Blais, Madeleine. "The Sly, Sexy Minimalism of Susan Minot's 'Lust.' " *Chicago Tribune* (June 11, 1989): 7.

Bonetti, Kay. "An Interview with Louise Erdrich and Michael Dorris." *Missouri Review*, 11, No. 2 (1988): 79–99.

Brown, Georgia. "Beauties and the Beast." *Mother Jones*, 14 (June 1989): 43–44.

Brown, Rosellen. "Arts in Review: The Year in Fiction, 1990." *Massachusetts Review*, 32 (1991): 123–46.

———. "The Emperor's New Fiction." *Boston Review* (August 1986): 7–8.

Bruchac, Joseph. [Review of *Love Medicine*.] *North Dakota Quarterly*, 53, No. 2 (Spring 1985): 254–57.

———. "Whatever Is Really Yours: An Interview with Louise Erdrich." *Survival This Way: Interviews with American Indian Poets*, ed. Joseph Bruchac. Tucson: University of Arizona Press, 1987, pp. 73–86.

Bruckner, D. J. R. "Books of the Times." *New York Times* (December 20, 1984): 21.

Bruner, Charlotte H. "Antigua." *World Literature Today*, 59 (1985): 644.

Buckley, Jerome Hamilton. *Season of Youth: The Bildungsroman from Dickens to Golding*. Cambridge: Harvard University Press, 1974.

Bucknell, Katherine. "The Children of Charm." *Times Literary Supplement* (September 5, 1986): 978.

Busch, Juan Daniel. "Self-Baptizing the Wicked Esperanza: Chicana Feminism and Cultural Contact in *The House on Mango Street*." *Mester*, 22, No. 2 (Fall 1993) and 23, No. 1 (Spring 1994): 123–34.

Butler, Robert Olen. *A Good Scent from a Strange Mountain*. New York: Henry Holt, 1992.

Cain, Michael S. [Review of *How the García Girls Lost Their Accents*.] *Multicultural Review*, 1 (January 1992): 43.

Castillo, Susan Pérez. "Postmodernism, Native American Literature and the Real: The Silko-Erdrich Controversy." *Massachusetts Review*, 32, No. 2 (Summer 1991): 285–94.

Chavkin, Allan, and Nancy Feyl Chavkin, eds. *Conversations with Louise Erdrich and Michael Dorris*. Jackson: University Press of Mississippi, 1994.

Chodorow, Nancy. *The Reproduction of Mothering: Psychoanalysis and the Sociology of Gender*. Berkeley: University of California Press, 1978.

Cisneros, Sandra. "Do You Know Me?: I Wrote *The House on Mango Street*." *Americas Review*, 15 (Spring 1987): 77–79.

———. "Ghosts and Voices: Writing from Obsession." *Americas Review*, 15 (Spring 1987): 69–73.

———. "Guadalupe: The Sex Goddess." *Ms.*, 7, No. 1 (July/August 1996): 43–46.

———. *The House on Mango Street*. New York: Vintage, 1991.

———. "Introduction." *The House on Mango Street*. New York: Knopf, 1994.

———. "Notes to a Younger Writer." *Americas Review*, 15 (Spring 1987): 74–76.

———. "Only Daughter." *Women's Voices from the Borderlands*, ed. Lillian Castillo-Speed. New York: Touchstone, 1995, pp. 157–60.

Coffey, Michael. "Tim O'Brien." *Publisher's Weekly*, 237 (February 16, 1990): 60–61.

Cole, Diane. "The Pick of the Crop: Five First Novels." *Ms.* (April 1985): 14.

Coltelli, Laura. *Winged Words: American Indian Writers Speak*. Lincoln: University of Nebraska Press, 1990.

Couser, G. Thomas. "*Going After Cacciato*: The Romance and the Real War." *Journal of Narrative Technique*, 13, No. 1 (1983): 1–10.

Cowley, Malcolm. "Faulkner Stories, in Amiable Mood." *New York Herald Tribune Books* (November 6, 1949): 7.

Cudjoe, Selwyn R. "Jamaica Kincaid and the Modernist Project: An Interview." *Caribbean Women Writers: Essays from the First International Conference*, ed. Selwyn R. Cudjoe. Wellesley: Calaloux, 1990, pp. 215–32.

Danziger, Edmund Jefferson Jr. *The Chippewas of Lake Superior*. Norman: University of Oklahoma Press, 1979.

Dark, Larry, ed. *Literary Outtakes*. New York: Fawcett Columbine, 1990, pp. 130–31.

Davis, Rocío G. "Identity in Community in Ethnic Short Story Cycles: Amy Tan's *The Joy Luck Club*, Louise Erdrich's *Love Medicine*, Gloria Naylor's *The Women of Brewster Place*." *Ethnicity and the American Short Story*, ed. Julie Brown. New York: Garland, 1997, pp. 3–23.

Densmore, Frances. *Chippewa Customs*. Minneapolis: Minnesota Historical Society Press, 1979.

Dooley, Susan. "Mah-Jong and the Ladies of the Club." *Washington Post Book World*, 19 (March 5, 1989): 7.

Dorris, Michael. "Mothers and Daughters." *Chicago Tribune Books* (March 12, 1989): Section 14, pp. 1, 11.

Dudar, Helen. "A Novel Partnership." *Wall Street Journal* (October 24, 1985): 62.

Dunn, Maggie, and Ann Morris. *The Composite Novel: The Short Story Cycle in Transition*. New York: Twayne, 1995.

Dutton, Wendy. "Merge and Separate: Jamaica Kincaid's Fiction." *World Literature Today*, 63, No. 3 (1989): 406–10.

Eder, Richard. " 'It Was Great, and Don't Call Me, I'll Call You.' " *Los Angeles Times* (June 25, 1989): 3.

———. "Seeing the Vietnamese." *Los Angeles Times Book Review* (March 29, 1992): 3, 7.

Elías, Eduardo F. "Sandra Cisneros." *Dictionary of Literary Biography: Chicano*

Writers, Second Series, ed. Francisco A. Lomelí and Carl R. Shirley. Detroit: Gale, 1992, pp. 77–81.

Erdrich, Louise. "The Beads." *North Dakota Quarterly*, 52 (Spring 1984): 54–61.

———. "Crown of Thorns." *Chicago*, 33, No. 9 (September 1984): 206–09, 238, 240.

———. "Love Medicine." *Ms.* 13 (November 1984): 74–84, 150.

———. *Love Medicine*. New York: Holt, Rinehart and Winston, 1984.

———. *Love Medicine: New and Expanded Version*. New York: Henry Holt, 1993.

———. "Lulu's Boys." *Kenyon Review*, 6, No. 3 (Summer 1984): 1–10.

———. "The Plunge of the Brave." *New England Review*, 7, No. 1 (Fall 1984): 120–36.

———. "The Red Convertible." *Mississippi Valley Review*, 11, No. 2 (1982): 10–17.

———. "Saint Marie." *Atlantic Monthly*, 253 (March 1984): 78–84.

———. "Scales." *North American Review*, 267, No. 1 (March 1982): 22–27.

———. "Where I Ought to Be: A Writer's Sense of Place." *New York Times Book Review* (July 28, 1985): 1, 23–24.

———. "Wild Geese." *Mother Jones*, 9 (October 1984): 21–22.

———. "The World's Greatest Fisherman." *Chicago*, 31, No. 10 (October 1982): 159–68.

Estrada, Mary Batts. "Four Sisters and a World of Difference." *Bookworld*, 21 (June 16, 1991): D11.

Eysturoy, Annie O. *Daughters of Self-Creation: The Contemporary Chicana Novel*. Albuquerque: University of New Mexico Press, 1996.

Ferguson, Moira. *Jamaica Kincaid: Where the Land Meets the Body*. Charlottesville: University Press of Virginia, 1994.

Fitzgerald, F. Scott. [Review of *In Our Time*.] *Bookman*, 63 (May 1926): 262–65.

Flavin, Louise. "Louise Erdrich's *Love Medicine*: Loving Over Time and Distance." *Critique*, 31, No. 1 (Fall 1989): 55–64.

Felski, Rita. *Beyond Feminist Aesthetics: Feminist Literature and Social Change*. Cambridge: Harvard University Press, 1989.

Freeman, Suzanne. "A Tightly Woven Tale of Love's Twists and Turns." *USA Today* (December 28, 1984): 3D.

Frieden, Sandra. "Shadowing/Surfacing/Shedding: Contemporary German Writers in Search of a Female *Bildungsroman*." *The Voyage In: Fictions of Female Development*, ed. Elizabeth Abel, Marianne Hirsch, and Elizabeth Langland. Hanover: University Press of New England, 1983, pp. 304–16.

Friedman, Norman. "Recent Short Story Theories: Problems in Definition." *Short Story Theory at a Crossroads*, ed. Susan Lohafer and Jo Ellyn Clarey. Baton Rouge: Louisiana State University Press, 1989, pp. 13–31.

Gates, David. "A Game of Show Not Tell." *Newsweek*, 113 (April 17, 1989): 68–69.

Gilbert, Harriett. "Mixed Feelings." *New Statesman* (February 8, 1985): 31.

Gilbert, Matthew. "Susan Minot Casts a Minimalist's Eye on Love." *Boston Globe* (June 9, 1989): 92.

Gilligan, Carol. *In a Different Voice: Psychological Theory and Women's Development.* Cambridge: Harvard University Press, 1982.

Gurney, A. R., Jr. "Men, Women and Children First." *New York Times Book Review* (April 27, 1986): 1, 27.

Harris, Robert R. "Too Embarrassed Not to Kill." *New York Times Book Review* (March 11, 1990): 8.

Hemingway, Ernest. *A Moveable Feast.* New York: Scribner's, 1964.

Heredia, Juanita. "Down These City Streets: Exploring Urban Space in *El Bronx Remembered* and *The House on Mango Street.*" *Mester*, 22 (Fall 1993) and 23 (Spring 1994): 93–105.

Herrera, Andrea O'Reilly. " 'Chambers of Consciousness': Sandra Cisneros and the Development of the Self in the BIG House on Mango Street." *Bucknell Review*, 39, No. 1 (1995): 191–204.

Herrera-Sobek, María. "The Politics of Rape: Sexual Transgression in Chicana Fiction." *Chicana Creativity and Criticism: New Frontiers in American Literature*, ed. Maria Herrera-Sobek and Helena María Viramontes. Albuquerque: University of New Mexico Press, 1996, pp. 171–81.

Herzog, Tobey C. "*Going After Cacciato*: The Soldier-Author-Character Seeking Control." *Critique*, 24, No. 2 (1983): 88–96.

Hickerson, Harold. *Chippewa Indians II: Ethnohistory of Mississippi Bands and Pillager and Winnibigoshish Bands of Chippewa.* New York: Garland, 1974.

Hinde, Thomas. "Bursts of Lucidity." *Books and Bookmen* (September 1986): 37.

Hirsch, Marianne. "Spiritual *Bildung*: The Beautiful Soul as Paradigm." *The Voyage In: Fictions of Female Development*, ed. Elizabeth Abel, Marianne Hirsch, and Elizabeth Langland. Hanover: University Press of New England, 1983, pp. 23–48.

Holt, Debra C. "Transformation and Continuance: Native American Tradition in the Novels of Louise Erdrich." *Entering the 90s: The North American Experience*, ed. Thomas E. Schirer. Sault Ste. Marie: Lake Superior University Press, 1991, pp. 149–61.

Hoy, Pat C. II. "Suffering and Desire." *Sewanee Review*, 100 (1992): cxvi–cxviii.

Ingram, Forrest L. *Representative Short Story Cycles of the Twentieth Century.* The Hague: Mouton, 1971.

Ismond, Patricia. "Jamaica Kincaid: 'First They Must Be Children.' " *World Literature Written in English*, 28, No. 2 (1988): 336–41.

Kaplan, Steven. *Understanding Tim O'Brien.* Columbia: University of South Carolina Press, 1995.

———. "The Undying Uncertainty of the Narrator in Tim O'Brien's *The Things They Carried.*" *Critique*, 35, No. 1 (1993): 43–52.

Kennedy, J. Gerald. "From Anderson's *Winesburg* to Carver's *Cathedral*: The Short Story Sequence and the Semblance of Community." In J. Gerald Kennedy, ed., *Modern American Short Story Sequences.* New York: Cambridge, 1995, pp. 194–215.

————. "Toward a Poetics of the Short Story Cycle." *Journal of the Short Story in English*, 11 (Autumn 1988): 9–25.

————, ed. *Modern American Short Story Sequences*. New York: Cambridge, 1995.

Kenney, Susan. "Paradise with Snake." *New York Times Book Review* (April 7, 1985): 6.

Kilgore, Kathleen. "How Others View Vietnam." *Christian Science Monitor* (September 4, 1992): 12.

Kilpatrick, Thomas L. [Review of *Love Medicine*.] *Library Journal* (October 1, 1984): 1860.

Kincaid, Jamaica. *Annie John*. New York: Farrar, Straus & Giroux, 1985.

————. *At the Bottom of the River*. New York: Vintage, 1985.

————. "The Circling Hand." *The New Yorker* (November 21, 1998): 50–57.

————. "Cold Heart." *The New Yorker* (June 25, 1990): 28–40.

————. "Columbus in Chains." *The New Yorker* (October 10, 1983): 48–52.

————. "Figures in the Distance." *The New Yorker* (May 9, 1983): 40–42.

————. "Gwen." *The New Yorker* (April 16, 1984): 34–53.

————. "The Long Rain." *The New Yorker* (July 30, 1984): 28–36.

————. "Lucy." *The New Yorker* (September 24, 1990): 44–50, 54, 56.

————. *Lucy*. New York: Farrar, Straus & Giroux, 1990.

————. "Mariah." *The New Yorker* (June 26, 1989): 32–38.

————. "Poor Visitor." *The New Yorker* (February 27, 1989): 28–30.

————. "The Red Girl." *The New Yorker* (August 8, 1983): 54–71.

————. *A Small Place*. New York: Farrar, Straus & Giroux, 1988.

————. "Somewhere, Belgium." *The New Yorker* (May 14, 1984): 44–51.

————. "The Tongue." *The New Yorker* (October 9, 1989): 44–54.

————. "A Walk to the Jetty." *The New Yorker* (November 5, 1984): 45–51.

Klein, Dianne. "Coming of Age in Novels by Rudolfo Anaya and Sandra Cisneros." *English Journal*, 81, No. 5 (September 1992): 21–26.

Lane, Mary T. [Review of Julia Alvarez, *How the García Girls Lost Their Accents*.] *Indiana Review*, 15, No. 2 (1992): 187–88.

"Laser Instinct." *Time* (July 10, 1989): 63.

Lehmann-Haupt, Christopher. "An Emotional Roadblock in the Heart of Lust." *New York Times* (June 8, 1989): 21.

Lewis, Clayton W. "Chronicles of War." *Sewanee Review*, 99 (1991): 296–302.

Luscher, Robert M. "The Short Story Sequence: An Open Book." *Short Story Theory at a Crossroads*, ed. Susan Lohafer and Jo Ellyn Clarey. Baton Rouge: Louisiana State University Press, 1989, pp. 148–67.

Lynn, Kenneth S. "Hemingway's Private War." *Commentary*, 72, No. 1 (1981): 24–33.

Lyons, Gene. "In Indian Territory." *Newsweek* (February 11, 1985): 68, 70.

Maitland, Sara. "Small Worlds." *New Statesman* (August 29, 1986): 25.

McCaffrey, Larry. "Interview with Tim O'Brien." *Dictionary of Literary Biography Documentary Series*, ed. Ronald Baughman. Vol. 9. Detroit: Bruccoli-Clark-Layman-Gale, 1991, pp. 153–64. Originally published in the *Chicago Review*, 33, No. 2 (1982): 129–49.

McCracken, Ellen. "Sandra Cisneros's *The House on Mango Street*: Community-Oriented Introspection and the Demystification of Patriarchal Violence." *Breaking Boundaries: Latina Writing and Critical Readings*, ed. Asunción Horno-Delgado, Eliana Ortega, and Nina M. Scott. Amherst: University of Massachusetts Press, 1989, pp. 62–71.

McKenna, Teresa. " 'Immigrants in Our Own Land': A Chicano Literature Review and Pedagogical Assessment." *ADE Bulletin*, No. 91 (Winter 1988): 30–38.

McNerney, Brian C. "Responsibly Inventing History: An Interview with Tim O'Brien." *War, Literature, & the Arts*, 6, No. 2 (1994): 1–26.

McWilliams, Dean. "Time in O'Brien's *Going After Cacciato*." *Critique*, 29, No. 4 (1988): 245–55.

Magalaner, Marvin. "Louise Erdrich: Of Cars, Time, and the River." *American Women Writing Fiction: Memory, Identity, Family, Space*, ed. Mickey Pearlman. Lexington: University Press of Kentucky, 1989, pp. 95–108.

Maitland, Sara. "Small Worlds." *New Statesman* (August 29, 1986): 25.

Mann, Susan Garland. *The Short Story Cycle: A Genre Companion and Reference Guide*. Westport: Greenwood, 1989.

Marsh, Pamela. "Ambivalence in Antigua: Leaving Childhood Behind." *Christian Science Monitor* (April 5, 1985): B2.

Maynard, Joyce. "The Young and Rootless." *Mademoiselle* (November 1986): 102, 104.

Mendelsohn, Jane. "Leaving Home: Jamaica Kincaid's Voyage Round Her Mother." *Village Voice Literary Supplement*, 89 (October 1990): 21.

Minot, Susan. "Accident." *The New Yorker* (November 7, 1983): 50–54.

———. "Allowance." *The New Yorker* (April 29, 1985): 37–41.

———. "Hiding." *Grand Street*, 2, No. 2 (1983): 19–32.

———. *Monkeys*. New York: E. P. Dutton, 1986.

———. "The Navigator." *Grand Street*, 4, No. 2 (1985): 90–100.

———. "The Silver Box." *Grand Street*, 5, No. 2 (1986): 26–33.

———. "Thanksgiving Day." *Grand Street*, 3, No. 3 (1984): 44–53.

———. "Thorofare." *The New Yorker* (June 27, 1983): 32–37.

Mitchell, David. "A Bridge to the Past: Cultural Hegemony and the Native American Past in Louise Erdrich's *Love Medicine*." *Entering the 90s: The North American Experience*, ed. Thomas E. Schirer. Sault Ste. Marie: Lake Superior University Press, 1991, pp. 162–70.

Morales, Ed. "Madam Butterfly: How Julia Alvarez Found Her Accent." *Village Voice Literary Supplement* (November 1994): 13.

Murdoch, H. Adlai. "Severing the (M)other Connection: The Representation of Cultural Identity in Jamaica Kincaid's *Annie John*." *Calloloo*, 13, No. 2 (1990): 325–40.

Mustard, Helen. *The Lyric Cycle in German Literature*. Morningside Heights: King's Crown Press, 1946.

Nagel, James. "Desperate Hopes, Desperate Lives: Depression and Self-Realization in Jamaica Kincaid's *Annie John* and *Lucy*." *Traditions, Voices, and Dreams: The American Novel Since the 1960s*, ed. Melvin J. Friedman and Ben Siegel. Newark: University of Delaware Press, 1995, pp. 237–53.

————. *Stephen Crane and Literary Impressionism*. University Park: Pennsylvania State University Press, 1980.

Naparsteck, Martin. "An Interview with Tim O'Brien." *Contemporary Literature*, 32 (1991): 1–11.

Natov, Roni. "Mothers and Daughters: Jamaica Kincaid's Pre-Oedipal Narrative." *Children's Literature*, 18 (1990): 1–16.

Novoa, Bruce. [Review of *How the García Girls Lost Their Accents*.] *World Literature Today*, 66 (Summer 1992): 516.

O'Brien, Tim. "The Ghost Soldiers." *Esquire* (March 1981): 90–93, 95–96, 98, 100.

————. "How to Tell a True War Story." *Esquire* (October 1987): 214.

————. *If I Die in a Combat Zone: Box Me Up and Ship Me Home*. New York: Laurel, 1969.

————. "In the Field." *Gentleman's Quarterly* (December 1989): 217, 220–22, 224, 227.

————. "The Lives of the Dead." *Esquire*, 111 (January 1989): 134, 136–39, 142.

————. "On the Rainy River." *Playboy*, 37 (January 1990): 97–98, 100, 108, 194–96.

————. "Speaking of Courage." *Massachusetts Review*, 17 (1976): 243–53.

————. "Spin." *The Quarterly*, 13 (1990): 3–13.

————. "Sweetheart of the Song Tra Bong." *Esquire* (July 1989): 94–103.

————. *The Things They Carried*. New York: Penguin, 1990.

————. "The Things They Carried." *Esquire* (August 1986): 76–81.

Olivares, Julián. "Entering *The House on Mango Street* (Sandra Cisneros)." *Teaching American Ethnic Literatures: Nineteen Essays*, ed. John R. Maitino and David R. Peck. Albuquerque: University of New Mexico Press, 1996, pp. 209–35.

————. "Sandra Cisneros' *The House on Mango Street* and the Poetics of Space." *Chicana Creativity and Criticism: Charting New Frontiers in American Literature*, ed. Maria Herrera-Sobek and Helena-Maria Viramontes. Houston: Arte Público, 1988, pp. 160–69.

Oliver, Bill. "From Tangents to Trespasses." *New England Review*, 15 (Summer 1993): 208–12.

O'Malley, Anne. "An Interview with Susan Minot." *Poets & Writers Magazine*, 15, No. 3 (1987): 11–15.

Ong, Caroline. "Roots Relations." *Times Literary Supplement* (December 29, 1989): 1447.

Onward, Ike. "Wising Up." *Times Literary Supplement* (November 29, 1985): 1374.

Packer, George. "From the Mekong to the Bayous." *New York Times Book Review* (June 7, 1992): 24.

Parini, Jay. "*Love Medicine* by Louise Erdrich." *Saturday Review* (November/ December 1984): 83.

Perry, Donna. "Initiation in Jamaica Kincaid's *Annie John.*" *Caribbean Women Writers: Essays from the First International Conference*, ed. Selwyn R. Cudjoe. Wellesley: Calaloux, 1990, pp. 245–53.

Portales, Marco. "People with Holes in Their Lives." *New York Times Book Review* (December 23, 1984): 6.

Pryor, Kelli. "The Story of Her Life: Writer Susan Minot Begins a New Chapter." *New York* (June 12, 1989): 52–55.

Rainwater, Catherine. "Reading Between Worlds: Narrativity in the Fiction of Louise Erdrich." *American Literature*, 62 (1990): 405–22.

Rebaza-Soraluz, Luis. [Review of *How the García Girls Lost Their Accents.*] *Hispanic Journal*, 14 (Spring 1993): 173–75.

Reid, Ian. *The Short Story*. New York: Barnes & Noble, 1977.

[Review of Julia Alvarez, *How the García Girls Lost Their Accents.*] *Publisher's Weekly*, 238 (April 5, 1991): 133.

[Review of Julia Alvarez, *How the García Girls Lost Their Accents.*] *Virginia Quarterly Review*, 68 (Winter 1992): 22.

[Review of Susan Minot's *Lust.*] *Kirkus Reviews*, 57 (March 15, 1989): 408–09.

[Review of Susan Minot's *Lust.*] *Library Journal*, 114 (May 15, 1989): 91.

[Review of Susan Minot's *Lust.*] *Publisher's Weekly*, 235 (April 14, 1989): 53.

Rifkind, Donna. "Speaking American." *New York Times Book Review*, 96 (October 6, 1991): 14.

Robison, James. "Tongue-Tied Lovers." *New York Times Book Review* (June 11, 1989): 24.

Rodríguez, Cecilia. "No Place like Home." *Women's Review of Books*, 8 (July 1991): 39.

Rosowski, Susan J. "The Novel of Awakening." *The Voyage In: Fictions of Female Development*, ed. Elizabeth Abel, Marianne Hirsch, and Elizabeth Langland. Hanover: University Press of New England, 1983, pp. 49–68.

Ross, Jean W. [Interview with Robert Olen Butler Jr.] *Contemporary Authors*, 112 (Detroit: Gale, 1985): 89–92.

Rubin, Merle. "Chinese-American 'Bridge Club.' " *Christian Science Monitor*, 81 (April 21, 1989): 13.

Sánchez, Reuben. "Remembering Always to Come Back: The Child's Wished-For Escape and the Adult's Self-Empowered Return in Sandra Cisneros's *House on Mango Street.*" *Children's Literature 23*, ed. Francelia Butler, R. H. W. Dillard, and Elizabeth Lennox Keyser. New Haven: Yale University Press, 1995, pp. 221–41.

Sanders, Scott R. [Commentary on *Love Medicine.*] *Studies in American Indian Literatures*, 9, No. 1 (1985): 6–11.

Sands, Kathleen M. [Commentary on *Love Medicine.*] *Studies in American Indian Literatures*, 9, No. 1 (1985): 12–24.

Schell, Orville. " 'Your Mother Is in Your Bones.' " *New York Times Book Review*, 94 (March 19, 1989): 3, 28.

See, Carolyn. "Drowning in America, Starving for China." *Los Angeles Times Book Review* (March 12, 1989): 3, 11.

Sheppard, R. Z. "Really Rosie." *Time* (June 9, 1986): 70–71.

Silberman, Robert. "Opening the Text: *Love Medicine* and the Return of the Native American Woman." *Narrative Chance: Postmodern Discourse on Native American Literatures*, ed. Gerald Vizenor. Albuquerque: University of New Mexico Press, 1989, pp. 101–20.

Simmons, Diane. *Jamaica Kincaid*. New York: Twayne, 1994.

Slabey, Robert M. *"Going After Cacciato*: Tim O'Brien's 'Separate Peace.' " *America Rediscovered: Critical Essays on Literature and Film of the Vietnam War*, ed. Owen W. Gilman Jr. and Lorrie Smith. New York: Garland, 1990, pp. 205–12.

Somogyi, Barbara, and David Stanton. "Amy Tan: An Interview." *Poets & Writers*, 19, No. 5 (1991): 24–32.

Starcevic, Elizabeth. "Talking About Language." *American Book Review*, 14 (August/September 1992): 15.

Stavans, Ilan. "Daughters of Invention." *Commonweal*, 119 (April 10, 1992): 23–25.

———. "Una Nueva Voz." *Commonweal*, 13 (September 1991): 524–25.

Stein, Dorothy. "Pieces of China." *Listener*, 122 (September 14, 1989): 25.

Stevens, Elisabeth. "Loving: Dangerous Liaisons." *Washington Post* (June 22, 1989): C8.

Stone, Les. "Kincaid, Jamaica 1949–." *Contemporary Authors*, 125 (1989): 256–57.

Streitfeld, David. "Never Done." *Washington Post Book World* (May 19, 1991): 15.

Takaki, Ronald. *A Different Mirror: A History of Multicultural America*. Boston: Little, Brown, 1993.

Tan, Amy. "End Game." *FM Five* (Spring 1986): 7–9, 12.

———. *The Joy Luck Club*. New York: G. P. Putnam's Sons, 1989.

———. "The Joy Luck Club." *Ladies' Home Journal*, 106 (March 1989): 98, 100, 102–6.

———. [On the Writing of *The Joy Luck Club*.] *Literary Outtakes*, ed. Larry Dark. New York: Fawcett Columbine, 1990, pp. 319–20.

———. "Rules of the Game." *Seventeen*, 45 (November 1986): 160–61, 177–79.

———. "Scar." *San Francisco Focus*, 35 (December 1988): 129, 170–74.

———. "Two Kinds." *Atlantic Monthly*, 263 (February 1989): 53–57.

Tapping, Craig. "Children and History in the Caribbean Novel: George Lamming's *In the Castle of My Skin* and Jamaica Kincaid's *Annie John*." *Kunapipi*, 11, No. 2 (1989): 51–59.

Taylor, Linda. "On- and Off-Reservation." *[London] Times Literary Supplement* (February 22, 1985): 196.

Tharp, Julie. "Women's Community and Survival in the Novels of Louise Erdrich." *Communication and Women's Friendships: Parallels and Intersections in Literature and Life*, ed. Janet Doubler Ward and JoAnna Stephens Mink. Bowling Green: Bowling Green State University Popular Press, 1993, pp. 165–80.

Timothy, Helen Pyne. "Adolescent Rebellion and Gender Relations in *At the Bottom of the River* and *Annie John*." *Caribbean Women Writers: Essays from the First International Conference*, ed. Selwyn R. Cudjoe. Wellesley: Calaloux, 1990, pp. 233–42.

Towers, Robert. "Far from Saigon." *New York Review of Books* (August 12, 1993): 40–41.

———. "Good News." *New York Review of Books* (June 26, 1986): 32–33, 35.

———. "Uprooted." *New York Review of Books* (April 11, 1985): 36.

Towery, Margie. "Continuity and Connection: Characters in Louise Erdrich's Fiction." *American Indian Culture and Research Journal*, 16, No. 4 (1992): 99–122.

Tyler, Anne. "The Art of Omission." *New Republic* (June 23, 1986): 34, 36.

Valdés, María Elena de. "The Critical Reception of Sandra Cisneros's *The House on Mango Street*." *Gender, Self, and Society*, ed. Renate von Bardeleben. Frankfort: Peter Lang, 1993, pp. 287–300.

———. "In Search of Identity in Cisneros's *The House on Mango Street*." *Canadian Review of American Studies*, 23, No. 1 (Fall 1992): 55–72.

Vannatta, Dennis. "Theme and Structure in Tim O'Brien's *Going After Cacciato*." *Modern Fiction Studies*, 28 (1982): 242–46.

Wang, Dorothy. "A Game of Show Not Tell." *Newsweek*, 113 (April 17, 1989): 69.

Wetherell, W. D. "Dubious Martyrdom." *Chicago Tribune Books* (March 11, 1990): 5.

White, Barbara A. *Growing up Female: Adolescent Girlhood in American Fiction*. Westport: Greenwood Press, 1985.

White, Evelyn C. "Growing Up Black." *Women's Review of Books*, 3, No. 2 (November 1985): 11.

Wiget, Andrew O. "Contemporary Native American Literature." *Choice* (June 1986): 1507–9.

Wiley, Catherine. [Review of *How the García Girls Lost Their Accents*.] *Bloomsbury Review*, 12 (March 1992): 9.

Willard, Nancy. "Tiger Spirits." *Women's Review of Books*, 6 (July 1989): 12.

Williams, Arnold. *The Drama of Medieval England*. East Lansing: Michigan State University Press, 1961.

Williamson, Barbara Fisher. "Book Notes." *Nation* (June 15, 1985): 748.

Wilson, Edmund. "Mr. Hemingway's Dry-Points." [Review of *in our time*.] *Dial*, 77 (October 1924): 340–41.

Wong, Hertha D. "An Interview with Louise Erdrich and Michael Dorris." *North Dakota Quarterly*, 55, No. 1 (1987): 196–218.

———. "Louise Erdrich's *Love Medicine*: Narrative Communities and the Short Story Sequence." In J. Gerald Kennedy, ed. *Modern American Short Story Sequences*. New York: Cambridge, 1995, pp. 170–93.

Woo, Elaine. "Striking Cultural Sparks." *Los Angeles Times* (March 12, 1989): Section 6, pp. 1, 14.

Wood, James. "Seeing Curt Lemon Blown Up." *London Review of Books* (July 26, 1990): 20.

Woolf, Rosemary. *The English Mystery Plays*. London: Routledge & Kegan Paul, 1972.

Wright, Austin M. "On Defining the Short Story: The Genre Question." *Short Story Theory at a Crossroads*, ed. Susan Lohafer and Jo Ellyn Clarey. Baton Rouge: Louisiana State University Press, 1989, pp. 46–53.

Yarbro-Bejarano, Yvonne. "Chicana Literature from a Chicana Feminist Perspective." *Chicana Creativity and Criticism: Charting New Frontiers in American Literature*, ed. María Herrera-Sobek and Helena María Viramontes. Houston: Arte Público Press, 1988, pp. 139–70.

Zappe, Jason. [Review of *How the García Girls Lost Their Accents*.] *Americas Review*, 19 (Winter 1991): 150–52.

Index

82 338BR 7808
08/05 04-172-00 GBC